Why Do You Need This New Edition?

If you're wondering why you should buy this new edition of *Along These Lines: Writing Sentences and Paragraphs*, Fifth Edition, here are some good reasons:

1. A new, bright, **visually appealing design** helps you find key concepts easily (especially in the writing process chapters) as you become an active and engaged learner.

2. An increased **focus on critical thinking and writing** helps you react to and understand the professional, personal, commercial, and informational writing that you see every day.

3. New **writing topics specifically designed to promote critical thinking** are included in the writing chapters. Addressing these topics by applying your analytical skills will be valuable preparation for the writing requirements in other departments.

4. New and varied exercises in every writing chapter **connect grammar principles to real-world writing**. These exercises will **help you avoid common grammar issues** down the road.

5. New **editing exercises** in every grammar chapter will enable you to strengthen grammatical skills and help you eliminate common errors from your writing.

6. New **photo-related writing topics** sharpen your perception and challenge your creativity.

7. **New and timely readings** on such topics as the power of pets in human therapy, the courage of a student writer who faced gang violence, and the advantages of getting to know your neighbors will catch your interest and lead you to your own topics for writing.

8. **Chapter Objectives, eText, and MyWritingLab:** Each chapter in *Along These Lines: Writing Sentences and Paragraphs* now opens with a listing of chapter objectives and ties them into Pearson's **MyWritingLab** (www.mywritinglab.com) and the eText. Now you can test your understanding of chapter content and truly master key concepts as MyWritingLab guides you to success!

PEARSON

W9-ATZ-352

| If practice makes perfect, imagine what *better* practice can do . . .

MyWritingLab™

MyWritingLab is an online learning system that provides better writing practice through progressive exercises. These exercises move students from literal comprehension to critical application to demonstration of their ability to write properly. With this better practice model, students develop the skills needed to become better writers!

When asked if they agreed with the following statements, here are how students responded:

"MyWritingLab helped me to improve my writing." **89%**

"MyWritingLab was fairly easy to use." **90%**

"MyWritingLab helped make me feel more confident about my writing ability." **83%**

"MyWritingLab helped me to better prepare for my next writing course." **86%**

"MyWritingLab helped me get a better grade." **82%**

"I wish I had a program like MyWritingLab in some of my other courses." **78%**

"I would recommend my instructor continue using MyWritingLab." **85%**

97%
The
MyWritingLab
Student-user
Satisfaction
Level

Student Success Story

"The first few weeks of my English class, my grades were at approximately 78%. Then I was introduced to MyWritingLab. I couldn't believe the increase in my test scores. My test scores had jumped from that low score of 78 all the way up to 100% (and every now and then a 99)."

—Exetta Windfield, *College of the Sequoias* (MyWritingLab student user)

TO PURCHASE AN ACCESS CODE, GO TO
WWW.MYWRITINGLAB.COM

Along These Lines

Writing Sentences and Paragraphs

Fifth Edition

John Sheridan Biays, professor emeritus of English
Broward College

Carol Wershoven, professor emerita of English
Palm Beach State College

PEARSON

Boston   Columbus   Indianapolis   New York   San Francisco   Upper Saddle River
Amsterdam   Cape Town   Dubai   London   Madrid   Milan   Munich   Paris   Montreal   Toronto
Delhi   Mexico City   Sao Paulo   Sydney   Hong Kong   Seoul   Singapore   Taipei   Tokyo

Editor in Chief: Eric Stano
Senior Acquisitions Editor: Matthew Wright
Assistant Editor: Amanda Dykstra
Senior Development Editor: Katharine Glynn
Marketing Manager: Kurt Massey
Supplements Editor: Cyndy Taylor
Executive Digital Producer: Stefanie Snajder
Digital Project Manager: Janell Lantana
Digital Editor: Robert St. Laurent
Project Coordination, Text Design,
  and Electronic Page Makeup: Rebecca Lazure / Laserwords
Senior Cover Design Manager: Nancy Danahy
Cover Art: Sunset viewing of Seventeen Arch Bridge in Imperial Summer Palace, Beijing, China / (c) China Image / Alamy
Text Permissions: Glenview / Heather Salus
Photo Research: PreMediaGlobal / Marta Johnson
Procurement Specialist: Mary Ann Gloriande
Printer/Binder: Courier / Kendallville
Cover Printer: Lehigh-Phoenix / Hagerstown

Credits and acknowledgments borrowed from other sources and reproduced, with permission, in this textbook appear on page 510.

Library of Congress Cataloging-in-Publication Data
Biays, John Sheridan.
    Along these lines : writing sentences and paragraphs / John Sheridan
    Biays, Carol Wershoven. -- 5th ed.
      p. cm.
    Includes bibliographical references and index.
    ISBN-13: 978-0-205-11020-9 (alk. paper)
    ISBN-10: 0-205-11020-7 (alk. paper)
      1. English language—Sentences. 2.   English language—Paragraphs.
      3. English language—Rhetoric.   I. Wershoven, Carol.   II. Title.
    PE1441   .B53 2011
    808'.042—dc23

                                            2011036831

10 9 8 7 6 5 4 3 2 —CRK —14 13 12

A la Carte Edition:
ISBN 10:   0-205-11059-2
ISBN 13: 978-0-205-11059-9

Student Edition:
ISBN 10:   0-205-11020-7
ISBN 13: 978-0-205-11020-9

Annotated Instructor's Edition:
ISBN 10:   0-205-11023-1
ISBN 13: 978-0-205-11023-0

www.pearsonhighered.com

Contents

v

Writing in Stages: The Process Approach   269

Appendix A: Readings for Writers   483

Appendix B: Grammar Practice for Nonnative Speakers   503

Photo Assignments to Accompany the Writing Chapters

Preface for Instructors

In this edition, we have integrated some new approaches for teaching developing writers but have maintained an emphasis on classroom-tested strategies for creative instruction and student success. Additionally, we offer a balance of group and individual assignments to vary the pace and focus for today's students accustomed to brief conversations and instant messages.

As students face the rigors of becoming confident, competent writers, their teachers strive to meet the needs of an ever-more diverse student population. In an unstable economy and an unpredictable job market, students have as many reasons for being in the classroom—training for a job, hoping for a career, learning to master a second language or a new set of career skills—as they have dreams or fears. Striking a balance between teaching these students creatively and meeting statewide or departmental "exit test" objectives can be challenging for any composition instructor. On a positive note, however, we are constantly amazed by the tireless efforts of so many educators who remain committed to quality developmental instruction despite drastic budget restraints and increasing class sizes. These dedicated instructors simply want their students to succeed, and when these professionals offer advice, we know we should pay close attention.

Based on the advice and support of fellow developmental educators, we have incorporated several new features and refinements aimed at motivating students to think critically, write coherently, and revise carefully. We have worked to make *Along These Lines: Writing Sentences and Paragraphs*, *5/e* the most comprehensive, user-friendly, pedagogically sound, and visually appealing text to date. Thank you very much for your continued interest in our work and for supporting developing education along *all* lines.

NEW FEATURES AND ENHANCEMENTS IN THE FIFTH EDITION

- **Increased emphasis on critical thinking and the writing process** as students react to types of professional, commercial, personal, and informational writing they encounter every day.
- **New grammar exercises in every chapter of the *Sentence-Level Skills* section.** *Practice* (individual sentence exercises), *Collaborate* (exercises to be completed with a partner or group), and *Connect* (editing and proofreading exercises) provide ample opportunity for skills reinforcement.
- **New and varied writing topics in every writing chapter,** enabling students to defend a point of view, imagine a certain scenario, or examine a trend. These assignments often draw on work, school, and home experiences to help students focus, generate details, and sharpen critical thinking skills.
- **New writing exercises in every chapter of the *Writing in Stages* section.** Students again work through *Practice*, *Collaborate*, and *Connect* activities as they engage in prewriting, planning, drafting and revising, editing, and proofreading.
- **New reading selections with follow-up discussion and writing topics** designed to spark students' imagination and promote critical thinking. Readings cover diverse subjects including the importance of neighbors getting to know each other, the power of pet therapy, and the courage of a student writer who faced gang violence and triumphed over adversity.

A SAMPLING OF PRAISE FROM *ALONG THESE LINES* ADOPTERS

*"**Along These Lines**' emphasis on the writing process is the text's strongest selling point. I love the chapters on the aims and modes of writing. [Throughout the book], the Info Boxes are not only helpful, they are critical. They are colorful and easy to find."*

Gretchen Polnac, University of Texas at Austin

*"**Along These Lines** is the best of all the books I've seen when it comes to grammar. My students really appreciate and enjoy the building-block approach because it makes sense to them."*

Anna Harrington, Jackson State Community College

*"The authors know the targeted population for **Along These Lines**, and their attention to detail is evident throughout the book. [Their style] lacks the pomposity or condescension found in other texts."*

Jonathan Lowndes, Broward College—South Campus

POPULAR FEATURES RETAINED

The Grammar Section

- Grammar concepts taught step-by-step, as in "Two Steps to Check for Sentence Fragments."
- A Chapter Test at the end of grammar chapters, ideal for class review or quick quizzes.

The Writing Section

- Visually appealing checklists, charts, and "Info Boxes."
- A lively conversational tone, including question-and-answer formats and dialogues.
- Framed examples of an outline, draft, and final version of an assignment in each chapter.
- A "Walk-Through" writing assignment at the end of each chapter that guides students, step-by-step, through the stages of the writing process.
- A Peer Review Form in most writing chapters so that students can benefit from a classmate's reaction to their drafts.

The Reading Section

- Reading selections grouped in a separate appendix (Appendix A) for easy reference.
- Vocabulary definitions based on the specific context of the writer's intent.
- Writing options, including critical thinking topics, sparked by a selection's content and designed to elicit informed responses.

Visual Enhancements

- Each grammar chapter opens with a "Quick Question" feature and includes an engaging photograph of students thinking, reading, studying, or interacting. Each quick question is related to the grammar principle covered in the chapter and provides an incentive to preview the content.

- Each writing chapter opens with a "Jumping In" feature that links an eye-catching, full-color photograph to the chapter's focus and initiates thinking, encourages discussion, and sparks prewriting about a particular rhetorical pattern.

ACKNOWLEDGMENTS

We are immensely grateful to the many individuals who helped us shape and refine the *Along These Lines* series. We thank the following new reviewers and survey respondents for their insightful and practical advice:

Marta Anderton	Jackson State Community College
Anna Harrington	Edison State College
Deedra Herington	Pensacola State College
Deanna Highe	Central Piedmont Community College
Lisa Jackson	Black River Technical College
Jonathan Lowndes	Broward College–South Campus
Linda Mobley	Bishop State Community College
Gretchen Polnac	University of Texas at Austin
Christine Prendergast	Pensacola State College
Sharon Rinkiewicz	Broward College–Central Campus
Carol Sinclair	Bainbridge College
Elizabeth Teagarden	Central Piedmont Community College
Melanie Thomas	Three Rivers Community College
Lisa Tittle	Harford Community College
Carmen Wong	John Tyler Community College

We are also indebted to Matt Wright, acquisitions editor for developmental English, for keeping us updated and on task throughout the revision process. He remained consistently upbeat about the scope of the series, and his faith in our work never waivered. We also want to thank Katharine Glynn, our development editor, for her insightful suggestions and for serving as our liason to Pearson headquarters.

We are very fortunate to have worked with Rebecca Lazure, our full-service production manager at Laserwords Maine. Rebecca somehow managed to resolve scheduling snags, tackle design challenges, meet page count mandates, and handle our venting sessions with grace and good humor. She gently reassured us that all would be fine, and we couldn't have been in kinder or more caring hands. Joan Foley, our project manager at Pearson headquarters, oversaw the entire enterprise, and we can't thank her enough for her calm but confident demeanor on several *ATL* editions over the years.

Any new edition relies on a wealth of expertise from talented individuals, and kudos are extended to Laura Patchkofsky, copy editor extraordinaire; Nancy Danahy, cover designer; Heather Salus, permissions specialist; Matt White, indexer; Kristen Pechtol, editorial assistant; and Megan Zuccarini, marketing assistant. We are also very grateful to Kurt Massey, marketing manager, for his enthusiastic support of the *Along These Lines* series and for coordinating presentations to sales teams and interested faculty.

Not only were we guided by Pearson's finest, we were also blessed to have the support of friends and family who tolerated our manic behavior as deadlines loomed with increasing frequency. We extend heartfelt thanks to Huck and Sophie Biays; Bill, Chris, and Yuki Childers; B. G., Nancy, and Pixie Thompson; Ted and Carol Cushmore; and Kathleen and Willow Bell for their patience and camaraderie along *all* lines.

Finally, and most importantly, we thank the countless developmental writing students who exemplify perseverance in the face of adversity. We sincerely hope that the *Along These Lines* series will continue to help developmental writers find their voice, accept new challenges, and reach their potential.

John Sheridan Biays
Carol Wershoven

The Simple Sentence

CHAPTER 1

Quick Question

True or False: In a simple sentence, the subject must come before the verb.

(After you study this chapter, you will be confident of your answer.)

Chapter Objectives

Students will be able to (1) identify subjects and verbs in both simple sentences and in ones with complicated word order; (2) recognize helping verbs, prepositional phrases, and infinitives; and (3) correct errors in faulty sentence construction.

Identifying the crucial parts of a sentence is the first step in many writing decisions: how to punctuate, how to avoid sentence fragments, and how to be sure that subjects and verbs *agree* (match). Moving forward to these decisions requires a few steps backward—to basics.

RECOGNIZING A SENTENCE

Let's start with a few definitions. A basic unit of language is a **word.**

> **examples:** cap, desk, tree

A group of related words can be a **phrase.**

> **examples:** battered baseball cap, on the desk, tall palm tree

When a group of words contains a subject and a verb, it is called a **clause.** When the word group has a subject and a verb and makes sense by itself, it is called a **sentence** or an independent clause.

2 Sentence-Level Skills   Grammar for Writers

If you want to check whether you have written a sentence and not just a group of related words, you first have to check for a subject and a verb. Locating the verbs first can be easier.

RECOGNIZING VERBS

Verbs are words that express some kind of action or being. **Action verbs** tell what somebody or something does.

> **action verbs:**
> Computers *hold* an amazing amount of information.
> We *call* our parents once a month.
> The boxer *exercises* at my local gym.
> You *missed* the bus yesterday.
> David *dented* the back of my car.
> He *drives* like a maniac.
> They *study* together on weekends.
> I *believe* her story.

Sometimes a verb tells what something or somebody is. Such verbs are called **being verbs**. Words like *feels*, *looks*, *seems*, *smells*, *sounds*, and *tastes* are part of the group called being verbs. Look at some examples of being verbs and their functions in the following sentences:

> **being verbs:**
> The computer *is* a great invention.
> The boxer *looks* tired today.
> You *sound* happy.
> David *is* a good candidate for traffic school.
> He *seems* unaware of traffic lights.
> They *are* the best students in my class.
> I *feel* confident about her story.
> Gossip *is* nasty and mean.

Exercise 1   Practice: Recognizing Action Verbs

Underline the action verbs in the following sentences.

1. The grandmother hugged the child.
2. On Friday, traffic blocked the intersection.
3. A kettle fell to the floor.
4. Old clothes remind me of the past.
5. The snake slithered into the tall grass.
6. Mitchell goes to a gym on the weekends.
7. A city bus takes me to work in the morning.
8. Karen needs your help today.
9. I locked the front door of the building.
10. One silly cartoon caused ten minutes of laughter.

Exercise 2 **Practice: Recognizing Being Verbs**

Underline the being verbs in the following sentences.

1. My study habits were not effective.

2. The homemade apple pie tastes delicious.

3. Your sister was a good and loyal friend.

4. The video seemed crude and nasty.

5. Jade Beach is a popular gathering place for students.

6. Professor Duvall is a well-known jazz musician.

7. Yesterday your plan sounded clear and reasonable.

8. The fall foliage looks magnificent today.

9. Weddings are sometimes stressful for the bride and groom.

10. My new wool socks feel like blankets around my cold feet.

Exercise 3 **Collaborate: Writing Sentences with Specific Verbs**

Collaborate

With a partner or group, write two sentences using each of the verbs listed below. Each sentence must have at least five words. When you have completed the exercise, share your answers with another group or with the class. The first one is done for you.

1. **verb:** dragged

   sentence 1: I dragged the heavy bag across the floor.

   sentence 2: Lori dragged herself out of a warm bed.

2. **verb:** smells

   sentence 1: _____

   sentence 2: _____

3. **verb:** argues

   sentence 1: _____

   sentence 2: _____

4. **verb:** seem

   sentence 1: _____

   sentence 2: _____

5. **verb:** slapped

   sentence 1: _____

   sentence 2: _____

6. **verb:** wins

   sentence 1: _____

   sentence 2: _____

7. verb: was

sentence 1: _____

sentence 2: _____

8. verb: were

sentence 1: _____

sentence 2: _____

9. verb: smiled

sentence 1: _____

sentence 2: _____

10. verb: annoys

sentence 1: _____

sentence 2: _____

Helping Verbs

The verb in a sentence can be more than one word. There can be **helping verbs** in front of the main verb (the action verb or being verb). Here is a list of some frequently used helping verbs:

INFO BOX: Common Helping Verbs

am	had	might	were
can	has	must	will
could	have	shall	would
did	is	should	
do	may	was	

Here are some examples of sentences with main and helping verbs:

> **main and helping verbs:**
> You *should have answered* the question. (The helping verbs are *should* and *have*.)
> Laurie *will notify* the lottery winner. (The helping verb is *will*.)
> Babies *can recognize* their mothers' voices. (The helping verb is *can*.)
> I *am thinking* about a career in medicine. (The helping verb is *am*.)

Exercise 4 **Practice: Recognizing the Complete Verb: Main and Helping Verbs**

Underline the complete verb (both main and helping verbs) in each of the following sentences.

1. On my birthday, I did expect some kind of gift from my girlfriend.

2. Several of my neighbors were planning a street party for Independence Day.

3. You will be taking your final exams next week.

4. Annette could have apologized for her rude remark to my uncle.

5. Gina and Larry are paying for their son's trip to Disney World.

6. My little nephew can sing several children's songs.

7. By Monday, you must make a decision about replacing the hot water heater.

8. At 7:30 A.M., my five-year-son was struggling with his jacket and cap.

9. I should have taken better care of my old car.

10. On Saturday, you may have left your credit card at the restaurant.

Exercise 5   **Collaborate: Writing Sentences with Helping Verbs**

Collaborate

Complete this exercise with a partner or group. First, ask one person to add at least one helping verb to the verb given. Then work together to write two sentences using the main verb and the helping verb(s). Appoint one spokesperson for your group to read all your sentences to the class. Notice how many combinations of main and helping verbs you hear. The first one is done for you.

1. **verb:** complained

   verb with helping verb(s): must have complained

   sentence 1: My supervisor must have complained about me.

   sentence 2: She must have complained twenty times yesterday.

2. **verb:** denying

   verb with helping verb(s): _____

   sentence 1: _____

   sentence 2: _____

3. **verb:** forgive

   verb with helping verb(s): _____

   sentence 1: _____

   sentence 2: _____

4. **verb:** said

   verb with helping verb(s): _____

   sentence 1: _____

   sentence 2: _____

5. **verb:** given

   verb with helping verb(s): _____

   sentence 1: _____

   sentence 2: _____

6. **verb:** expecting

   verb with helping verb(s): _____

   sentence 1: _____

   sentence 2: _____

7. **verb:** broken

verb with helping verb(s): _____

sentence 1: _____

sentence 2: _____

8. **verb:** encourage

verb with helping verb(s): _____

sentence 1: _____

sentence 2: _____

9. **verb:** growing

verb with helping verb(s): _____

sentence 1: _____

sentence 2: _____

10. **verb:** caused

verb with helping verb(s): _____

sentence 1: _____

sentence 2: _____

More Than One Main Verb

Helping verbs can make the verb in a sentence longer than one word, but there can also be more than one main verb.

more than one main verb:
Antonio *begged* and *pleaded* for mercy.
I *ran* to the car, *tossed* my books on the back seat, and *jammed* the key in the ignition.
My dog *steals* my shoes and *chews* on them.

Exercise 6 Practice: Recognizing Main Verbs

Some of the sentences below have one main verb; some have more than one main verb. Underline all the main verbs in each sentence.

1. Every night, my brother drives to his girlfriend's house, honks his car horn, and waits for her in his car.

2. Edward Kansky and Nick Stamos sell silver jewelry and leather belts at the flea market.

3. Alicia borrowed my clothes but rarely returned them.

4. My favorite place for breakfast is a pancake house with seven kinds of pancakes and eight flavors of syrup.

5. Your mother called and invited us to dinner tomorrow night.

6. A drunk driver shattered one car's taillight, smashed another's front end, and skidded into a trash can.

7. Felice ordered a salad for lunch and cut the lettuce into tiny pieces.

8. Some of the animals in his paintings look like dragons or other fantastic creatures from an imaginary world.

9. My oldest friend understands my problems, accepts my weaknesses, and believes in my strengths.

10. Marty is close to his sister and talks to her at least once a week.

Exercise 7 **Practice: Recognizing Verbs in a Selection from "The Tell-Tale Heart"**

This selection is from "The Tell-Tale Heart," a horror story by Edgar Allan Poe. In it, an insane murderer has killed an old man and buried him under the floor. When the police arrive, they find nothing, but the murderer is convinced that he—and the police—can hear the old man's heart beating under the floor. In this selection, the murderer describes what he feels as he hears the heart beat louder and louder.

Underline all of the verbs in the selection. Notice how a careful choice of verbs can make writing exciting and suspenseful.

The officers were satisfied. My manner had convinced them. I was singularly at ease. They sat, and while I answered cheerfully, they chatted of familiar things. But, ere* long, I felt myself getting pale and wished them gone. My head ached, and I fancied* a ringing in my ears: but still they sat and still chatted. The ringing became more distinct: —it continued and became more distinct: I talked more freely to get rid of the feeling: but it continued and gained definitiveness—until, at length,* I found that the noise was not within my ears.

No doubt I now grew very pale; —but I talked more fluently, and with a heightened voice. Yet the sound increased—and what could I do? . . . I gasped for breath—and yet the officers heard it not. I talked more quickly, more vehemently*; but the noise steadily increased. I arose and argued about trifles, in a high key and with violent gesticulations,* but the noise steadily increased. Why would they not be gone? I paced the floor to and fro with heavy strides, as if excited to fury by the observation of the men—but the noise steadily increased. Oh God! What could I do?

I foamed—I raved—I swore! . . . It grew louder—louder—louder! And still the men chatted pleasantly, and smiled. Was it possible they heard not? Almighty God! —no, no! They heard! —they suspected! —they knew!

***ere:** before
***fancied:** imagined
***at length:** after a time
***vehemently:** furiously
***gesticulations:** gestures

RECOGNIZING SUBJECTS

After you learn to recognize verbs, you can easily find the subjects of sentences because subjects and verbs are linked. If the verb is an action verb, for example, the **subject** will be the word or words that answer the question "Who or what is doing that action?" Follow these steps to identify the subject:

> **sentence with an action verb:**
> The cat slept on my bed.
>
> **Step 1:** Identify the verb: *slept*
>
> **Step 2:** Ask, "Who or what slept?"
>
> **Step 3:** The answer is the subject: The *cat* slept on my bed. The *cat* is the subject.

If the verb is a being verb, the same steps apply to finding the subject.

> **sentence with a being verb:**
> Clarice is his girlfriend.
>
> **Step 1:** Identify the verb: *is*
>
> **Step 2:** Ask, "Who or what is his girlfriend?"
>
> **Step 3:** The answer is the subject: *Clarice* is his girlfriend. *Clarice* is the subject.

Just as there can be more than one verb, there can be more than one subject.

> **examples:** *Coffee* and a *doughnut* are a typical breakfast for me.
>
> His *father* and *grandfather* own a landscaping service.

Exercise 8 **Practice: Recognizing Subjects in Sentences**

Underline the subjects in the following sentences.

1. The pudding tastes like caramel and cream.

2. Sylvia Jong might have left a message on my cell phone.

3. Grease and dirt stuck to the surface of the stove.

4. Something woke me in the middle of the night.

5. Lorraine and Pierre have family members in Haiti.

6. Smoking is becoming an expensive and socially unacceptable habit.

7. Greed and arrogance led William to a series of bad decisions.

8. Peanuts can cause dangerous allergic reactions in some people.

9. They brought their cousin to our engagement party.

10. A quilt can be a valuable piece of family history.

| Exercise 9 | **Collaborate: Adding Subjects to Sentences** |

Collaborate

Working with a partner or group, complete the paragraph below by adding subjects to the blank lines. Before you fill in the blanks, discuss your answers and try to come to an agreement about the worst movie, the worst music video, and so on. When you have completed the paragraph, share your answers with another group or with the class.

This year has seen many achievements in the arts and entertainment, but it has

also seen many creative disasters. On movie screens, there have been some ter-

rible movies. Without a doubt, _____ was the worst movie of the year.

It should never have been made. On television, _____ was the worst

and also the most irritating show. Every time I see it, I want to turn it off or kick

in the television screen. _____ and _____ take the prize for

the worst actor and actress of the year. They should consider other careers. In the

field of music, _____ ranks as the least successful music video of the

year. _____ is the most annoying song because the radio played it far

too often. Last, _____ is the most annoying singer.

MORE ABOUT RECOGNIZING SUBJECTS AND VERBS

Recognizing the Core Subject

When you look for the subject of a sentence, look for the core word or words; do not include descriptive words around the subject. Look for the subject, not for the words that describe it.

> **the core subject:**
> Light blue *paint* will brighten these walls.
> Cracked *sidewalks* and rusty *railings* made the old school dangerous
> for children.

Prepositions and Prepositional Phrases

Prepositions are usually short words that often signal a kind of position or possession, as shown in the following list.

INFO BOX: Some Common Prepositions

about	before	by	inside	on	under
above	below	during	into	onto	up
across	behind	except	like	over	upon
after	beneath	for	near	through	with
among	beside	from	of	to	within
around	between	in	off	toward	without
at	beyond				

A **prepositional phrase** is made up of a preposition and its object. Here are some prepositional phrases. In each one, the first word is the preposition; the other words are the object of the preposition.

prepositional phrases:

about the movie	of mice and men
around the corner	off the wall
between two lanes	on the mark
during recess	up the chimney
near my house	with my sister and brother

An old memory trick can help you remember prepositions. Think of a chair. Now, think of a series of words you can put in front of the chair:

around the chair	*with* the chair
by the chair	*to* the chair
behind the chair	*near* the chair
between the chairs	*under* the chair
of the chair	*on* the chair
off the chair	*from* the chair

These words are prepositions.

You need to know about prepositions because they can help you identify the subject of a sentence. Here is an important grammar rule about prepositions:

Nothing in a prepositional phrase can ever be the subject of a sentence.

Prepositional phrases describe people, places, or things. They may also describe the subject of a sentence, but they never *include* the subject. Whenever you are looking for the subject of a sentence, begin by putting parentheses around all the prepositional phrases:

parentheses and prepositional phrases:
The park (behind my apartment) has a playground (with swings and slides).

Nothing in the prepositional phrase can be the subject. Once you have eliminated these phrases, you can follow the steps to find the subject of the sentence.

Step 1: Identify the verb: *has*

Step 2: Ask, "Who or what has?"

Step 3: The answer is the subject: The *park*. The *park* is the subject.

By marking off the prepositional phrases, you are left with the core of the sentence. There is less to look at.

(Across the street) a *child* (with a teddy bear) sat (among the flowers).
subject: *child*

The *student* (from Jamaica) won the contest (with ease).
subject: *student*

Exercise 10   **Practice: Recognizing Prepositional Phrases, Subjects, and Verbs**

Put parentheses around the prepositional phrases in the following sentences. Then underline the subjects and verbs, putting *S* above the subject and *V* above the verb.

1. Two of my friends graduated from Western High School in 2004.

2. My puppy raced down the stairs and skidded across the wet floor into my arms.

3. A bunch of flowers and a card lay on the kitchen counter.

4. The girl with the long black hair was the most attractive stranger at my brother's party.

5. The mud on the side of my car came from a deep puddle at the end of the street.

6. Nothing except a sincere apology from that man can soothe the anger in my heart.

7. The children climbed over a crumbling wall onto the decaying property with the haunted cabin behind the tall trees.

8. At one point, the troops were driving through dangerous territory without clear directions.

9. Near the end of class, I looked under my desk and saw a mouse among the books on the floor.

10. One of my friends completes his reading assignments between classes, writes his papers around midnight, and studies for his tests on the weekends.

Exercise 11   **Collaborate: Writing Sentences with Prepositional Phrases**

Collaborate

Do this exercise with a partner. First, add one prepositional phrase to the core sentence. Then ask your partner to add a second prepositional phrase to the same sentence. For the next sentence, switch places. Let your partner add the first phrase; you add the second. Keep switching places throughout the exercise. When you have completed the exercise, share your sentences (the ones with two prepositional phrases) with the class. The first one is done for you.

1. **core sentence:** Employees are concerned.

    Add one prepositional phrase: Employees are concerned about their paychecks.

    Add another prepositional phrase: Employees at the central plant are concerned about their paychecks.

2. **core sentence:** Eduardo ran.

    Add one prepositional phrase: _____

    _____

    Add another prepositional phrase: _____

    _____

3. **core sentence:** A huge truck skidded.

    Add one prepositional phrase: _____

    _____

    Add another prepositional phrase: _____

    _____

4. **core sentence:** Kelly called me.

    Add one prepositional phrase: _____

    _____

    Add another prepositional phrase: _____

    _____

5. **core sentence:** Young adults should be ready.

    Add one prepositional phrase: _____

    _____

    Add another prepositional phrase: _____

    _____

6. **core sentence:** A man in black appeared.

    Add one prepositional phrase: _____

    _____

    Add another prepositional phrase: _____

    _____

Word Order

When we speak, we often use a very simple word order: first, the subject; then, the verb. For example, someone would say, "He lost the key." *He* is the subject that begins the sentence; *lost* is the verb that comes after the subject.

However, not all sentences use such a simple word order. Prepositional phrases, for example, can change the word order. To identify the subject and verb, follow these steps:

prepositional phrase and changed subject–verb order:
Behind the cabinet was a box of coins.

Step 1: Mark off the prepositional phrases with parentheses: (Behind the cabinet) was a box (of coins). Remember that nothing in a prepositional phrase can be the subject of a sentence.

Step 2: Find the verb: *was*

Step 3: Who or what was? A box was. The subject of the sentence is *box*.

After you change the word order of this sentence, you can see the subject (S) and the verb (V) more easily.

     S   V

A *box* of coins *was* behind the cabinet.

    (Even though *coins* is a plural word, you must use the singular verb *was* because *box* is the singular subject.)

Exercise 12   **Practice: Finding Prepositional Phrases, Subjects, and Verbs in Complicated Word Order**

Put parentheses around the prepositional phrases in the following sentences. Then underline the subjects and verbs, putting an *S* above each subject and a *V* above each verb.

1. Across the street from my grandmother's apartment is an empty lot with cracked cement.

2. By a border of white roses stood a small dog without a collar.

3. Behind all Mario's bragging and bluster hid a shy man with a longing for approval.

4. Inside the crumpled envelope lay a rusty key on a thin gold chain.

5. From the back of the auditorium came the loud sound of someone snoring happily.

6. Among the items in the old wooden chest is a faded photograph of my grandparents on their wedding day.

7. Through the halls echoed the sound of excited schoolchildren on their way to the lunchroom.

8. Down the snow-covered street raced two boys on shiny new sleds.

9. Under the pile of leaves slithered a thin silver snake with black markings.

10. Within walking distance of my house stands a famous monument to the soldiers of World War II.

More on Word Order

The expected word order of a subject followed by a verb will change when a sentence starts with *There is/are, There was/were, Here is/are,* or *Here was/were.* In such cases, look for the subject after the verb:

S–V order with *There is/are, Here is/are*:

> V   S   S
> There *are* a *supermarket* and a *laundromat* near my apartment.

> V   S
> Here *is* my best *friend.*

To understand this pattern, you can change the word order:

> S   S   V
> A *supermarket* and a *laundromat* *are* there, near my apartment.

> S   V
> My best *friend is* here.

You should also note that even when the subject comes after the verb, the verb has to *match* the subject. For instance, if the subject refers to more than one thing, the verb must refer to more than one thing:

> There are a *supermarket* and a *laundromat* near my apartment. (Two things, a supermarket and a laundromat, *are* near my apartment.)

Word Order in Questions

Questions may have a different word order. The main verb and the helping verb may not be next to each other.

Word order in questions:

question: Did you study for the test?
subject: *you*
verbs: *did, study*

To understand this concept, you can think about answering the question. If someone accused you of not studying for the test, you might say, "I *did study* for it." You would use two words as verbs.

question: Will she call her mother?
subject: *she*
verbs: *will, call*

question: Is Charles making the coffee?
subject: *Charles*
verbs: *is, making*

Exercise 13 **Practice: Recognizing Subjects and Verbs in Questions and**
Here is/are, There is/are **Word Order**

Underline the subjects and verbs in the following sentences, putting an *S*
above each subject and a *V* above each verb.

1. There is somebody with a package at the front door.

2. Have we driven off the main road and missed the right exit?

3. Do you expect an answer to your letter?

4. Here is our chance for a family vacation.

5. Would Mrs. Sung like a gift card for her birthday?

6. On the left side of the street there are a barber shop and an
   electronics store.

7. There was a long line at the college bookstore today.

8. Can Amber take me to the doctor's office on Friday?

9. Has your new boss told you the rules for overtime pay?

10. Here are George's old photograph album and Marisol's first
    crayon drawings.

Words That Cannot Be Verbs

Sometimes there are words that look like verbs in a sentence but are not
verbs. Such words include *adverbs* (words like *always, often, nearly, never,
ever*) that are placed close to the verb but are not verbs. Another word that
is placed between a helping verb and a main verb is *not. Not* is not a verb.
When you are looking for verbs in a sentence, be careful to eliminate words
like *often* and *not*.

> They will not accept his apology. (The complete verb is *will
> accept*.)
> Matthew can often repair his truck by himself. (The complete verb is
> *can repair*.)

Be careful with *contractions*.

> He hasn't called me in a long time. (The complete verb is *has called*.
> *Not* is not a part of the verb, even in contractions.)
> Don't you speak Spanish? (The complete verb is *do speak*.)
> Won't you come inside? (The complete verb is *will come. Won't* is a
> contraction for *will not*.)

Recognizing Main Verbs

If you are checking to see if a word is a main verb, try the pronoun test. Combine your word with this simple list of pronouns: *I, you, he, she, it, we, they*. A main verb is a word such as *look* or *pulled* that can be combined with the words on this list. Now try the pronoun test.

> For the word *look:* I look, you look, he looks, she looks, it looks, we look, they look
> For the word *pulled:* I pulled, you pulled, he pulled, she pulled, it pulled, we pulled, they pulled
> But the word *never* can't be used alone with the pronouns:
> ~~I never, you never, he never, she never, it never, we never, they never~~
> (Never did what?)
> *Never* is not a verb. *Not* is not a verb either, as the pronoun test indicates:
> ~~I not, you not, he not, she not, it not, we not, they not~~ (These combinations don't make sense because *not* is not a verb.)

Verb Forms That Cannot Be Main Verbs

There are forms of verbs that can't be main verbs by themselves either. An *-ing* verb by itself cannot be the main verb, as the pronoun test shows.

> For the word *taking:* ~~I taking, you taking, he taking, she taking, it taking, we taking, they taking~~

If you see an *-ing* verb by itself, correct the sentence by adding a helping verb.

> He ~~taking~~ his time. (*Taking*, by itself, cannot be a main verb.)
> **correction:** He *is taking* his time.

Another verb form, called an *infinitive*, also cannot be a main verb. An infinitive is the form of the verb that has *to* placed in front of it.

INFO BOX: Some Common Infinitives

to call	to eat	to live	to smile
to care	to fall	to make	to talk
to drive	to give	to run	to work

Try the pronoun test and you'll see that infinitives can't be main verbs:

> For the infinitive *to live:* ~~I to live, you to live, he to live, she to live, we to live, they to live~~

So if you see an infinitive being used as a verb, correct the sentence by adding a main verb.

> He ~~to live~~ in a better house.
> **correction:** He *wants* to live in a better house.

The infinitives and the *-ing* verbs just don't work as main verbs. You must put a verb with them to make a correct sentence.

Exercise 14   Practice: Correcting Problems with Infinitive or *-ing* Verb Forms

Most—but not all—of the following sentences are faulty; an *-ing* verb or an infinitive may be taking the place of a main verb. Correct the sentences that have errors.

1. Nobody in the store paying attention to the jumbled piles of merchandise on the sales tables.

2. A lack of jobs in our state sending many people into debt, bankruptcy, and homelessness.

3. Mark's talent for putting people at ease was a real asset in his volunteer work at the free clinic near the edge of town.

4. In the middle of a cold winter, my father wondering about a move to a state with a warmer climate.

5. For me, the most challenging parts of the charity walkathon to be the hot weather and the hills along the route.

6. At the end of the weekend, I thinking about the responsibilities of the days ahead.

7. A tropical storm with strong winds and heavy rain is expected to move into our area in the next two or three days.

8. Sixteen-year-old Callie to get her driver's license during the summer vacation.

9. Kind strangers, patient coworkers, and warm-hearted neighbors are turning my first weeks in a new town into a series of good experiences.

10. Inside a laundry basket two playful white kittens tumbling over one another on a pile of white towels.

Exercise 15   Practice: Finding Subjects and Verbs: A Comprehensive Exercise

Underline the subjects and verbs in the following sentences, putting an *S* above each subject and a *V* above each verb.

1. My sisters don't like to shop at any supermarket with spoiled tomatoes or a smelly fish counter.

2. Behind all the bragging and the smart talk is an insecure young man with a need for acceptance.

3. Keith has always wanted a career in the U.S. Navy.

4. Matt hoped to send a message to his wife before her meeting with the cardiologist.

5. Didn't you ever think about the risks of traveling in a war-torn country?

6. There are a few problems with buying a used laptop from a pawn shop.

7. Deep love and constant patience helped my parents to survive the first years of a marriage between two people with opposing temperaments.

8. Where did you and Tina go after our geography class on Thursday afternoon?

9. At the back of my closet is a pile of old baseball caps from my teen years on several local teams.

10. Andre should have told me about his arrest for drunk driving.

Exercise 16   **Practice: Finding Subjects and Verbs: A Comprehensive Exercise**

Underline the subjects and verbs in the following sentences, putting an *S* above each subject and a *V* above each verb.

1. Beneath the pile of dirty clothes was a pair of old leather boots in terrible condition.

2. In the summer, Wallace drives to the mountains and hikes on trails at McLendon Park.

3. The Cuban coffee and pastries at Sylvia's restaurant attracted customers from miles away.

4. Without Peter's help, Jamie might never have gotten the chance to start a new career.

5. Below street level is an underground mall with fifty shops and restaurants.

6. Paul's love for his children has made him into a generous and compassionate man.

7. There was a gold border around the rim of the blue vase.
V   *S*

8. Isaac's cat leaped onto my lap and became a blissful ball of orange fur.
V S   *S*

9. Haven't you ever seen the view from the top of Randall Hill?
S   *V*

10. Without a ticket for the evening show, you don't have a chance of
S

getting into the club.

Exercise 17   **Collaborate: Creating Your Own Text**

Do this exercise with a partner or a group. Following is a list of rules you have just studied. Write two examples for each rule. When your group has completed the examples for each rule, trade your group's completed exercise with another group's and check their examples while they check yours. The first rule has been done for you.

Rule 1: The verb in a sentence can express some kind of action.

  example 1: My cousin studies biology in college.

  example 2: Yesterday the rain destroyed the rose bushes.

Rule 2: The verb in a sentence can express some state of being.

  example 1: _____

  example 2: _____

Rule 3: The verb in a sentence can consist of more than one word.

  example 1: _____

  example 2: _____

Rule 4: There can be more than one subject in a sentence.

  example 1: _____

  example 2: _____

Rule 5: If you take out the prepositional phrases, it is easier to identify the subject of a sentence because nothing in a prepositional phrase can be the subject of a sentence. (Write sentences containing at least one prepositional phrase. Put parentheses around the prepositional phrases.)

  example 1: _____

  example 2: _____

Rule 6: Not all sentences have the simple word order of first subject, then verb. (Give examples of sentences with more complicated word order.)

  example 1: _____

  example 2: _____

Rule 7: Words like *not, never, often, always,* and *ever* are not verbs. (Write sentences using one of those words, but put a *V* above the correct verb.)

example 1: _____

example 2: _____

Rule 8: An *-ing* verb form by itself or an infinitive (*to* preceding the verb) cannot be a main verb. (Write sentences with *-ing* verb forms or infinitives, but put a *V* above the main verb.)

example 1: _____

example 2: _____

Connect

Exercise 18 **Connect: Recognizing Subjects and Verbs in a Paragraph**

Underline the subjects and verbs in the following paragraph, putting an *S* above each subject and a *V* above each verb.

A major event in our town is the annual weekend of hot rod racing. From every part of the state come thousands of people. Neighboring states also send their share of competitors and spectators. During this weekend there are huge economic benefits to our town. Many visitors arrive in their campers. Consequently, the local campgrounds fill with every kind of recreational vehicle. Other racing fans stay at nearby hotels and motels. Everyone in town for the races needs to eat, too. During this weekend, the restaurants and supermarkets in our town never complain about a lack of business. Other places sell souvenirs. There are shirts, caps, cups, stickers, bandanas, and flags for sale in every service station, drug store, and superstore. Visitors, merchants, and hotelkeepers love race weekend. In addition, many local residents love this time, too. Thousands of old timers in town have never missed a visit to the races. Without the fun and action of this event, our town would be a sad place.

Connect

Exercise 19 **Connect: Recognizing Subjects and Verbs in a Paragraph**

Underline the subjects and verbs in the following paragraph, putting an *S* above each subject and a *V* above each verb.

My brother has an irritating habit of removing all the change from his pockets at the end of each day. He saves this change for a rainy day. On that day, he will take all the change to the bank and come home with paper money in the same amount. That rainy day has never arrived. For years, mounds of nickels, dimes, pennies, and quarters have appeared in every part of the house. These piles fill every container in the house, from a huge coffee mug in the kitchen to a plastic drinking glass in the bathroom. Inside the kitchen cabinets are freezer storage bowls with heavy piles of coins under their plastic lids. My brother's stash of spare change is filling our home with heavy deposits of coins. He should sort and exchange the heavy metal for some lighter, paper cash.

Chapter Test The Simple Sentence

Underline the subjects and verbs in the following sentences, putting an *S* above each subject and a *V* above each verb.

1. With a strong reliance on common sense, a person will nearly always find a way to handle tough decisions.

2. Shouldn't Maria take an early morning flight to Atlanta and rent a car at the airport?

3. From the back of the audience at the comedy came the loudest laughter of anyone in the room.

4. Without a penny in his pocket, my grandfather arrived in a strange country and found work.

5. Mosquitoes have been making my life miserable during the endless hot and rainy days of a South Carolina summer.

6. Beyond the glamorous sights and sounds of the city center are abandoned apartment buildings and empty shops in a state of decay.

7. Won't you get a little sentimental after seeing the videos of your fifth birthday party in our old house?

8. After a few minutes of assessing the situation, the plumber went to his truck, grabbed his tools, and started the long process of fixing the leak.

9. In the dark hours of one winter's night, an eerie sound penetrated the silence of the frozen landscape and caused me to shiver in fear.

10. After 5:00 P.M., Will always remembers to call me to tell me about traffic delays or extra hours at work.

MyWritingLab™ For support in meeting this chapter's objectives, log in to www.mywritinglab.com and select **Subjects and Verbs** and **Sentence Structure.**

Beyond the Simple Sentence: Coordination

CHAPTER 2

Quick Question

Which sentence(s) is/are correct?

A. Carla made coffee, and she offered us some cookies.

B. Carla made coffee and offered us some cookies.

(After you study this chapter, you will be confident of your answer.)

Chapter Objectives

Students will be able to identify and apply sentence-combining techniques that rely on coordinating conjunctions and conjunctive adverbs.

A group of words containing a subject and a verb is called a **clause.** When that group makes sense by itself, it is called a sentence or an independent clause. A sentence that has one independent clause is called a **simple sentence.** If you rely too heavily on a sentence pattern of simple sentences, you risk writing paragraphs like this:

> My father never got a chance to go to college. He had to struggle all his life. He struggled to make a good living. He dreamed of sending his children to college. He saved his money for their education. Today, all three of his children are in college. Two of them are working toward degrees in business. My father is very proud of them. His third child has pleased my father the most. The third child, my brother, is majoring in education. My father will be proud of his son the teacher. He thinks a teacher in the family is a great gift.

instead of

> My father never got a chance to go to college, and he had to struggle all his life to make a good living. He dreamed of sending his children to college, so he saved his money for their education. Today, all three of his children are in college. Two of them are working toward degrees in business. My father is very proud of them, yet his third child has pleased my father the most. The third child, my brother, is majoring in education. My father will be proud of his son the teacher, for he thinks a teacher in the family is a great gift.

If you read the two paragraphs aloud, you'll notice how choppy the first one sounds. The second one is smoother. The first one is made up of simple sentences, while the second one combines some simple sentences for a more flowing style.

OPTIONS FOR COMBINING SIMPLE SENTENCES

Good writing involves **sentence variety.** This means mixing a simple sentence with a more complicated one and using both short and long sentences. Sentence variety is easier to achieve if you can combine related, short sentences into one.

Some students avoid such combining because they're not sure how to do it. They don't know how to punctuate the new combinations. It's true that punctuating involves memorizing a few rules, but once you know them, you'll be able to use them automatically and write with more confidence. Here are three options for combining simple sentences followed by the punctuation rules you need to use in each case.

OPTION 1: USING A COMMA WITH A COORDINATING CONJUNCTION

You can combine two simple sentences with a comma and a coordinating conjunction. The coordinating conjunctions are *for, and, nor, but, or, yet,* and *so.*

To **coordinate** means to *join equals.* When you join two simple sentences with a comma and a coordinating conjunction, each half of the combination remains an **independent clause,** with its own subject (S) and verb (V).

Here are two simple sentences:

>   S   V   S   V
> *Joanne drove* the car. *Richard studied* the map.

Here are two simple sentences combined with a comma and with the word *and,* a coordinating conjunction (CC).

>   S   V   , CC S   V
> *Joanne drove* the car, *and Richard studied* the map.

The combined sentences keep the form they had as separate sentences; that is, they are still both independent clauses, with a subject and verb and with the ability to stand alone.

The word that joins them is the **coordinating conjunction.** It is used to join *equals.* Look at some more examples. These examples use a variety of coordinating conjunctions to join two simple sentences (also called independent clauses).

sentences combined with *for:*

```
     S        V            ,  CC       S       V
```
My *mother was* furious, *for* the *doctor was* two hours late. (Notice
   that *for* means *because.*)

sentences combined with *nor:*

```
   S      V      V              ,  CC    V    S    V
```
We couldn't see the stage, *nor could we hear* the music. (Notice what
   happens to the word order when you use *nor.*)

sentences combined with *but:*

```
    S       V            ,  CC   S     V
```
She brought a cake, *but she forgot* a cake slicer.

sentences combined with *or:*

```
      S        V              ,  CC   S      V
```
Mr. Chang can call my office, *or he can write* me.

sentences combined with *yet:*

```
 S    V          ,  CC  S         V
```
I loved botany, *yet I* never *got* a good grade in it. (Notice that *yet*
   means *but* or *nevertheless.*)

sentences combined with *so:*

```
      S       V                ,  CC  S      V
```
Marshall brought her flowers, *so she forgave* him for his rudeness.
   (Notice that *so* means *therefore* or *as a result.*)

Note: One easy way to remember the coordinating conjunctions is to call them,
as a group, **fanboys** (*for*, **a**nd, **n**or, **b**ut, **o**r, **y**et, **s**o).

Where Does the Comma Go?

The comma goes *before* the coordinating conjunction (*for, and, nor, but, or,
yet, so*). It comes before the new idea—the second independent clause. It
goes where the first independent clause ends. Try this punctuation check.
After you've placed the comma, look at the combined sentences. For example,

   John saved his money, and he bought a new car.

Now split it into two sentences at the comma:

   John saved his money. And he bought a new car.

If you put the comma in the wrong place, after the coordinating conjunction,
like this:

comma in wrong place:

~~John saved his money and, he bought a new car.~~

Your split sentences would look like this:

   John saved his money and. He bought a new car. (The split doesn't
      make sense.)

This test helps you see whether the comma has been placed correctly—where the first independent clause ends. (Notice that, in addition to starting a sentence with *and*, you can also begin a sentence with *for*, *nor*, *but*, *or*, *yet*, or *so*—as long as you've written a complete sentence.)

Caution: Do *not* use a comma every time you use the words *for*, *and*, *nor*, *but*, *or*, *yet*, *so*; use one only when the coordinating conjunction joins independent clauses. Do not use a comma when the coordinating conjunction joins words:

> tea or coffee
> exhausted but relieved
> love and happiness

Do not use a comma when the coordinating conjunction joins phrases:

> on the patio or in the garden
> in the glove compartment and under the seats
> with harsh words but without anger

A comma is used when the coordinating conjunction joins two independent clauses. Another way to state this rule is to say that a comma is used when the coordinating conjunction joins two simple sentences.

Placing the Comma by Using S–V Patterns

An independent clause, or simple sentence, follows this basic pattern:

> S (subject)   V (verb)

Here is an example:

> S V
> *He ran.*

You can add to the basic pattern in several ways:

> S   S V
> *He and I ran.*
> S V   V
> *He ran and swam.*
> S   S V   V
> *He and I ran and swam.*

Study all the examples above, and you'll notice that you can draw a line separating the subjects on one side and the verbs on the other:

S	V
SS	V
S	VV
SS	VV

So whether the simple sentence has one subject (or more than one), the pattern is subject(s) followed by verb(s).

Compound Sentences

When you combine two simple sentences, the pattern changes:

two simple sentences:

> S V
> *He swam.*

S   V
I ran.

two simple sentences combined:
S   V   S   V
He swam, but *I ran.*

In the new pattern, SVSV, you can't draw a line separating all the subjects on one side and all the verbs on the other. The new pattern is called a **compound sentence:** two simple sentences, or independent clauses, combined into one.

Learning the Coordinating Conjunctions

You've just studied one way to combine simple sentences. If you are going to take advantage of this method, you need to memorize the coordinating conjunctions—*for, and, nor, but, or, yet, so*—so that your use of them, with the correct punctuation, will become automatic.

Exercise 1   **Practice: Recognizing Compound Sentences and Adding Commas**

Add commas only where they are needed in the following sentences.

1. Denise decorated her room in shades of green, but I chose purple as the color for my room.

2. An acquaintance at the music store told me about a sale on guitars, and advised me about the best deals.

3. At the end of the month, Robin pays all his bills, for he fears getting into debt.

4. Some of my mother's old clothes from her high school days are back in style, but they don't fit her anymore.

5. The chef at the vegetarian restaurant creates meals with great flavor, yet very little fat or salt.

6. My boyfriend spent Saturday afternoon at a soccer match, so I went to the movies with my cousin.

7. Phil must not see his sister before Saturday, or he will ruin the surprise about the farewell party.

8. The actor wasn't particularly handsome, nor was he a typical action hero.

9. You can take my car, and I'll stay home.

10. Anthony called me after work, and asked me to switch tomorrow's schedules with him.

Exercise 2   **Practice: More on Recognizing Compound Sentences and Adding Commas**

Add commas only where they are needed in the following sentences.

1. Mr. Mendoza and Mr. Polsky arranged the transportation, and provided the refreshments for the children's field trip to the science museum.

2. My next door neighbor has neither a sense of humor, nor a tolerance for young people's parties.

3. Coffee gets me started in the morning, but too much caffeine leaves me with a bad headache.

4. Ricky's sister can take Ricky to work on Tuesday, or he can get a ride with me.

5. The tea kettle was screeching, so Miriam ran to turn off the heat on the stove.

6. My four-year-old dropped his bowl of oatmeal on the floor, and I reached for the roll of paper towels.

7. I will never speak to Frank again, for he betrayed my trust in him.

8. Patrick loves to watch NASCAR events on television, so I got him tickets to a live race for his birthday.

9. Alan's presentation at the city council was a nervous, yet moving appeal for a homeless shelter in our town.

10. My history teacher is thinking about giving our class a take-home final examination, or assigning a final paper.

Collaborate

Exercise 3 **Collaborate: Writing and Punctuating Compound Sentences**

Working with a partner or a group, write the compound sentences described below. Be sure to punctuate them correctly. When you have completed the exercise, share your answers with another group or with the class.

1. Write a compound sentence using the coordinating conjunction *for*.

~~The boy ate the apple, and the girl at~~
The boy ate the apple, for the girl gave it to him.

2. Write a compound sentence using the coordinating conjunction *and*.

The boy ate the apple, and the girl ate the orange.

3. Write a compound sentence using the coordinating conjunction *nor*.

The boy couldn't eat the apple, nor the orange.

4. Write a compound sentence using the coordinating conjunction *but*.

The boy tried to eat the apple, but the girl stole it.

5. Write a compound sentence using the coordinating conjunction *or*.

You can have the apple, or the orange.

6. Write a compound sentence using the coordinating conjunction *yet*.

The boy wanted to eat the apple, yet he ate the orange.

7. Write a compound sentence using the coordinating conjunction *so*.

The boy ate the apple, so the girl couldn't.

OPTION 2: USING A SEMICOLON BETWEEN TWO SIMPLE SENTENCES

Sometimes you want to combine two simple sentences (independent clauses) without using a coordinating conjunction. If you want to join two simple sentences that are related in their ideas and you do not want to use a coordinating conjunction, you can combine them with a semicolon.

two simple sentences:

S   V   S   V
I washed the floor. *He dusted* the furniture.

two simple sentences combined with a semicolon:

S   V   ; S   V
I washed the floor; *he dusted* the furniture.

Here are more examples of this option in use:

S   V   ; S   V
He swam; I ran.

S   V   V   ; S   V   V
Jacy couldn't sleep; she was thinking about her job.

S   V   ; S   V
Skindiving is expensive; *you need* money for equipment.

Notice that when you join two simple sentences with a semicolon, the second sentence begins with a lowercase letter, not a capital letter.

Exercise 4   **Practice: Recognizing Compound Sentences and Adding Semicolons**

Add semicolons only where they are needed in the following sentences.

1. I took my dog to the veterinarian's office and asked the doctor about flea medication.

2. David doesn't like Italian food; he prefers Indian cooking.

3. Today has been horrible; everything has gone wrong.

4. Anita's fear of driving on the freeway is hurting her chances for a position in sales; many salespeople must travel frequently as part of their jobs.

5. The weekend at my brother's house was wonderful; we had some good conversations and laughed at each other's stories.

6. You might need glasses; you seem to be squinting often.

7. A doctor examined my ankle but seemed unconcerned about the possibility of broken bones.

8. My boyfriend is in jail; last night he was arrested for driving with an expired license.

9. In the middle of July, my air conditioner broke; I sweated in my tiny apartment for one miserable weekend.

10. A barbecue will be a pleasant way to celebrate Labor Day and a chance to see old friends.

Exercise 5   **Practice: More on Recognizing Compound Sentences and Adding Semicolons**

Add semicolons only where they are needed in the following sentences.

1. Sammy gossips about all his friends; I can never trust him with a secret.

2. Tamara sometimes changes the oil in the car; Phil never does.

3. Jessica or her cousin could invite their aunt to dinner, and pay a little attention to the elderly woman.

4. Everything in our bedroom is dusty or dirty, we really need to clean.

5. My clothes don't fit me anymore, and are not worth giving away to a charity.

6. Bill won't marry again, he is afraid of getting hurt and wants to protect himself from rejection.

7. A kind little man with a huge heart and a tough-talking lady guided me through some terrible times, and inspired me to change.

8. It's raining hard, we need our umbrellas.

9. Marrying young can satisfy your immediate needs, it can also lead you to a whole new set of needs.

10. My psychology class introduced me to different ways to understand other people's behavior, and taught me how to recognize my own motives.

OPTION 3: USING A SEMICOLON AND A CONJUNCTIVE ADVERB

Sometimes you may want to join two simple sentences (independent clauses) with a connecting word or phrase called a **conjunctive adverb.** This word points out or clarifies a relationship between the sentences.

INFO BOX: Some Common Conjunctive Adverbs

also	furthermore	likewise	otherwise
anyway	however	meanwhile	similarly
as a result	in addition	moreover	still
besides	in fact	nevertheless	then
certainly	incidentally	next	therefore
consequently	indeed	now	thus
finally	instead	on the other hand	undoubtedly

You can put a conjunctive adverb (CA) between simple sentences, but when you do, you still need a semicolon in front of the adverb.

two simple sentences:

S V   S V
I got a tutor for College Algebra. *I improved* my grade.

two simple sentences joined by a conjunctive adverb and a semicolon:

S V   ; CA S   V
I got a tutor for College Algebra; *then I improved* my grade.

S V   ;   CC   S   V
I got a tutor for College Algebra; *consequently, I improved* my grade.

Punctuating After a Conjunctive Adverb

Notice the comma after the conjunctive adverb in the sentence, *I got a tutor for college algebra; consequently, I improved my grade.* Here's the generally accepted rule:

> **Put a comma after the conjunctive adverb if the conjunctive adverb is more than one syllable long.**

For example, if the conjunctive adverb is a word like *consequently, furthermore,* or *moreover,* you use a comma. If the conjunctive adverb is one syllable, you do not have to add a comma after it. One-syllable conjunctive adverbs are words like *then* or *thus.*

punctuating with conjunctive adverbs:

Every month, I paid my whole credit card debt; *thus* I avoided paying interest.
Every month, I paid my whole credit card debt; *consequently,* I avoided paying interest.

Exercise 6   **Practice: Recognizing and Punctuating Compound Sentences with Conjunctive Adverbs**

Add semicolons and commas only where they are needed in the following sentences.

1. We worked on our plans for a trip to the beach, meanwhile the rain poured onto the roof and into the gutters.

2. We worked on our plans for a trip to the beach, then the rain poured onto the roof and into the gutters.

3. I hate writing with ballpoint pens; in fact, I always carry a gel or felt-tip pen.

4. My commute to college is a long bus ride; however, it gives me time to study.

5. Lindsay used to read stacks of romance novels, now she is involved in her own love story.

6. My car has been making a strange noise; undoubtedly, I should get the car checked by a mechanic.

7. Kevin's girlfriend nags him about his clothes, but refuses to go clothes shopping with him.

8. Last semester I waited too long to apply for financial aid; consequently, I am applying one month ahead of this semester's deadline.

9. Rick is a friend but never stops talking about himself, and his latest girlfriend.

10. We could celebrate our anniversary at an expensive restaurant, on the other hand we could have a romantic evening at home.

Exercise 7 **Practice: More on Recognizing and Punctuating Compound Sentences with Conjunctive Adverbs**

Add semicolons and commas only where they are needed in the following sentences.

1. Jim has always been a loyal friend to Adam; certainly he will come to Adam's wedding.

2. Jonetta's love of animals certainly played a role in her choice of a college major.

3. Greg might work in his father's landscaping business, and even study accounting at night.

4. I'll wash my clothes on Saturday morning; next I'll treat myself to breakfast at the Pancake Palace.

5. Keira begged and pleaded with her father; still he would not lend her the money for a tattoo.

6. Al never seems to have any money on him, yet always wears expensive clothes.

7. We'll go shopping; then we can meet your brother at the mall.

8. Tina is not interested in me; besides she already has a boyfriend.

9. Steve lived at home and worked at a full-time job for a year as a result; he saved enough money for college tuition.

10. Jerry was the best of all the contestants in the hip-hop contest; incidentally he is my cousin.

Exercise 8 **Practice: Selecting the Correct Conjunctive Adverb**

In the sentences below, underline the conjunctive adverb that expresses the meaning given in the hint. The first one is done for you.

1. Hint: Select the word that means *yet*.

   The best vegetarian restaurant is Fresh and Fabulous Food; (moreover, <u>however</u>), it's too expensive for a person on a budget.

2. Hint: Select the word that means *as a substitute*.

   Nathan has stopped smoking cigarettes; (<u>instead</u>, incidentally), he chews nicotine gum to deal with his cravings.

3. Hint: Select the word that means *in the same way or manner*.

   San Diego has a nearly perfect climate; (undoubtedly, <u>similarly</u>), the weather in the Bahamas is mild and welcoming.

4. Hint: Select the word that means *at the same time*.

   I ran to turn off the water in the overflowing bathtub; (<u>meanwhile</u>, anyway), Denise gathered a pile of dry towels and began wiping up the mess.

5. Hint: Select the word that means *without question*.

   My daughter has more training in dance than the other contestants; (otherwise, <u>undoubtedly</u>), she will win the dance competition.

6. Hint: Select the word that means *in spite of that*.

Mitchell doesn't have much money to buy clothes; (likewise, <u>nevertheless</u>), he always looks clean and neat.

7. Hint: Select the word that means *as a result*.

I worked in the kitchen of a pizza restaurant all summer; (<u>therefore</u>, furthermore), I am ready for a job in a less stifling atmosphere.

8. Hint: Select the word that means *at this moment*.

A year ago I did not speak much English; (<u>now</u>, next) I can hold a conversation with any speaker of the language.

9. Hint: Select the word that means *afterward*.

Miranda was my brother's girlfriend for two years; (thus, <u>then</u>) she met a handsome salesman at the local Ford dealership.

10. Hint: Select the word that means *without a doubt*.

My father is the best choice for the job of team leader; (<u>certainly</u>, furthermore), he has more experience than any of the other applicants.

Exercise 9   **Collaborate: Writing Sentences with Conjunctive Adverbs**

Collaborate

Working with a partner or group, write one sentence for each of the conjunctive adverbs below. When you have completed this exercise, share your answers with another group or with the class. The first one is done for you.

1. Write a compound sentence using *instead*.

She couldn't find her notes for her speech to the jury; instead, she relied

on her memory.

2. Write a compound sentence using *then*.

The boy ate the apple then, the boy ate another apple

3. Write a compound sentence using *furthermore*.

The boy ate the apple; furthermore, he was full.

4. Write a compound sentence using *on the other hand*.

The boy wanted to eat the apple; on the other hand he also had an orange.

5. Write a compound sentence using *otherwise*.

You'd better eat the apple; otherwise, you'll go hungry

6. Write a compound sentence using *therefore*.

He was hungry; therefore, he ate the apple

7. Write a compound sentence using *thus*.

We had sex; thus, we had a baby.

8. Write a compound sentence using *in addition*.

He ate the apple, in addition, he also ate apple pie.

9. Write a compound sentence using *undoubtedly*.

He likes apples; undoubtedly, he likes apple juice.

10. Write a compound sentence using *certainly*.

If you give him an apple, certainly he will want another

Exercise 10 Practice: Combining Simple Sentences Three Ways

Add (1) a comma, (2) a semicolon, or (3) a semicolon and a comma to the following sentences. Do not add, change, or delete any words. Just add the correct punctuation.

1. Send a sympathy card to Uncle Leo, then call him in a few days.

2. I admire my father very much, but some of his ideas about raising a family seem old-fashioned.

3. Melissa is out of town, so I am taking care of her tropical fish and walking her terrier for a few days.

4. Nothing is happening this weekend consequently, I am bored and restless.

5. Ryan used to be engaged to the star of a reality television show; anyway, he brags about this love affair all the time.

6. We may not get to Spring Hills before dark; still, we can try.

7. I have to use a special cream rinse on my hair; otherwise the top of my head looks like a thatch of dead grass.

8. We've decorated the house for the holiday, now the fun begins.

9. A snake found its way into our yard, it was lying in a sunny patch of leaves.

10. Thick, rich chocolate syrup covered the vanilla ice cream, and chunks of chocolate cookies crowded against the edges of the ice cream bowl.

Exercise 11 Practice: More on Combining Simple Sentences Three Ways

Add (1) a comma, (2) a semicolon, or (3) a semicolon and a comma to the following sentences. Do not add, change, or delete any words. Just add the correct punctuation.

1. Sandra might have run into bad weather on the highway, or she might have gotten a late start.

2. Eli called every paint store in town; finally he found a place with the right color of latex paint.

3. My mother never pays attention to family gossip, thus she remains friends with everyone in our large family.

4. I am tired of getting up early in the morning, in fact I would like to sleep until noon every day for a year.

5. The new shoe store is in a great location, yet it hasn't attracted many customers.

6. Yesterday, Shareena was flirting with me, now she walks by without talking to me.

7. Lionel was hungry, so he made some toast, with strawberry jelly.

8. My husband and his brother cleaned out our garage on Saturday, and I sorted through the boxes in the basement.

9. My grandfather walks two miles every day; in addition he belongs to a bicycle club and rides on weekends.

10. I took my sister to her favorite restaurant, then I asked her for a big favor.

Exercise 12　**Collaborate: Combining Simple Sentences**

Collaborate

Following are pairs of simple sentences. Working with a partner or group, combine each pair into one sentence. Remember the three options for combining sentences: (1) a comma and a coordinating conjunction, (2) a semicolon, (3) a semicolon and a conjunctive adverb. When you have combined each pair into one sentence, exchange your exercise with another group. Write a new sentence below each sentence prepared by the other group. The first one is done for you.

1. Takeout pizza for a family of six is expensive.

    My children and I make our own pizza at home.

    combination 1: Takeout pizza for a family of six is expensive, so my children and I make our own pizza at home.

    combination 2: Takeout pizza for a family of six is expensive; instead, my children and I make our own pizza at home.

2. Alicia recently earned her G.E.D.

    She is thinking about taking some college courses.

    combination 1: _____

    _____

    combination 2: _____

    _____

3. You never kept your friends' secrets.

    Most people no longer trust you.

    combination 1: _____

    _____

combination 2: _____

_____

4. Mrs. Garcia's house was always a mess.

Everyone loved the warmth and happiness in her home.

combination 1: _____

_____

combination 2: _____

_____

5. My parents were divorced after four years of marriage.

I never knew my father well.

combination 1: _____

_____

combination 2: _____

_____

6. Andrea never complained about being poor.

She did not want sympathy from others.

combination 1: _____

_____

combination 2: _____

_____

7. The community center has been closed for three years.

Teens have nowhere to go after school.

combination 1: _____

_____

combination 2: _____

_____

8. We can go to a movie at the multiplex.

We can play games at the arcade.

combination 1: _____

_____

combination 2: _____

_____

9. Charlotte Ling is a great chess player.

She started playing chess in elementary school.

combination 1: _____

_____

combination 2: _____

_____

10. We have run out of sugar.

I can put honey in my tea.

combination 1: _____

_____

combination 2: _____

_____

Exercise 13 **Connect: Punctuating Compound Sentences in a Paragraph** **Connect**

Add commas and semicolons only where they are needed in the paragraph below.

Losing a dog is a terrible experience finding one can be a stressful occasion, too. One morning, a woman from the neighborhood came to our door. She had a small, fluffy dog in her arms. She knew that we had a small poodle and she had found the fluffy dog wandering in the street. Did the dog in her arms belong to us? she asked. We said no but we offered to take the lost dog to our veterinarian's office. Our vet keeps part of her office for rescuing lost or abandoned pets however the rescue part accepts strays only in the late afternoon. In the meantime, we waited and worried. Our first worry concerned our dog she did not like the newcomer. The intruder dog sniffed our poodle consequently our dog growled. Soon the lost dog was exiled to our screened porch. We gave him water and food. He lapped the water enthusiastically then he peered through the sliding glass door of the porch and gazed lovingly at our dog. Our dog growled meanwhile we worried about the little stranger. We thought about dogs without homes and worried about a dog's life in a shelter. We went to the porch and petted the little dog immediately our dog growled. Soon the time came for taking the strange dog to our veterinarian's shelter. Fortunately, this story has a happy ending. The next day, the dog's owner checked the shelter. The lost dog became the found dog. All the humans felt relieved and two dogs were safe in their own homes.

Connect

Exercise 14 **Connect: Punctuating Compound Sentences in a Paragraph**

Add commas and semicolons only when they are needed in the paragraph below.

A habitually late friend or family member can be irritating but certain strategies can reduce the stress of family and friends in dealing with the latecomer. One such strategy is the lie. A punctual person can lie about the time of a movie or party as a result the habitually late person may actually show up on time. Unfortunately, the latecomer could soon discover this trick so it may not work for long. Another strategy is more dramatic but more exhausting for the punctual person. In this strategy, the punctual person shouts or screams at the late person. In some cases, the punctual person may also threaten the late person. Unfortunately, dramatic scenes may frighten the latecomer but they will not lead to a change in his or her behavior. Finally, the most useful strategy is a type of surrender. A punctual person can simply arrive late, too. Of course, doubling the number of late arrivals will ultimately lead to more friends and family missing the beginning of movies, offending the hosts of parties, and getting the worst seats in clubs. These consequences are not pleasant nevertheless they may result in a change in a habitually late person's behavior. At some time, he or she may want to see the beginning of a film or get a good seat at a club then Mr. or Ms. Tardiness may arrive early.

Chapter Test Beyond the Simple Sentence: Coordination

Add a comma, a semicolon, or a semicolon and a comma to the following sentences. Do not add, change, or delete any words; just add the correct punctuation.

1. On her birthday, Carlotta received a call from her father still she would have preferred a visit from him.

2. It rained for six hours on Saturday night finally the rain stopped on Sunday morning.

3. Ben wouldn't talk about his childhood in foster homes nor would he discuss his years as a runaway.

4. Your boyfriend is a kind and understanding person certainly he will support you in this sad time.

5. Many of the stores at Tower Mall are losing business for a new shopping center has opened nearby.

6. I will get better grades on my next two chemistry tests anyway I will study harder.

7. Most of the clothes in my closet were dirty some of them were smelly.

8. Carlton has a barbecue grill in his back yard thus he can invite his friends for cookouts during the summer.

9. You should go to the doctor and have your swollen wrist examined otherwise it could develop into a serious problem.

10. Kelly is always friendly and kind at work yet she never talks about herself.

CHAPTER 3

Avoiding Run-on Sentences and Comma Splices

Quick Question

True or False: A comma splice is an error that occurs when a writer forgets to use a comma where it is needed.

(After you study this chapter, you will be confident of your answer.)

Chapter Objectives

Students will be able to recognize and correct run-on sentences and comma splices.

RUN-ON SENTENCES

If you run two independent clauses together without the necessary punctuation, you make an error called a **run-on sentence.** This error is also called a **fused sentence.**

> **run-on sentence error:**
> I worked hard in the class I earned a good grade.

> **run-on sentence error corrected:**
> I worked hard in the class, and I earned a good grade. (To correct this error, you need a comma before the coordinating conjunction *and.*)

> **run-on sentence error:**
> I worked hard in the class I earned a good grade.

run-on sentence error corrected:

I worked hard in the class; I earned a good grade. (To correct this
error, you need a semicolon between the two independent clauses.)

run-on sentence error:

I worked hard in the class I earned a good grade.

run-on sentence error corrected:

I worked hard in the class. I earned a good grade. (To correct this
error, you need to create two sentences with a period after "class"
and a capital letter to begin the second sentence.)

Steps for Correcting Run-on Sentences

When you edit your writing, you can correct run-on sentences by following
these steps:

Step 1: Check for two independent clauses.

Step 2: Check that the clauses are separated by either a coordinating
conjunction (*for, and, nor, but, or, yet, so*) and a comma, or by
a semicolon.

Follow the steps in checking this sentence:

Spaghetti is cheap I buy it often.

Step 1: Check for two independent clauses. You can do this by checking for the subject–verb, subject–verb pattern that indicates
two independent clauses.

S   V   S V
Spaghetti is cheap *I buy* it often.

The pattern indicates that you have two independent clauses.

Step 2: Check that the clauses are separated by either a coordinating
conjunction (*for, and, nor, but, or, yet, so*) and a comma, or by
a semicolon.

There is no punctuation between the independent clauses, and there is no
coordinating conjunction. You therefore have a run-on sentence. You can
correct it three ways:

**run-on sentence corrected with a coordinating conjunction and
a comma:**

Spaghetti is cheap, *so* I buy it often.

run-on sentence corrected with a semicolon:

Spaghetti is cheap; I buy it often.

run-on sentence corrected with a period and a capital letter:

Spaghetti is cheap. I buy it often.

Follow the steps once more, checking this sentence:

I bought a new computer it is too complicated for me.

Step 1: Check for two independent clauses. Do this by checking the
subject–verb, subject–verb pattern.

S V   S V
I bought a new computer *it is* too complicated for me.

Step 2: Check that the clauses are separated by either a coordinating conjunction (*for, and, nor, but, or, yet, so*) and a comma, or by a semicolon.

There is no punctuation between the independent clauses. There is no coordinating conjunction, either. Without the proper punctuation, this is a run-on sentence. Correct it three ways:

> **run-on sentence corrected with a coordinating conjunction and a comma:**
> I bought a new computer, *but* it is too complicated for me.

> **run-on sentence error corrected with a semicolon:**
> I bought a new computer; it is too complicated for me.

> **run-on sentence error corrected with a period and a capital letter:**
> I bought a new computer. It is too complicated for me.

Using the steps to check for run-on sentences can also help you to avoid unnecessary punctuation. Consider this sentence:

> Alan stuffed the papers into the trash and carried the trash bag to the curb.

Step 1: Check for two independent clauses. Do this by checking the subject–verb, subject–verb pattern.

> S   V   V
> *Alled stuffed* the papers into the trash and *carried* the trash bag to the curb.

The pattern is SVV, not SV, SV. You have one independent clause, not two. The sentence is not a run-on sentence.

Following the steps in correcting run-on sentences can help you avoid a major grammatical error.

Exercise 1 **Practice: Correcting Run-on Sentences**

Some of the sentences below are correctly punctuated. Some are run-on (fused) sentences—two simple sentences run together without any punctuation. If a sentence is correctly punctuated, write *OK* in the space provided. If it is a run-on sentence, put an *X* in the space provided and correct the sentence above the lines.

1. _____ My father never went to college yet knows a great deal about the history of World War II.

2. _____ The elderly lady looked exhausted there were dark circles around her eyes.

3. _____ Water was leaking from the bottom of the refrigerator and spreading across the kitchen floor.

4. _____ The high price of fuel makes long road trips more difficult for vacationers but hasn't resulted in more people traveling by air.

5. _____ Marcus could visit his family during the spring he could wait until the summer months.

6. _____   I like writing with gel pens they write more smoothly than ballpoint pens and require less pressure than pencils.

7. _____   Nobody was home at my parents' house I opened the front door with my house key.

8. _____   My brother's baby is a beautiful boy the baby's picture should be on the label of jars of baby food.

9. _____   Kevin O'Connor exercises at the gym for an hour each morning he is in great shape.

10. _____   Tell Steve the truth he will probably forgive you.

Exercise 2   **Practice: More on Correcting Run-on Sentences**

Some of the following sentences are correctly punctuated. Some are run-on (fused) sentences—two simple sentences run together without any punctuation. If the sentence is correctly punctuated, write *OK* in the space provided. If it is a run-on sentence, put an *X* in the space provided and correct the sentence above the lines.

1. _____   Water was coming in through a leak in the window frame it was dripping down the newly painted wall.

2. _____   I'm going to get my hair cut tomorrow I want to look good for Emily's party.

3. _____   The store detective looked at me with suspicion and asked to see the contents of my bag.

4. _____   My car radio is not working right I can get only two radio stations.

5. _____   Tom complained about his brother Rick's clothes Rick wears Tom's clothes now.

6. _____   Sabrina still thinks about her first love she sighs over old photographs of the two of them together and listens to their special songs.

7. _____   I studied my psychology notes for an hour then I fell asleep in my chair.

8. _____   Waiting in line to register for classes and standing in line at the financial aid office can take several hours.

9. _____   My sister is shy thus some people mistakenly believe she is snobbish.

10. _____   Coffee and iced tea contain caffeine and can keep me awake at night.

COMMA SPLICES

A **comma splice** is an error that occurs when you punctuate with a comma but should use a semicolon instead. If you are joining two independent clauses without a coordinating conjunction, you *must use* a semicolon. A comma isn't enough.

comma splice error:
The rain fell steadily, the valley filled with water.

comma splice error corrected:
The rain fell steadily; the valley filled with water.

comma splice error:
I lost my umbrella, now I have to buy a new one.

comma splice error corrected:
I lost my umbrella; now I have to buy a new one.

Correcting Comma Splices

When you edit your writing, you can correct comma splices by following these steps:

Step 1: Check for two independent clauses.

Step 2: Check that the clauses are separated by a coordinating conjunction (*for, and, nor, but, or, yet, so*). If they are, then a comma in front of the coordinating conjunction is sufficient. If they are not separated by a coordinating conjunction, you have a comma splice. Correct it by changing the comma to a semicolon.

Follow the steps to check for a comma splice in this sentence:

The puppy jumped up, he licked my face.

Step 1: Check for two independent clauses. You can do this by checking for the subject–verb, subject–verb pattern that indicates two independent clauses.

S   V   S   V

The *puppy jumped* up, *he licked* my face.

Step 2: Check that the clauses are separated by a coordinating conjunction.

There is no coordinating conjunction. To correct the comma splice error, you must use a semicolon instead of a comma:

comma splice error corrected:
The puppy jumped up; he licked my face.

Be careful not to mistake a short word like *then* or *thus* for a coordinating conjunction. Only the seven coordinating conjunctions (*for, and, nor, but, or, yet, so*) with a comma in front of them can join independent clauses.

comma splice error:
Suzanne opened the letter, then she screamed with joy.

comma splice error corrected:
Suzanne opened the letter; then she screamed with joy.

Then is not a coordinating conjunction; it is a conjunctive adverb. When it joins two independent clauses, it needs a semicolon in front of it.

Also remember that conjunctive adverbs that are two or more syllables long (such as *consequently, however, therefore*) need a comma after them *as well as* a semicolon in front of them when they join independent clauses.

Anthony passed the placement test; consequently, he can take
Advanced Mathematics.

(For a list of some common conjunctive adverbs, see Chapter 2.)

Sometimes writers use commas before and after a conjunctive adverb
and think the commas are sufficient. Check this sentence for a comma splice
by following the steps:

The van held all my tools, however, it used too much gas.

Step 1: Check for two independent clauses by checking for the subject–verb, subject–verb pattern.

S   V   S   V

The van held all my tools, however, it used too much gas.

Step 2: Check for a coordinating conjunction.

There is no coordinating conjunction. *However* is a conjunctive adverb, not
a coordinating conjunction. Without a coordinating conjunction, a semicolon
is needed between the two independent clauses.

comma splice corrected:
The van held all my tools; however, it used too much gas.

Following the steps in correcting comma splices can help you avoid a major
grammar error.

Exercise 3   Practice: Correcting Comma Splices

Some of the following sentences are correctly punctuated. Some contain
comma splices. If the sentence is correctly punctuated, write *OK* in the space
provided. If it contains a comma splice, put an *X* in the space provided and
correct the sentence. To correct the sentence, you do not need to add words;
just correct the punctuation.

1. _____ We don't need an expensive television, nor should we spend
   any money on a new and faster computer.

2. _____ The soft kitten jumped into my lap, then it dug its sharp
   little claws into my arm.

3. _____ Sandra's little brother was reading all her email, also,
   he was telling his friends about some of the romantic
   messages.

4. _____ I lost my wallet, then I had to take quick action to protect
   my identity and savings.

5. _____ Eric spent most of his life in Norway, so he never complains
   about a few days of snow.

6. _____ You have to attend every one of your accounting classes,
   otherwise, you will miss too much explanation and be
   hopelessly lost.

7. _____ Bob loves spreading gossip at work, but he is extremely
   protective of his own privacy.

8. _____ The children's chorus worked on its spring concert for
   months, then very few people came to hear the program.

9. _____ We must invite your friends for dinner, otherwise, we will hurt their feelings.

10. _____ A piece of cake at a special dinner won't hurt you, a piece of cake after every dinner can add unhealthy fat, sugar, and empty calories.

Exercise 4 Practice: More on Correcting Comma Splices

Some of the following sentences are correctly punctuated. Some contain comma splices. If the sentence is correctly punctuated, write *OK* in the space provided. If it contains a comma splice, put an *X* in the space provided and correct the sentence. To correct the sentence, you do not need to add words; just correct the punctuation.

1. _____ My two-year-old has a cold, so I can't drop him off at his preschool today.

2. _____ Mr. Scheindlin enjoys Greek food, he comes to the annual Greek festival every year.

3. _____ Patrick and Claudia have three cats, moreover, they have a large Doberman.

4. _____ Jeans with status labels cost too much, I buy my jeans at a discount store.

5. _____ Someone broke into my parents' house, as a result, my parents have to get all their locks changed.

6. _____ I have been seeing Lisa for six months, yet I sometimes think about my former girlfriend.

7. _____ Pete wouldn't go to the fair with me, however, he promised he would meet me for breakfast next week.

8. _____ Andre always borrowed money from me and my sister, then he found a good job and paid us back.

9. _____ Eric handed me a small velvet box, it contained a pair of sparkling earrings.

10. _____ I'll call you tomorrow after school, or you can email me anytime.

Collaborate

Exercise 5 Collaborate: Completing Sentences

With a partner or group, write the first part of each of the following incomplete sentences. Make your addition an independent clause. Be sure to punctuate your completed sentences correctly. The first one is done for you.

1. My candle suddenly blew out; _____ then I saw the ghost.

2. _____ meanwhile, someone screamed.

3. _____ yet he kept smiling at me.

4. _____ next we'll plan a wedding.

5. _____ now I can't sleep.

6. _____ consequently, he won't speak to me.

7. _____ for I'm really hungry.

8. _____but the shadowy figure followed us.

9. _____ instead, you can be honest.

10. _____ and a swarm of bees appeared.

Exercise 6   **Connect: Editing a Paragraph for Run-on Sentences and Comma Splices**

Connect

Edit the following paragraph for run-on sentences and comma splices. There are eight errors.

Waiting in line at a crowded restaurant can provide a lesson in personality types and in keeping the peace. First of all, there are the calm people, they wait patiently and quietly. Unfortunately, the calm people are often outnumbered by the other types. Some people see the wait as a social opportunity they like to make new friends. Social types start conversations they will talk to anyone. Such people are generally kind and don't mean any harm. They have sweet dispositions, however, a few shy or very private people may feel uneasy around the social people. A more irritating type is the loud cell phone conversationalist. The conversationalist needs to be on the phone all the time. Unfortunately, the conversationalist loves an audience. With a captive audience of people in line, the conversationalist is elated. He or she will reveal family secrets and disturbing emotional problems and never blink, meanwhile, the listeners in line are horrified. No one knows whether to look at the speaker or to look away. The last kind of line personality is physically aggressive. Restless and impatient people in line may push others, they may even jump to the head of the line. Line jumpers often try to look confident they walk boldly to the front, ask a question of a staff member, and then stay at the front of the line. With cell phone dramatics and line jumping, even patient people can become distressed. A mix of impatience and irritation can be dangerous but everyone in line should remember the value of peaceful coexistence and think of the delicious food to come.

Connect

Exercise 7 **Connect: Editing a Paragraph for Run-on Sentences and Comma Splices**

Edit the following paragraph for run-on sentences and comma splices. There are five errors.

Working on the weekends can be a great fit for one person's schedule and a terrible strain on another person's time. My experiences have shown both the advantages and disadvantages of such a schedule. I was quite happy working long weekend hours last semester, at that time, I had a light course load at college. I was able to do my assigned reading and studying during the week then I could put in many weekend hours as a pizza delivery person. The money was good, and I managed to get fairly good grades for the term. This semester is a much more difficult one, I am taking an advanced math class and a chemistry class. Both of these classes demand hours of study the extra study time stretches well into the weekend. I had to reduce my hours at the pizza shop later, I had to quit the job. Next semester, I have to take another chemistry class and a challenging physics class. During that semester, I will look for part-time work on week nights and save my weekends for hours of study.

Chapter Test Avoiding Run-on Sentences and Comma Splices

Some of the sentences below are correctly punctuated. Some are run-on sentences, and some contain comma splices. If a sentence is correctly punctuated, write *OK* in the space provided. If it is a run-on sentence or contains a comma splice, put an *X* in the space provided and correct the sentence above the lines. To correct a sentence, add the necessary punctuation. Do not add any words.

1. _____ Someone at the back of the room sneezed loudly I began to worry about the recent flu epidemic.

2. _____ Ella met a kind, bright, and attractive man at college in Chicago and became engaged to him at the end of her sophomore year.

3. _____ My dog is getting older, consequently, I worry about her capacity for long walks and other vigorous exercise.

4. _____ You forgot our anniversary such thoughtlessness hurts me.

5. _____ It's too late for a big meal, so let's have soup and a salad.

6. _____ My bedroom is dark, in fact, it's the darkest room in the house.

7. _____ Calvin doesn't drink alcohol thus he saves money on visits to bars and clubs.

8. _____ My mother is not fond of her older brother, nevertheless, she invites him to all the family gatherings.

9. _____ Brian will love moving to Arizona, for he is an experienced mountain climber with a true appreciation for nature.

10. _____ Manny gave his little girl a compliment about her drawing of a horse instantly the child smiled with pride.

CHAPTER 4

Beyond the Simple Sentence: Subordination

Quick Question

Which sentence(s) is/ are correct?

A. Unless my sore throat improves, I can't sing in the chorus tomorrow.

B. I can't sing in the chorus tomorrow unless my sore throat improves.

(After you study this chapter, you will be confident of your answer.)

Chapter Objectives

Students will be able to (1) identify sentence-combining techniques that rely on subordinating conjunctions, (2) distinguish between dependent and independent clauses, and (3) generate and punctuate sentences correctly.

MORE ON COMBINING SIMPLE SENTENCES

You may remember these principles of grammar:

- A clause has a subject and a verb.
- An independent clause is a simple sentence; it is a group of words, with a subject and a verb, that makes sense by itself.

Chapter 2 described three options for combining simple sentences (independent clauses). There is another kind of clause called a **dependent clause.** It has a subject and a verb, but it does not make sense by itself. It cannot stand alone because it is not complete by itself. That is, it *depends* on the rest of the sentence to give it meaning. You can use a dependent clause in another option for combining simple sentences.

OPTION 4: USING A DEPENDENT CLAUSE TO BEGIN A SENTENCE

Often, you can combine simple sentences by changing an independent clause into a dependent clause and placing it at the beginning of the new sentence.

two simple sentences:

S   V   S V
I missed my bus. *I slept* through my alarm.

changing one simple sentence into a beginning dependent clause:

S V   S   V
Because *I slept* through my alarm, *I missed* my bus.

OPTION 5: USING A DEPENDENT CLAUSE TO END A SENTENCE

You can also combine simple sentences by changing an independent clause into a dependent clause and placing it at the end of the new sentence:

S   V   S V
I missed my bus because *I slept* through my alarm.

Notice how one simple sentence can be changed into a dependent clause in two ways:

two simple sentences:

S   V   S   V
Nicholas played his guitar. *Jared sang* an old song.

changing one simple sentence into a dependent clause:

S   V   S   V
Nicholas played his guitar while *Jared sang* an old song.

or

S   V   S   V
While *Jared sang* an old song, *Nicholas played* his guitar.

Using Subordinating Words: Subordinating Conjunctions

Changing an independent clause to a dependent one is called **subordinating.** How do you do it? You add a subordinating word, called a **subordinating conjunction,** to an independent clause, which makes it dependent—less "important"—or subordinate, in the new sentence.

Keep in mind that the subordinate clause is still a clause; it has a subject and a verb, but it doesn't make sense by itself. For example, here is an independent clause:

S   V
David cooks

Somebody (David) does something (cooks). The statement makes sense by itself. But if you add a subordinating conjunction to the independent clause, the clause becomes dependent—incomplete, unfinished—like this:

When David cooks (When he cooks, what happens?)
Unless David cooks (Unless he cooks, what will happen?)
If David cooks (If he cooks, what will happen?)

Now, each dependent clause needs an independent clause to finish the idea:

dependent clause   independent clause
When David cooks, he makes wonderful meals.

dependent clause   independent clause
Unless David cooks, you will not get a decent dinner.

dependent clause   independent clause
If David cooks, dinner will be delicious.

There are many subordinating conjunctions. When you put any of these words in front of an independent clause, you make that clause dependent. Here is a list of some subordinating conjunctions.

INFO BOX: **Subordinating Conjunctions**

after	before	so that	whenever
although	even though	though	where
as	if	unless	whereas
as if	in order that	until	whether
because	since	when	while

If you pick the right subordinating conjunction, you can effectively combine simple sentences (independent clauses) into a more sophisticated sentence pattern. Such combining helps you add sentence variety to your writing and helps to explain relationships between ideas.

simple sentences:

S V   V   S V
Emily had never *studied* art. *She was* a gifted painter.

new combination:

dependent clause   independent clause
Although Emily had never studied art, she was a gifted painter.

simple sentences:

S V   S   V
I bought a new leash last night. My *puppy chewed* up his old one.

new combination:

independent clause   dependent clause
I bought a new leash last night because my puppy chewed up his old one.

Punctuating Complex Sentences

The new combination, which has one independent clause and one or more dependent clauses, is called a **complex sentence.** Complex sentences are very easy to punctuate. See if you can figure out the rule for punctuating by yourself. Look at the following examples. All are punctuated correctly:

dependent clause   independent clause
Whenever I visit my mother, I bring flowers.

independent clause   dependent clause
I bring flowers whenever I visit my mother.

dependent clause   independent clause
While he was talking, I was daydreaming.

independent clause   dependent clause
I was daydreaming while he was talking.

In the examples above, look at the sentences that have a comma. Now look at the ones that don't have a comma. Both kinds of sentences are punctuated correctly. Do you see the rule?

When a dependent clause comes at the beginning of a sentence, the clause is followed by a comma. When a dependent clause comes at the end of a sentence, the clause does not need a comma.

Here are some correctly punctuated complex sentences:

Although he studied hard, he failed the test.
He failed the test although he studied hard.
Until I started running, I was out of shape.
I was out of shape until I started running.

Exercise 1 Practice: Punctuating Complex Sentences

All of the following sentences are complex sentences—they have one independent and one or more dependent clauses. Add a comma to each sentence that needs one.

1. Unless I get a part-time job during the summer, I won't have enough money for fall tuition and fees at college.

2. Bring me some fresh orange juice, when you go to the supermarket.

3. After Victoria heard about the robbery on the other side of town, she stopped jogging through the local park on her own.

4. When daylight savings time begins, I feel disoriented for a few days.

5. Andrew struggled with depression, after he returned from military service in Afghanistan.

6. Before Aunt Ella saw a physician, my aunt had no idea of the dangers of diabetes.

7. Whenever the weather changes, suddenly allergy sufferers are likely to experience symptoms.

8. Pedestrians huddled against the walls of the nearest buildings, as a sudden storm blasted through the city.

9. My father hasn't had anything to eat since he grabbed coffee, and a doughnut this morning at 6:00 P.M.

10. As we agreed last month, you are going to pay for the gas on our weekend trip to Daytona Beach.

Exercise 2 **Practice: More on Punctuating Complex Sentences**

All of the following sentences are complex sentences—they have one independent and one or more dependent clauses. Add a comma to each sentence that needs one.

1. Although the area once had a reputation for criminal activity, and urban decay it is slowly renewing itself and emerging as an attractive neighborhood.

2. Lewis is taking care of his two nephews, while his sister is in the hospital.

3. Maybe Marcie can tell me where Leonard put the box of envelopes.

4. Toby smiled at me, as if he had a wonderful secret.

5. Since there's nothing I want to watch on television, I'm going to listen to some music.

6. Even if Laura can't find the perfect job, she can earn money and learn about her field in a less attractive job.

7. Ardese called me last night, because she is worried about her father's health.

8. Tom will drive me to Tulsa next week, unless he has to fill in for someone at the station.

9. Because my parents spoke Spanish at home, I grew up knowing two languages.

10. I want to research used cars on the Internet, before I visit any car dealerships.

Exercise 3 **Practice: Combining Sentences**

Combine each pair of sentences below into one smooth, clear sentence. The new combination should include one independent and one dependent clause and an appropriate subordinating word.

1. I am hoping for sunny weather on Saturday. I can spend the afternoon at the beach.

combined: _____ So that _____

2. Angela rehearsed her speech in front of family members and friends. She became more confident about giving the speech in front of her speech class.

combined: because _____

3. Cameron has been saving a little money each month. He wants to buy a bus ticket home to Alabama.

   combined: _because_ _____

   _____

4. Eric developed a sudden interest in the theater. He met a pretty and dynamic drama student.

   combined: _when_ _____

   _____

5. You never admit your mistakes. They always come to my attention in some way.

   combined: _so that_ _____

   _____

6. We lose our electricity during the storm. We have plenty of battery-powered lights and lanterns.

   combined: _however_ _____

   _____

7. I plan on a quiet Saturday night. My sister asks me to babysit for her toddlers.

   combined: _unless_ _____

   _____

8. Omar called and told me an enormous lie about his weekend plans. I heard his roommate laughing in the background.

   combined: _because_ _____

   _____

9. Broiled fish is a healthy and low-fat food. I never eat it.

   combined: _whereas_ _____

   _____

10. Lisa took many advanced classes in mathematics and science. She could be accepted into a prestigious technology program at a nearby college.

    combined: _so that_ _____

    _____

Exercise 4   **Collaborate: Creating Complex Sentences**

Collaborate

Do this exercise with a partner or group. Each item below lists a dependent clause. Write two different sentences that include the dependent clause. One sentence should begin with the dependent clause; the other sentence should end with the dependent clause. The first one is done for you.

1. **dependent clause:** whenever I visit my grandmother

   sentence 1: _Whenever I visit my grandmother, she tells me stories about life in Havana._

sentence 2: _I bring a box of chocolates whenever I visit my grandmother._
_____

2. **dependent clause:** even if Kevin apologizes

   sentence 1: _____

   _____

   sentence 2: _____

   _____

3. **dependent clause:** as shots were fired at the soldiers

   sentence 1: _____

   _____

   sentence 2: _____

   _____

4. **dependent clause:** before our baby is born

   sentence 1: _____

   _____

   sentence 2: _____

   _____

5. **dependent clause:** since I have to work overtime this weekend

   sentence 1: _____

   _____

   sentence 2: _____

   _____

6. **dependent clause:** after he spent a year in prison

   sentence 1: _____

   _____

   sentence 2: _____

   _____

7. **dependent clause:** while the family slept

   sentence 1: _____

   _____

   sentence 2: _____

   _____

8. **dependent clause:** unless you can think of a better place

   sentence 1: _____

   _____

   sentence 2: _____

   _____

9. **dependent clause:** although my room is a mess

   sentence 1: _____

   _____

sentence 2: _____

_____

10. **dependent clause:** because my boss was a kind person

sentence 1: _____

_____

sentence 2: _____

_____

Exercise 5   **Connect: Editing a Paragraph with Complex Sentences**   Connect

Edit this paragraph by adding or omitting commas. There are eight places that contain errors.

For fifteen years, my family has moved often and has had to deal with mixed effects of constant change. Because my parents and I have seen many parts of the country, we have learned about different places. We know about the beauty of Northern California, and the friendliness of people in small Southern towns. We have learned how to adjust quickly to a new house, or a new town, so that we can feel secure and stable. We have learned not to judge strangers before we get to know them. While some people have been known to judge us too quickly, we have tried to understand them. Although our many travels have widened our perspective and brought us happiness, we have missed a few important parts of a stable life. My parents suffered whenever they were forced to look for new jobs. Since I changed schools six times, I never enjoyed an enduring friendship. Loneliness followed us from place to place, even though we found good people in each city or town. Fortunately, my family has now settled for good in a warm and safe community, where we can develop permanent friendships and deep bonds.

Exercise 6   **Connect: Editing a Paragraph with Complex Sentences**   Connect

Edit this paragraph by adding commas or omitting commas. There are six places that contain errors.

When long hair looks good on a man he should not think about cutting it. Russell had always been known for his attractive head of long, sleek brown hair with its red, sunburnt glints. Russell began to think about cutting his hair, when a few of his friends teased him about looking like a girl. They encouraged him to follow the latest styles and get rid of his extra hair. These friends had recently

shaved their heads and did not look very attractive after their style change.

Although Russell would not agree to join them in their bald state he did consent to

a haircut. His friends cheered him, while the stylist clipped, shaped, and snipped

Russell's hair. The result was a short cut. After the session at the hair salon was

complete Russell looked stylish. Unfortunately, he looked like hundreds of men

with the same haircut. Russell will not be the real Russell, until he lets his hair

grow again.

Chapter Test Beyond the Simple Sentence: Subordination

All of the following sentences are complex sentences, but some are not correctly punctuated. Write *OK* next to the ones that are correctly punctuated and *X* next to the ones that are not.

1. _____ My grandmother could barely walk, before she started physical therapy at the orthopedic center.

2. _____ Whenever the doorbell rings my dog hides.

3. __X__ Everyone at school treats me as if I had a contagious disease.

4. _____ I can't wait until my husband gets back from active duty in Iraq and can see our new baby.

5. _____ Since her hair is thick and unmanageable, my cousin spends a great deal of money on hair products and visits to hair salons.

6. _____ A garbage truck made its early morning rounds through the neighborhood, while I covered my ears and tried to block out the noise of creaky metal crashing against metal.

7. _____ After you finish summer school, you can take a short break and relax.

8. _____ Let me know, if you need a ride to work.

9. _____ Whether Emmanuel decides to forgive you or stays angry, you have done the right thing.

10. _____ Eddie is a terrible cook, even though he brags about his barbecuing expertise.

MyWritingLab™ For support in meeting this chapter's objectives, log in to www.mywritinglab.com and select **Parts of Speech, Phrases and Clauses**, and **Combining Sentences**.

Combining Sentences: A Review of Your Options

Chapter Objectives

Students will be able to (1) recognize compound and complex sentence patterns and (2) incorporate an effective balance of long and short sentences in their writing.

Combining sentences helps you to avoid a choppy writing style in which all your sentences are short. The pattern of one short sentence after another makes your writing repetitive and boring. When you mix the length of sentences, using some long ones and some short ones, you use a strategy called **sentence variety.**

You can develop a style that includes sentence variety by combining short, related sentences clearly and smoothly. There are several ways to combine sentences. The following chart helps you to see them all at a glance. It also includes the punctuation necessary for each combination.

INFO BOX: Options for Combining Sentences

Coordination

Option 1

Independent clause
{
, for
, and
, nor
, but
, or
, yet
, so
}
independent clause.

Option 2

Independent clause
{
;
}
independent clause.

Option 3

Independent clause
{
; also,
; anyway,
; as a result,
; besides,
; certainly,
; consequently,
; finally,
; furthermore,
; however,
; in addition,
; in fact,
; incidentally,
; indeed,
; instead,
; likewise,
; meanwhile,
; moreover,
; nevertheless,
; next
; now
; on the other hand,
; otherwise,
; similarly,
; still
; then
; therefore,
; thus
; undoubtedly,
}
independent clause.

Subordination

	After	
	Although	
	As	
	As if	
	Because	
	Before	
	Even though	
	If	
	In order that	
Option 4	Since	dependent clause, independent clause. (When you begin with a dependent clause, put a comma at the end of the dependent clause.)
	So that	
	Though	
	Unless	
	Until	
	When	
	Whenever	
	Where	
	Whereas	
	Whether	
	While	

	after	
	although	
	as	
	as if	
	because	
	before	
	even though	
	if	
	in order that	
Option 5	since	dependent clause
Independent clause	so that	
	though	
	unless	
	until	
	when	
	whenever	
	where	
	whereas	
	whether	
	while	

Note: In Option 4, words are capitalized because the dependent clause will begin your complete sentence.

Exercise 1   **Practice: Combining Simple Sentences**

Following are pairs of simple sentences. Combine each pair of sentences into one clear, smooth sentence. Create two new combinations for each pairing. The first one is done for you.

1. My car wouldn't start yesterday.

   The car battery was dead.

   combination 1: My car wouldn't start yesterday because the battery was dead.

   _____

   combination 2: The car battery was dead; as a result, my car wouldn't start yesterday.

2. Allison was afraid to be alone.

   She tolerated her boyfriend's selfish behavior.

   combination 1: _____

   _____

   combination 2: _____

   _____

3. My brother has to get up early to go to work every day.

   He feels lucky to have a little job security.

   combination 1: _____

   _____

   combination 2: _____

   _____

4. Professor Montand is friendly and understanding.

   He demands his students' best work.

   combination 1: _____

   _____

   combination 2: _____

   _____

5. My brother and his friends get together on Sunday afternoons.

   They talk about sports for hours.

   combination 1: _____

   _____

   combination 2: _____

   _____

6. I cooked some fish last night.

   My cat started circling the kitchen.

   combination 1: _____

   _____

combination 2: _____

_____

7. You can go to the new action film.

You won't like it much.

combination 1: _____

_____

combination 2: _____

_____

8. My four-year-old nephew found the salt shaker.

He sprinkled the entire living room carpet with salt.

combination 1: _____

_____

combination 2: _____

_____

9. Sam's grandmother is a cranky woman.

He visits her regularly.

combination 1: _____

_____

combination 2: _____

_____

10. I am sleeping on my sister's couch.

I was evicted from my apartment.

combination 1: _____

_____

combination 2: _____

_____

| Exercise 2 | **Collaborate: Create Your Own Text** |

Collaborate

Following is a list of rules for sentence combining through coordinating and subordinating sentences. Working with a group, create two examples of each rule and write those sentences on the lines provided. After your group has completed this exercise, share your examples with another group.

Option 1: You can join two simple sentences (two independent clauses) into a compound sentence with a coordinating conjunction and a comma in front of it. (The coordinating conjunctions are *for, and, nor, but, or, yet, so.*)

example 1: _____

_____

example 2: _____

_____

Option 2: You can combine two simple sentences (two independent clauses) into a compound sentence with a semicolon between independent clauses.

example 1: _____

_____

example 2: _____

_____

Option 3: You can combine two simple sentences (two independent clauses) into a compound sentence with a semicolon and a conjunctive adverb between independent clauses. (Some common conjunctive adverbs are _also, anyway, as a result, besides, certainly, consequently, finally, furthermore, however, in addition, in fact, incidentally, indeed, instead, likewise, meanwhile, moreover, nevertheless, next, now, on the other hand, otherwise, similarly, still, then, therefore, thus,_ and _undoubtedly._)

example 1: _____

_____

example 2: _____

_____

Option 4: You can combine two simple sentences (two independent clauses) into a complex sentence by making one clause dependent. The dependent clause starts with a subordinating conjunction. If the dependent clause begins the sentence, the clause ends with a comma. (Some common subordinating conjunctions are _after, although, as, because, before, even though, if, in order that, since, though, unless, until, when, whenever, where, whereas, whether, while._)

example 1: _____

_____

example 2: _____

_____

Option 5: You can combine two simple sentences (two independent clauses) into a complex sentence by making one clause dependent. If the dependent clause comes after the independent clause, no comma is needed.

example 1: _____

_____

example 2: _____

_____

| **Exercise 3** | **Connect: Combining Sentences in a Paragraph** |

Connect

In the following paragraph, combine each pair of underlined sentences into one clear, smooth sentence. Write your combination in the space above the old sentences.

I made my choice of careers years ago. I was a child. My parents gave me a puppy for my seventh birthday, and I fell in love. Most children love puppies instantly. Most children lose interest in the dogs or take them for granted. I was not like most children. My dog became my best friend. I took responsibility for his care. I loved to walk him, feed him, and brush him. Soon I wanted my dog to have a little brother or sister. I brought home a stray dog. At age ten, I had three dogs, two cats, and three hamsters. My parents accepted all these new members of the family. They could see my love for animals. At fourteen, I volunteered to walk the dogs at the animal shelter. I saw the kindness of the staff. I recognized the needs of the helpless animals. I wanted to do more than walk the dogs. From my first puppy to my teen work at the shelter, I had been moving toward one goal. Today, I am closer to that goal. I am studying veterinary science.

| **Exercise 4** | **Connect: Editing a Paragraph with Compound and Complex Sentences** |

Connect

Edit the following paragraph, adding commas and semicolons where they are necessary and taking out unnecessary commas. There are nine errors.

My situation makes it difficult for me to meet people. I am a commuter student at a nearby college. In addition, I am the single parent of two children, and have a job. Because I am juggling so many responsibilities I have very little social life. I don't meet anyone at work, where I sit in front of a computer screen all day. I attend classes at night and on weekends. I rush to classes then, I rush home to my children. Most of my relatives are married and middle-aged. They don't know many young people so I meet few people of my age through my family. My friends have good intentions but I hate "fixed-up" dates. At this time in my life, I must focus on raising my children, finishing my education, and getting a better job. Now there is no time or opportunity for romance on the other hand I may find it later.

Exercise 5 **Connect: Editing a Paragraph with Compound and Complex Sentences**

Edit the following paragraph, adding semicolons and commas where they are necessary and taking out unnecessary commas. There are nine errors.

I have recently started to notice the size and weight of women's bags I am amazed at and horrified by these monstrous accessories. My sister carries a huge canvas shoulder bag, whenever she leaves the house. I tried to pick it up the other day, after she dropped it on the couch. It weighed about twenty pounds. It must have been full of rocks undoubtedly, she uses it as a weapon against muggers. I feel sorry for any purse snatcher with a plan to rob my sister for he or she would wind up with a severe injury. In fact, I think my sister's shoulder is sinking under the weight of her bag. My girlfriend is another woman burdened by her bag. Unlike my sister, she carries a handbag however, it bulges with electronics, cell phone accessories, and even a tiny umbrella. It weighs about as much as my sister's bag, and seems to be dragging my girlfriend's arm down. Since I've become more conscious of women's bags I've noticed many women struggling under the weight of huge, bulky handbags and shoulder bags. Observing this trend has made me feel sympathy for women but it has also made me glad to leave home with only keys, a wallet, and a cell phone in my pockets.

Chapter Test Combining Sentences: A Review of Your Options

All of the following sentences are compound or complex sentences, but some are not correctly punctuated. Write *OK* next to the ones that are correctly punctuated and *X* next to the ones that are not.

1. _____ I cannot resist a gooey chocolate brownie, although it is full of fat and sugar.

2. _____ Rafael told me a lie, then he covered it up with another lie.

3. _____ The singer was a role model for many young Latinas, for she had great talent, a strong spirit, and a big heart.

4. _____ Unless we get stuck in heavy traffic, we should make it to the stadium on time.

5. _____ My girlfriend can be stubborn and demanding; on the other hand, she is loyal and loving.

6. _____ Charlie doesn't know much about living on his own because, his mother cooked his meals, cleaned his room, and did all his laundry.

7. _____ While Danny stared at the phone bill in horror; I pretended not to notice his reaction.

8. _____ Somebody drove through a red light, then I heard sirens behind me.

9. _____ My grandfather just completed a yoga class; now he is taking a course in creative writing.

10. _____ Clarissa rarely changes the style of her beautiful, curly hair, nor does she wear a great deal of makeup.

Avoiding Sentence Fragments

Chapter Objectives

Students will be able to recognize and correct sentence fragments.

A **sentence fragment** is a group of words that looks like a sentence, is punctuated like a sentence, but is not a sentence. Writing a sentence fragment is a major error in grammar because it reveals that the writer is not sure what a sentence is. The following groups of words are all fragments:

fragments:
Because parents with small children want a car with room for a car seat, stroller, diaper bags, and toys.
Her father being an open-minded individual.
For example, the controversy over the safety of air bags.

There are two simple steps that can help you check your writing for sentence fragments.

INFO BOX: Two Steps in Recognizing Sentence Fragments

Step 1: Check each group of words punctuated like a sentence; look for a subject and a verb.

Step 2: If you find a subject and a verb, check that the group of words makes a complete statement.

RECOGNIZING FRAGMENTS: STEP 1

Check for a subject and a verb. Some groups of words that look like sentences may actually have a subject but no verb, or they may have a verb but no subject, or they may have no subject *or* verb.

fragments:
The bowl with the bright gold rim. (*Bowl* could be the subject of the sentence, but there is no verb.)
Can't be a friend of mine from college. (There is a verb, *Can be*, but there is no subject.)
On the tip of my tongue. (There are two prepositional phrases, *On the tip* and *of my tongue*, but there is no subject or verb.)

Remember that an *-ing* verb by itself cannot be the main verb in a sentence. Therefore, groups of words like the following ones may look like sentences but are missing a verb and are really fragments.

fragments:
The man cooking the Texas chili for the barbecue contest.
A few brave souls taking the plunge into the icy lake in mid-March.
My friend Cynthia being loyal to her selfish and manipulative sister.

An infinitive (*to* plus a verb) cannot be a main verb in a sentence, either. The following groups of words, which contain infinitives, are also fragments.

fragments:
Next week a representative of the airlines to meet with travel agents from across the country.
My hope to help the children of the war-torn nation.
Something nutritious to eat for supper.

Groups of words beginning with words such as *also, especially, except, for example, for instance, in addition,* and *such as* need subjects and verbs. Without subjects and verbs, these groups can be fragments, like the ones below:

fragments:
Also a dangerous neighborhood in the late hours of the evening.
Especially a house with a large basement.
For example, a box of high-priced chocolates.

Checking for subjects and verbs is the first step in recognizing the major sentence errors called fragments.

Exercise 1 Practice: Checking Groups of Words for Subjects and Verbs

Some of the following groups of words have subjects and verbs; these are sentences. Some groups are missing subjects, verbs, or both; these are fragments. Put an *S* next to each sentence; put an *F* next to each fragment.

1. _____ Especially someone with an extreme fear of heights.

2. _____ For example, homeowners struggle to meet their mortgage payments in a time of economic uncertainty.

3. _____ Certainly shouldn't think about a trip to a country with an unstable government and armed rebels in the countryside.

4. _____ The thin walls between the apartments allowing the noise of each apartment to travel into the adjoining ones and preventing residents from getting to sleep at night.

5. _____ The new exit on the highway reduces the typical rush hour congestion.

6. _____ From the shimmering costumes of the dance team to the precision of the marching band.

7. _____ Will's need for attention being stronger than his desire to earn his parents' respect.

8. _____ Except for the support of my loving family and the encouragement of the staff at the physical therapy center in Monroe.

9. _____ Can't we come to an agreement about the price of your three-year-old Camry?

10. _____ At a bowling alley near a rundown strip of tattoo parlors and takeout restaurants.

Exercise 2 Practice: More on Checking Groups of Words for Subjects and Verbs

Some of the following groups of words have subjects and verbs; these are sentences. Some groups are missing subjects, verbs, or both; these are fragments. Put an *S* next to each sentence; put an *F* next to each fragment.

1. _____ Learning a language takes practice.

2. _____ A hint of sadness appeared in his paintings.

3. _____ Needs a used car with low mileage and a good safety record.

4. _____ Mr. Sabatino's explanation for the fire being an electrical problem in the basement.

5. _____ Especially a woman with a good education and excellent references from previous employers.

6. _____ From the end of the line came a loud voice.

7. _____ Might have chosen a partner with more common sense.

8. _____ One conflict with little chance of a resolution in the next few months.

9. _____ Linda is spreading a rumor around the neighborhood.

10. _____ Except for my mother, no one likes cornbread.

RECOGNIZING FRAGMENTS: STEP 2

If you are checking a group of words to see if it is a sentence, the first step is to look for a subject and a verb. If you find a subject and a verb, step 2 is to check that the group of words makes a complete statement. Many groups of words have both a subject and a verb but don't make sense by themselves. They are **dependent clauses.**

How can you tell if a clause is dependent? After you've checked each group of words for a subject and a verb, check to see if it begins with one of the subordinating conjunctions that start dependent clauses.

> **INFO BOX:** **Subordinating Conjunctions**
>
> | | | | |
> |---|---|---|---|
> | after | before | so that | whenever |
> | although | even though | though | where |
> | as | if | unless | whereas |
> | as if | in order that | until | whether |
> | because | since | when | while |

A clause that begins with a subordinating conjunction is a dependent clause. When you punctuate a dependent clause as if it were a sentence, you have a kind of fragment called a **dependent-clause fragment.** These fragments do not make a complete statement.

dependent-clause fragments:

After she gave him a kiss. (What happened after she gave him a kiss?)
Because lemonade tastes better than limeade. (What will happen because lemonade tastes better than limeade?)
Unless you leave for the movie right now. (What will happen unless you leave for the movie right now?)

It is important to remember both steps in checking for fragments:

Step 1: Check for a subject and a verb.

Step 2: If you find a subject and a verb, check that the group of words makes a complete statement.

Exercise 3   **Practice: Checking for Dependent-Clause Fragments**

Some of the following groups of words are sentences. Some are dependent clauses punctuated like sentences; these are sentence fragments. Put an *S* next to each sentence and an *F* by each fragment.

1. _____ Whenever I hear an old song from my senior year at Washington High School.

2. _____ At the birthday party for my boyfriend was a woman with an obvious interest in attracting his attention.

3. _____ Whether I can get more child support from the father of my twins.

4. _____ Making a fuss is my sister's way of coping with anxiety.

5. _____ On Saturdays I always have good intentions about catching up on household chores.

6. _____ If you can pick Denise up at the airport next Sunday at 9:30 P.M.

7. _____ Behind all the gossip about Russell is resentment of his sudden success.

8. _____ Before the paint had dried on the bathroom walls.

9. _____ Although the chances of a hurricane hitting our area in late October are slim.

10. _____ Because golf is a boring sport for most television viewers.

| Exercise 4 | **Practice: More on Checking for Dependent-Clause Fragments** |

Some of the following groups of words are sentences. Some are dependent clauses punctuated like sentences; these are sentence fragments. Put an *S* next to each sentence and an *F* by each fragment.

1. _____ Then the kitten licked the sleeping child.

2. _____ Unless Claudia asks for a transfer to another department.

3. _____ From my grandfather I inherited a love of fishing.

4. _____ Even though the prices at Classic Style can be high.

5. _____ Until somebody complained about the broken traffic light at the intersection of River Road and Carson Boulevard.

6. _____ Without Darrell there wouldn't be a party.

7. _____ Since Pete signed up for a class in electrical engineering.

8. _____ After Tower College opened a branch campus near Westburg and started offering weekend classes.

9. _____ When the price of nearly everything rises and my salary stays at the same low figure.

10. _____ Inside your heart is a warm spot for your first love.

| Exercise 5 | **Practice: Using Two Steps to Recognize Sentence Fragments** |

Some of the following are complete sentences; some are sentence fragments. To recognize the fragments, check each group of words by using the two-step process:

Step 1: Check for a subject and a verb.

Step 2: If you find a subject and a verb, check that the group of words makes a complete statement.

Then put an *S* next to each sentence and an *F* next to each fragment.

1. _____ One of the great features in the nature preserve being a wooden boardwalk across an area of wetlands.

2. _____ Doing the dishes is not a job for careless or sloppy people.

3. _____ When the wind blows at night and shakes the branches of the tree outside my window.

4. _____ On the top of the wedding cake were real roses in shades of yellow and peach.

5. _____ Without any hesitation or fear of the consequences of his difficult decision.

6. _____ A small group of people sacrificing their safety for the well-being of millions of citizens.

7. _____ As if Dina knew a secret about her former boss and was ready to tell it.

8. _____ The mayor of our town to open the Summer Music Series at Langdon Park on Saturday.

9. _____ Some of the students in my English class want to plead for an extension on the due date of our latest assignment.

10. _____ For instance, someone with a highly contagious form of liver disease.

Exercise 6 **Practice: More on Using Two Steps to Recognize Sentence Fragments**

Some of the following are complete sentences; some are sentence fragments. To recognize the fragments, check each group of words by using the two-step process:

Step 1: Check for a subject and a verb.

Step 2: If you find a subject and a verb, check that the group of words makes a complete statement.

Then put an *S* next to each sentence and an *F* next to each fragment.

1. _____ Some of the most distinguished heart surgeons in the country to meet in San Francisco next month and study new ways to prevent heart disease.

2. _____ In the middle of the crowd stood a man in a bumblebee costume and another man dressed as the team mascot.

3. _____ The reason being a lack of interest in participating in a talent show.

4. _____ Bargaining over the price of a car can be stressful.

5. _____ At times Christopher can be annoying or rude.

6. _____ Whenever my grandparents bring out the old photographs of the Jamaican branch of the family.

7. _____ Out of the drawer jumped a small green lizard.

8. _____ Because half the clothes in my closet are hand-me-downs from my two sisters.

9. _____ Has to get a doctor to examine the bruise on his leg.

10. _____ Turning into an argument over the responsibilities of a son to a distant and demanding father.

CORRECTING FRAGMENTS

You can correct fragments easily if you follow the two steps for identifying them.

Step 1: Check for a subject and a verb. If a group of words is a fragment because it lacks a subject or a verb, or both, *add what is missing*.

fragment: Jonette giving ten percent of her salary. (This fragment lacks a main verb.)

corrected: Jonette gave ten percent of her salary. (The verb *gave* replaces *giving*, which is not a main verb.)

fragment: Can't study with the television on. (This fragment lacks a subject.)

corrected: Salvatore can't study with the television on. (A subject, *Salvatore*, is added.)

fragment: Especially at the end of the day. (This fragment has neither a subject nor a verb.)

corrected: I often feel stressed, especially at the end of the day. (A subject, *I*, and a verb, *feel*, are added.)

Step 2: If you find a subject and a verb, check that the group of words makes a complete statement. To correct the fragment, you can turn a dependent clause into an independent one by removing the subordinating conjunction, *or* you can add an independent clause to the dependent one to create a statement that makes sense by itself.

fragment: When Mrs. Diaz offered him a job. (This statement does not make sense by itself. The subordinating conjunction *when* leads the reader to ask, "What happened when Mrs. Diaz offered him a job?" The subordinating conjunction makes this a dependent clause, not a sentence.)

corrected: Mrs. Diaz offered him a job. (Removing the subordinating conjunction makes this an independent clause—a sentence.)

corrected: When Mrs. Diaz offered him a job, he was very happy. (Adding an independent clause to the end of the sentence turns this into a statement that makes sense by itself.)

corrected: He was very happy when Mrs. Diaz offered him a job. (Adding an independent clause to the beginning of the sentence turns this into a statement that makes sense by itself.)

Note: Sometimes you can correct a fragment by adding it to the sentence before or after it.

---

fragment (in italics): *Even if he lowers the price.* I can't afford that car.

corrected: Even if he lowers the price, I can't afford that car.

fragment (in italics): Yvonne hates large parties. *Like the one at Matthew's house.*

corrected: Yvonne hates large parties like the one at Matthew's house.

You have several choices for correcting fragments. You can add words, phrases, or clauses; you can take words out or combine independent and dependent clauses. You can change fragments into simple sentences or create compound or complex sentences. If you create compound or complex sentences, be sure to use correct punctuation.

Exercise 7 Practice: Correcting Fragments

Correct each sentence fragment below in the most appropriate way.

1. I am tired of wasting my time on nasty relatives. Such as your brother and my aunt.

corrected: _____

_____

2. If you can lend me twenty dollars. I will pay you back on Saturday.

corrected: _____

_____

3. Seeing my brother and sister-in-law celebrating their tenth wedding anniversary. I hoped for a lasting relationship of my own.

corrected: _____

_____

4. Brian will eat any kind of chicken. Except chicken livers.

corrected: _____

_____

6. If we get a big dog with a loud bark.

corrected: _____

_____

7. My obnoxious little brother scraping all the icing off the beautifully decorated birthday cake.

corrected: _____

_____

8. I need to see a tax adviser. To get some help in completing my income tax form.

corrected: _____

_____

9. As we ran toward the student center. Hail hit the sidewalk.

corrected: _____

_____

10. After years of working in low-paying jobs, two of my friends thinking about going back to school.

corrected: _____

_____

Exercise 8 Collaborate: Correcting Fragments Two Ways

Collaborate

The following groups of words all contain fragments. With a partner or group, construct two ways to eliminate the fragment. You can add words, phrases, or clauses; take out words; combine independent and dependent clauses; or attach a fragment to the sentence before or after it. When you have completed the exercise, be ready to share your answers with another group or with the class. The first one is done for you.

1. While my children sat in the back of the car and tried to slap each other.

corrected: While my children sat in the back of the car and tried to slap each other, I tried to keep my eyes on the road.

corrected: I tried to keep my eyes on the road while my children sat in the back of the car and tried to slap each other.

2. After a group of firefighters had extinguished the fire. The family members surveyed the damage to their home.

   corrected: _____

_____

   corrected: _____

3. If anyone asks about my black eye.

   corrected: _____

_____

   corrected: _____

_____

4. Jay considering a job offer in Austin, Texas.

   corrected: _____

_____

   corrected: _____

_____

5. Whenever my partner talks about a trip to the rainforest. I think about exotic animals.

   corrected: _____

_____

   corrected: _____

_____

6. Carmen lit the candles on the cake. As the guests sang "Happy Birthday."

   corrected: _____

_____

   corrected: _____

_____

7. At the end of a busy day, when Jimmy was tired and irritable.

   corrected: _____

_____

   corrected: _____

_____

8. Unless it rains within the next week. Our plants will die.

   corrected: _____

_____

   corrected: _____

_____

9. Although nothing is wrong with the leftover chili.

corrected: _____

_____

corrected: _____

_____

10. When my car started making strange noises.

corrected: _____

_____

corrected: _____

_____

Connect

Exercise 9 **Connect: Editing a Paragraph to Eliminate Fragments**

Edit the paragraph below, correcting the sentence fragments by writing in
the space above each fragment. There are six fragments.

All my closest friends are optimists. Such as my cousin Jared. Jared is always

willing to expect the best outcome in a school, family, or work crisis. As a child,

Jared had cancer, yet he seemed to be the strongest member of the family. Even

though he suffered terrible pain and endured surgery, chemotherapy, and radiation

treatments. Jared stayed calm and tough. He was an inspiration to me. Recently,

Jared giving me strength and a positive attitude. I lost my job at the movie theater

and was depressed about finding work. However, Jared encouraged me to trans-

form my loss. Into an opportunity to find a job better suited to my personality. His

support led me to make an active and thorough job search. After a few months,

I got a position at a computer store. Where I enjoy helping the customers choose

the best technology. I like the work; in addition, I appreciate the rise in salary. My

loss turned into a gain. Because I took the advice of a close friend and acted on it.

Connect

Exercise 10 **Connect: Editing a Paragraph to Eliminate Fragments**

Edit the paragraph below, correcting the sentence fragments by writing in
the space above each fragment. There are six fragments.

Andy is a man who appeals to women. But not for the generally expected

reasons. Andy is not extremely good looking. In addition, not a rich man. He has a

job in a plumbing supply company. Where he has worked since high school. While

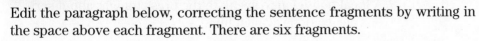

many women are attracted by a man's intelligence, Andy is not particularly smart, either. Yet he always has a girlfriend and many female friends who are buddies. Andy's appeal comes from a long list of good qualities. Women like him. Because he always listens to them. He enjoys a woman's company. While many men stare into the distance as soon as a woman begins to talk. In addition, Andy treats women as more than conquests. For example, never cheating on a girlfriend. When he and a woman part, they remain friends. Andy appeals to many women who want friendship and trust as well as romance.

Chapter Test Avoiding Sentence Fragments

Some of the following are complete sentences; some are sentence fragments. Put an *S* by each sentence and an *F* by each fragment.

1. _____ Next to an attractive little house on Whittier Drive, an empty lot full of weeds, concrete blocks, and old tires.

2. _____ About five hundred feet ahead of me was a car stopped on the side of the road.

3. _____ In order that the local police can reach people in trouble and get to the scene of an accident or crime as quickly as possible.

4. _____ When a dozen squirrels scampered on the lawn and munched on the treasures fallen from the bushes and the trees.

5. _____ Then an angry man complained loudly about the long lines at the cash register.

6. _____ The rising price of cigarettes prompting many smokers to sign up for smoking cessation programs or to try to quit on their own.

7. _____ Except for an overcooked selection of vegetables, the meal at Maureen's house was tasty.

8. _____ If someone wants my old computer table, he or she can have it.

9. _____ Until Eliot finds a way to pay for the repairs on his bike, he can borrow my brother's old bike.

10. _____ A local politician to speak to the press tonight about serious accusations against him.

Using Parallelism in Sentences

Chapter Objectives

Students will be able to recognize parallel structure and use it to revise awkwardly worded sentences.

Parallelism means balance in sentences. To create sentences with parallelism, remember this rule:

Similar points should get similar structures.

Often, you will include two or more points—related ideas, examples, or details—in one sentence. If you express these ideas in a parallel structure, they will be clearer, smoother, and more convincing.

Here are some pairs of sentences with and without parallelism:

not parallel: Of all the household chores, the ones I hate the most are cooking, to iron, and dusting.

parallel: Of all the household chores, the ones I hate the most are *cooking*, *ironing*, and *dusting*. (Three words are parallel.)

not parallel: When I need a pencil, I look in my purse, the table, and beside the telephone.

parallel: When I need a pencil, I look *in my purse*, *on the table*, and *beside the telephone*. (Three prepositional phrases are parallel.)

> **not parallel:** Inez should get the promotion because she gets along with her coworkers, she works hard, and a knowledge of the business.
>
> **parallel:** Inez should get the promotion because *she gets along with her coworkers*, *she works hard*, and *she knows the business*. (Three clauses are parallel.)

From these examples you can see that parallelism involves matching the structures of parts of your sentence. There are two steps that can help you check your writing for parallelism.

INFO BOX: **Two Steps in Checking a Sentence for Parallel Structure**

Step 1: Look for the list in the sentence.

Step 2: Put the parts of the list into a similar structure.

You may have to change or add something to get a parallel structure.

ACHIEVING PARALLELISM

Let's correct the parallelism of the following sentence:

> **not parallel:** If you want to pass the course, you have to study hard, taking good notes, and attendance at every class.

To correct this sentence, we'll follow the steps.

> **Step 1:** Look for the list. If you want to pass the course, you have to do three things. Here's the list:
> 1. study hard
> 2. taking good notes
> 3. attendance at every class
>
> **Step 2:** Put the parts of the list into a similar structure.
>
> 1. *to study* hard
> 2. *to take* good notes
> 3. *to attend* every class

Now revise to get a parallel sentence.

> **parallel:** If you want to pass the course, you have *to study* hard, *to take* good notes, and *to attend* every class.

If you follow steps 1 and 2, you can also write the sentence like this:

> **parallel:** If you want to pass the course, you have to *study* hard, *take* good notes, and *attend* every class.

But you can't write the sentence like this:

> **not parallel:** If you want to pass the course, you have to study hard, take good notes, and to attend every class.

Think of the list again. You can have
If you want to pass the course, you have

1. to study
2. to take   } parallel
3. to attend

Or you can have
> If you want to pass the course, you have to
>
> > 1. study
> > 2. take   } parallel
> > 3. attend

But your list can't be
> If you want to pass the course, you have to
>
> > 1. study
> > 2. take   } not parallel
> > 3. to attend

In other words, use *to* once (if it fits every part of the list) or use it with *every* part of the list.

Note: Sometimes making ideas parallel means adding something to the sentence because all the parts of the list cannot match exactly.

> **not parallel:** After the toddler threw his bowl of cereal, oatmeal splattered down the walls, the floor, and the table.

> **Step 1:** Look for the list. After the toddler threw his bowl of cereal, oatmeal splattered
>
> > 1. down the walls
> > 2. the floor
> > 3. the table

As this sentence is written, *down* goes with *walls*, but it doesn't go with *floor* or *table.* Check the sense of this sentence by looking at each part of the list and how it is working in the sentence: "After the toddler threw his bowl of cereal, oatmeal splattered *down the walls*" is clear. But "oatmeal splattered *down the floor*"? Or "oatmeal splattered *down the table*"? These parts of the list are not right.

> **Step 2:** The sentence needs some words added to make the structure parallel.

> **parallel:** After the toddler threw his bowl of cereal, oatmeal splattered *down* the walls, *on* the floor, and *under* the table.

When you follow the two steps to check for parallelism, you can write clear sentences and improve your style.

Exercise 1   **Practice: Revising Sentences for Parallelism**

Some of the following sentences need to be revised so they have parallel structures. Revise the ones that need parallelism. Write *OK* for sentences that already have parallel structures.

> 1. Getting up early in the morning is not as bad as when you get up in the middle of the night.

> revised: _____

_____

2. Colin can be immature and irritating at times, yet he can also be sympathetic and generous.

revised: _____

_____

3. My older brother warned me about flirting with his friends and to let myself fall in love with one, but I didn't listen.

revised: _____

_____

4. Shane's outgoing personality, being naturally confident, and athletic ability made him popular in high school.

revised: _____

_____

5. In my family, children were taught to say "please" and "thank you," be kind to animals, and always telling the truth.

revised: _____

_____

6. André could grow up to be a man with strong principles and a heart that is filled with generosity.

revised: _____

_____

7. I keep running into Mrs. Kelly on the bus, the movies, and in the hall.

revised: _____

_____

8. If my favorite entertainer ever goes on tour in the Southwest, I will travel to one of his concerts by car or plane.

revised: _____

_____

9. When I am bored, I waste my time calling all my friends, eat large quantities of junk food, and watching endless hours of bad television.

revised: _____

_____

10. My final exams start on December 12; December 19 is when they end.

revised: _____

_____

Collaborate

Exercise 2 **Collaborate: Writing Sentences with Parallelism**

With a partner or group, complete each sentence. Begin by brainstorming a draft list; then revise the list for parallelism. Finally, complete the sentence in a parallel structure. You may want to assign one task (brainstorming a draft list, revising it, etc.) to each group member, then switch tasks on the next sentence. Following is a sample of how to work through each question, from list to sentence.

sample incomplete sentence: The three parts of college I like best are

Draft List

1. new friends
2. doing well in English
3. Fridays off

Revised List

1. making new friends
2. doing well in English
3. having Fridays off

sentence: The three parts of college I like best are making new friends, doing well in English, and having Fridays off.

1. Three reasons for getting regular exercise are

Draft List

1. _____
2. _____
3. _____

Revised List

1. _____
2. _____
3. _____

sentence: _____

_____

2. Two suggestions for fighting a cold are

Draft List

1. _____
2. _____

Revised List

1. _____
2. _____

sentence: _____

_____

3. Three signs that a person is lying are

Draft List

1. _____
2. _____
3. _____

Revised List

1. _____
2. _____
3. _____

sentence: _____

_____

4. When parents get a divorce, young children struggle because

Draft List

1. _____

   _____

2. _____

   _____

Revised List

1. _____

   _____

2. _____

   _____

3. _____   3. _____

   _____   _____

sentence: _____

_____

_____

5. Four ways you can use old bath towels

Draft List   **Revised List**

1. _____   1. _____

2. _____   2. _____

3. _____   3. _____

   _____   _____

4. _____   4. _____

sentence: _____

_____

Collaborate

Exercise 3 **Collaborate: Recognizing Parallelism in Famous Speeches**

Some of the most famous speeches in history contain parallel structures. This parallelism adds emphasis and dignity to the points expressed. Working in a group, have one member read each segment of a speech aloud while the others listen carefully. Then underline all the words, phrases, clauses, or sentences that are in parallel form. When you have completed the exercise, share your answers with another group.

1. **Inaugural Address**

   John F. Kennedy

President John F. Kennedy delivered this speech when he was inaugurated on January 20, 1961. His theme was the renewal of American values and the changes and challenges we must face.

   Let the word go forth from this time and place, to friend and foe alike, that the torch has been passed to a new generation of Americans—born in this century, tempered* by war, disciplined by a hard and bitter peace, proud of our ancient heritage—and unwilling to witness or permit the slow undoing of those human rights to which this nation has always been committed, and to which we are committed today at home and around the world.

*tempered** means hardened, toughened

2. **I Have a Dream**

   Martin Luther King, Jr.

Martin Luther King, Jr., a Southern minister, was a leading advocate of civil rights in the 1960s. He delivered this speech to 200,000 people in Washington, D.C., where they had gathered to demonstrate peacefully for the cause of equality.

I have a dream that one day every valley shall be exalted, every hill and mountain shall be made low, the rough places shall be made plain, and the crooked places shall be made straight, and the glory of the Lord will be revealed, and all flesh shall see it together.

This is our hope. This is the faith that I go back to the South with. With this faith we will be able to hew* out of the mountain of despair a stone of hope. With this faith, we will be able to transform the jangling discords of our nation into a beautiful symphony of brotherhood.

With this faith we will be able to work together, to pray together, to go to jail together, to stand up for freedom together, knowing that we will be free one day.

****hew** means to make or shape with cutting blows

Connect

| Exercise 4 | **Connect: Combining Sentences and Creating a Parallel Structure** |

In the paragraph below, some sentences should be combined in a parallel structure. Combine each cluster of underlined sentences into one sentence with a parallel structure. Write your sentences in the lines above the old ones.

At my college, footwear suits the role of each group of people. For example, students have to come to class. They sit in a classroom. Listening to lectures is a major duty of being a student. Students are an important part of campus, and there are hundreds of them everywhere. Most of them dress in a similar style. <u>Their footwear tends to be flip flops in warm weather. Students wear sneakers when it gets cold outside.</u> Like students, most teachers wear a specific type of footwear. Their shoes have to be comfortable. <u>Teachers stand in front of the classroom. Sometimes they walk around the room. Heavy books and papers are often in their arms as they go from one classroom to another.</u> They need shoes that are stronger than flip flops and a little more formal than scuffed athletic shoes. These shoes tend to be loafers or another comfortable but professional-looking shoe. <u>Administrators deal with students and faculty. They interact with other administrators. Also, they are representatives of the college in the community.</u> They wear more traditional, businesslike footwear. <u>For example, male administrators tend to wear stiff black shoes. Black shoes also appear on female administrators. They wear black high heels.</u> Of course, not all college students, teachers, or administrators wear the same types of footwear. There are some professors in ratty-looking athletic shoes. In addition, some students come to class directly from their jobs and may appear in dressier shoes. However, most of the time, shoes tell the place of each person in the college community.

Connect

Exercise 5 **Connect: Revising a Paragraph for Parallelism**

The following paragraph contains sentences with errors in parallelism. In the space above the lines, correct the sentences that contain errors in parallelism. There are five sentences with errors.

My favorite restaurant is hard to classify. It is not a part of a restaurant chain like Burger King or a fancy restaurant like the expensive steakhouse outside of town. It has roomy booths, tables made of wood, and colorful curtains. In good weather, a patio offers outdoor seating. The outdoor spots fill up quickly because a cluster of oak trees offer shade, and a soft breeze comes with the trees. This restaurant is in an old section of town. The place is famous for barbecue. Customers stand in line for seats or take out the homemade dinners. I love all the choices: barbecued pork, beef, chicken, or barbecued shrimp. A customer can eat one kind of barbecue or enjoy a mixed platter. The smoky smell of barbecue fills the air for miles, and people are called to the restaurant. This barbecue place regularly calls me back for more because of its relaxed atmosphere, reasonable prices, and the food that is irresistible.

Connect

Exercise 6 **Connect: Revising a Paragraph for Parallelism**

The following paragraph contains sentences with errors in parallelism. In the space above the lines, correct the sentences that contain errors in parallelism. There are four sentences with errors.

Staying out of debt was never a problem for me until recently. Today money worries appear and reappear like wicked gremlins. The price of gas has risen, there's a higher rent on my apartment, and my heating bill has nearly doubled. At the same time, my salary remains low. Each day I struggle with money decisions. For instance, if I fill up my gas tank, I may not have enough cash to get a haircut. Sometimes, I have to think hard before I spend money at a pizza restaurant when I can save money by eating at home. The greatest temptation is to rely on credit cards, but I have seen the worst aspects of debt. My father used to juggle two or three credit cards, to pay a little each month, get deeper into debt, and then, out of desperation, sign up for another card. I have one credit card and use it only for emergencies. So far, I have

managed to live within my means, but I miss the days when I could buy a movie

ticket, a CD, or t-shirt without considering the effects on my budget. By the end of

each pay period, my head is filled with money worries. Worse, each new paycheck

seems to disappear as soon as I deposit it. By the time I pay my rent, put gas in my

car, stocking the refrigerator with food, and settle my utility bills, I am broke again.

Chapter Test **Using Parallelism in Sentences**

Some of the following sentences have errors in parallelism; some are correct.
Put *OK* next to the correct sentences and *X* by the sentences with errors in
parallelism.

1. _____ After a long day of arguing with his parents, trying to sell
shoes at a nearly empty store, and losing his car keys, Eric
was exhausted.

2. _____ Horror movies can be ridiculous, love stories are often
phony, and to sit through a long war movie bores me, so
I rarely go to the movies.

3. _____ Every Halloween my parents put up the old ghost decora-
tions, buying huge bags of candy, and string spooky lights
across the front yard so that the local children can have fun.

4. _____ A huge insect darted across the kitchen floor and hid under
the stove.

5. _____ A dried-up tube of lip gloss, a collection of ratty cotton balls in
a yellowed plastic bag, an ancient hairbrush, and half-empty
bottle of cough medicine fell out of the rusty medicine cabinet.

6. _____ After my chemistry class, I always notice some of the students gathering in the hall, whispering complaints about the
grading policy, and I hear them worrying about the next test.

7. _____ Somehow a cat from New Mexico turned up in Chicago,
was taken to a shelter, was identified by a microchip in his
body, and got a plane ride home to New Mexico.

8. _____ Ben goes to Miranda's Palace every weekend because the
place offers live music, the low price of the tasty food, and
the atmosphere is friendly.

9. _____ My brother hated high school because the peer pressure
was constant, nasty gossip filled the halls, and the bullying
of vulnerable students.

10. _____ Before my early morning class, I gulp a strong cup of
coffee, race to campus, and concentrate on staying alert.

Using Adjectives and Adverbs

Chapter Objectives

Students will be able to identify adjectives and adverbs and incorporate them correctly in their writing.

WHAT ARE ADJECTIVES?

Adjectives describe nouns (words that name persons, places, or things) or pronouns (words that substitute for a noun).

adjectives:
She stood in a *dark* corner. (*Dark* describes the noun *corner.*)
I need a *little* help. (*Little* describes the noun *help.*)
She looked *happy.* (*Happy* describes the pronoun *she.*)

An adjective usually comes before the word it describes.

He gave me a *beautiful* ring. (*Beautiful* describes *ring.*)

Sometimes an adjective comes after a *being* verb, a verb that tells what something is. Being verbs are words like *is, are, was, am, has been.* Words like *feels, looks, seems, smells, sounds,* and *tastes* are part of the group called being verbs.

He seems *unhappy.* (*Unhappy* describes *he* and follows the being verb *seems.*)

Alan was *confident.* (*Confident* describes *Alan* and follows the being verb *was.*)

Your tires are *bald.* (*Bald* describes *tires* and follows the being verb *are.*)

| Exercise 1 | Practice: Recognizing Adjectives |

Circle the adjective in each of the following sentences.

1. A bowl of rice in the refrigerator smelled rotten.
2. Rick walked across the hot sand.
3. My mother bought me an expensive bracelet for my birthday.
4. The old tires on your car need to be replaced.
5. Uncle Frank feels tired in the afternoon.
6. The lavish praise embarrassed Cynthia.
7. A tiny lizard slipped under the fence.
8. Something in the sauce tastes bitter.
9. A bright moon tempted us to go fishing in the dark.
10. Pablo and Katherine seemed upset about the news.

| Exercise 2 | Practice: More on Recognizing Adjectives |

Circle the adjective in each of the following sentences.

1. Aggressive salespeople can frighten shoppers.
2. The children look excited about the trip to the zoo.
3. Dirty windows blocked the sun.
4. My boss gave me a small raise.
5. That man is wearing an expensive watch.
6. Curly hair runs in my family.
7. The top of the table feels sticky.
8. Your offer for the car sounds fair.
9. Our journey took us to an ancient site.
10. The foolish remark hurt Eva.

ADJECTIVES: COMPARATIVE AND SUPERLATIVE FORMS

The **comparative** form of an adjective compares two persons or things. The **superlative** form compares three or more persons or things.

comparative: Your car is *cleaner* than mine.
superlative: Your car is the *cleanest* one in the parking lot.

comparative: Hamburger is *cheaper* than steak.
superlative: Hamburger is the *cheapest* meat on the menu.

comparative: Lisa is *friendlier* than her sister.
superlative: Lisa is the *friendliest* of the three sisters.

For most adjectives of one syllable, add *-er* to form the comparative and add *-est* to form the superlative.

The weather is *colder* today than it was yesterday, but Friday was the *coldest* day of the year.

Orange juice is *sweeter* than grapefruit juice, but the *sweetest* juice is grape juice.

For longer adjectives, use *more* to form the comparative and *most* to form the superlative.

I thought College Algebra was *more difficult* than English; however, Beginning Physics was the *most difficult* course I ever took.

My brother is *more outgoing* than my sister, but my father is the *most outgoing* member of the family.

The three forms of adjectives usually look like this:

Adjective	Comparative (two)	Superlative (three or more)
sweet	sweeter	sweetest
fast	faster	fastest
short	shorter	shortest
quick	quicker	quickest
old	older	oldest

Or they may look like this:

Adjective	Comparative (two)	Superlative (three or more)
confused	more confused	most confused
specific	more specific	most specific
dangerous	more dangerous	most dangerous
confident	more confident	most confident
beautiful	more beautiful	most beautiful

However, there are some *irregular forms* of adjectives:

Adjective	Comparative (two)	Superlative (three or more)
good	better	best
bad	worse	worst
little	less	least
many, much	more	most

Exercise 3   **Practice: Selecting the Correct Adjective Forms**

Write the correct form of the adjective in each of the following sentences.

1. When money is involved, my sister has always been _____ (smart) about spending than my brother is.

2. The red-haired boy in the back row of the classroom was the _____ (funny) of all the students.

3. My truck gets _____(good) gas mileage than my husband's van.

4. Which of our five visits to the amusement park was the _____ (little) expensive?

5. Ignoring a nagging toothache can lead to _____ (bad) trouble than going to a dentist would.

6. Although my first apartment had many attractive features, my second one had even _____ (many) stylish and modern features.

7. Andrew's performance at the talent show was _____ (confident) than his first try at singing in public.

8. In the Jackson family, Jill is _____ (good) at playing video games than Ben, but their father is the _____ player in the family.

9. My sister has _____ (little) faith in the power of Vitamin C to prevent colds.

10. Of all the special moments in my life, the birth of my daughter was the _____ (joyful).

Exercise 4   **Collaborate: Writing Sentences with Adjectives**

Collaborate

Working with a partner or group, write a sentence that correctly uses each of the following adjectives. Be prepared to share your answers with another group or with the class.

1. more dangerous _____

_____

2. best _____

_____

3. sillier _____

_____

4. most talented _____

_____

5. brightest _____

_____

6. more stubborn _____

_____

7. cleaner _____

_____

8. worst _____

_____

9. wiser _____

_____

10. most capable _____

_____

WHAT ARE ADVERBS?

Adverbs describe verbs, adjectives, or other adverbs.

> **adverbs:**
> As she spoke, Steve listened *thoughtfully*. (*Thoughtfully* describes the verb *listened*.)
> I said I was *really* sorry for my error. (*Really* describes the adjective *sorry*.)
> The cook worked *very* quickly. (*Very* describes the adverb *quickly*.)

Adverbs answer questions like "How?" "How much?" "How often?" "When?" "Why?" and "Where?"

Exercise 5 **Practice: Recognizing Adverbs**

Circle the adverbs in the following sentences.

1. At a children's concert, I heard a naturally talented, seven-year-old pianist.

2. Offered a free ticket to a hockey game, Mitchell was not very enthusiastic.

3. We'll rent a movie tomorrow.

4. The women looked suspiciously at the man with a briefcase full of cheap designer watches.

5. Pamela smiled shyly as the new boy looked at her.

6. If the traffic is heavy, the drive home can be really frustrating.

7. My boss is usually tolerant about sick days and other emergencies.

8. When the family needed help, the community responded generously.

9. Cory behaved very foolishly after his girlfriend left him.

10. The senior class heard truly inspiring advice from a former graduate.

Exercise 6 **Practice: More on Recognizing Adverbs**

Circle the adverbs in the following sentences.

1. The bathroom was painted in a particularly bright shade of orange.

2. An exceptionally hot day forced everyone on the block to seek relief outdoors in the shade.

3. Before her first plane trip, my great aunt waited anxiously for the call to board the aircraft.

4. Ella often forgets to turn off the porch lights.

5. When the manager opened the doors to the new superstore, a crowd of shoppers immediately filled the aisles.

6. Food at the popular new sports bar is ridiculously overpriced.

7. Tell me honestly about your reaction to my offer of help.

8. A good haircut does not have to be an extremely expensive one.

9. My cousin from North Carolina called me yesterday .

10. Scott is deliberately ignoring my calls and texts.

Exercise 7   **Collaborate: Writing Sentences with Adverbs**

Collaborate

Working with a partner or group, write a sentence that correctly uses each of the following adverbs. Be prepared to share your answers with another group or with the class.

1. usually _____

_____

2. exceptionally _____

_____

3. never _____

_____

4. magically _____

_____

5. mostly _____

_____

6. intentionally _____

_____

7. badly _____

_____

8. barely _____

_____

9. sometimes _____

_____

10. impatiently _____

_____

Hints About Adjectives and Adverbs

Do not use an adjective when you need an adverb. Some writers make the mistake of using an adjective when they need an adverb.

not this: Talk to me ~~honest~~.
but this: Talk to me honestly.

not this: You can say it ~~simple~~.
but this: You can say it simply.

not this: He was breathing ~~deep~~.
but this: He was breathing deeply.

Exercise 8 **Practice: Changing Adjectives to Adverbs**

In each pair of sentences, change the underlined adjective in the first sentence to an adverb in the second sentence. The first one is done for you.

1. a. That light is <u>bright</u>.

    b. That light gleams ___brightly___.

2. a. The traffic officer made a <u>tactful</u> reply.

    b. The traffic officer replied _____.

3. a. Two mechanics did a <u>thorough</u> check of the race car.

    b. Two mechanics checked the race car _____.

4. a. The senator has a <u>decisive</u> way of speaking.

    b. The senator speaks _____.

5. a. Miguel has a <u>beautiful</u> voice.

    b. Miguel sings _____.

6. a. Taylor makes <u>constant</u> references to his luck with women.

    b. Taylor _____ refers to his luck with women.

7. a. Amy has a <u>simple</u> style of dressing.

    b. Amy dresses _____.

8. a. My son can be <u>impatient</u> in his actions.

    b. My son can act _____.

9. a. Parker's complaints about his job are <u>rare.</u>

    b. Parker _____ complains about his job.

10. a. The differences between coffee and tea are <u>significant.</u>

    b. Coffee and tea are _____ different.

Do Not Confuse *Good* and *Well*, *Bad* and *Badly*

Remember that *good* is an adjective; it describes nouns. It also follows being verbs like *is*, *are*, *was*, *am*, and *has been*. Words like *looks*, *seems*, *smells*, *sounds*, and *tastes* are part of the group called being verbs. *Well* is an adverb; it describes verbs. (The only time *well* can be used as an adjective is when it means *healthy*, as in *I feel well today.*)

not this: You ran that race ~~good~~.
but this: You ran that race well.

not this: I cook eggs ~~good~~.
but this: I cook eggs well.

not this: How ~~good~~ do you understand grammar?
but this: How well do you understand grammar?

Bad is an adjective; it describes nouns. It also follows being verbs like *is*, *are*, *was*, *am*, and *has been*. Words like *feels*, *looks*, *seems*, *smells*, *sounds*, and *tastes* are part of the group called being verbs. *Badly* is an adverb; it describes verbs.

not this: He feels ~~badly~~ about his mistake.
but this: He feels bad about his mistake. (*Feels* is a being verb; it is followed by the adjective *bad.*)

not this: That soup smells ~~badly~~.
but this: That soup smells bad. (*Smells* is a being verb; it is followed by the adjective *bad.*)

not this: He dances ~~bad~~.
but this: He dances badly.

Exercise 9   **Practice: Using Good and Well, Bad and Badly**

Write the appropriate word in the following sentences.

1. Jonelle has been sick with the flu; she seemed really _____ (bad, badly) yesterday.

2. That room _____ (bad, badly) needs a new coat of paint.

3. Let me know if you feel _____ (good, well) enough to drive to Omaha next week.

4. André is behaving _____ (good, well) in his kindergarten class.

5. My chances of getting more financial aid look _____ (bad, badly).

6. Something in the kitchen smells _____ (good, well).

7. When Terrance asked you an embarrassing question, you answered it _____ (good, well).

8. After the team performed _____ (bad, badly) in the first half, the fans began to lose hope.

9. That new jacket looks _____ (good, well) on you.

10. The music of the new Jamaican group sounds _____ (bad, badly).

Do Not Use *More* + *-er,* or *Most* + *-est*

Be careful. Never write both an *-er* ending and *more*, or an *-est* ending and *most.*

not this: I want to work with someone ~~more smarter~~.
but this: I want to work with someone smarter.

not this: Alan is the ~~most richest~~ man in town.
but this: Alan is the richest man in town.

Use *Than*, Not *Then*, in Comparisons

When you compare things, use *than. Then* means *at a later time.*

not this: You are taller ~~then~~ I am.
but this: You are taller than I am.

not this: I'd like a car that is faster ~~then~~ my old one.
but this: I'd like a car that is faster than my old one.

When Do I Need a Comma Between Adjectives?

Sometimes you use more than one adjective to describe a noun:

> I visited a cold, dark cave.
> The cat had pale blue eyes.

If you look at the examples above, one uses a comma between the adjectives *cold* and *dark*, but the other doesn't have a comma between the adjectives *pale* and *blue*. Both sentences are correctly punctuated. To decide whether you need a comma, try one of these tests:

Test 1: Try to put *and* between the adjectives. If the sentence still makes sense, put a comma between the adjectives.

> **Check for comma:** I visited a cold, dark cave. (Do you need the comma? Add *and* between the adjectives.)
> **Add *and*:** I visited a cold and dark cave. (Does the sentence still make sense? Yes. You need the comma.)
> **Correct sentence:** I visited a cold, dark cave.

> **Check for comma:** The cat had pale blue eyes. (Do you need the comma? Add *and* between the adjectives.)
> **Add *and*:** The cat had pale and blue eyes. (Does the sentence still make sense? No. You do not need the comma.)
> **Correct sentence:** The cat had pale blue eyes.

Test 2: Try to reverse the order of the adjectives. If the sentence still makes sense, put a comma between the adjectives.

> **Check for comma:** I visited a cold, dark cave. (Do you need the comma? Reverse the order of the adjectives.)
> **Reverse the order of the adjectives:** I visited a dark, cold cave. (Does the sentence still make sense? Yes. You need the comma.)
> **Correct sentence:** I visited a cold, dark cave.

> **Check for comma:** The cat had pale blue eyes. (Do you need a comma? Reverse the order of the adjectives.)
> **Reverse the order of the adjectives:** The cat had blue pale eyes. (Does the sentence still make sense? No. You don't need a comma.)
> **Correct sentence:** The cat had pale blue eyes.

You can use Test 1 or Test 2 to determine whether you need a comma between adjectives.

Exercise 10 **Practice: A Comprehensive Exercise on Using Adjectives and Adverbs**

Correct any errors in the use of adjectives and adverbs (including punctuation errors) in the following sentences. Write your corrections in the space above the errors. Some sentences do not need correcting.

1. Both Alan and Meghan are excellent swimmers, but Meghan is the best one.

2. Katrina feels badly about her last conversation with her boyfriend.

3. In the dog world, there is no dog more smarter than Archer, my uncle's fox hound.

4. Cocoa tastes good on a cold night in December.

5. I found a cheap kitchen table at a neighborhood garage sale.

6. Charlie was the least trustworthy of my two former boyfriends.

7. I will eat any kind of chocolate, but I like milk chocolate better then dark chocolate.

8. Emily gave me an evasive nervous answer when I asked her about last night.

9. My little girl performed beautifully in the dance program at her school.

10. In a crisis, David is a real loyal friend.

Exercise 11   **Practice: Another Comprehensive Exercise on Using Adjectives and Adverbs**

Correct any errors in the use of adjectives and adverbs (including punctuation errors) in the following sentences. Write your corrections in the space above the errors. Some sentences do not need correcting.

1. I like your new cologne; it smells good.

2. Peter is more happier than he was in his previous job.

3. Luisa and John have three dogs; the little brown dachshund is the smartest.

4. We have been having a terrible winter; last Monday was the most coldest day since 1989.

5. Evan grew up in a poorly constructed apartment building in a bad neighborhood.

6. The little boy asked me nice if he could have a cookie.

7. The real story behind the crime is a deep dark secret.

8. My girlfriend is the less athletic person I have ever known.

9. Noah dreams of something better then the life his parents led.

10. I got up late, so I barely had time for a quick cup of coffee.

Exercise 12   **Connect: Editing a Paragraph for Errors in Adjectives and Adverbs**

Connect

Edit the following paragraph, correcting all the errors in the use of adjectives and adverbs. Write your corrections in the space above the errors. There are eight errors.

Sometimes loneliness hurts me bad. I am a general outgoing person and choose to spend my time with friends. However, sometimes everyone is busy.

I tend to feel nervously when I have to face an afternoon alone at home. Saturday evenings by myself are even worst. Of course, I can send emails or text messages, but those connections don't satisfy me. At such times, I don't know what I want. I start feeling bored. Soon I wonder why everyone is having a best time then I am. Sitting alone, I feel jealous and sorry for myself. Then loneliness creeps into my brain. Being alone creates a terrible emptiness for me. My idea of happiness is being with others and sharing extremely, wild adventures. To me, a day alone is never a well day.

Connect

Exercise 13 **Connect: Editing a Paragraph for Errors in Adjectives and Adverbs**

Edit the following paragraph, correcting all the errors in the use of adjectives and adverbs. Write your corrections in the space above the lines. There are seven errors.

An old photograph in the right frame can combine to create a beautiful thoughtful gift. Everyone has at least one packet or box of photographs stashed in a closet or attic. When people take the time to look through older photos, they typical react with pleasure. Reactions such as "Oh, that was your brother at four. Wasn't he a sweet little boy?" or "Don't we look ridiculously in our costumes?" are common. Unfortunately, the photos generally end up back in a dusty box or packet. When a friend or family member takes the time to choose a special photo, the difficult part of the gift-giving process is complete. Finding a suitable frame is simple and even inexpensive. Photo frames are sold nearly everywhere, from drug stores to discount superstores to craft shops. Any frame is better then an unframed photo stuck in a box, but the most best frame is a careful chosen one. The gift of a framed photograph brings the past into the present, and that photograph will sit proud on someone's mantel, bureau, or desk.

Chapter Test   Using Adjectives and Adverbs

Some of the following sentences have errors in the use of adjectives and adverbs. Some are correct. Put *OK* by the correct sentences and *X* by the sentences with an error.

1. _____ I have eaten all kinds of cakes, but the most delicious cake of all was one called Raspberry Surprise, a mix of white cake, butter cream icing, and raspberry filling.

2. _____ The people in the corner house were particularly proud of their careful maintained lawn.

3. _____ One candidate for governor gave a really good explanation of her position on offshore oil drilling.

4. _____ Lamar was confident about his performance on the multiple-choice test, but he wasn't sure how good he did on the essay test.

5. _____ My four cousins are all excellent musicians, but the youngest is the more talented of the group.

6. _____ I'm considering a class in graphic design or one in advertising, but I'm not sure which one is a better choice for me.

7. _____ Mason has a big, red bump on his forehead and some scratches on his hands.

8. _____ When my brother explained the math problem to me, he spoke very sarcastic.

9. _____ Tom is handsome when he wears a blazer and slacks; he doesn't look as well in shorts and a t-shirt.

10. _____ Whitney wants to meet a man more taller than she is.

Correcting Problems with Modifiers

Chapter Objectives

Students will be able to identify modifiers within sentences and correct misplaced or dangling modifiers.

Modifiers are words, phrases, or clauses that describe (modify) something in a sentence. All of the following italicized words, phrases, and clauses are modifiers.

> **modifiers:**
> the *black* cat (word)
> the cat *in the corner* (phrase)
> the cat *that he adopted* (clause)

Sometimes modifiers limit another word. They make another word (or words) more specific.

> the basket *in the boy's bedroom* (tells which basket)
> *twenty* cookies (tells how many cookies)
> the card *that she gave me* (tells which card)
> They *seldom* visit. (tells how often)

Exercise 1   **Practice: Recognizing Modifiers**

In each of the following sentences, underline the modifiers (words, phrases, or clauses) that describe the italicized word.

1. David's overweight orange *cat*, with its fluffy tail, crept into the kitchen and rubbed against my leg.

2. Peering into the window, *Ethan* saw someone asleep in a rocking chair.

3. A thin *man* in an overcoat waited at the end of a long line.

4. Yesterday a kind *stranger* returned my lost wallet.

5. Swept away by the flood, the *house* fell into pieces.

6. Ryan spent years in the jungles of South America, so he can tell amazing *stories*.

7. I want a *cake* covered in vanilla icing.

8. The *passengers* stuck at the airport waited for the storm to pass.

9. Alone on the stage stood a *woman* in an evening gown.

10. The latest action *movie* at the multiplex offered Simon a chance to escape his worries.

Exercise 2   **Practice: Finding Modifiers in Professional Writing**

Following is an excerpt from an essay by Pat Mora, a Chicana educator and writer. It is a remembrance of her favorite aunt, Lobo. The writing makes effective use of specific details, particularly through the use of modifiers. After you read the selection, underline the modifiers that describe each italicized word or phrase.

We called her "Lobo." The word means "wolf" in Spanish, an odd name for a generous and loving *aunt*. Like all names it became synonymous* with her, and to this day returns me to my child self. Although the name seemed perfectly *natural* to us and to our friends, it did cause *frowns* from strangers throughout the years. I particularly remember one hot *afternoon* when on a crowded *streetcar* between the border cities of El Paso and Juarez, I momentarily *lost* sight of her. "Lobo! Lobo!" I cried in panic. Annoyed faces peered at me, disappointed at such disrespect to a white-haired woman.

Actually the fault was hers. She lived with us for years, and when she arrived home from work in the evening, she'd knock on the front *door* and ask, "Donde estan mis lobitos?" "Where are my little *wolves?*" Gradually she became our lobo, a spinster* aunt who gathered the four of us around her, tying us to her life by giving us all she had.

*__synonymous__ means having the same or a similar meaning

*__spinster__ means an unmarried woman

CORRECTING MODIFIER PROBLEMS

Modifiers can make your writing more specific and more vivid. Used effectively and correctly, modifiers give the reader a clear picture of what you want to say, and they help you to say it precisely. But modifiers have to be used correctly. You can check for errors with modifiers as you revise your sentences.

INFO BOX: **Three Steps in Checking for Sentence Errors with Modifiers**

Step 1: Find the modifier.

Step 2: Ask, "Does the modifier have something to modify?"

Step 3: Ask, "Is the modifier in the right place, as close as possible to the word, phrase, or clause it modifies?"

If you answer no to either step 2 or step 3, you need to revise your sentence.

Review the three steps in the following example:

sample sentence: They were looking for a man walking a dog smoking a cigar.

Step 1: Find the modifier. The modifiers are *walking a dog* and *smoking a cigar*.

Step 2: Ask, "Does the modifier have something to modify?" The answer is yes. The man is walking a dog. The man is smoking a cigar. Both modifiers go with *man*.

Step 3: Ask, "Is the modifier in the right place?" The answer is yes and no. One modifier is in the right place:

a man *walking a dog*

The other modifier is not in the right place:

a dog *smoking a cigar*

The dog is not smoking a cigar. The sentence needs to be revised.

revised sentence: They were looking for a man *smoking a cigar and walking a dog.*

Here is another example of how to apply the three steps:

sample sentence: Slathered in whipped cream and nuts, she ate the hot fudge sundae.

Step 1: Find the modifiers. The modifiers are *Slathered in whipped cream and nuts* and *hot fudge*.

Step 2: Ask, "Does the modifier have something to modify?" The answer is yes. The sundae is *slathered in whipped cream and nuts* and the sundae is *hot fudge*.

Step 3: Ask, "Is the modifier in the right place?" The answer is yes and no. The phrase *hot fudge* is in the right place:

hot fudge sundae

But *Slathered in whipped cream and nuts* is in the wrong place:

Slathered in whipped cream and nuts, she

She is not slathered in whipped cream and nuts. The sundae is. The sentence needs to be revised.

revised sentence: She ate the *hot fudge* sundae *slathered in whipped cream and nuts.*

Caution: Be sure to put words like *almost, even, exactly, hardly, just, merely, nearly, only, scarcely,* and *simply* as near as possible to what they modify. If you put them in the wrong place, you may write a confusing sentence.

---

confusing sentence: Brian only wants to buy toothpaste and shampoo. (The modifier that creates confusion here is *only.* Does Brian have only one goal in life—to be a toothpaste and shampoo buyer? Or are these the only items he wants to buy? To create a clearer sentence, move the modifier.)

revised sentence: Brian wants to buy *only* toothpaste and shampoo.

The preceding examples show one common error in using modifiers. This error involves **misplaced modifiers**—words that describe something but are not where they should be in the sentence. Here is the rule to remember:

Put the modifier as close as possible to the word, phrase, or clause it modifies.

Exercise 3   Practice: Correcting Sentences with Misplaced Modifiers

Some of the following sentences contain misplaced modifiers. Revise any sentences that have a misplaced modifier by putting the modifier as close as possible to whatever it modifies.

1. Slow-cooked in a large pot, Manny enjoyed the stew.

   revised: _____

   _____

2. On my first day of college, I nearly sat in the wrong classroom for an hour.

   revised: _____

   _____

3. Lewis used to know a beautiful woman with a rare disease named Lucinda.

   revised: _____

   _____

4. Cooking in a tiny kitchen all day, the chef became dizzy and dehydrated.

    revised: _____

    _____

5. My cousins like to study dinosaurs on their visits to the natural history museum.

    revised: _____

    _____

6. With a can of paint, all of the bathroom walls were brightened by a smart decorator.

    revised: _____

    _____

7. Leticia will regret today's foolish decision in later years.

    revised: _____

    _____

8. I learned about the oil spill on my cell phone.

    revised: _____

    _____

9. My boyfriend had good intentions and had nearly finished all his reading assignments in history class but didn't write a required book report.

    revised: _____

    _____

10. After slipping on the ice, a few kind strangers asked me if I needed help.

    revised: _____

    _____

Correcting Dangling Modifiers

The three steps for correcting modifier problems can help you recognize another kind of error. For example, let's use the steps to check the following sentence.

> **sample sentence:** Cruising slowly through the Everglades, two alligators could be seen.

> **Step 1:** Find the modifier. The modifiers are *Cruising slowly through the Everglades* and *two*.

> **Step 2:** Ask, "Does the modifier have something to modify?" The answer is yes and no. The word *two* modifies *alligators*. But who or what is *cruising slowly through the Everglades*? There is no person mentioned in the sentence. The alligators are not cruising.

This kind of error is called a **dangling modifier.** It means that the modifier does not have anything to modify; it just dangles in the sentence. If you want to correct this kind of error, just moving the modifier will not work.

> **still incorrect:** Two alligators could be seen cruising slowly through the Everglades. (There is still no person cruising, and the alligators are not cruising.)

The way to correct this kind of error is to add something to the sentence. If you gave the modifier something to modify, you might come up with several correct sentences.

> **revised sentences:** *As we cruised slowly through the Everglades,* two alligators could be seen.
>
> Two alligators could be seen *when the visitors were cruising slowly through the Everglades.*
>
> *Cruising slowly through the Everglades, the people on the boat* saw two alligators.

Try the process for correcting dangling modifiers once more:

> **sample sentence:** Having struggled in the snow all day, hot coffee was welcome.

> **Step 1:** Find the modifier. The modifiers are *Having struggled in the snow all day* and *hot.*

> **Step 2:** Ask, "Does the modifier have anything to modify?" The answer is yes and no. *Hot* modifies *coffee,* but *Having struggled in the snow all day* doesn't modify anything. Who struggled? There is nobody mentioned in the sentence. To revise, put somebody in the sentence.

> **revised sentences:** Having struggled in the snow all day, Dan welcomed hot coffee.
> After we struggled in the snow all day, hot coffee was welcome.

Remember that you cannot correct a dangling modifier just by moving the modifiers. You have to give the modifier something to modify, so you must add something to the sentence.

Exercise 4 Practice: Correcting Sentences with Dangling Modifiers

Some of the following sentences use modifiers correctly, but some have dangling modifiers. Revise the sentences that have dangling modifiers. To revise, you will have to add words and change words.

1. When meeting people for the first time, highly personal questions are out of place.

   revised: _____

   _____

2. To finish a complicated task, small steps are useful.

   revised: _____

   _____

3. Motivated by fear and the pressure of my family's expectations, there was nothing but misery ahead.

revised: _____

_____

4. Lost in a forest and without warm clothes, the chances of surviving the night were slim.

revised: _____

_____

5. Preparing for a career in the military, good health is essential.

revised: _____

_____

6. Wrapped in an old blanket, the cat slept peacefully on the car's back seat.

revised: _____

_____

7. Without advanced training in electronics, a job at the new plant will be difficult to get.

revised: _____

_____

8. Shaken by the news of his brother's arrest, Aidan was lost and sad.

revised: _____

_____

9. At the age of ten, my father gave me a beautiful bicycle.

revised: _____

_____

10. After making an unintentionally cruel remark, an instant apology is needed.

revised: _____

_____

REVIEWING THE STEPS AND THE SOLUTIONS

It is important to recognize problems with modifiers and to correct these problems. Modifier problems can result in confusing or even silly sentences, and when you confuse or unintentionally amuse your reader, the reader misses your point.

Remember to check for modifier problems by using the three steps and to correct each kind of problem appropriately.

INFO BOX: **A Summary of Modifier Problems**

Checking for Modifier Problems

Step 1: Find the modifier.

Step 2: Ask, "Does the modifier have something to modify?"

Step 3: Ask, "Is the modifier in the right place?"

Correcting Modifier Problems

- If a modifier is in the wrong place (a misplaced modifier), put it as close as possible to the word, phrase, or clause it modifies.

- If a modifier has nothing to modify (a dangling modifier), add or change words so that it has something to modify.

Exercise 5 **Practice: Revising Sentences with Misplaced or Dangling Modifiers**

All of the sentences below have some kind of modifier problem. Write a new, correct sentence for each one. You can move, remove, add, or change words. The first one is done for you.

1. Chewing on an old shoe, Lincoln discovered his puppy.

   revised: Lincoln discovered his puppy chewing on an old shoe.

   _____

2. Climbing several flights of old, steep stairs, aches and pains began to afflict the tourists.

   revised: _____

   _____

3. Worried by endless rain, flooding was constantly in the residents' thoughts.

   revised: _____

   _____

4. Dancing through the aisles of the theater, the audience applauded the performers.

   revised: _____

   _____

5. An old car turned up in an abandoned barn that could be a classic Ford.

   revised: _____

   _____

6. Completing the calculus test nearly took me an hour.

   revised: _____

   _____

7. Wrapped in plastic, Lisa saw a huge stuffed teddy bear.

   revised: _____

   _____

8. To make friends, money or good looks are not required.

   revised: _____

   _____

9. Falling from the giant trees, David saw the red, orange, and yellow leaves of autumn.

   revised: _____

   _____

10. Cracked during the move from the museum, Andrea picked up the antique platter.

    revised: _____

    _____

Collaborate

| Exercise 6 | **Collaborate: Completing Sentences with Modifiers**

Do this exercise with a partner or group. Below are the beginnings of sentences. Complete each sentence by adding your own words. Be sure that each new sentence is free of modifier problems. When you have completed the exercise, share your sentences with another group or with the class. The first one is done for you.

1. Scorched and dry, the toasted English muffin tasted like a chunk of charcoal.

2. Furious about his friend's betrayal, _____

   _____

3. Sitting around the campfire on a starless night, _____

   _____

4. When making an excuse, _____

   _____

5. Stuck at work until 9:00 P.M., _____

   _____

6. To make friends in a new town, _____

   _____

7. Suddenly encountering a huge bear, _____

   _____

8. Loved by millions, _____

   _____

9. While trying to install a ceiling fan, _____

   _____

10. Filled with money, _____

    _____

Exercise 7 **Connect: Revising for Modifier Problems**

The following paragraph has some modifier problems. Correct the errors by writing above the lines. There are eight errors.

Moving is a terrible experience for me. Decisions about what to keep face me. I must decide also which unwanted possessions to throw away and which to donate to charity. Caught in these dilemmas, hours go by. The next major problem is packing. I just want to finish packing. I do not wish to spend hours or days accumulating enough boxes to hold my clothes, CDs, books, furniture, dishes, sheets, and towels. Another major category, bathroom items must be considered. Packing my collection of hair products, hair dryers, teeth whiteners, shaving cream, razors, tissues, skin lotions, and skin cream takes time. Sometimes I give up the struggle to acquire enough boxes, and I stuff most of my possessions into large plastic garbage bags. Having dumped my belongings into bags, several other duties must be performed. I must remember to fill out a change-of-address form; otherwise, my mail will be floating somewhere in the unknown. Then there is the horror of cleaning out the refrigerator. Seeing jars and plastic containers full of green and purple mold, fear and disgust strike me. Last, the actual move creates tension. Stuffing my belongings into a car, truck, SUV, or moving van makes me nervous. At my new residence, fitting my furniture and bulging plastic bags through narrow doors, hallways, and staircases is always a challenge. After enduring all the stages of the process, a reward ends my day. The pleasure of unpacking and enjoying the sight of my old belongings in a new setting is great. When I have to move again, I only hope I remember the good part of a move: the end.

Exercise 8 **Connect: Revising for Modifier Problems**

The following paragraph has some modifier problems. Correct the errors by writing above the lines. There are five errors.

Going online, the time speeds by. I am capable of sitting at my computer for five hours and losing all sense of the passing of time. After checking my messages, replies must be sent to all my friends. Involved in the resulting conversations, a new world is entered, one without clocks. I can spend hours on my favorite sites and blogs. I can play games, chat, watch videos, listen to music, and shop. My computer offers a new world for me. In this world, I can choose what I want to see and hear. First becoming popular years ago, some people worried about the power of television. They worried about television's ability to fascinate huge audiences. However, spending hours in front of a television does not erase a person's sense of time. An online experience can only do that.

Chapter Test   Correcting Problems with Modifiers

Some of the sentences below have problems with modifiers; some are correct. Put *OK* by each correct sentence and *X* by each sentence with a modifier problem.

1. _____ When I was short of cash, I took almost all the coins out of the cookie jar in the kitchen.

2. _____ With no sense of direction, getting lost on a huge campus was typical behavior for Sam.

3. _____ While taking a shower, a lizard crawled out of the drain.

4. _____ Broken-hearted, Lisa had difficulty learning to trust others again.

5. _____ Clutching his identification papers, the visitor to the United States waited at the end of a long line.

6. _____ Blended with strawberries and bananas, Sarah sipped the tropical drink.

7. _____ Constantly looking behind him, fear drove the escaped prisoner into a panic.

8. _____ At four years old, Callie's mother introduced her to the pleasures of dancing.

9. _____ To lose weight, motivation must be matched with self-discipline.

10. _____ You exactly were right about the value of the old silver tray.

Verbs: The Four Main Forms

CHAPTER 10

Quick Question

Which sentence(s) is/ are correct?

A. Amanda laid the stolen cash under a stack of sweaters in her bottom drawer.

B. Most of the time, Trevor do not speak to his father.

(After you study this chapter, you will be confident of your answer.)

Chapter Objectives

Students will be able to (1) identify standard and irregular verb forms and (2) recognize errors in verb tense or consistency.

Verbs are words that show some kind of action or being:

> **verb**
> My brother *washes* my car.

> **verb**
> The teddy bear *is* his oldest toy.

> **verb**
> Your cinnamon cake *smells* wonderful.

Verbs also tell about time:

> **verb**
> My brother *will wash* my car. (The time is future.)

> **verb**
> The teddy bear *was* his oldest toy. (The time is past.)

> **verb**
> Your cinnamon cake *smells* wonderful. (The time is present.)

111

The time of a verb is called its **tense.** You can say a verb is in the **present tense,** the **future tense,** the **past tense,** or many other tenses.

Using verbs correctly involves knowing which form of the verb to use and choosing the right verb tense.

USING STANDARD VERB FORMS

Many people use nonstandard verb forms in everyday conversation. But everyone who wants to write and speak effectively should know different levels of language, from the slang and dialect of everyday conversation to the **standard English** of college, business, and professional environments.

In everyday conversation, you might use nonstandard forms like the ones that follow:

Nonstandard Verb Forms

it seem	I faces	we was	you was
we goes	they doesn't	they talks	she work
you be	I be	he sell	it don't

But these are not correct forms in standard English. To become more familiar with standard verb forms, start with a review of the present tense.

THE PRESENT TENSE

Following are the standard verb forms of the verb *walk.*

INFO BOX: Standard Verb Forms in the Present Tense

I walk	we walk
you walk	you walk
he, she, it walks	they walk

Take a closer look at the standard verb forms. Only one form is different:

he, she, it *walks*

This is the only form that ends in *-s* in the present tense.

In the present tense, use an *-s* or *-es* ending on the verb only when the subject is *he, she,* or *it,* or the equivalent of *he, she,* or *it.*

examples:
He *drives* to the store on Saturdays.
Larry *walks* his dog on Saturdays. (*Larry* is the equivalent of *he.*)
The cat *chases* the birds in my garden. (The *cat* is the equivalent of *it.*)
She *reminds* me of my sister.
It *looks* like a new car.

Your engine *sounds* funny. (The word *engine* is the equivalent of *it.*)
My daughter *watches* the news on television. (The word *daughter* is
the equivalent of *she.*)

Take another look at the present tense. If the verb is a standard verb,
like *work*, it will follow this form in the present tense:

I *work* on the weekends.   It *works* on solar power.
You *work* too hard.   We *work* well together.
He *works* for his father.   You two boys *work* with Joe.
They *work* near the mall.   She *works* in a bakery.

Exercise 1   Practice: Picking the Right Verb in the Present Tense

To familiarize yourself with standard verb forms in the present tense, underline
the subject and circle the correct verb form in each of the following sentences.

1. The sound of a car horn (wake / wakes) me up every morning.

2. Andrea is always thinking of her future; each week she (put / puts)
   a few dollars into a savings account.

3. Before every family barbecue, my father (prepare/ prepares) his
   famous hot sauce.

4. My job responsibilities (seem / seems) to grow every week.

5. Meeting at my house for dinner (give / gives) us a chance to catch
   up on the latest local gossip.

6. Cynthia and her sister (look / looks) like twins.

7. On sunny days, I (wear / wears) a hat to protect my face from too
   much exposure to damaging rays.

8. He (need / needs) a new best friend.

9. Ricardo and his uncle (own / owns) a towing company.

10. A mouse in the garage regularly (chew / chews) tiny holes in a bag
    of dog food.

Exercise 2   Practice: More on Picking the Right Verb in the Present Tense

To familiarize yourself with standard verb forms in the present tense, underline the subject and circle the correct verb form in each of the following
sentences.

1. On Thanksgiving, the restaurant (serve / serves) dinners
   to the poor.

2. A week without studying (seem / seems) impossible.

3. Her quick temper (cause / causes) problems in the family.

4. Next week, you (drive / drives) Callie to Orlando.

5. Anthony (look / looks) worried about the sociology exam.

6. In the attic of the old house (live / lives) a raccoon.

7. Your bathroom (smell / smells) like a beauty salon.

8. They rarely (offer / offers) me any advice.

9. At a party, I usually (spend / spends) most of my time with friends.

10. Constant jealousy (damage / damages) any relationship.

Collaborate

Exercise 3 **Collaborate: Writing Sentences with Verbs in the Present Tense**

Below are pairs of verbs. Working with a partner or group, write a sentence using each verb. Be sure your verbs are in the present tense, and make your sentences at least five words long. When you have completed the exercise, share your sentences with another group. The first one is done for you.

1. **verbs:** ignore, ignores

   sentence 1: _Sometimes I ignore Jay's constant complaining._ _____

   _____

   sentence 2: _Alan regularly ignores his mother's warnings about eating too_ much fatty food. _____

2. **verbs:** forget, forgets

   sentence 1: _____

   _____

   sentence 2: _____

   _____

3. **verbs:** demand, demands

   sentence 1: _____

   _____

   sentence 2: _____

   _____

4. **verbs:** reveal, reveals

   sentence 1: _____

   _____

   sentence 2: _____

   _____

5. **verbs:** spoil, spoils

   sentence 1: _____

   _____

   sentence 2: _____

   _____

6. **verbs:** remain, remains

   sentence 1: _____

   _____

   sentence 2: _____

   _____

7. verbs: lose, loses

sentence 1: _____

_____

sentence 2: _____

_____

8. verbs: prepare, prepares

sentence 1: _____

_____

sentence 2: _____

_____

9. verbs: look, looks

sentence 1: _____

_____

sentence 2: _____

_____

10. verbs: intend, intends

sentence 1: _____

_____

sentence 2: _____

_____

Exercise 4   **Connect: Revising a Paragraph for Errors in the Present Tense**

Connect

The following paragraph contains nine errors in the present tense verb forms. Correct the errors in the spaces above the lines.

A sick person often take medicine to get well, but sometimes liquids

tastes disgusting and pills gets stuck in a person's throat. When I feel nau-

seous, I take a pink liquid. Swallowing this liquid cause me to consider spitting

it out. Surely, other people with indigestion wonders about taking a nasty cure.

In addition, my doctor sometimes prescribes pills when I suffers from the flu

or a migraine headache. These medications seems much bigger than a tiny

aspirin or a cold pill. Most adults fear choking on such enormous pills. After

symptoms appears, I and other people wants a quick end to colds, infections,

allergies, and pain. However, the remedies often seem almost as unpleasant as

the ailment.

THE PAST TENSE

The past tense of most verbs is formed by adding *-d* or *-ed* to the verb.

INFO BOX: Standard Verb Forms in the Past Tense

I walked	we walked
you walked	you walked
he, she, it walked	they walked

Add *-ed* to *walk* to form the past tense. For some other verbs, you may add *-d*.

> The zookeeper *chased* the chimpanzee.
> I *trembled* with excitement.
> Paul *baked* a birthday cake for his daughter.

Exercise 5   **Practice: Writing the Correct Form of the Past Tense**

To familiarize yourself with the past tense, write the correct past tense form of each verb in the blank space.

1. After planning a visit to a national park, my parents _____ (count) on good weather.

2. Before our wedding, my fiancé and I _____ (receive) many beautiful gifts.

3. When she was a child, my mother _____ (suffer) from a problem with her spine.

4. Last weekend, my car _____ (stall) in heavy traffic.

5. During my first semester of college, I _____ (learn) about the differences between high school and higher education.

6. Once in summer school, someone _____ (pull) the fire alarm in a classroom building.

7. At the end of the party, a friend _____ (offer) me a ride home.

8. In kindergarten, my older sister _____ (love) her teacher and the entire experience of school.

9. At my last job, no one _____ (expect) our supervisor to quit and move to Montana.

10. Ten years ago, my cousin _____ (play) a terrible trick on me.

Exercise 6   **Practice: More on Writing the Correct Form of the Past Tense**

To familiarize yourself with the past tense, write the correct past tense form of each verb in the blank space.

1. During the early morning hours, someone _____ (knock) on my door.

2. At the beginning of class, one brave student _____ (ask) to postpone the test.

3. Two weeks ago, Jessica _____ (promise) me a ride in her new car.

4. All afternoon, my cat _____ (stare) at the birds perched on the outdoor bird feeder.

5. Last night at a family dinner, I _____ (spill) tomato sauce on my mother's best tablecloth.

6. After hours of hard, physical labor, Calvin _____ (long) for a hot shower and a good night's sleep.

7. An old girlfriend from my high school days _____ (reappear) in my life last fall.

8. In 1999, Beth Cho _____ (create) a popular cartoon character and a nationally known comic strip.

9. Upset by all the rumors and criticism, Taylor _____ (resign) from the team yesterday.

10. At the end of the meeting, no one _____ (stay) to chat.

Exercise 7   **Collaborate: Writing Sentences with Verbs in the Present and Past Tense**

Collaborate

Below are pairs of verbs. Working with a partner or group, write a sentence using each verb. Each sentence should be five or more words long. When you have completed the exercise, share your sentences with another group. The first one is done for you.

1. **verbs:** criticizes, criticized

   sentence 1: <u>Every time I see my grandfather, he criticizes my clothes.</u>

   _____

   sentence 2: <u>After our first visit to the Italian restaurant, Daniel and I</u>

   <u>criticized the texture of the pizza.</u>

2. **verbs:** convey, conveyed

   sentence 1: _____

   _____

   sentence 2: _____

   _____

3. **verbs:** refuses, refused

   sentence 1: _____

   _____

   sentence 2: _____

   _____

4. **verbs:** remains, remained

   sentence 1: _____

   _____

sentence 2: _____

_____

5. **verbs:** deceive, deceived

sentence 1: _____

_____

sentence 2: _____

_____

6. **verbs:** chase, chased

sentence 1: _____

_____

sentence 2: _____

_____

7. **verbs:** raises, raised

sentence 1: _____

_____

sentence 2: _____

_____

8. **verbs:** copes, coped

sentence 1: _____

_____

sentence 2: _____

_____

9. **verbs:** define, defined

sentence 1: _____

_____

sentence 2: _____

_____

10. **verbs:** reject, rejected

sentence 1: _____

_____

sentence 2: _____

_____

Connect

Exercise 8 **Connect: Rewriting a Paragraph, Changing the Verb Tense**

Rewrite the following paragraph, changing all the present tense verbs to the past tense. Write the changes in the lines above the original words.

Every time my Aunt Christina meets a woman in her twenties, my aunt immediately imagines her as a possible wife for me. She wants to know whether the woman is single, what the woman does for a living, and whether she likes children. If my aunt gets the answers she desires, she proceeds with her scheme. She brags about her handsome, smart, and single nephew. Of course, the personal questions and aggressive tactics do not put a woman at ease. In addition, they create a picture of me as a desperate man. I find Aunt Christina's tactics crude and embarrassing. As a result, I avoid any contact with my aunt if the meeting involves young, single women. I love Aunt Christina, but she is not my idea of a matchmaker. In addition, I know how to find true love by myself.

THE FOUR MAIN FORMS OF A VERB

When you are deciding what form of a verb to use, you will probably rely on one of four verb forms: the present tense, the past tense, the present participle, or the past participle. You will use one of these forms or add a helping verb to it. As an example, look at the four main forms of the verb *walk*.

INFO BOX: The Four Main Forms of a Verb

Present	Past	Present Participle	Past Participle
walk	walked	walking	walked

You use the four verb forms—present, past, present participle, and past participle—alone or with helping verbs to express time (tense). Forms of regular verbs like *walk* are easy to remember.

Use the **present** form for the present tense:
They *walk* three miles every day.

The **past** form expresses past tense:
Steve *walked* to work yesterday.

The **present participle,** or *-ing* form, is used with helping verbs:
He *was walking* in a charity fundraiser.
I *am walking* with a neighbor.
You *should have been walking* faster.

The **past participle** is the form used with the helping verbs *have, has,* or *had:*
I *have walked* down this road before.
She *has walked* to church for years.
The children *had walked* the dog before they went to school.

Of course, you can add many helping verbs to the present tense.

present tense:
We *walk* in a beautiful forest.

add helping verbs:
We *will* walk in a beautiful forest.
We *must* walk in a beautiful forest.
We *can* walk in a beautiful forest.

In **regular verbs,** the four verb forms are simple: the past form is created by adding *-d* or *-ed* to the present form. The present participle is formed by adding *-ing* to the present form, and the past participle is the same as the past form.

Collaborate

Exercise 9 **Collaborate: Writing Sentences Using the Four Main Forms of a Verb**

Do this exercise with a partner or group. Below are pairs of verbs. Write a sentence for each verb. Your sentences should be at least five words long. When you have completed this exercise, share your answers with another group or with the class. The first one is done for you.

1. verbs: worry, worrying

    sentence 1: I rarely worry about my health or fitness.

    _____

    sentence 2: Colleen's parents could have been worrying about her reckless

    behavior.

2. verbs: request, requested (Put *had* in front of *requested.*)

    sentence 1: _____

    _____

    sentence 2: _____

    _____

3. verbs: scattered, scattering

    sentence 1: _____

    _____

    sentence 2: _____

    _____

4. verbs: distort, distorted

    sentence 1: _____

    _____

    sentence 2: _____

    _____

5. verbs: praise, praised (Put *has* in front of *praised.*)

    sentence 1: _____

    _____

sentence 2: _____

_____

6. **verbs:** disclose, disclosed (Put *had* in front of *disclosed.*)

sentence 1: _____

_____

sentence 2: _____

_____

7. **verbs:** survive, surviving

sentence 1: _____

_____

sentence 2: _____

_____

8. **verbs:** restore, restoring

sentence 1: _____

_____

sentence 2: _____

_____

9. **verbs:** implying, implied (Put *has* in front of *implied.*)

sentence 1: _____

_____

sentence 2: _____

_____

10. **verbs:** expressing, expressed

sentence 1: _____

_____

sentence 2: _____

_____

IRREGULAR VERBS

The Present Tense of *Be, Have, Do*

Irregular verbs do not follow the same rules for creating verb forms that regular verbs do. Three verbs that we use all the time—*be*, *have*, and *do*—are irregular verbs. You need to study them closely. Look at the present tense forms for all three, and compare the standard present tense forms with the nonstandard ones. *Remember to use the standard forms for college or professional writing.*

present tense of *be:*

Nonstandard	Standard
~~I be or I is~~	I am
~~you be~~	you are
~~he, she, it be~~	he, she, it is
~~we be~~	we are
~~you be~~	you are
~~they be~~	they are

present tense of *have:*

Nonstandard	Standard
~~I has~~	I have
~~you has~~	you have
~~he, she, it have~~	he, she, it has
~~we has~~	we have
~~you has~~	you have
~~they has~~	they have

present tense of *do:*

Nonstandard	Standard
~~I does~~	I do
~~you does~~	you do
~~he, she, it do~~	he, she, it does
~~we does~~	we do
~~you does~~	you do
~~they does~~	they do

> **Caution:** Be careful when you add *not* to *does.* If you're using the contraction of *does not*, be sure you write *doesn't* instead of *don't.* Contractions should be avoided in most formal reports and business writing courses. Always check with your instructor about the appropriate use of contractions in your assignments.

not this: He don't call me very often.

but this: He doesn't call me very often.

Exercise 10   **Practice: Choosing the Correct Form of *Be, Have,* and *Do* in the Present Tense**

Circle the correct form of the verb in each sentence.

1. After my boyfriend and I argue, we (are / be) ashamed of our bad tempers.

2. Leon, my friend from high school, (has / have) a job at the airport.

3. My new cell phone (do / does) everything but cook.

4. Stacks of books (be / are) extremely heavy items for carrying to class.

5. As we enter North Ridge, we (has / have) a beautiful view of hills and trees.

6. When I see my husband come home from his night class, I (am / be) proud of his determination.

7. At the club house, two or three members (does / do) a little cleaning once a month.

8. Once a year, the local library (has / have) a giant used book sale.

9. Nelson must learn some manners if he (is / be) thinking of a job in a hotel.

10. After dark, my sister (don't / doesn't) walk through our neighborhood alone.

Exercise 11 **Practice: More on Choosing the Correct Form of *Be, Have,* and *Do* in the Present Tense**

Circle the correct form of the verb in each sentence.

1. Mark likes to talk too much, but he (do / does) tell a good story.

2. I (have / has) not had a raise in two years.

3. I love my speech class, so I (am / be) thinking about taking another class in public speaking.

4. Both colleges offer the classes you want; you (has / have) a choice to make.

5. The coffeemaker in the lunch room (is / be) making a strange sound.

6. Sondra (do / does) everything to make her children happy.

7. Every time I see Marlon, he (has / have) another story about his new baby.

8. Whenever I see a terrible movie, I (is / am) determined never to waste my money on trash again.

9. If I stay out too late, my brain (doesn't / don't) work well in the morning.

10. The band members at Sequoia High School (have / has) practice tomorrow morning.

Exercise 12 **Connect: Revising a Paragraph with Errors in the Present Tense of *Be, Have,* and *Do***

Connect

The following paragraph contains nine errors in the use of the present tense forms of *be, have,* and *do.* Correct the errors above the lines.

A small park at the back of my apartment complex be causing some problems in our neighborhood. The park have swing sets, a slide, and a jungle gym designed for children in kindergarten or elementary school, but neighborhood teens has an interest in the park. The teens does not have a gathering place of their own, so they be regular visitors to the children's park. Sometimes the teens frighten the small children. In addition, the playground equipment be not designed to hold the weight of older children, so the swing sets, slide, and even the jungle gym has dents and cracks. The parents of the young children do not like this invasion of the park, but the teens are now in control of the property. It do not seem fair that small children are now the outsiders at a park for small children. On the other hand, local teens does not want to be stuck with no gathering place except the streets.

The Past Tense of *Be, Have,* and *Do*

The past tense forms of these irregular verbs can be confusing. Again, compare the nonstandard forms with the standard forms. *Remember to use the standard forms for college or professional writing.*

past tense of *be:*

Nonstandard	Standard
~~I were~~	I was
~~you was~~	you were
~~he, she, it were~~	he, she, it was
~~we was~~	we were
~~you was~~	you were
~~they was~~	they were

past tense of *have:*

Nonstandard	Standard
~~I has~~	I had
~~you has~~	you had
~~he, she, it have~~	he, she, it had
~~we has~~	we had
~~you has~~	you had
~~they has~~	they had

past tense of *do:*

Nonstandard	Standard
~~I done~~	I did
~~you done~~	you did
~~he, she, it done~~	he, she, it did
~~we done~~	we did
~~you done~~	you did
~~they done~~	they did

Exercise 13 **Practice: Choosing the Correct Form of *Be, Have,* and *Do* in the Past Tense**

Circle the correct verb form in each sentence.

1. After Katrina paid her traffic ticket, she (have / had) very little money in her bank account.

2. Jay apologized to his girlfriend, but he (did / done) nothing to break his habit of criticizing her.

3. When I entered college, I (was / were) unsure about my goals.

4. After the tornado, the neighbors (did / done) their best to salvage the pieces of their shattered homes.

5. A few months ago, I took my six-year-old nephew to a carnival, and we (had / has) a wonderful time.

6. My children stayed up late last night, so they (was / were) reluctant to get out of bed this morning.

7. Today you are a respected citizen, but years ago you (was / were) a troubled teenager.

8. Before we got married, we (did / done) nothing but argue about trivial matters.

9. When they moved to Pennsylvania, my parents (had / has) never seen snow.

10. The heating system broke last night, and my apartment (have / had) no alternate source of heat such as a fireplace.

Exercise 14 **Practice: More on Choosing the Correct Form of _Be, Have,_ and _Do_ in the Past Tense**

Circle the correct verb form in each sentence.

1. Lisa and Danny (done / did) most of the work in the office; the other members of the staff were on the road most of the time.

2. After my grandmother retired, she finally (have / had) the time to enjoy her favorite hobbies: photography and ballroom dancing.

3. For two years, I (was / were) the proud owner of a large snake.

4. When I first saw my sister's cats, they (was / were) tiny kittens curled up in an old baseball cap.

5. My brothers never helped with chores around the house; they always (have / had) a million excuses for getting out of housework.

6. The cake at Kelly's birthday party (was / were) so large that we all took leftover pieces home.

7. For months, Saul and his friends (done / did) nothing but complain about their bad luck.

8. Because our parents died young, my sister and I (has / had) very little guidance in our teen years.

9. A month after we moved into our new house, we (was / were) still unpacking boxes of clothes, dishes, and other household items.

10. Getting a cell phone (did / done) nothing to make my day easier.

Exercise 15 **Connect: Revising a Paragraph with Errors in the Past Tense** **Connect** **of _Be, Have,_ and _Do_**

The following paragraph contains twelve errors in the use of the past tense of _be, have,_ and _do_. Correct the errors above the lines.

Yesterday I stood up to Jamie, my older brother, and I done it for some good reasons. First, Jamie were an obnoxious person all afternoon. He ridiculed me, and he done it for hours. He were especially cruel because he done the verbal bullying when my fiancée were present. I were convinced that he meant to shame me in front of her, and I were full of rage. In addition, the hurt of many years of Jamie's abuse seemed to collect in my heart. These two factors was enough to provoke me to fight back. I done nothing physical, but I stood my ground. "Watch it, Jamie," I said. "You has gone too far with your meanness." He glared at me in silence, but I did not back off. "Watch your words," I said, and my brother have nothing else to say. I felt free and strong for the first time in years, and I plan to keep challenging my brother's cruelty.

More Irregular Verb Forms

Be, have, and *do* are not the only verbs with irregular forms. There are many such verbs, and everybody who writes uses some form of an irregular verb. When you write and you are not certain you are using the correct form of a verb, check the following list of irregular verbs.

For each verb listed, the *present,* the *past,* and the *past participle* forms are given. The present participle isn't included because it is always formed by adding *-ing* to the present form.

Irregular Verb Forms

Present	Past	Past Participle
(Today I arise.)	(Yesterday I arose.)	(I have/had arisen.)
arise	arose	arisen
awake	awaked, awoke	awaked, awoken
bear	bore	born, borne
beat	beat	beaten
become	became	become
begin	began	begun
bend	bent	bent
bite	bit	bitten
bleed	bled	bled
blow	blew	blown
break	broke	broken
bring	brought	brought
build	built	built
burst	burst	burst
buy	bought	bought
catch	caught	caught
choose	chose	chosen

Present	Past	Past Participle
come	came	come
cling	clung	clung
cost	cost	cost
creep	crept	crept
cut	cut	cut
deal	dealt	dealt
draw	drew	drawn
dream	dreamed, dreamt	dreamed, dreamt
drink	drank	drunk
drive	drove	driven
eat	ate	eaten
fall	fell	fallen
feed	fed	fed
feel	felt	felt
fight	fought	fought
find	found	found
fling	flung	flung
fly	flew	flown
freeze	froze	frozen
get	got	got, gotten
give	gave	given
go	went	gone
grow	grew	grown
hear	heard	heard
hide	hid	hidden
hit	hit	hit
hold	held	held
hurt	hurt	hurt
keep	kept	kept
know	knew	known
lay (to put)	laid	laid
lead	led	led
leave	left	left
lend	lent	lent
let	let	let
lie (to recline)	lay	lain
light	lit, lighted	lit, lighted
lost	lost	lost
make	made	made
mean	meant	meant
meet	met	met
pay	paid	paid
ride	rode	ridden
ring	rang	rung
rise	rose	risen
run	ran	run
say	said	said
see	saw	seen
sell	sold	sold
send	sent	sent
sew	sewed	sewn, sewed
shake	shook	shaken
shine	shone, shined	shone, shined
shrink	shrank	shrunk
shut	shut	shut

continued

Present	Past	Past Participle
sing	sang	sung
sit	sat	sat
sleep	slept	slept
slide	slid	slid
sling	slung	slung
speak	spoke	spoken
spend	spent	spent
stand	stood	stood
steal	stole	stolen
stick	stuck	stuck
sting	stung	stung
stink	stank, stunk	stunk
string	strung	strung
swear	swore	sworn
swim	swam	swum
teach	taught	taught
tear	tore	torn
tell	told	told
think	thought	thought
throw	threw	thrown
wake	waked, woke	waked, woken
wear	wore	wore
win	won	won
write	wrote	written

Exercise 16   Practice: Choosing the Correct Form of Irregular Verbs

Write the correct form of the verb in parentheses in the following sentences. Be sure to check the list of irregular verbs.

1. The environmental scientist has _____ (draw) a clear picture of the danger to our lakes and rivers.

2. Before my grandfather designed his house in Boulder, he had already _____ (build) two houses in South Dakota.

3. Yesterday the mayor _____ (stand) on the stage and tried to calm the fears of a crowd of residents.

4. I usually take some kind of dessert to a family gathering, but last weekend I _____ (bring) a scalloped potato casserole.

5. Colin had _____ (give) his wife a piece of jewelry every year until recently, when she divorced him.

6. I'm not sure that I can _____ (find) a cheap table at the used furniture store.

7. By the end of the month, Sarah had _____ (tell) me three different stories about her family background.

8. The temperature was so low that the water in the birdbath was _____ (freeze).

9. Jesse _____ (slide) a plastic container of ketchup across the counter until my mother scolded him.

10. Last week, I _____ (think) about looking for a better job.

Exercise 17 Practice: More on Choosing the Correct Form of Irregular Verbs

Write the correct form of the verb in parentheses in the following sentences. Be sure to check the list of irregular verbs.

1. When the spotlight turned to me, I _____ (shake) with nervousness.

2. Be careful; that little puppy has _____ (bite) me with his sharp little teeth.

3. In the summer, I _____ (sling) an old sheet over the curtain rod on my bedroom window to keep out the early morning sun.

4. When the storm hit, the wind _____ (blow) through the smallest cracks in the log cabin's walls.

5. After class, Alicia _____ (go) to the computer lab to work on her political science assignment.

6. My mother saved old buttons and _____ (string) them together to make a necklace for her little granddaughter.

7. I have never _____ (sleep) on the top bunk of a bunk bed.

8. For years, my father has _____ (rise) at 5:30 A.M. and cooked himself a large breakfast.

9. By the time dinner was served, the children had _____ (eat) so many snacks that they were no longer hungry.

10. Yesterday my husband _____ (buy) our toddler a tiny basketball.

Exercise 18 Collaborate: Writing Sentences with Correct Verb Forms

Collaborate

With a partner or with a group, write two sentences that correctly use each of the following verb forms. Each sentence should be five or more words long. In writing these sentences, you may add helping verbs to the verb forms, but you may *not* change the verb form itself. When your group has completed the exercise, share your answers with another group or with the class. The first one has been done for you.

1. **verb:** bit

    sentence 1: _Dozens of mosquitoes bit me while I walked in the woods._

    _____

    sentence 2: _While he was eating a peach, Emilio bit into the pit and chipped_

    his tooth. _____

2. **verb:** written

    sentence 1: _____

    _____

    sentence 2: _____

    _____

3. verb: torn

sentence 1: _____

_____

sentence 2: _____

_____

4. verb: taught

sentence 1: _____

_____

sentence 2: _____

_____

5. verb: meant

sentence 1: _____

_____

sentence 2: _____

_____

6. verb: beat

sentence 1: _____

_____

sentence 2: _____

_____

7. verb: chosen

sentence 1: _____

_____

sentence 2: _____

_____

8. verb: bore

sentence 1: _____

_____

sentence 2: _____

_____

9. verb: chose

sentence 1: _____

_____

sentence 2: _____

_____

10. verb: begin

sentence 1: _____

_____

sentence 2: _____

_____

Exercise 19 Connect: Revising a Paragraph That Contains Errors in Irregular Verb Forms

Connect

Thirteen of the irregular verb forms in the following paragraph are incorrect. Write the correct verb forms in the space above the lines.

When the pipes bursted in our house, panic breaked loose among the family members. The disaster occurred on a Saturday evening while we were in the kitchen. As we sitted at the kitchen table, our supper was interrupted by a sudden flow of water. Within minutes, the water had covered the floor. Because we were so shooked up, no one knowed what to do. My mother was the first to act. She flinged kitchen mats, chairs, pet bowls, and other objects onto higher spaces such as the table and kitchen counters. The rest of us keeped trying to figure out the cause of the damage. Meanwhile, the amount of water just growed. Of course, because this mess hit us on a Saturday night, we had a hard time finding a plumber. Finally, we finded a person who came to our rescue. The damage was extensive, and repairing it costed a great deal of money. Once the kitchen was repaired and restored, my sister and I still shrinked from sitting at the kitchen table. We remembered the awful time when the water stinked and our kitchen was tored apart. Today, three years after the flood, I still spend very little time in the kitchen.

Exercise 20 Connect: Revising Another Paragraph That Contains Errors in Irregular Verb Forms

Connect

Nine of the irregular verb forms in the following paragraph are incorrect. Write the correct verb forms in the space above the lines.

Waiting for a loved one to come out of surgery can mean spending hours filled with emotions. When I waited for my sister as she was undergoing surgery for breast cancer, the time seemed endless. Impatience builded in me until I wanted to hit something. I tried to distract myself by observing the other people waiting for loved ones, but they all appeared calm and even unconcerned. Two people, for example, talked and drinked cans of soda as if they had no worries. Another woman sleeped in her chair for an hour. Meanwhile, I growed more tense and impatient. I knowed the surgeon was supposed to come out and talk to me and my aunt when he had finished the operation. I began to think he had gave up on my sister

and didn't want to talk to us. Fear replaced my anger. I feeded my imagination with

all kinds of horrible situations such as funerals and burials. Hours later, my sister's

surgeon come through the swinging doors. He had good news. Now I felt intense

joy and, underneath it, relief. I could not have beared the loss of my sister.

Chapter Test Verbs: The Four Main Forms

Some of the sentences use verbs correctly; others do not. Put *OK* by each
correct sentence and *X* by each sentence with an error in using verbs.

1. _____ After the argument at my house, my sister and her boyfriend done nothing to improve family relations.

2. _____ The comedian has hid his intelligence behind a mask of
foolishness.

3. _____ Matthew and Lisa could have went to a discount store to
buy their window air conditioner.

4. _____ Even though Michael is a strict parent, he do have a warm
heart and great love for his children.

5. _____ If you are ready to leave at 6:30 A.M., we can avoid the
morning rush hour on Cade Boulevard.

6. _____ The horror movie had a lingering effect on me; it gave me
nightmares for a week.

7. _____ Serena swum in the city pool whenever she had some free
time.

8. _____ By the time I saw Enrique again, he had grown a full beard.

9. _____ Although your best friend showed a lack of respect for your
privacy, you was wrong to react with such anger.

10. _____ At the garden center, one of the clerks slung a large bag of
mulch over his shoulder and carried it to my car.

More on Verb Tenses

CHAPTER 11

Quick Question

Which sentence(s) is/
are correct?

  A. Maria wished
     she will find a
     good job soon.

  B. If you had
     called an
     ambulance
     sooner, Daniel
     could have
     reached the
     hospital earlier.

(After you study this
chapter, you will be
confident of your
answer.)

Chapter Objectives

Students will be able to (1) identify proper subject–verb agreement, (2) recognize fixed-form helping verbs, and (3) distinguish between various perfect and progressive verb tenses.

HELPING VERBS AND VERB TENSES

The main verb forms—present, past, present participle, and past participle—can be combined with **helping verbs** to create more verb tenses. Following is a list of some common helping verbs.

INFO BOX: Some Common Helping Verbs

is	was	does	have
am	were	did	had
are	do	has	

These verbs change their form, depending on the subject:

> She *is* calling the ticket booth.
> I *am* calling the ticket booth.

Fixed-Form Helping Verbs

Some other helping verbs always keep the same form, no matter what the subject. These are the **fixed-form helping verbs.** Following are the fixed-form helping verbs.

INFO BOX: Fixed-Form Helping Verbs

can	will	may	shall	must
could	would	might	should	

Notice how the helping verb *can* is in the same form even when the subject changes:

> She *can* call the ticket booth.
> I *can* call the ticket booth.

Helping Verbs *Can* and *Could, Will* and *Would*

Can is used to show the present tense:
> Today, David *can* fix the washer.

Could is used to show the past tense:
> Yesterday, David *could* fix the washer.

Could is also used to show a possibility or a wish:
> David *could* fix the washer if he had the right tools.
> Harry wishes he *could* fix the washer.

Will points to the future from the present:
> Cecilia is sure she *will* win the case. (Today, in the present, Cecilia is sure she will win, in the future.)

Would points to the future from the past:
> Cecilia was sure she *would* win the case. (In the past, Cecilia was sure she would win, in the future.)

Would is also used to show a possibility or a wish:
> Cecilia *would* win the case if she prepared for it.
> Cecilia wishes she *would* win the case.

Exercise 1 **Practice: Recognizing Helping Verbs**

Underline the helping verbs in the following sentences.

1. Cameron does dress well, but he never looks stylish.

2. The cooking smells in the seafood restaurant have given me a headache several times.

3. Before our baby was born, we could count on sleeping through the night.

4. You might find a cheap dining room table at the flea market.

5. I hear loud music; we must be near the party at the park.

6. Before I signed up for the bus trip, some of my friends had enjoyed the same tour.

7. My brother likes to argue for the sake of arguing, but last night he did make a valid point about the price of gas.

8. Because our landlord is raising the rent, my roommate and I are thinking about moving.

9. His homeland is torn by fighting, so Andre shall cancel his plans for a visit to the area.

10. Lynette and Aaron were traveling on a crowded highway when their truck got a flat tire.

> **Exercise 2** **Practice: Selecting *Can* or *Could, Will* or *Would***

In each of the following sentences, circle the correct helping verb.

1. When I was young, I (can / could) eat fattening foods and never gain weight.

2. Terrence (will / would) pass the final math exam if he studied more.

3. Even when he was eight years old, Manny was sure he (will / would) become a pilot.

4. The weather is so beautiful today that I (can / could) not stay indoors.

5. Kevin was never sure that he (can / could) speak frankly to his father.

6. Miriam is convinced that she (will / would) find a job in her field.

7. After you activate the alarm system, no one (can / could) enter the house in silence.

8. All your friends know that you (will / would) always be kind and generous.

9. Only one man knew the riverfront (will / would) flood before daybreak.

10. Last night Eric (can / could) not get to sleep until midnight.

PRESENT PROGRESSIVE TENSE

The **present progressive tense** uses the present participle (the *-ing* form of the verb) plus some form of *to be*. Following are examples of the present progressive tense.

INFO BOX: Present Progressive Tense

I am walking		we are walking	
you are walking	singular	you are walking	plural
he, she, it is walking		they are walking	

All of these forms of the present progressive tense use an *-ing* form of the verb (*walking*) plus a present form of *to be* (*am, is, are*).

Be careful not to confuse the present progressive tense with the present tense:

present tense: Terry *listens* to music. (This sentence means that Terry *does* listen to music, but it does not say she is doing so at this moment.)

present progressive: Terry *is listening* to music. (This sentence means that Terry is listening to music at this moment.)

The present progressive tense shows us that the action is happening right now. The present progressive tense can also show future time.

Terry *is listening* to music later. (This sentence means that Terry will be listening to music in the future.)

> **Exercise 3** **Practice: Distinguishing Between the Present Tense and the Present Progressive Tense**

Circle the correct verb tense in each of the following sentences. Be sure to look carefully at the meaning of each sentence.

1. Occasionally, my parents (are traveling / travel) to Maine in the summer.

2. I can talk to my advisor right now, she (is sitting / sits) in her office with the door open.

3. At twilight, the crickets outside my house (are making / make) a terrible noise.

4. At this moment, my best friend (is starting / starts) his first day in the U.S. Navy.

5. Clea and William seem content; evidently, they (are adjusting / adjust) to the challenges of moving to a new city.

6. When it gets cold, Lisa (is getting / gets) her daily exercise by walking at a huge indoor mall.

7. Occasionally you (are making / make) sarcastic remarks about my father.

8. It's too hot to cook indoors, so I (am grilling / grill) hot dogs in the back yard.

9. Every Saturday night, my father (is playing / plays) cards with his friends.

10. Leon can't come to the phone right now; he (is taking / takes) a shower.

PAST PROGRESSIVE TENSE

The **past progressive tense** uses the present participle (the -*ing* form of the verb) plus a past form of *to be* (*was, were*). Following are examples of the past progressive tense.

INFO BOX: Past Progressive Tense

I was walking			we were walking		
you were walking	}	singular	you were walking	}	plural
he, she, it was walking			they were walking		

Be careful not to confuse the past progressive tense with the past tense:

past tense: George *walked* carefully. (This sentence implies that George has stopped walking.)

past progressive tense: George *was walking* carefully when he slipped on the ice. (This sentence says that George was in the process of walking when something else happened: he slipped.)

Use the progressive tenses, both present and past, when you want to show that something was or is in progress.

Exercise 4   **Practice: Distinguishing Between the Past Tense and the Past Progressive Tense**

Circle the correct verb tense in each of the following sentences. Be sure to look carefully at the meaning of each sentence.

1. Last week, the trip to Houston (was taking / took) more time than usual.

2. Eric (was packing / packed) his duffle bag last night.

3. After Kelly's trip to North Carolina, she (was talking / talked) about nothing but the beautiful mountains.

4. The hurricane (was devastating / devastated) parts of coastal Texas before it moved to the Florida Panhandle.

5. You (wore / were wearing) a hideous yellow sweater when we first met.

6. When I was a child, I (was loving / loved) cartoons with animal characters.

7. More than a month ago, Bill (was promising / promised) to pay his debt to me within twenty-four hours.

8. I (was typing / typed) my essay when the power went out.

9. Before I could grab the hamburger patty, my dog (was snatching / snatched) it off the floor.

10. One winter, I (wore / was wearing) my heavy jacket every day.

PRESENT PERFECT TENSE

The **present perfect tense** is made up of the past participle form of the verb plus *have* or *has* as a helping verb. Following are examples of the present perfect tense.

INFO BOX: Present Perfect Tense

I have walked		we have walked	
you have walked	singular	you have walked	plural
he, she, it has walked		they have walked	

Be careful not to confuse the present perfect tense with the past tense:

> **past tense:** Jacqueline *studied* yoga for two years. (This sentence means that Jacqueline doesn't study yoga anymore, but she did study it in the past.)
>
> **present perfect tense:** Jacqueline *has studied* yoga for two years. (This sentence means that Jacqueline started studying yoga two years ago; she is still studying it.)

The present perfect tense is used to show an action that started in the past but is still going on in the present.

> ### Exercise 5   Practice: Distinguishing Between the Past and the Present Perfect Tense

Circle the correct verb tense in each of the following sentences. Be sure to look carefully at the meaning of each sentence.

1. Yesterday, the mayor (declared / has declared) that all city departments would work four days a week, with each day lasting ten hours.

2. My grandmother (cooked / has cooked) at a local Cuban restaurant for ten years before she opened her own catering business.

3. For many years now, my parents (celebrated / have celebrated) their anniversary with a huge family party.

4. At the supermarket, my little girl (demanded / has demanded) a new, sugar-filled type of cereal, but I ignored her words.

5. A nervous jogger on the Emerson Trail called campus security and (reported / has reported) strange noises coming from a dark grove of pines.

6. For some months now, the old hamburger drive-through near the mall (was / has been) closed and shuttered.

7. Lisa Quinn and her brother Bill (studied / have studied) accounting at Crandon College for four years, and they are now joining their father's accounting firm in Phoenix.

8. Germaine (visited / has visited) seven car dealerships and decided to buy a used car from the one with the best service department.

9. For two days, we (tried / had tried) to win the radio call-in contest but gave up in frustration yesterday.

10. Since he married my mother five years ago, my stepfather (gave / has given) me money on my birthday.

PAST PERFECT TENSE

The **past perfect tense** is made up of the past participle form of the verb with *had* as a helping verb. You can use the past perfect tense to show more than one event in the past; that is, you can use it to show when two or more events happened in the past but at different times.

> **past tense:** Alan *cut* the grass.
>
> **past perfect tense:** Alan *had cut* the grass by the time David arrived. (Alan cut the grass *before* David arrived. Both events happened in the past, but one happened earlier than the other.)

past tense: The professor *lectured* for an hour.

past perfect tense: The professor *had lectured* for an hour when he pulled out a surprise quiz. (Lecturing came first; pulling out a surprise quiz came second. Both actions are in the past.)

The past perfect is especially useful because you write most of your essays in the past tense, and you often need to get further back into the past. Just remember to use *had* with the past participle of the verb, and you'll have the past perfect tense.

Exercise 6   **Practice: Distinguishing Between the Past and the Past Perfect Tense**

Circle the correct verb tense in the following sentences. Be sure to look carefully at the meaning of each sentence.

1. I was surprised when Lisa offered me another slice of her birthday cake before I finished / had finished eating my first slice.

2. Carlos suspected that his girlfriend (went / had gone) though his bureau drawers before he came home.

3. By the time I finished washing my car, the sky (turned / had turned) dark and cloudy.

4. At the movie, my brother (talked / had talked) on his cell phone while I tried to concentrate on the film.

5. Every Friday, my friends at work (met / had met) for a meal at a local Asian restaurant.

6. My father wondered if I (met / had met) any soccer players at school.

7. As Alan (wailed /had wailed) about the dismal performance of his favorite team, he clenched his fists in rage.

8. By the time we got to the airport, our flight (left / had left) the runway.

9. Callie felt that Paul's recent efforts to stop smoking (were / had been) only half-hearted.

10. When the new baby cried, both parents (raced / had raced) in to check on him.

A Few Tips About Verbs

There are a few errors that people tend to make with verbs. If you are aware of these errors, you will be on the lookout for them as you edit your writing.

Used to: Be careful when you write that someone *used to* do, say, or feel something. It is incorrect to write *use to*.

not this: Wendy ~~use to~~ make pancakes for breakfast.
but this: Wendy *used to* make pancakes for breakfast.

not this: They ~~use to~~ live on my street.
but this: They *used to* live on my street.

Supposed to: Be careful when you write that someone is *supposed to* do, say, or feel something. It is incorrect to write *suppose to*.

not this: He was ~~suppose to~~ repair my watch yesterday.
but this: He was *supposed to* repair my watch yesterday.

>   **not this:** I am ~~suppose to~~ make dinner tomorrow.
>   **but this:** I am *supposed to* make dinner tomorrow.

Could have, should have, would have: Using *of* instead of *have* is another error with verbs.

>   **not this:** He ~~could of~~ sent me a card.
>   **but this:** He *could have* sent me a card.

>   **not this:** You ~~should of~~ been more careful.
>   **but this:** You *should have* been more careful.

>   **not this:** Norman ~~would of~~ enjoyed the music.
>   **but this:** Norman *would have* enjoyed the music.

Would have/had: If you are writing about something that might have been possible but that did not happen, use *had* as the helping verb.

>   **not this:** If he ~~would have~~ been friendlier, he would not be alone now.
>   **but this:** If he *had* been friendlier, he would not be alone now.

>   **not this:** I wish the plane fare ~~would have~~ cost less.
>   **but this:** I wish the plane fare *had* cost less.

>   **not this:** If David ~~would have~~ controlled his temper, he would be a free man today.
>   **but this:** If David *had* controlled his temper, he would be a free man today.

Connect

Exercise 7 Connect: Editing a Paragraph for Common Errors in Verbs

Correct the six errors in *used to*, *supposed to*, *could have*, *should have*, *would have*, and *would have/had* in the following paragraph. Write your corrections above the lines.

When I fell in love for the first time, I was so overcome with emotion

that I made a fool of myself. Of course, I was twelve years old at the time, and

I had never spoken to the boy. He was in my class at middle school. I use to

stare at him while our teacher was talking, and I could of sworn that the boy

saw my adoring gaze. Now I know that a girl in love is suppose to be aloof and

cold. Then the man of her dreams is expected to notice her. Unfortunately, this

twelve-year-old boy of my dreams never noticed me at all. All my gazing and fan-

tasizing had no effect on him. I could of worn face paint to class and he wouldn't

of noticed. Of course, if I would have just waited a few years, that boy might

have noticed me at last.

Exercise 8   **Collaborate: Writing Sentences with the Correct Verb Forms**   Collaborate

Do this exercise with a partner or with a group. Write or complete each of the following sentences. When you have finished the exercise, be ready to share your answers with another group or with the class.

1. Complete this sentence and add a verb in the correct tense: Ethan had never seen the ocean until he

_____

_____

2. Write a sentence that uses the words *given me the same birthday gift* in the middle of the sentence.

_____

_____

3. Complete this sentence and add a verb in the correct tense: I was falling asleep at my desk when

_____

_____

4. Write a sentence that includes the phrases *has guided* and *for many years.*

_____

_____

5. Complete this sentence: If only you had asked me,

_____

_____

6. Write a sentence that contains the words *should have.*

_____

_____

7. Write a sentence that includes both these helping verbs: *will* and *would.*

_____

_____

8. Complete this sentence: By the time the battle ended, six soldiers

_____

_____

9. Write a sentence that includes the words *for weeks* and *have been nagging.*

_____

_____

10. Write a sentence that includes the words *movies used to.*

_____

_____

Connect

Exercise 9 **Connect: A Comprehensive Exercise in Editing a Paragraph for Errors in Verb Tense**

Correct the seven errors in verb tense in the following paragraph. Write your corrections in the space above the lines.

Anne hopes she would succeed as a fashion designer when she finishes studying at an art school, but she is prepared for some challenges. First, she understands that she could not expect a quick rise to the top of the fashion world. Although she worked in the clothing department of a popular discount store for three years now, she is aware of the odds against her becoming a design star. Competition for jobs in the fashion world has become fierce since television first packed many channels with programs about style, designers, fashion shows, models, and makeovers a few years ago. Anne use to watch those programs, and they motivated her to dream of a career in fashion. When she finished high school, friends and family had urged her to choose a "safe" course of study in a field such as health or business. However, by that time, the safe, sensible choice appealed to Anne less than ever. Anne was convinced that by settling for a career that held no appeal for her, she would always feel cheated. Unless she took the risks of following her dream, she would always have wondered what might be.

Connect

Exercise 10 **Connect: A Comprehensive Exercise in Editing a Paragraph for Errors in Verb Tense**

Correct the six errors in verb tense in the following paragraph. Write your corrections above the lines.

Too much quiet can be hard on a person's nerves. If a person has walked into a totally quiet department store, for example, he or she would suspect a robbery was in progress. Similarly, a person who entered a classroom full of silent students will feel uneasy. The person can fear that a boring lecture or a tough exam was in progress. Sitting in an airport lounge at night after most of the passengers and staff departed is a strange experience, too. In addition, many parents are having a hard time dealing with the silence in the house after the last child has left home. Places that are usually full of sound had become strange and even sinister when they are quiet.

Chapter Test   More on Verb Tenses

Some of the sentences below are correct; some have errors in verb tenses or other common errors. Put *OK* next to the correct sentences and *X* next to the sentences with errors.

1. _____ After a bumpy ride on a cramped, stuffy airplane, I wished I would have driven to my cousin's wedding.

2. _____ Every weekend, Carter is taking his mother to visit his father's grave.

3. _____ My cousin is helping me paint my basement tomorrow so that I can use the space as a game room.

4. _____ My math professor wondered if I had forgotten last week's assignment.

5. _____ Allison was determined that she will find a good preschool for her son.

6. _____ Henry was convinced he will persuade Linda to go to Idaho with him.

7. _____ Shane has spent thirty minutes in front of the mirror, tried to style his hair, and then gave up.

8. _____ Jeffrey and Ron were in a good mood when I saw them at the game.

9. _____ For as long as I've lived in Plainfield, Mason's Café has been my favorite place for breakfast.

10. _____ When my brother was a parking lot attendant at the Regal Auditorium, he was making most of his money in tips.

Verbs: Consistency and Voice

Chapter Objectives

Students will be able to (1) maintain verb tense consistency in their writing, (2) distinguish between active and passive voice, and (3) correct any shifts in voice.

Remember that your choice of verb form indicates the time (tense) of your statements. Be careful not to shift from one tense to another unless you have a reason to change the time.

CONSISTENT VERB TENSES

Staying in one tense (unless you have a reason to change tenses) is called **consistency of verb tense.**

> **incorrect shifts in tense:**
> He *raced* through the yellow light, *stepped* on the gas, and *cuts* off a driver in the left lane.
> A woman in a black dress *holds* a handkerchief to her face and *moaned* softly.

You can correct these errors by putting all the verbs in the same tense.

consistent present tense:

He *races* through the yellow light, *steps* on the gas, and *cuts* off a
driver in the left lane.

A woman in a black dress *holds* a handkerchief to her face and
moans softly.

consistent past tense:

He *raced* through the yellow light, *stepped* on the gas, and *cut* off a
driver in the left lane.

A woman in a black dress *held* a handkerchief to her face and
moaned softly.

Whether you correct the errors by changing all the verbs to the present
tense or by changing them all to the past tense, you are making the tense
consistent. Consistency of verb tenses is important when you describe events
because it helps the reader understand what happened and when it happened.

| Exercise 1 | **Practice: Correcting Sentences That Are Inconsistent in Tense** |

In each sentence that follows, one verb is inconsistent in tense. Cross it out
and write the correct tense above. The first one is done for you.

1. Even though food ~~tasted~~ **tastes** better when I am hungry, food still tastes

   good whenever I eat it.

2. Our first dog was exceptionally intelligent: he learned commands

   within weeks, adjusts to our schedule almost immediately, and

   sensed our moods quickly.

3. When autumn arrives, I brought out my sweaters and flannel shirts

   and prepare to enjoy the changing colors of the leaves, the brisk

   morning temperatures, and the deep blue skies.

4. For five days, I woke up at 3:00 A.M., struggled to get back to sleep,

   and wind up awake and exhausted.

5. My brother and I share a bedroom, so he usually knew when

   I wake up.

6. Andy missed most of the gossip at school because he paid no

   attention to rumors and never enjoys a nasty story about a rival.

7. For many years, Mike sent his niece a gift on her birthday and tol-

   erated her lack of gratitude, but when she does not invite him to

   her wedding, he lost his patience.

8. My older sister accuses me of gossiping about her and refuses to share any news with me when I called her.

9. Because the state legislature cut funding, the local shelter for abused children postpones the start of its expansion, the county delayed its planned road repairs, and the fire department canceled its plans to hire more firefighters.

10. Yesterday evening, my husband cooked spaghetti and meatballs for our two children, gave them baths, but foolishly allows them to stay up long past their bedtime.

Connect

Exercise 2 **Connect: Editing a Paragraph for Consistency of Tense**

Read the following paragraph. Then cross out any verbs that are inconsistent in tense and write the corrections above them. The paragraph has five errors.

Every Friday evening, Sam calls me to ask about my plans for Saturday night. Almost always, I told him the same thing: I have no plans. After a brief sigh of disappointment, Sam bombards me with a list of suggestions for filling the Saturday evening hours. He mentioned the same old activities every week. They included going to a game, playing cards, meeting women at a club, or driving around aimlessly. When I tell him about my lack of money for socializing or filling the gas tank of my car, Sam admits his own lack of funds. At that point, we come to a realistic decision. We planned to meet at my house and watch an old movie. This dialogue and its outcome occur each week, and I thought they always happen for the same reason. Each time, Sam and I are hoping for a better outcome.

Connect

Exercise 3 **Connect: Editing a Paragraph for Consistency of Tense**

Read the following paragraph. Then cross out any verbs that are inconsistent in tense and write the corrections above them. The paragraph has six errors.

Last night, someone did me a great favor, and I never got to thank that person. At 10:00 P.M., when I came home from work, I park my car in the parking lot next to my apartment and settled in for the night. After eating a microwave pizza and some cookies, I checked my e-mail, listen to some music, and fell into a deep sleep by midnight. When my alarm rings at 7:00 A.M., I was still sleepy. Half awake, I

stumbled into the shower, brush my teeth, and threw on some clothes. Grabbing

a cold can of Coke, I walked to my car in a daze. I was about to turn the key in the

ignition when I see a note placed under one of the windshield wipers. Irritated, I

thought it was another advertising flyer and planned to crumple it up and toss it in

the back of my car. However, it was a handwritten note that warned me about my

left front tire, which was nearly flat. That note kept me from driving off, still half

asleep and unaware of any danger, with a bad tire. Thanks to a stranger, I was able

to take care of my tire before I wind up stuck on the highway—or worse.

Exercise 4   Collaborate: Rewriting a Paragraph for Consistent Verb Tenses

Collaborate

The following paragraph has some inconsistencies in verb tenses: it shifts
between past and present tenses. With a partner or a group, correct the errors
in consistency by writing all the verbs in the past tense. You can write your
corrections in the space above the errors. When you have completed the corrections, have one member of the group read the paragraph aloud as a final check.

When my parents bought an old house in a decrepit neighborhood, I had my

doubts about their decision. I think the house was a hopeless wreck and I imagine

my parents struggling to fix it up. Nothing about their plan seemed practical.

I imagined a terrible struggle to deal with rotted wood, broken tiles, a leaky roof,

bad plumbing, and an overgrown yard. I also believe that the other houses in the

area are not worth repairing or restoring. I was wrong. Almost immediately after

they bought the house, my parents started serious work on the property, and the

changes are remarkable. Eventually, I was impressed and joined the group of

family members who transformed the house and yard. My surprise grew when the

changes spread to neighboring properties. Several people in the community watch

my parents work and begin improving their homes. All my doubts about the power

of hope, work, and determination are foolish, as my parents' efforts showed.

PASSIVE AND ACTIVE VOICE

Verbs not only have tenses; they have voices. When the subject in the sentence is doing something, the verb is in the **active voice.** When something
is done to the subject, the verb is in the **passive voice.**

active voice:

I designed the album cover. (*I*, the subject, did it.)

My friends from college raised money for the homeless shelter. (*Friends*, the subject, did it.)

passive voice:

The album cover was designed by me. (The *cover*, the subject, didn't do anything. It received the action—it was designed.)

Money for the homeless shelter was raised by my friends from college. (*Money*, the subject, didn't do anything. It received the action—it was raised.)

Notice what happens when you use the passive voice instead of the active voice:

active voice: I designed the album cover.

passive voice: The album cover was designed by me.

The sentence in the passive voice is two words longer than the one in the active voice. Yet the sentence that used the passive voice doesn't say anything different, and it doesn't say it more clearly than the one in the active voice.

Using the passive voice can make your sentences wordy, it can slow them down, and it can make them boring. The passive voice can also confuse readers. When the subject isn't doing anything, readers may have to look carefully to see who or what *is doing* something. Look at this sentence, for example:

A famous city landmark is being torn down.

Who is tearing down the landmark? In this sentence, it's impossible to find the answer to that question.

Of course, there will be times when you have to use the passive voice. For example, you may have to use it when you don't know who did something, as in these sentences:

Lana's car was stolen last week.

A bag of garbage was scattered all over my neighbor's lawn.

But, in general, you should avoid using the passive voice; instead, rewrite sentences so they are in the active voice.

Collaborate

Exercise 5 **Collaborate: Rewriting Sentences, Changing the Passive Voice to the Active Voice**

Do this exercise with a partner or group. In the following sentences, change the passive voice to the active voice. If the original sentence doesn't tell you who or what performed the action, add words that tell you who or what did it. The first one is done for you.

1. One of Shakespeare's plays was performed at Peace River High School last night.

   rewritten: Students at Peace River High School performed one of Shakespeare's plays last night.

2. A series of safety measures was recommended by the superintendent of the Water Management District.

   rewritten: _____

   _____

3. Tremendous effort went into restoring the historic house.

   rewritten: _____

   _____

4. A new contract for workers at the plant has been proposed.

   rewritten: _____

   _____

5. A decision was made not to hire more security guards for the shopping center.

   rewritten: _____

   _____

6. A famous musician has been invited to speak at the college graduation ceremony.

   rewritten: _____

   _____

7. On most days, my mail is delivered after 5:00 P.M.

   rewritten: _____

   _____

8. Advice for dealing with stress was offered by a local psychologist.

   rewritten: _____

   _____

9. Cigarette butts, plastic bottles, and soda cans had been tossed on the sand.

   rewritten: _____

   _____

10. Several options for reducing traffic in the downtown area were proposed by the city manager.

   rewritten: _____

   _____

Exercise 6   **Collaborate: Rewriting a Paragraph, Changing It to the Active Voice**

Collaborate

Do this exercise with a partner or group. Rewrite the paragraph below, changing all the verbs that are in the passive voice to the active voice. To make these changes, you may have to add words, omit words, and change the structure of sentences. Write your changes in the space above the lines. Be ready to read your new version of the paragraph to another group or to the class.

A better system for ensuring residents' safety has been initiated at Cedar Forest

Apartments. The change was designed by the Responsible Management Company

as a quick response to residents' concerns about recent burglaries and damages to vehicles at the Cedar Forest site. Beginning next month, all residents will receive an electronic card that will enable them to pass through a new gated entrance to the community. A small electronic gatehouse will be installed by the Responsible Management Company (RMC) next week. An introductory period of transition from an open community to a gated one has been planned for the following week. During this period, the gated entrance will be made accessible to all residents and visitors. This period was planned by RMC to familiarize residents with the new structure. A telephone line to the resident apartment manager will also be installed by management so that any discomfort with the new process can be minimized. When the gated entrance system is initiated by RMC next month, the structure will include a phone. Using this phone, a visitor to the apartments may call a resident and gain entry. Any further questions about the new system can be answered by your resident manager.

Avoiding Unnecessary Shifts in Voice

Just as you should be consistent in the tense of verbs, you should be consistent in the voice of verbs. Do not shift from active to passive, or vice versa, without a good reason to do so.

>   **active**   **passive**
> **shift:** *Carl wrote* the song, but the *credit was taken* by Tom.
>
>   **active**   **active**
> **rewritten:** *Carl wrote* the song, but *Tom took* the credit.
>
>   **passive**
> **shift:** Several *suggestions were made* by the vice president, yet the
>   **active**
> *president rejected* all of them.
>
>   **active**
> **rewritten:** The *vice president made* several suggestions, yet the
>   **active**
> *president rejected* all of them.

Being consistent can help you to write clearly and smoothly.

Exercise 7 **Practice: Rewriting Sentences to Correct Shifts in Voice**

Rewrite the following sentences so that all the verbs are in the active voice. You may change the wording to make the sentences clear, smooth, and consistent in voice.

    1. André Hall was awarded a scholarship by the New Vistas Organization; André is a remarkable young man.

        rewritten: _____

        _____

2. My mother and her friends are obsessed with one television show; its stars and plots are constantly analyzed by the women.

   rewritten: _____

   _____

3. The drill sergeant bullied the new recruits, and the last drop of energy was squeezed from them.

   rewritten: _____

   _____

4. If plans for a holiday party were made by my parents, they didn't include me in their arrangements.

   rewritten: _____

   _____

5. Palmer Heights was a desirable place to live until the area was struck by a series of violent robberies.

   rewritten: _____

   _____

6. The spectators roared with approval as sports history was made by the pitcher.

   rewritten: _____

   _____

7. It has been arranged by volunteer firefighters to sponsor a food drive next week; they will collect canned goods.

   rewritten: _____

   _____

8. Because Kelly is so eager to please her boyfriend, her ambitions can easily be stifled by him.

   rewritten: _____

   _____

9. A wallet was found in the vacant hotel room; the housekeeping staff also discovered a diamond ring.

   rewritten: _____

   _____

10. When the art school rejected my application for admission, my dreams of a career in fashion were shattered.

    rewritten: _____

    _____

Exercise 8 **Connect: Editing a Paragraph for Consistency in Voice**

Connect

The following paragraph contains six unnecessary shifts to the passive voice. Write your corrections in the space above the errors. You can add words, omit words, or change words.

Employees were told by managers not to worry when a vice president of the department store chain visited our location. It was assumed by most employees that he was bringing bad news. The rumors focused on the term "reorganization," and that term is usually taken to mean cutting back on staff. However, the vice president announced changes that did not frighten the workers. The company has plans to improve the appearance of each store and to redesign the flow of customer traffic. These improvements will be appreciated by customers and employees. A store that looks brighter and is easier to navigate will attract more customers. In addition, the need for such improvements has been sensed by most workers for several years. While most visits from top management result in misery to many, this one signaled hope. The surprisingly positive news was appreciated by every employee at the store.

Connect

Exercise 9 **Connect: A Comprehensive Exercise: Editing a Paragraph for Errors in Consistent Verb Tense and Voice**

The following paragraph has seven errors related to verb tense and voice. Correct the errors in the space above the lines.

I live in a town where college football dominates the autumn weekends. Our local college's team is valued by the students and the community partly because the team has a decent record of success. Whether the team was playing at home or away, the team colors dominate the landscape before each game. Flags with the colors are flown on cars, trucks, and even motorcycles, and of course these colors appear in clothing. Babies are dressed in the colors by enthusiastic parents, and the babies' strollers carry team-colored streamers. Even dogs wore collars or coats with pictures of the team mascot. On game days, floral arrangements in the team colors are sold at local supermarkets. Football fever is always fun because it linked thousands of people of all ages and backgrounds.

Chapter Test **Verbs: Consistency and Voice**

Some of the sentences below are correct; others have errors related to consistency in verb tense or voice. Put *OK* next to the correct sentences and *X* next to the sentences with errors.

1. _____ When Martin called me, he sounded tired and avoided the topic of his divorce.

2. _____ Sarah smiles at me and asks me about my family every time I see her at the supermarket.

3. _____ Although the heavy rain was good for my lawn, I want it to end because my basement is filling with water.

4. _____ When we have a family dinner at my sister's house, I bring the lemonade and soda, my mother cooked the main course, my sister prepares dessert, and my father supplies cheese and crackers.

5. _____ Sushi is considered delicious and healthy by millions of people in many parts of the world; however, I hate the thought of eating it.

6. _____ When I have a writing assignment, I like to complete it as quickly as possible; however, my rush to finish is criticized by my roommate, an English major.

7. _____ My father patted me on the back, my mother hugged me, and my dog gave me a slobbery kiss when I left home to start my first job in a neighboring state.

8. _____ After class last night, I took a chance and asked the woman sitting next to me if she wanted to go out, but she stares at me without saying a word.

9. _____ My uncle cuts my hair because he owns a barber shop in the neighborhood and knows how to tame my mess of curls and frizz.

10. _____ Before I traveled to Cozumel, my Mexican-born grandfather taught me a few important words and phrases in Spanish.

Making Subjects and Verbs Agree

Chapter Objectives

Students will be able to (1) correct simple errors in subject–verb agreement, (2) isolate prepositional phrases to determine the subject of a sentence, and (3) determine the correct verb form to use when the subject is a collective noun or an indefinite pronoun.

Subjects and verbs have to agree in number. That means a singular subject must be matched with a singular verb form; a plural subject must be matched with a plural verb form.

> singular subject, singular verb
> *Nicole races* out of the house in the morning.

> plural subject,   plural verb
> *Christine, Michael, and Marie take* the train to work.

> singular subject, singular verb
> The old *song reminds* me of Mexico.

> plural subject, plural verb
> Greasy *hamburgers upset* my stomach.

> **Caution:** Remember that a regular verb has an -*s* ending in one singular form in the present tense—the form that goes with *he, she, it,* or their equivalents.

s endings in the present tense:

He *takes* good care of his dog.
She *concentrates* on her assignments.
It *looks* like a nice day.
Eddie *buys* high-octane gasoline.
Nancy *seems* pleased.
The apartment *comes* with cable television.

PRONOUNS USED AS SUBJECTS

Pronouns can be used as subjects. **Pronouns** are words that take the place of nouns. When pronouns are used as subjects, they must agree in number with verbs.

Following is a list of subject pronouns and the regular verb forms that agree with them in the present tense.

INFO BOX: Subject Pronouns and Present Tense Verb Forms

pronoun	verb	
I	walk	
you	walk	(all singular forms)
he, she, it	walks	
we	walk	
you	walk	all plural forms
they	walk	

In all the following sentences, the pronoun used as the subject of the sentence agrees in number with the verb:

singular pronoun, singular verb
I take good care of my daughter.

singular pronoun, singular verb
You sing like a professional entertainer.

singular pronoun, singular verb
She argues with conviction and courage.

plural pronoun, plural verb
We want a better deal on the apartment.

plural pronoun, plural verb
They accept my decision about moving.

| Exercise 1 | Connect: Editing a Paragraph for Simple Errors in Subject–Verb Agreement |

Connect

There are seven errors in subject–verb agreement in the following paragraph. If the verb does not agree with the subject, cross out the incorrect verb form and write the correct one above it.

A few children likes to get up when their parents wake them, but most children, including mine, resist and stalls as long as they can. My older son, for example, believe that my words about waking up signals a warning, but not a final statement. He requires two or three more "warnings" before he slides out of bed. My younger boy simply ignores my wake-up calls. He seem to have the power to incorporate my words into a dream and to keep on dozing. Naturally, school days at my house often deteriorates into a series of frustrations and confrontations. Of course, I keeps my own secret from my boys: I love to sleep late, and I want their few extra minutes in bed.

SPECIAL PROBLEMS WITH AGREEMENT

Agreement seems fairly simple, doesn't it? If a subject is singular, use a singular verb form; if a subject is plural, use a plural verb form. However, certain problems with agreement will come up in your writing. Sometimes it is difficult to find the subject of a sentence; at other times, it can be difficult to determine if a subject is singular or plural.

Finding the Subject

When you are checking for subject–verb agreement, you can find the real subject of the sentence by first eliminating the prepositional phrases. To find the real subject, put parentheses around the prepositional phrases. Then it will be easy to find the subject because nothing in a prepositional phrase can be the subject of a sentence.

prepositional phrases in parentheses:

    S   V
A *person* (with good math skills) *is* a good candidate (for the job).

    S   V
One (of the children) (from the village) (in the hills) *is* my cousin.

          S   V
The *restaurant* (down the road) (from Cindy's house) *is* open all night.

    S   V
Roy, (with his charm and style), *is* popular (with the ladies).

> **Exercise 2** **Practice: Finding the Subject and Verb by Recognizing Prepositional Phrases**

Put parentheses around all the prepositional phrases in the following sentences, and identify the subject and verb by writing an *S* or a *V* above them.

1. During my drive to North Dakota, I saw very little sunshine

   between the ominous gray clouds.

2. Cathy strolled through the garden with a watering can in her hand.

3. Before the end of winter, I sometimes wore a bright t-shirt under

   my heavy sweater and coat in an attempt at bringing some

   brightness into the day.

4. The happiest day of my life came at the end of my father's military

   duty in a dangerous part of the Middle East.

5. A box of castoff clothes and shoes turned into fabulous costumes for

   two little girls with lively imaginations and a love of playing roles.

6. The best barbecued ribs in the area are at a family restaurant

   between a horse pasture and a farmers' supply store.

7. Someone with an extensive knowledge of genealogy spoke at the

   local library last week.

8. From her first appearance in our tenth-grade classroom to her

   warm good-bye at graduation, Mrs. Klein was the most generous

   and caring mentor among many caring coaches and teachers.

9. In a time of constant worry and stress, Jose, with his sense of humor

   and positive attitude, kept me from falling into misery and self-pity.

10. On an icy January night, I enjoy a movie about intrigue on a

    tropical island.

Exercise 3   **Practice: Selecting the Correct Verb Form by Identifying
                   Prepositional Phrases**

In the following sentences, put parentheses around all the prepositional
phrases; then circle the verb that agrees with the subject.

1. A representative of the insurance company (was / were) explaining the

   change in benefits to a group of employees during a staff meeting.

2. The miners' survival at the bottom of a deep, dark pit (is / are) almost unbelievable in a time of natural and man-made disasters, from earthquakes to oil spills.

3. Frowning at me from the other side of the room (was / were) my mother, with the look of someone in an extremely bad mood.

4. In the early morning hours, Bill's good intentions about cramming for his exams (do / does) not keep him alert or even awake.

5. The sight of red ants on the picnic table and in the cake and salads (was / were), without a doubt, a horror beyond my worst fears.

6. A cup of coffee from the vending machine at the site of our evening classes (make / makes) a person think about dish water.

7. Between the closing of the tile factory on Saturday afternoon and its opening on Monday morning, one of the back doors (was / were) pried open.

8. A crack in the foundation of my brother's house (has / have) caused him hours of worry about the need for major repairs.

9. One of the most irritating sensations (is / are) the buzz of a swarm of mosquitoes around my head.

10. Carly, with all her faults, (remain / remains) a dear friend in good times and bad.

Changed Word Order

You are probably used to looking for the subject of a sentence in front of the verb, but not all sentences follow this pattern. Questions, sentences beginning with words like *here* or *there*, and other sentences change the word order. Therefore, you have to look carefully to check for subject–verb agreement.

sentences with changed word order:

       V   S

Where *are* the *packages?*

       V   S   V

When *is Mr. Hernandez giving* the exam?

                 V   S
Behind the trees *is* a picnic *table.*

        V   S
There *are crumbs* on the floor.

        V   S
There *is* an *answer* to your question.

Exercise 4 **Practice: Making Subjects and Verbs Agree in Sentences
with Changed Word Order**

In each of the following sentences, underline the subject; then circle the
correct verb form.

1. Here (comes / come) my favorite niece and nephew in their new
car.

2. There (is / are) freedom and optimism in my soul when I begin my
summer vacation.

3. When (do / does) the new discount auto center open?

4. Among the most cherished items in my closet (was / were) my first
baseball glove.

5. Here (was / were) an unopened pack of playing cards from my
grandfather's gambling days.

6. There (is / are) several reasons for Emilio's loss of interest in joining the U.S. Air Force.

7. At the top of my list of favorite places (is / are) the community pool
in the summer season.

8. Below Tyler Hill (stands / stand) a small monument with the names
of local heroes of World War I.

9. Where (is / are) the candles for the top of Lindsay's birthday cake?

10. Near the back of the auditorium (was / were) an ancient film
projector on a decrepit rolling cart.

Collaborate

Exercise 5 **Collaborate: Writing Sentences with Subject–Verb Agreement
in Changed Word Order**

Do this exercise with a partner or group. Complete the following, making
each into a sentence. Be sure the subject and verb agree. The first one is
done for you.

1. From the back of the room came *three loud cheers.* _____

2. Behind the castle wall lurks _____

3. Here are _____

4. Under the pile of old newspapers was _____

5. With the famous basketball star come _____

6. After the scream, there was _____

7. Into the glass skylight crashes _____

8. At the top of the mountain are _____

9. Toward me run _____

10. Where is my _____

Compound Subjects

A **compound subject** is two or more subjects joined by *and*, *or*, or *nor*.

When subjects are joined by *and*, they are usually plural.

compound subjects joined by *and*:

> S   S   V
> *Bill* and *Chris are* good tennis players.

> S   S   V
> The *garage* and the *basement are* full of water.

> S   S   V
> A *restaurant* and a *motel are* across the road.

Caution: Be sure to check for a compound subject when the word order changes.

---

compound subjects in changed word order:

> V   S   S
> There *are* a *restaurant* and a *motel* across the road. (Two things, a restaurant and a motel, are across the road.)

> V   S   S
> Here *are* your *notebook* and *pencil*. (Your notebook and pencil, two things, are here.)

When subjects are joined by *or*, *either . . . or*, *neither . . . nor*, *not only . . . but also*, the verb form agrees with the subject closest to the verb.

compound subjects with *or*, *either . . . or*, *neither . . . nor*, *not only . . . but also*:

> singular S   plural S, plural V
> *Christine* or the *neighbors are* making dinner.

> plural S   singular S, singular V
> The *neighbors* or *Christine is* making dinner.

> singular S   plural S, plural V
> Not only my *mother* but also my *brothers were* delighted with the gift.

> plural S   singular S, singular V
> Not only my *brothers* but also my *mother was* delighted with the gift.

> plural S   singular S, singular V
> Either the *tenants* or the *landlord has* to back down.

> singular S   plural S, plural V
> Either the *landlord* or the *tenants have* to back down.

> plural S   singular S, singular V
> Neither the rose *bushes* nor the lemon *tree fits* in that corner of the yard.

> singular S   plural S, plural V
> Neither the lemon *tree* nor the rose *bushes fit* in that corner of the yard.

Exercise 6   **Practice: Making Subjects and Verbs Agree: Compound Subjects**

Underline the correct form of the verb in each of the following sentences.

1. While the physician examined the accident victim, his mother and sister (was / were) panicking in the emergency waiting room.

2. Either anger at losing my job or money problems (has / have) caused me to clench my jaw until it hurts.

3. There (is / are) a quick, risky way and a longer, safer way to fix a broken windshield.

4. Neither my sisters nor my mother (is / are) interested in cosmetic surgery.

5. In the kitchen drawer (is / are) an extra set of house keys and a small flashlight.

6. The next door neighbors or my father (takes / take) care of my cat when I am away.

7. Not only your shoes but also your coat (is / are) splashed with mud.

8. Here (is / are) a warm wool hat and a thick scarf for your long walk in the snow.

9. State Representative William O'Dowd or State Treasurer Ann Pulaski (is / are) expected to run for governor next year.

10. Carlene's lack of interest in sports and her superior attitude (was / were) factors in my decision to end our relationship.

Exercise 7   **Practice: Recognizing Subjects and Verbs: A Review**

Being sure that subjects and verbs agree often depends on recognizing subjects and verbs in sentences with changed word order, prepositional phrases, and compound subjects. To review the subject–verb patterns of sentences, underline all the subjects and verbs in the following selection. Put an *S* above the subjects and a *V* above the verbs.

The following excerpt is from an essay by Edna Buchanan, a former prize-winning journalist for the *Miami Herald* and now a famous crime novelist.

Miami's Most Dangerous Profession

Miami's most dangerous profession is not police work or fire fighting; it is driving a cab. For taxi drivers, many of them poor immigrants, murder is an occupational hazard. All-night gas station attendants and convenience store clerks used to be at high risk, but steps were taken to protect them. All gas pumps now switch to self-serve after dark, with exact change only, and the attendants are locked in bullet-proof booths. Convenience stores were redesigned, and drop safes were installed, leaving little cash available.

But the life of a taxi driver is just as risky as it was twenty years ago when I covered my first killing of a cabbie.

Bullet-proof glass could be placed between the driver and passengers, but most owners say it is too expensive, and besides, there is no foolproof way to protect oneself totally from somebody riding in the same car.

Indefinite Pronouns

Certain pronouns, called **indefinite pronouns,** always take a singular verb.

INFO BOX:	Indefinite Pronouns			
one	everyone	somebody	anything	each
anyone	nobody	everybody	something	either
someone	anybody	nothing	everything	neither

If you want to write clearly and correctly, you must memorize these words and remember that they always use singular verbs. Using common sense isn't enough because some of these words seem plural: for example, *everybody* seems to mean more than one person, but in grammatically correct English, it takes a singular verb. Here are some examples of the pronouns used with singular verbs:

indefinite pronouns and singular verbs:

singular S   singular V
Each of my friends *is* athletic.

singular S   singular V
Everyone in the supermarket *is looking* for a bargain.

singular S   singular V
Anybody from our Spanish class *is* capable of translating the letter.

singular S   singular V
Someone from the maintenance department *is working* on the heater.

singular S   singular V
One of Roberta's nieces *is* in my sister's ballet class.

singular S   singular V
Neither of the cakes *is* expensive.

You can memorize the indefinite pronouns as the *-one, -thing,* and *-body* words—*everyone, everything, everybody,* and so on—plus *each, either,* and *neither.*

> **Exercise 8** **Practice: Making Subjects and Verbs Agree: Using Indefinite Pronouns**

Underline the correct verb in the following sentences.

    1. Here (is / are) everyone in our study group.

    2. Nobody in high heels (enjoys / enjoy) standing in line for thirty-five minutes.

3. Everybody from the two neighboring towns (knows / know) about the old rivalry between the two high schools.

4. (Has / Have) anyone from the doctor's office called?

5. Last night at the movies, somebody in one of the back rows (was / were) throwing popcorn at me.

6. Take some time to see the Lincoln Memorial; nothing in the thousands of photographs and film clips (do / does) justice to its magnificence.

7. Unfortunately, neither of my sons (has / have) an interest in joining the family business.

8. Each of my best dresses (needs / need) to be sent to a good dry cleaning establishment.

9. Everyone in my neighborhood (is / are) familiar with the sound of sirens in the middle of the night.

10. Years ago, my uncles Calvin and Henry lent my father money to start a business; today, each of them (is / are) still ready to help a friend or family member in need.

Exercise 9   **Practice: Another Exercise on Making Subjects and Verbs Agree: Using Indefinite Pronouns**

Underline the correct verb in the following sentences.

1. Sal and Todd are both trustworthy and discreet; either (makes / make) a good listener when you are in trouble.

2. Anyone from our old graduating class still (remembers / remember) Mrs. Marciano, the sweetest lady in the cafeteria.

3. Each of the sequined t-shirts (costs / cost) more than my weekly paycheck.

4. Fortunately, neither of my sisters (has / have) inherited my mother's restless spirit.

5. Be sure to read the entire contract; nothing in all those pages (covers / cover) electrical problems.

6. Somebody from the airlines (was / were) explaining the flight delays.

7. (Has /Have) anyone in the office made coffee yet?

8. Everybody in my math class (complains / complain) about all the homework.

9. Nobody with money problems (needs / need) to be bombarded with offers for more credit cards.

10. There (is /are) everyone from your old softball team.

Exercise 10   **Connect: Editing for Subject–Verb Agreement in a Paragraph with Indefinite Pronouns**

Connect

The following paragraph has six errors in the agreement of indefinite pronouns and verbs. Correct the errors in the spaces above the lines.

Many people would suspect that something are wrong with a small house containing one woman and five cats. However, the stereotype of a weird, witchlike old lady and her mysterious animals does not fit this situation. The woman is Tamika, my sister, and she is a veterinarian with a big heart. Because she is a veterinarian, everybody in her neighborhood are eager to get her advice on animals. In addition, someone are always likely to bring her a stray kitten or a pregnant mother cat. Nothing touch my sister's emotions like a cat in trouble. Most of the time, she brings these homeless pets to her workplace: a no-kill animal shelter. There they receive care and a good chance at adoption. At times she is so touched by a kitten's helplessness or a mother cat's bravery that everything in her heart tell her to invite the newcomer into her home. Neither my parents' advice nor her own common sense keep her from nurturing her five cats. They are the most damaged or the least likely to be adopted, but in my sister's house they are loved.

Collective Nouns

Collective nouns refer to more than one person or thing.

INFO BOX: Some Common Collective Nouns

team	audience	family	government
class	company	jury	group
committee	corporation	council	crowd

Collective nouns usually take a singular verb.

collective nouns and singular verbs:

> singular S, singular V
> The *class is meeting* in the library today.

> singular S, singular V
> The *audience was* bored.

> singular S, singular V
> The *jury is examining* the evidence.

A singular verb is used because the group is meeting, or feeling bored, or examining, *as one unit*.

Collective nouns take a plural verb *only* when the members of the group are acting individually, not as a unit.

collective noun with a plural verb:

plural S,   plural V
The football *team are arguing* among themselves. (The phrase *among themselves* shows that the team is not acting as one unit.)

Exercise 11 **Practice: Making Subjects and Verbs Agree: Using Collective Nouns**

Circle the correct verb in each of the following sentences.

1. The Saddle Club (wants / want) all the members to support the local horse rescue organization.

2. West Valley's advisory board (has / have) suggested constructing a safety fence around the community's playground area.

3. Morrison Tee Shirts Company (designs / design) commemorative tees for birthdays, festivals, and local softball teams.

4. After the plans are approved, a group of volunteers (intends / intend) to begin building a new women's shelter.

5. The tourists from China (was / were) scheduled to visit Disney World in two days.

6. The jury (is / are) quarrelling among themselves; a swift verdict is unlikely.

7. Two generations of millionaire investors recently announced that, because of distrust within the family, several members (was / were) dividing the family assets.

8. After the comedian returned for the second curtain call, the audience (was / were) more appreciative than ever.

9. Whenever the home team scored, the crowd of local supporters (was /were) elated.

10. A family of five (is / are) adopting two child survivors of the Haitian earthquakes.

MAKING SUBJECTS AND VERBS AGREE: A REVIEW

As you have probably realized, making subjects and verbs agree is not as simple as it first appears. But if you can remember the basic ideas in this section, you will be able to apply them automatically as you edit your own writing. Following is a quick summary of subject–verb agreement.

> **INFO BOX: Making Subjects and Verbs Agree: A Summary**
>
> 1. Subjects and verbs should agree in number: singular subjects get singular verbs; plural subjects get plural verbs.
>
> 2. When pronouns are used as subjects, they must agree in number with verbs.
>
> 3. Nothing in a prepositional phrase can be the subject of a sentence.

continued

4. Questions, sentences beginning with *here* or *there*, and other sentences can change word order.

5. Compound subjects joined by *and* are usually plural.

6. When subjects are joined by *or, either . . . or, neither . . . nor, not only . . . but also*, the verb form agrees with the subject closest to the verb.

7. Indefinite pronouns always take singular verbs.

8. Collective nouns usually take singular verbs.

Exercise 12 **Practice: A Comprehensive Exercise on Subject–Verb Agreement**

This exercise covers all the rules on subject–verb agreement. Underline the correct verb form in the following sentences.

1. If the restless crowd (is / are) pushing and shoving among themselves, then the security staff will have to act.

2. A popular fruit juice company from the Hawaiian Islands (is / are) thinking of opening a chain of juice bars in California.

3. How (was / were) the sound system and lighting at the auditorium?

4. Sometimes, when a bad day at work leaves me frustrated, a good dinner and my boyfriend's sympathy (soothes / soothe) my nerves.

5. Anybody with a taste for deep-fried seafood (loves / love) my cooking.

6. Behind all Simon's jokes and foolish behavior (is / are) an insecure man with a hunger for acceptance.

7. Each of the trucks for sale at the used car lot (needs / need) some major repairs.

8. Neither a bad cold nor occasional backaches (keeps / keep) Pete from his daily workout.

9. A college student with a heavy schedule of classes and a load of responsibilities at home or work (needs / need) a strong support system of family or friends.

10. Until winter ends and the snow melts, someone in this family (has / have) to shovel the ice and snow from our sidewalks.

Exercise 13 **Practice: Another Comprehensive Exercise on Subject–Verb Agreement**

This exercise covers all the rules on subject–verb agreement. Underline the correct verb form in the following sentences.

1. Occasionally, famous celebrities (wants / want) nothing more than privacy.

2. After spring break, everyone in school (was / were) longing for the semester to end.

3. If you want to send your girlfriend a picture of you, either of the photographs from the picnic (is / are) an excellent choice.

4. Where on earth (is / are) my license and registration?

5. Every week, there (is / are) a classic film and a discussion group at the National Cinema.

6. For years, the United States (has / have) offered free public libraries in each state.

7. At the end of the term, the early childhood education class (gives / give) a party for children at a local daycare center.

8. To me, nothing in Mario's apology (seems / seem) sincere.

9. There (is / are) an empty box of tissues and a yellowed newspaper on the floor of your car.

10. Either the hot water heater or the pipes (is / are) making a strange noise.

Collaborate

Exercise 14	Collaborate: Writing Sentences with Subject–Verb Agreement: A Comprehensive Exercise

With a partner or group, write two sentences for each of the following phrases. Use a verb that fits and put it in the present tense. Be sure that the verb agrees with your subject. The first one is done for you.

1. A group of Ecuadoran students visits my high school once a year in the fall.

   A group of Ecuadoran students corresponds with a group of high school seniors from Milwaukee.

2. Nothing at the movies _____

   _____

   Nothing at the movies _____

   _____

3. My cell phone provider _____

   My cell phone provider _____

   _____

4. Anyone with common sense _____

   _____

   Anyone with common sense _____

   _____

5. Each of my children _____

   _____

   Each of my children _____

   _____

6. Not only my mother but also the neighbors _____

   _____

   Not only my mother but also the neighbors _____

   _____

7. Everyone on the stairs _____

_____

Everyone on the stairs _____

_____

8. The group by the copy machine _____

_____

The group by the copy machine _____

_____

9. Neither the eggs nor the bacon _____

_____

Neither the eggs nor the bacon _____

_____

10. Books about sports or a sports DVD_____

_____

Books about sports or a sports DVD _____

_____

Collaborate

Exercise 15 **Collaborate: Create Your Own Text on Subject–Verb Agreement**

Work with a partner or group to create your own grammar handbook. Following is a list of rules on subject–verb agreement. Write two sentences that are examples of each rule. Write an *S* above the subject of each sentence and a *V* above the verb. After you've completed this exercise, trade it for another group's exercise. Check that group's examples while it checks yours. The first one is done for you.

Rule 1: Subjects and verbs should agree in number: singular subjects get singular verb forms; plural subjects get plural verb forms.

     S V
example 1: An apple is a healthy snack. _____

_____

     S V
example 2: Runners need large quantities of water. _____

_____

Rule 2: When pronouns are used as subjects, they must agree in number with verbs.

example 1: _____

_____

example 2: _____

_____

Rule 3:   Nothing in a prepositional phrase can be the subject of a sentence.

example 1: _____

_____

example 2: _____

_____

Rule 4:   Questions, sentences beginning with *here* or *there*, and other sentences can change word order.

example 1: _____

_____

example 2: _____

_____

Rule 5:   Compound subjects joined by *and* are usually plural.

example 1: _____

_____

example 2: _____

_____

Rule 6:   When subjects are joined by *or, either ... or, neither ... nor,* or *not only ... but also,* the verb form agrees with the subject closest to the verb.

example 1: _____

_____

example 2: _____

_____

Rule 7:   Indefinite pronouns always take singular verbs.

example 1: _____

_____

example 2: _____

_____

Rule 8:   Collective nouns usually take singular verbs.

example 1: _____

_____

example 2: _____

_____

Connect

Exercise 16   **Connect: A Comprehensive Exercise: Editing a Paragraph for Subject–Verb Agreement**

The following paragraph has eight errors in subject–verb agreement. Correct the errors in the spaces above the lines.

The City Cares Club are known for giving time and money to various projects in the community. Last week, third-grade students at Kennedy Community School were pleasantly surprised to receive a gift from the club members. The president and five other people involved in the gift arrived at the school with boxes of goodies. The goodies, however, was not edible. Brain food arrived in the boxes. Each of the third graders were startled to receive a dictionary. The students' teacher quickly focused the students' attention by asking them to look up the meaning of two words: "dangerous" and "enormous." Within minutes, several students quickly found both words; every student in the class were excited. One of the excited students were anxious to know if she could bring her dictionary home. "Of course," said the club's president, "The City Cares Club want every student to own a book." Neither the teacher nor the students was able to remember a better surprise. The third-grade class at Kennedy Community School are likely to remember this day for a long time.

Connect

Exercise 17   **Connect: Another Comprehensive Exercise: Editing a Paragraph for Subject–Verb Agreement**

The following paragraph has six errors in subject–verb agreement. Correct the errors in the spaces above the lines.

One of the cashiers at the local market are known for her great disposition. Kathleen Monaghan greets all her customers with a big smile and a cheery "Hey! How are you doing?" If she knows the customer, she will add a compliment such as "You're looking good today." Strangers will hear Kathleen shout, "Hi! Come on in!" Something about her tone make people feel special. Once a shopper arrives at Kathleen's checkout counter, he or she see more of Kathleen's sunny personality. She will chat about the weather, sports, or local news. Her conversation is always upbeat. There is too many high points in every day for a person to focus

on low moments, she believes. By the time Kathleen hands a customer a receipt

and change, he or she are in a good mood. "Good bye, Honey," she calls to each

customer who walks out the door. She adds, "Have a great day." Neither the old-

timers nor the first-time customer are able to leave without smiling.

Chapter Test   Making Subjects and Verbs Agree

Some of the sentences below are correct; others have errors in making subjects and verbs agree. Put *OK* next to the correct sentences and *X* next to
the sentences with errors.

1. _____ Where is the leftover turkey and cranberry sauce from
Thanksgiving dinner?

2. _____ Each of Eva's elaborate hairstyles take her at least an hour
to create.

3. _____ Two sneaky squirrels or one very large blue jay empties my
birdfeeder minutes after I fill it.

4. _____ There are a large black snake and a speckled lizard relaxing
on the sunny patio.

5. _____ The celebrity chef, with all his television fame and popular
cookbooks, has never cooked red beans and rice.

6. _____ Every time the temperature falls below freezing, not only
my cat but also my dogs crawls into my bed.

7. _____ Something in the taste and texture of the soup makes me
wonder about the ingredients.

8. _____ Our local government must find a way to limit its spending
until the economy improves.

9. _____ Neither two long weekends nor one week are enough time
for me to spend with my family.

10. _____ Here are a small blue bowl and a blue mug.

CHAPTER 14

Using Pronouns Correctly: Agreement and Reference

Chapter Objectives

Students will be able to (1) recognize proper pronoun case; (2) identify pronoun antecedents, indefinite pronouns, and collective nouns; and (3) correct errors in pronoun agreement and reference.

Pronouns are words that substitute for nouns. A pronoun's **antecedent** is the word or words it replaces.

pronouns and antecedents:

antecedent   pronoun
George is a wonderful father; *he* is loving and kind.

           antecedent   pronoun
Suzanne wound *the clock* because *it* had stopped ticking.

       antecedent   pronoun
Talking on the phone is fun, but *it* takes up too much of my time.

       antecedent   pronoun
Joanne and David know what *they* want.

     antecedent   pronoun
Christopher lost *his* favorite baseball cap.

       antecedent   pronoun
The *horse* stamped *its* feet and neighed loudly.

Exercise 1 **Practice: Identifying the Antecedents of Pronouns**

In each of the following sentences, a pronoun is underlined. Circle the w͏
or words that are the antecedent of the underlined pronoun.

1. Elizabeth and her mother loved to shop together; however, t͏
didn't have the same taste in clothes.

2. My brother hates the sound of sirens; however, <u>it</u> doesn't bother me͏

3. Dancing to loud music energizes Sheila; <u>it</u> allows her to shake off
her worries and cares.

4. Fortunately, the travelers were able to find <u>their</u> way to a police
station and report the incident.

5. Kelly, will <u>you</u> promise me one thing?

6. Over the weekend my girlfriend and I had a new experience; <u>we</u>
spent two days at the auto races.

7. Halloween left <u>its</u> mark in my house in the form of bags of extra
candy.

8. Anxious children sometimes fear that <u>they</u> will be abandoned.

9. The German shepherds danced and pranced when their owner
returned home, and <u>he</u> felt a rush of happiness.

10. A few of my classmates were getting together to share <u>their</u> notes
on the material covered on the final exam.

AGREEMENT OF A PRONOUN AND ITS ANTECEDENT

A pronoun must agree in number with its antecedent. If the antecedent is
singular, the pronoun must be singular. If the antecedent is plural, the pronoun must be plural.

singular antecedents, singular pronouns:

singular antecedent   singular pronoun
The *dog* began to bark wildly; *it* hated being locked up in the cellar.

singular antecedent   singular pronoun
Maria spends most of *her* salary on rent.

plural antecedents, plural pronouns:

plural antecedent   plural pronoun
Carlos and Ronnie went to Atlanta for a long weekend; *they* had
a good time.

plural antecedent   plural pronoun
Cigarettes are expensive, and *they* can kill you.

SPECIAL PROBLEMS WITH AGREEMENT

Agreement of pronoun and antecedent seems fairly simple: If an antecedent is singular, use a singular pronoun; if an antecedent is plural, use a plural pronoun. There are, however, some special problems with agreement of
pronouns, and these problems will come up in your writing. If you become

familiar with the explanations, examples, and exercises that follow, you'll be ready to handle special problems.

Indefinite Pronouns

Certain words, called **indefinite pronouns,** are always singular. Therefore, if an indefinite pronoun is the antecedent, the pronoun that replaces it must be singular. Here are the indefinite pronouns:

INFO BOX: Indefinite Pronouns				
one	everyone	somebody	anything	each
anyone	nobody	everybody	something	either
someone	anybody	nothing	everything	neither

You may think that *everybody* is plural, but in grammatically correct English, it is a singular word. Therefore, if you want to write clearly and correctly, memorize these words as the *-one*, *-thing*, and *-body* words: *everyone, everything, everybody, anyone, anything,* and so on, plus *each, either,* and *neither.* If any of these words is an antecedent, the pronoun that refers to it is singular.

indefinite pronouns as antecedents:

indefinite pronoun antecedent   singular pronoun
Each of the women skaters did *her* best in the Olympic competition.

indefinite pronoun antecedent   singular pronoun
Everyone nominated for Father of the Year earned *his* nomination.

Avoiding Gender Bias

Consider this sentence:

Everybody in the cooking contest prepared _____ best dish.

How do you choose the correct pronoun to fill this blank? You can write:

Everybody in the cooking contest prepared *his* best dish.

if everybody in the contest is male. Or you can write:

Everybody in the cooking contest prepared *her* best dish.

if everybody in the contest is female. Or you can write:

Everybody in the cooking contest prepared *his or her* best dish.

if the contest has male and female entrants.

In the past, most writers used *his* to refer to both men and women when the antecedent was an indefinite pronoun. Today, many writers try to use *his or her* to avoid gender bias. If you find using *his or her* is getting awkward and repetitive, you can rewrite the sentence and make the antecedent plural.

Correct: *The entrants* in the cooking contest prepared *their* best dishes.

But you cannot shift from singular to plural:

Incorrect: ~~Everybody in the cooking contest prepared their best dish.~~

Exercise 2   Practice: Making Pronouns and Their Antecedents Agree:
Simple Agreement and Indefinite Pronouns

In each of the following sentences, write the appropriate pronoun in the blank
space. Look carefully for the antecedent before you choose the pronoun.

1. After Joshua decided to study for a degree in sports management,
_____ felt free of stress.

2. Most of my relatives spend _____ vacations at home, doing home
repairs or yard work.

3. A resident at the women's shelter regained some of _____ confidence by attending group therapy sessions.

4. Has anybody from the men's club lost _____ membership card?

5. My daughters are going to a free concert at the park; _____ will
enjoy the music and sunshine.

6. Either of my brothers would have offered me _____ support in
these tough times.

7. One of the men on the train dropped _____ glasses on the floor
and broke one of the lenses.

8. A divorced father with children in a distant state and little cash
may miss _____ children terribly.

9. Relying on frozen food and a microwave for your meals can be
depressing, however, _____ saves time and money.

10. Each of my sisters likes _____ hamburgers cooked rare.

Exercise 3   Connect: Editing a Paragraph for Errors in Agreement:
Indefinite Pronouns

Connect

The following paragraph contains seven errors in agreement where the antecedents are indefinite pronouns. Correct the errors in the space above the lines.

When one of the classroom buildings at my college lost their power yesterday,

a brief period of excitement, uncertainty, and amusement followed. In my math

class, everyone was sitting quietly, listening to the professor explain some new

material, when the lights went out. At first, nobody expressed their surprise.

Then somebody got out of their chair and walked toward the windows. Suddenly

another person began to talk, and soon a wave of conversation spread through the

room. Our teacher remained calm. He called the maintenance department, but nei-

ther an employee in the central maintenance building nor one in our dark building

was able to say much. By this time, several people in our classroom had tried to

open the windows and found them hard to unstick. Meanwhile, everyone began to fan themselves with a lightweight textbook or notebook. Next, somebody left their chair and, in near darkness, headed to the hall. Almost immediately, each student grabbed their belongings and stumbled into the windowless third-floor hallway. That area was lighted only by small emergency exit markers. Fortunately, at the same moment when the entire class was stumbling around the hall, electricity was restored. Nobody had to suffer in the darkness and heat anymore, but everybody had to be seated and return their attention to the mathematics lesson.

Collective Nouns

Collective nouns refer to more than one person or thing.

INFO BOX: Some Common Collective Nouns

team	audience	family	government
class	company	jury	group
committee	corporation	council	crowd

Most of the time, collective nouns take a singular pronoun.

> **collective nouns and singular pronouns:**
>
> collective noun   singular pronoun
> The *jury* in the murder trial announced *its* verdict.

> collective noun   singular pronoun
> The *company* I work for has been in business a long time; *it* started in Atlanta, Georgia.

Collective nouns are usually singular because the group is announcing a verdict or starting a business as one, as a unit. Collective nouns take a plural *only* when the members of the group are acting individually, not as a unit.

> **collective noun and a plural pronoun:**
>
> collective noun plural pronoun
> The *team* signed *their* contracts yesterday. (The members of the team sign contracts individually.)

Connect

Exercise 4   **Connect: Making Pronouns and Antecedents Agree: Collective Nouns**

Underline the correct pronoun in each of the following sentences.

1. The Morton Company is having (its / their) holiday party early this year.

2. My favorite team began to suffer many losses when the players began to quarrel among (itself / themselves).

3. When the featured singer arrived an hour late, the audience lost (its / their) faith in the show.

4. Several of the pharmaceutical corporations agreed to donate part of (its / their) profits to medical research.

5. Over the years, bad feelings broke the family apart; (it / they) never resolved an old feud and lost touch with one another.

6. Aqua Sports created a cheaper version of (its / their) popular personal watercraft.

7. The Helping Hands Club lost (its / their) president last week.

8. The committee that interviewed me for the job will let me know (its / their) decision next week.

9. The Air Force brings (its / their) best jets to the air show.

10. My son's kindergarten class had (its / their) graduation party yesterday.

Exercise 5	Connect: Editing a Paragraph for Errors in Agreement: Collective Nouns

Connect

The following paragraph contains five errors in agreement where the antecedent is a collective noun. Correct the errors in the spaces above the lines.

Last summer, the Student Conduct Committee of our county's school board made a controversial decision. They decided that mandatory school uniforms would bring harmony and better behavior to the county's schools. Of course, families with school-age children had their own reactions to this plan. A small group quickly expressed their approval. On the other hand, a much larger crowd loudly expressed its disapproval and horror. Meanwhile, hundreds of students marched, spoke, and wrote about the issue. Letters to the editor of the local newspaper blasted the Conduct Committee for forcing students into clothing that would suppress their individuality and stifle their creativity. On the other hand, some writers praised the uniforms as a way to place all students, rich and poor, at the same level. These writers argued that low-income students cannot afford the latest "hot" clothing styles and labels and may endure ridicule or bullying from classmates. By the end of the summer, the Student Conduct Committee had not responded to the complaints. Finally, days before the school term began, the committee issued their final decision. Uniforms became the rule. However, the anti-uniform crowd won on a few of their points. Today, school uniforms are simply dark or khaki pants or shorts for males; dark or khaki pants, shorts, or skirts for females; and a variety of solid-colored polo shirts for everyone. Compromise has not made everyone happy, but the students have adjusted. In addition, each class has their share of students who like being freed from the daily decision of what to wear to school.

Collaborate

Exercise 6 **Collaborate: Writing Sentences with Pronoun–Antecedent Agreement**

With a partner or with a group, write a sentence for each of the following pairs of words, using each pair as a pronoun and its antecedent(s). The first pair is done for you.

1. men . . . their

   sentence: *The men at the dance were wearing their best clothes.* _____

   _____

2. The Eastville Sheriff's Department . . . its

   sentence: _____

   _____

3. parrot . . . its

   sentence: _____

   _____

4. anyone . . . his or her

   sentence: _____

   _____

5. Graciela and Brandon . . . their

   sentence: _____

   _____

6. nothing . . . its

   sentence: _____

   _____

7. neither . . . her

   sentence: _____

   _____

8. bragging . . . it

   sentence: _____

   _____

9. everyone . . . his or her

   sentence: _____

   _____

10. celebrities . . . they

sentence: _____

_____

PRONOUNS AND THEIR ANTECEDENTS: BEING CLEAR

Remember that pronouns are words that replace or refer to other words, and those other words are called *antecedents*.

Make sure that a pronoun has one clear antecedent. Your writing will be vague and confusing if a pronoun appears to refer to more than one antecedent or if a pronoun doesn't have any specific antecedent to refer to. Such confusing language is called a problem with *reference of pronouns*.

When a pronoun refers to more than one thing, the sentence can become confusing or silly.

pronouns below refer to more than one thing (unclear antecedent):
Carla told Elaine that her car had a flat tire. (Whose car had a flat tire? Carla's? Elaine's?)
Josh woke to the shrieking alarm clock, buried his head in his pillow, and threw it across the room. (What did Josh throw? The pillow? The clock? His head?)

If there is no one, clear antecedent, you must rewrite the sentence to make the reference clear. Sometimes the rewritten sentence may seem repetitive, but a little repetition is better than a lot of confusion.

unclear: Carla told Elaine that her car had a flat tire.
clear: Carla told Elaine that Carla's car had a flat tire.
clear: Carla told Elaine that Elaine's car had a flat tire.
clear: Carla told Elaine, "Your car has a flat tire."
clear: Carla told Elaine, "My car has a flat tire."

unclear: Josh woke to the shrieking alarm clock, buried his head in his pillow, and threw it across the room.
clear: Josh woke to the shrieking alarm clock, buried his head in his pillow, and threw the clock across the room.

Sometimes the problem is a little more confusing. Can you spot what's wrong with this sentence?

Linda was able to negotiate for a raise, which pleased her. (What pleased Linda? The raise? Or the fact that she was able to negotiate for it?)

Be very careful with the pronoun *which*. If there is any chance that using *which* will confuse the reader, rewrite the sentence and get rid of *which*.

clear: Linda was pleased that she was able to negotiate for a raise.
clear: Linda was pleased by the raise she negotiated.

Sometimes a pronoun has nothing to refer to; it has no antecedent.

pronouns with no antecedent:
When Mary took the television to the repair shop, they said the television couldn't be repaired. (Who are "they"? Who said the television couldn't be repaired? The television service personnel? The customers? The repairmen?)

I have always been interested in designing clothes and have decided that's what I want to be. (What does "that" refer to? The only word it could refer to is *clothes.* You certainly don't want to be clothes. You don't want to be a dress or a suit.)

If a pronoun lacks an antecedent, add an antecedent or eliminate the pronoun.

> **add an antecedent:** When Mary took the television to the repair shop and asked *the service personnel* for an estimate, they said the television couldn't be repaired.

> **eliminate the pronoun:** I have always been interested in designing clothes and have decided I want to be a fashion designer.

To check for clear reference of pronouns, underline any pronouns that may not be clear. Then try to draw a line from that pronoun to its antecedent. Are there two or more possible antecedents? Is there no antecedent? In either case, you need to rewrite.

Exercise 7   Practice: Rewriting Sentences for Clear Reference of Pronouns

Rewrite the following sentences so that the pronouns have clear references. You can add, take out, or change words.

1. Alice rarely has a free weekend, which depresses her.

   rewritten: _____

   _____

2. Charlie warned his brother that his money was running out.

   rewritten: _____

   _____

3. They didn't tell me that late registration had ended.

   rewritten: _____

   _____

4. Mark dropped a china candlestick on the glass coffee table, but it didn't break.

   rewritten: _____

   _____

5. Natalie quizzed Deanna, trying to find out what Adam had said about her.

   rewritten: _____

   _____

6. My sister stopped speaking to Stephanie because she has a quick temper.

   rewritten: _____

   _____

7. My parents want me to consider the health-care field, but I don't want to be one.

   rewritten: _____

   _____

8. Bill returned the expensive new truck, which infuriated his wife.

   rewritten: _____

   _____

9. Valerie always buys her groceries at Daria's Market because they have good deals on meat and produce.

   rewritten: _____

   _____

10. Lauren complained to Chantelle that her room was a mess.

    rewritten: _____

    _____

Exercise 8   **Collaborate: Revising Sentences with Problems in Pronoun Reference: Two Ways**

Collaborate

Do this exercise with a partner or group. Each of the following sentences contains a pronoun with an unclear antecedent. Because the antecedent is unclear, the sentence can have more than one meaning. Rewrite each sentence twice to show the different meanings. The first one is done for you.

1. Mrs. Klein told Mrs. Yamaguchi her dog was digging up the flower beds.

   sentence 1: Mrs. Klein told Mrs. Yamaguchi, "Your dog is digging up the flower beds."

   sentence 2: Mrs. Klein told Mrs. Yamaguchi that Mrs. Klein's dog was digging up the flower beds.

2. Jimmy asked Lewis if he could bring a friend to the party.

   sentence 1: _____

   _____

   sentence 2: _____

   _____

3. Patty ran into her mother at her favorite restaurant.

   sentence 1: _____

   _____

   sentence 2: _____

   _____

4. Leonard took a five-dollar bill out of the envelope and gave it to me.

   sentence 1: _____

   _____

   sentence 2: _____

5. Once the guests had petted the dogs, they left the room.

   sentence 1: _____

   _____

   sentence 2: _____

   _____

6. Pete soon got a new job, which brightened his mood.

   sentence 1: _____

   _____

   sentence 2: _____

   _____

7. Yolanda told Melissa she worried too much about little things.

   sentence 1: _____

   _____

   sentence 2: _____

   _____

8. When Jolene picked up her little daughter, she began to cry.

   sentence 1: _____

   _____

   sentence 2: _____

   _____

9. Emma's sister asked her to bring her big cooler to the picnic.

   sentence 1: _____

   _____

   sentence 2: _____

   _____

10. After my two beagles met my sister's bossy cats, they were never
    the same.

    sentence 1: _____

    _____

    sentence 2: _____

    _____

Exercise 9   **Connect: Editing a Paragraph for Errors in Pronoun Reference**

Connect

The following paragraph contains five errors in pronoun reference. Correct the errors in the spaces above the lines.

When I needed minor surgery recently, they were kind and caring at the outpatient clinic. As soon as I arrived in the lobby, a receptionist called the patient preparation center and a nursing attendant came right out. My sister was allowed to follow me through the swinging doors into the pre-surgery area. Soon I was taken to a private cubicle where a nurse dressed me in a hospital gown and hooked me up to an IV. Someone else helped me onto a hospital bed and covered me in blankets. I found comfort in it. Next, someone with a clipboard arrived to ask me a string of questions, which confused me. Then a lady in a volunteer's uniform came to keep me company. One of the nurses soon arrived to take my blood pressure. She could barely get into my cubicle because of all the attention I was receiving from my sister and the volunteer. A few minutes later, they said that I would soon be taken to the operating room. I became anxious because I was afraid of undergoing surgery without getting an anesthetic. The volunteer laughed and said they had put an anesthetic into the IV fluid when I had first entered my cubicle. Once I learned about my anesthetic, I began to feel sleepy. I vaguely remember being rolled into surgery for my brief and successful procedure.

Exercise 10   **Connect: Editing a Paragraph for Errors in Agreement and Reference**

Connect

The following paragraph contains five errors in pronoun agreement and reference. Correct the errors in the space above the lines.

A pet can be a terrible nagger. Although I love my animals, each of the critters can be a torment at various times. If my dog Chance wants to go outside, for instance, he knows how to tell me. Whenever he looks out the window and sees a squirrel playing in the yard, he whines and paws the glass until I let him outside. Chance is sure that whatever I am doing, even if it is studying for a test or standing on a ladder to change a light bulb, cannot be as important as chasing a squirrel. When Chance sees a squirrel, nothing matter. He has to go out and chase that pesky creature. My cat Ethel is equally impatient when she wants to be fed. Unfortunately, she has decided that she wants to be fed at 3:00 A.M. At that ghastly hour, she sits next to my head on the pillow and repeatedly licks my face with her sandpaper tongue, which makes me crazy. When I finally crawl out of bed and stagger to the kitchen, Puffy, my parrot, wakes up. Puffy resents the early wake-up call and begins to scold me. He squawks until my cat and I have left the room and quiet has returned to the kitchen. Everyone who hears about my pets' little imperfections has their own opinion about animal behavior and training. But I know that each of my pets has demonstrated their capacity to learn and grow. Unfortunately, the group of animals in my house have learned how to train *me*.

Chapter Test **Using Pronouns Correctly: Agreement and Reference**

Some of the sentences below are correct; others have errors in pronoun agreement or reference. Put *OK* next to the correct sentences and *X* next to the sentences with errors.

1. _____ Drinking too many soft drinks can be bad for your weight; it can also be bad for your teeth.

2. _____ Each of the Clemons brothers had their own brand of charm.

3. _____ Everything in the Florida Keys lost its appeal for me when I experienced a hurricane in Key West.

4. _____ I ordered a slice of pizza and a small salad, but it wasn't very tasty.

5. _____ My mother and her sister met to discuss her recent divorce.

6. _____ Last week, the Fantastic Toys Company announced their new line of miniature robots.

7. _____ My four-year-old loves to visit the library because they always have new books and videos.

8. _____ Someone in our neighborhood has posted fliers about his or her missing cat.

9. _____ Cleaning houses has become a popular way for college students to make money, but I don't want to be one.

10. _____ My little sister got her nostril pierced and wears a small nose ring, which infuriates my parents.

Using Pronouns Correctly: Consistency and Case

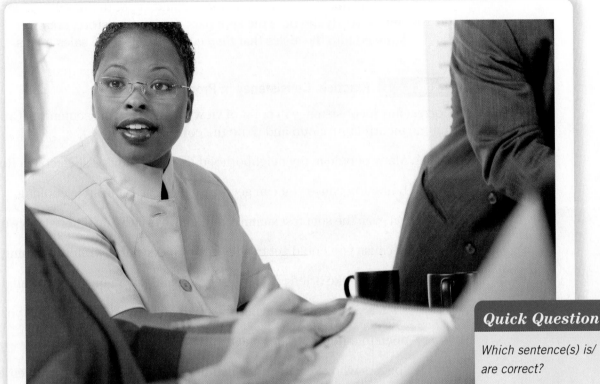

CHAPTER 15

Quick Question

Which sentence(s) is/ are correct?

A. You can get a ride to the mountains with Damian and me.

B. I've stopped going to that club because you have to wait in line for an hour to get inside.

(After you study this chapter, you will be confident of your answer.)

Chapter Objectives

Students will be able to (1) recognize first, second, and third-person points of view; (2) correct errors in pronoun consistency; and (3) use appropriate pronoun cases in their writing.

When you write, you write from a point of view, and each point of view gets its own form. If you write from the first person point of view, your pronouns are in the *I* (singular) or *we* (plural) forms. If your pronouns are in the second person point of view, your pronouns are in the *you* form, whether they are singular or plural. If you write from the third person point of view, your pronouns are in the *he, she,* or *it* (singular) or *they* (plural) forms.

Different kinds of writing may require different points of view. When you are writing a set of directions, for example, you might use the second person (*you*) point of view. For an essay about your childhood, you might use the first person (*I*) point of view.

Whatever point of view you use, be consistent in using pronouns. That is, do not shift the form of your pronouns without some good reason.

not consistent: The last time *I* went to that movie theater, the only seat *you* could get was in the front row.

consistent: The last time *I* went to that movie theater, the only seat *I* could get was in the front row.

not consistent: By the time the shoppers got into the store, *they* were so jammed into the aisles that *you* couldn't get to the sales tables.

consistent: By the time the shoppers got into the store, *they* were so jammed into the aisles that *they* couldn't get to the sales tables.

Exercise 1 Practice: Consistency in Pronouns

Correct any inconsistency in point of view in the following sentences. Cross out the incorrect pronoun and write the correct one above it.

1. Many people in my neighborhood like to eat at the Stagecoach Restaurant because you can get a good deal on homestyle cooking.

2. On even the sunniest summer day, I always carry an umbrella to work because you could get caught in a thunderstorm without warning.

3. After I spoke briefly to a salesperson making an unsolicited call, I soon realized that allowing one company to make contact left you open to a flood of sales calls.

4. Joggers who exercise in the middle of the day have to watch their intake of fluids because you can easily become dangerously dehydrated.

5. Twice a year, I went to a giant sale at the local library; it offered used books, magazines, DVDs, CDs, and videos, and you could get as many as ten items for ten dollars.

6. I'm planning to finish school next summer and then look for a job in the city, but you can't make plans too far ahead of time and then expect them to work out.

7. Children trusted the teacher's aide because you would always get a kind word of encouragement from her.

8. Whenever Charlene gives me a compliment, you know she wants something from me.

9. We went to the show sponsored by several college clubs, but the sound system was so poor that you couldn't understand any of the comedian's jokes.

10. Nathan tried to build his career in music, but you could not make the right contacts in a small, rural town.

Exercise 2   **Collaborate: Rewriting Sentences with Consistency Problems**   Collaborate

Do this exercise with a partner or group. Rewrite the following sentences, correcting any errors in the consistency of pronouns. To make the corrections, you may have to change, add, or take out words.

1. I don't see why I should give Ella another chance; after she makes new promises, she always hurts you again.

   rewritten: _____

   _____

   _____

2. Once my father has sauteed the onions, you add them to the grilled steaks and buns, and he serves his famous steak sandwiches.

   rewritten: _____

   _____

   _____

3. The first time I worked in the kitchen at the pizza place, the pace of the workers was so fast that you could hardly keep up.

   rewritten: _____

   _____

   _____

4. The most rewarding part of my job at the daycare center is seeing the children run to you when they enter the door.

   rewritten: _____

   _____

   _____

5. Customers who want to take advantage of the store's weekly sales and special offers must remember to present your discount cards at the register.

   rewritten: _____

   _____

   _____

6. Samantha isn't going to invite her cousin Rick to her graduation party because he'll just make you want to scream if he keeps following her around with his camera.

   rewritten: _____

   _____

   _____

7. Parents who return to school need support, for you can get lost balancing school, home, and work responsibilities.

   rewritten: _____

   _____

   _____

8. Manny's favorite holiday is the Fourth of July when you can relax in shorts and a t-shirt, get some sun, and, if he has the energy, go to the park and see the fireworks.

   rewritten: _____

   _____

   _____

9. You knew this was a happy family as soon as we walked in and saw the children helping their parents set the table.

   rewritten: _____

   _____

   _____

10. Drivers on the Tillotson Expressway this weekend are advised to keep a close eye on your speedometers because the Highway Patrol will be ticketing speeders.

    rewritten: _____

    _____

    _____

Connect

Exercise 3   **Connect: Editing a Paragraph for Pronoun Consistency**

The following paragraph has five errors in consistency of pronouns. Correct the errors above the lines.

When I started volunteering at a convalescent and therapeutic center for

veterans, I expected something totally different from the reality I experienced.

I thought that old men would be slouched in wheelchairs and dozing in hospital

beds. I thought that you would rarely see an alert man. I expected to be depressed.

Every one of my expectations was wrong. First of all, you could see all types of

veterans: old, young, male, and female. Many of them were undergoing gruel-

ing physical therapy, and even those in wheelchairs worked out. The sight of

amputees engaged in tough, demanding exercises made me rethink your image

of a wounded warrior. Of course, my first experience of so many people fighting

disability and pain caused me to feel strong emotions. However, you didn't feel

depressed. Instead, admiration and awe led you to a sense of gratitude for being

able to play a minor role at this place for healing and transformation.

CHOOSING THE CASE OF PRONOUNS

Pronouns have forms that show number and person, and they also have forms that show **case.** Following is a list of three cases of pronouns:

INFO BOX: Pronouns and Their Case

Singular Pronouns

	Subjective case	Objective case	Possessive case
First person	I	me	my
Second person	you	you	your
Third person	he, she, it	him, her, it	his, her, its

Plural Pronouns

	Subjective case	Objective case	Possessive case
First person	we	us	our
Second person	you	you	your
Third person	they	them	their

Rules for Choosing the Case of Pronouns

The rules for choosing the case of pronouns are simple:

1. When a pronoun is used as a subject, use the subjective case.

2. When a pronoun is used as the object of a verb or the object of a preposition, use the objective case.

3. When a pronoun is used to show possession, use the possessive case.

   Here are some examples of the correct use of pronouns:

   pronouns used as subjects:
   She calls the office once a week.
   Sylvia wrote the letter, and *we* revised it.
   When Guy called, *I* was thrilled.

   pronouns used as objects:
   The loud noise frightened *me.*
   The card was addressed to *him.*
   Sadie's dog always traveled with *her.*

   pronouns used to show possession:
   The criticism hurt *her* feelings.
   Our car is nearly new.
   The restaurant changed *its* menu.

Exercise 4   **Practice: Choosing the Correct Pronoun Case: Simple Situations**

Underline the correct pronoun in each of the following sentences.

1. After years of struggle, my mother earned what (she / her) had wanted for years: her citizenship in the United States of America.

2. Dave can call me tomorrow; (he / him) has my number.

3. Three hikers from our town got lost in the mountains; (they / them / their) survived on one bottle of water and three granola bars until searchers in a plane saw (they / them / their) three days later.

4. Don't forget to bring (you / your) sunscreen.

5. After my mother put (I / me / my) in bed for the night, (I / me / my) went to sleep within minutes.

6. Uncle Eddie is an artist; (he / him / his) paintings are in galleries throughout the country.

7. Kathleen and Andy took (they / them / their) dog to the veterinarian yesterday.

8. A police officer was very kind to (we / us / our) when (we / us / our) got lost in a strange place.

9. Two food stalls at the market sell fresh fruit, but (they / them / their) prices are high.

10. Sam lied to (he / him / his) parents when (he / him / his) went out to a party with me.

PROBLEMS CHOOSING PRONOUN CASE

Choosing the Correct Pronoun Case in a Related Group of Words

You need to be careful in choosing pronoun case when the pronoun is part of a related group of words. If the pronoun is part of a related group of words, isolate the pronoun. Next, try out the pronoun choices. Then decide which pronoun is correct and write the correct sentence. For example, which of these sentences is correct?

> Diane had a big surprise for Jack and *I*.
> > or
> Diane had a big surprise for Jack and *me*.

To choose the correct sentence, follow these steps:

Step 1: Isolate the pronoun. Eliminate the related words *Jack and*.

Step 2: Try each case.

> Diane had a big surprise for *I*.
> > or
> Diane had a big surprise for *me*.

Step 3: Decide which pronoun is correct and write the correct sentence.

correct sentence: Diane had a big surprise for Jack and *me*.

The pronoun acts as an object, so it takes the objective case.

To be sure that you understand the principle, try working through the steps once more. Which of the following sentences is correct?

> Next week, my sister and *me* will start classes at Bryant Community College.
> > or
> Next week, my sister and *I* will start classes at Bryant Community College.

Step 1: Isolate the pronoun. Eliminate the related words *my sister and*.

Step 2: Try each case.

> Next week, *me* will start classes at Bryant Community College.
> Next week, *I* will start classes at Bryant Community College.

Step 3: Decide which pronoun is correct and write the correct sentence.

correct sentence: Next week, my sister and *I* will start classes at Bryant Community College.

Common Errors with Pronoun Case

In choosing the case of pronouns, be careful to avoid these common errors:

1. *Between* is a preposition. The pronouns that follow it are objects of the preposition: between *us*, between *them*, between *you and me*. It is never correct to write between *you and I*.

   examples:
   not this: What I'm telling you must be kept strictly between you and ~~I~~.
   but this: What I'm telling you must be kept strictly between you and me.

2. Never use *myself* as a replacement for *I* or *me*.

   examples:
   not this: My family and ~~myself~~ are grateful for your expressions of sympathy.
   but this: My family and I are grateful for your expressions of sympathy.

   not this: The scholarship committee selected Nadine and ~~myself~~.
   but this: The scholarship committee selected Nadine and me.

3. The possessive pronoun *its* has no apostrophe.

   examples:
   not this: The stale coffee lost ~~it's~~ flavor.
   but this: The stale coffee lost its flavor.

Exercise 5 **Practice: Choosing the Correct Pronoun Case: Problems with Pronoun Case**

Underline the correct pronoun in each of the following sentences.

1. Carlos was pleased with the gift from Kate and (me / myself).

2. Rebecca used to have beautiful skin, but too much sunbathing has had (it's / its) effect on her complexion.

3. I told Henry that he could go to town with Tom and (I / me).

4. After Mike gave the dogs a bath, he took (they / them) and the neighbor's Labrador Retriever to the dog park.

5. Blinded by sunlight beating against the windshield, Mr. Abbot and (she / her) could not see the fallen tree in the road.

6. On behalf of (me / myself) and Mrs. Kline, I want to thank you for your outstanding work in customer service.

7. One of my neighbors smiles at Sandra and (I / me) whenever we pass him in the street, but I've forgotten his name.

8. My parents and (we / us) have been thinking about renting a cabin in one of the national parks.

9. Authentic Chinese food is always a treat for Tony and (I / me).

10. You and (I / me) just need a little time to figure out the budget for our trip.

Exercise 6 **Practice: More on Choosing the Correct Pronoun Case: Problems with Pronoun Case**

Underline the correct pronoun in each of the following sentences.

1. Did you think that the anniversary party was to be a secret between you and (I / me)?

2. My brother and (I / myself) have hired an accountant to look into the files at the office.

3. I used to love bowling in a bowling league, but the sport has lost (it's / its) appeal for me.

4. My mother warned me to stay out of the quarrel between my sister and brother or I would end up hurting (me / myself).

5. Without the unpaid labor of Tony and (I / me), my brother's basement would never have been renovated.

6. By midnight, (she / her) and Sal had studied every assigned chapter in their speech communications textbook.

7. Joe's decision to leave Minneapolis was a total shock to Robert and (I / me).

8. At the end of the month, Leon and (he / him) needed to make a decision about renewing their lease.

9. The past six months have presented several challenges for my children and (I / me).

10. Arthur may get a promotion at work, but he says (it's / its) too soon to tell.

Collaborate

Exercise 7 **Collaborate: Write Your Own Text on Pronoun Case**

With a partner or group, write two sentences that could be used as examples for each of the following rules. The first one is done for you.

Rule 1: When a pronoun is used as a subject, use the subjective case.

example 1: They study for tests in the math lab.

example 2: Caught in the rain, she ran for cover.

Rule 2: When a pronoun is used as the object of a verb or the object of a preposition, use the objective case. (For examples, write one sentence in which the pronoun is the object of a verb and one in which the pronoun is the object of a preposition.)

example 1: _____

example 2: _____

Rule 3: When a pronoun is used to show ownership, use the possessive case.

example 1: _____

example 2: _____

Rule 4: When a pronoun is part of a related group of words, isolate
the pronoun to choose the case. (For examples, write two sentences in which the pronoun is part of a related group of words.)

example 1: _____

example 2: _____

Exercise 8 **Connect: Editing a Paragraph for Correct Pronoun Case**

Connect

The following paragraph has six errors in pronoun case. Correct the errors
above the lines.

Nothing is more awful than an air conditioner losing it's power to cool dur-

ing a three-day holiday weekend in July. This terrible scenario happened to my

sister and I over the recent Independence Day weekend. Of course, trying to

schedule a repair during the Independence Day period is terrible. My sister and

myself first realized we were in trouble when the air in our air conditioning vents

became uncomfortably warm. We turned down the thermostat, but warm and then

even warmer air kept pushing through the vents. Being optimists, my sister and I

continued to hope that some miracle would occur and our system would suddenly

regain it's power to cool. After panting and wallowing in our own perspiration,

we decided to accept reality and beg for emergency assistance. Most places we

called simply offered us a recorded message about calling back after the weekend;

another offered us hope when a person answered the phone. Unfortunately, he

could offer us service only after the Monday holiday. Meanwhile, the house was

getting hotter. Out of desperation, me and my sister chose the only sensible solu-

tion: we went home to our parents' house where the big, reliable air conditioning

system was pumping it's heart out.

Exercise 9   **Connect: Editing a Paragraph for Pronoun Consistency and Correct Pronoun Case**

The following paragraph has six errors in pronoun consistency and case. Correct the errors above the lines.

I love to go to the movies, but I am disgusted by the condition of the movie theaters. Even before you find a seat, the sticky floors make me wonder what I've just stepped on or into. The mess could be gum, melted candy, or half-dried cola. The noise of a crackle or an oozy texture under your shoe as I make my way down the aisle does not welcome me into the room. The fact that the room is dark makes the search for a seat even more unpleasant. In a theater with stadium seating, you face the possibility of sliding on a slick substance and falling down the stairs. After I find a seat, two more problems confront me. One is more trash. Last week, me and my girlfriend climbed into two seats in the middle of a row and had to fight our way around half-empty boxes of popcorn, huge paper cups, and crumpled paper plates. When we finally got to the center seats, they were covered in another sticky substance. My girlfriend and myself felt as if we were sitting on garbage in a trash heap. On another occasion, I found another problem: broken seats. I sat back, expecting to relax in a rocking-chair seat, but I relaxed a little too far. The seat had no spring attached, and I slid into an endless slope. Feeling like a fool and hoping no one had noticed me, I scrambled to another seat. It, too, was damaged. This time, the armrest fell off the chair. I know that movie theaters get a large, continuous stream of patrons. I also know that the ushers and cleaners work hard and fast between showings so that the theaters will be fresh. But between you and I, I must confess that, after my recent experiences, renting DVDs is looking better than movie-going.

Chapter Test **Using Pronouns Correctly: Consistency and Case**

Some of the sentences below are correct; others have errors in pronoun consistency or case. Put *OK* next to the correct sentences and *X* next to the sentences with errors.

1. _____ Vincent likes to go to the city, where you never know what can happen.

2. _____ A string of arguments over silly misunderstandings caused my boyfriend and I to separate for a few months.

3. _____ Fighting a deadly virus had its effect on Daniel, who lost weight and physical strength.

4. _____ Sometimes when I try to reason with my father, I feel that you can't change the mind of someone living in the past.

5. _____ When Cara and I were in our teens, we kept a terrible secret between me and her.

6. _____ The teacher reminded us to bring your textbook to class for every class meeting or we would miss some important lessons.

7. _____ My partner and myself are astonished at winning the award for best design.

8. _____ I and my large bloodhound took a long walk in the woods yesterday.

9. _____ Whenever Tim has a little extra cash, him and his brother run out and spend it.

10. _____ Vincent likes to go to places where you never know what can happen.

Chapter Objectives

Students will be able to demonstrate proficiency in basic punctuation skills, including (but not limited to) the proper use of commas, semicolons, colons, apostrophes, parentheses, numbers, capital letters, and abbreviations.

You probably know much about punctuation already. In fact, you probably know many of the rules so well that you punctuate your writing automatically. However, there are times when every writer wonders, "Do I need a comma here?" or "Should I capitalize this word?" The following review of the basic rules of punctuation can help you answer such questions.

THE PERIOD

Periods are used two ways:

1. Use a period to mark the end of a sentence that makes a statement.

   examples:
   My father gave me an exciting new book.
   After the dance, we went to a coffeehouse for a snack.

196

2. Use a period after abbreviations.

examples:
Mr. Vinh
Carlos Montoya, Sr.
11:00 A.M.
Dr. J. T. Mitchell

THE QUESTION MARK

Use a question mark after a direct question.

examples:
Do you have any spare change?
Wasn't that song beautiful?

If a question is not a direct question, do not use a question mark.

examples:
I wonder if it will rain tonight.
Nadine asked whether I had cleaned the kitchen.

Exercise 1 **Practice: Punctuating with Periods and Question Marks**

Add the necessary periods and question marks to the following sentences.

1. Why isn't Cecilia at work today

2. Dr. Michalski was appointed to the Water Management Board

3. The mail carrier wanted to know if the people next door had

   moved away

4. When does the plane from LaGuardia Airport arrive

5. My brother was out until 4:00 AM, so I don't think he wants to play

   basketball this morning

6. Carmine and Rosanna wondered whether the little dog on the

   street belonged to anyone

7. Mr Sutton has a BA in African History

8. If you have a minute, can you explain this math problem to me

9. I am not sure when I will be able to go back to work

10. Patrick questioned the truth of Leon's account of the accident

Exercise 2 **Collaborate: Punctuating with Periods and Question Marks**

Collaborate

Do this exercise with a partner. First, by yourself, write a paragraph that
needs periods and question marks, but leave out those punctuation marks.
Then exchange paragraphs with your partner, and add the necessary periods

and question marks to your partner's paragraph. Finally, you and your partner should check each other's punctuation.

Write a paragraph of at least six sentences, using the topic sentence below.

New students have many questions about college, but their questions are soon answered. _____

_____

_____

_____

_____

_____

_____

THE SEMICOLON

There are two ways to use semicolons:

1. Use a semicolon to join two independent clauses.

    examples:
    Aunt Celine can be very generous; she gave me fifty dollars for my
        birthday.
    The ice storm was horrible; our town endured five days without
        electricity.

If the independent clauses are joined by a conjunctive adverb, you still need a semicolon. You will also need a comma after the conjunctive adverb if the conjunctive adverb is more than one syllable long.

    examples:
    I called the towing service; then I waited impatiently for the tow truck
        to arrive.
    Stephen forgot about the exam; therefore, he was not prepared
        for it.

2. If a list contains commas and the items on it need to be clarified, use
    a semicolon to separate the items. Note how confusing the following
    lists would be without the semicolons.

    examples:
    The student government presidents at the conference represented
        Mill Valley High School, Springfield; Longfellow High School, River-
        dale; Kennedy High School, Deer Creek; and Martin Luther King
        High School, Rocky Hills.
    The members of the musical group were Janet Reese, guitar;
        Richelle Dennison, drums; Sandy Simon, bass; and Lee Vickers,
        vocalist.

Exercise 3 **Practice: Punctuating with Semicolons**

Some of the following sentences need semicolons; some do not. Add the necessary semicolons. (You may need to change some commas to semicolons.)

1. Bananas are a great snack they are full of potassium and fiber.

2. If you go to the beach tomorrow, be sure to bring heavy sunscreen, a big towel or blanket, several bottles of water, and a hat.

3. Give me the jar I can open it for you.

4. Riding a bicycle to work or school can help you lose weight and can keep you fit.

5. In the summer, my mother took us to free concerts in the park thus we grew up loving all kinds of music.

6. Yesterday, the Neighborhood Crime Watch Association elected these officers: Pierre Nilon, president, Estelle Moreno, vice president, Stanley Rosen, treasurer, and Alan Chang, secretary.

7. Edward spent all afternoon looking for some paint for the kitchen but couldn't decide on the right shade of blue.

8. Dr. Wing has all the academic qualifications for the job of head of the pediatrics department furthermore, he is devoted to his patients.

9. The guests at Kimberly's wedding came from as far away as San Francisco, California, Portland, Oregon, Denver, Colorado, and Honolulu, Hawaii.

10. A handsome man answered the door he looked at me suspiciously.

Exercise 4 **Connect: Punctuating with Semicolons**

Connect

Add semicolons where they are needed in the following paragraph. You may need to change some commas to semicolons.

When Sean started work at the Rose Inn, he struggled to adapt to the personalities and demands of his bosses. At work, Sean had to answer to four people: Alice Lejeune, the head of reservations, Don Davis, the day manager, Catherine Chinn, the night manager, and John Carney, the chief accountant. As a new member of the reservations staff, Sean had to learn how to deal with the hotel guests in addition, he had to learn what each of his superiors required from him. John Carney, for example, cared about money problems he did not want Sean to make any promises of discounts or refunds to customers. If Sean worked the night shift, Catherine Chinn wanted him to be lively and energetic when guests checked in late at night. The day manager was a calm and tolerant man, consequently, Sean learned to relax around Mr. Davis. On the other hand, Alice Lejeune, the head of reservations, expected the best of her staff. Sean worked extra hard to please Ms. Lejeune as a result, he became a competent and confident staff member. For Sean, dealing with the hotel guests was a challenge dealing with four bosses was an education.

Exercise 5 Connect: Punctuating with Semicolons

Add semicolons where they are needed in the following paragraph. You may need to change some commas to semicolons.

After many years of hard work, Jonathan Reilly was able to buy a home, next, he wanted to create a good life for his children. He felt that he could provide opportunities that he had never had to Crystal, seven years old, Marcus, four years old, and Anthony, eighteen months old. Mr. Reilly never gave his children expensive clothes, fancy cars, or lavish vacations. Mr. Reilly didn't believe that a childhood full of luxuries would open doors for his sons and daughter instead, he focused on their education. Even if he had to work at two jobs, he found a way to save the money for three children's college educations. From their earliest years, Crystal, Marcus, and Anthony learned to focus on their academic strengths and improve their academic weaknesses. Mr. Reilly challenged his children to open their minds, in addition, he showed them the pleasures of learning. Books filled the Reilly home, and the children learned the pleasures of stargazing, exploring nature, camping, and caring for animals. By the time they were old enough for college, the Reilly children had focused on their career paths. Crystal chose veterinary science, Marcus decided to become a writer. The third child, Anthony, focused on marine biology. Jonathan Reilly lived to see his children find fulfillment and happiness. The Reillys are a remarkable family. I know them intimately. Jonathan is my grandfather Anthony is my father. One day, I hope to be as hardworking and committed as they are.

THE COMMA

There are four main ways to use a comma, and there are other, less important ways. Memorize the four main ways. If you can learn and understand these four rules, you will be more confident and correct in your punctuation. That is, you will use a comma only when you have a reason to do so; you will not be scattering commas in your sentences simply because you think a comma might fit, as many writers do. The four main ways to use a comma are as a *lister*, a *linker*, an *introducer*, or an *inserter* (two commas).

1. **Comma as a lister**
   Commas separate items in a series. These items can be words, phrases, or clauses.

   commas between words in a list:
   Charles was fascinated by Doreen because she was smart, sassy, and funny.

   commas between phrases in a list:
   I wanted a house on a quiet street, in a friendly neighborhood, and with a school nearby.

   commas between clauses in a list:
   In a single year my uncle joined the army, he fought in the Gulf War, and he was decorated for valor.

Note: In a list, the comma before *and* is optional, but many writers use it.

Exercise 6   **Practice: Using the Comma as a Lister**

Add commas only where they are needed in the following sentences.

1. Living on my own turned out to be stressful scary and difficult, but it was also exciting liberating and fun.

2. After they heard the news, Melanie was upset Robert got angry and Henry felt guilty.

3. By the time I was ten, my family had lived in four cities: Miami Orlando Atlanta and Charlotte.

4. Babysitting a toddler working in a preschool and volunteering at a children's hospital are all good training for becoming a parent.

5. Brian always checked the tires changed the oil washed the windshield and changed the filters on his sister's old car.

6. With very little money, Aunt Eva serves large tasty and nutritious meals to her family of six.

7. When my grandmother was young, the only good jobs available to most women were secretary nurse and teacher.

8. Get me some shampoo toothpaste deodorant and cough drops when you go to the drug store.

9. Billy could be at his father's house at the movies or at the gym.

10. Thinking planning and revising are all part of the writing process.

2. **Comma as a linker**
   A comma and a coordinating conjunction link two independent clauses. The coordinating conjunctions are *for, and, nor, but, or, yet, so*. The comma goes before the coordinating conjunction.

comma before coordinating conjunctions:

Norbert was thrilled by the A in Organic Chemistry, for he had studied really hard all semester.

You can pick up the pizza, and I'll set the table.

Our house had no basement, nor did it have much of an attic.

The movie was long, but it was action-packed.

Diane will fly home for summer vacation, or her parents will visit her.

Mr. Weinstein has lived in the neighborhood for a year, yet no one knows him very well.

The front door was open, so I went right in.

> **Note:** Before you use a comma, be careful that the coordinating conjunction is linking two independent clauses.

no comma: Veronica wrote poetry and painted beautiful portraits.

use a comma: Veronica wrote poetry, and she painted beautiful portraits.

Exercise 7 **Practice: Using the Comma as a Linker**

Add commas only where they are needed in the following sentences.

1. I really need a haircut but I can't afford one right now.

2. Thomas rarely says much yet he always seems quite intelligent.

3. The new neighbors painted the exterior of their house and they planted some bushes in the front yard.

4. Some of my friends from work get together on Fridays and have dinner at a Caribbean restaurant.

5. My dentist rarely hurts me nor does he give me any anesthetic.

6. Sam is shy so he sometimes appears arrogant or aloof.

7. Many people have dealt with addiction in their own families or have seen friends cope with substance abuse.

8. We have to call an electrician for we need to check the wiring in the basement.

9. Callie checked her email several times last night but didn't find any messages from Mercedes.

10. The kitten loves people and it is already litter-trained.

3. **Comma as an introducer**
    Put a comma after introductory words, phrases, or clauses in a sentence.

    comma after an introductory word:
    No, I can't afford that car.

    comma after an introductory phrase:
    In my opinion, that car is a lemon.

    comma after an introductory clause:
    When the baby smiles, I am the happiest father on earth.

Exercise 8 **Practice: Using the Comma as an Introducer**

Add the necessary commas to the following sentences.

1. With no apology the stranger cut ahead of me in the ticket line.

2. Before you go to bed lock the doors.

3. Fortunately I have never had to borrow money from my family.

4. On the first day of spring Amanda married her childhood sweetheart.

5. Laughing with pleasure Mitchell recognized some old friends at the surprise party in his honor.

6. On a cold winter day I want to stay in my warm bed forever.

7. When my instructor asks me a question I hesitate before answering him.

8. If someone at the college is advertising for a roommate I might call the number on the advertisement.

9. As soon as I drank some water I stopped coughing and choking.

10. Sure you can borrow my notes from psychology class.

4. **Comma as an inserter**

   When words or phrases that are not necessary are inserted into a sentence, put a comma on *both* sides of the inserted material.

   commas around inserted material:
   Her science project, a masterpiece of research, won first prize.
   Selena's problem, I believe, is her fear of failure.
   Julio, stuck by the side of the road, waited for the tow truck.
   Artichokes, a delicious vegetable, are not always available at the local market.

Using commas as inserters requires that you decide what is *essential* to the meaning of the sentence and what is *nonessential.*

> **If you do not need material in a sentence, put commas around the material.**
>
> **If you need material in a sentence, do not put commas around the material.**

For example, consider this sentence:

   The woman who was promoted to captain was Jack's wife.

Do you need the words *who was promoted to captain* to understand the meaning of the sentence? To answer this question, write the sentence without the words:

   The woman was Jack's wife.

Reading the shorter sentence, you might ask, "What woman?" The words *who was promoted to captain* are essential to the sentence. Therefore, you do not put commas around them.

   correct: The woman who was promoted to captain was Jack's wife.

Remember that the proper name of a person, place, or thing is always sufficient to identify it. Therefore, any information that follows a proper name is inserted material; it is not essential and gets commas on both sides.

> **proper names and inserted material:**
> Gloria Chen, who lives in my apartment building, won the raffle at Dominion High School.
> Suarez Electronics, which just opened in the mall, has great deals on color televisions.

Inserted material often begins with one of these **relative pronouns:** *who, which, that.* If you have to choose between *which* and *that, which* usually begins inserted material that is not essential:

> The movie, which was much too long, was a comedy.

That usually begins inserted material that is essential.

> The puppy that I want is a miniature poodle.

Note: Sometimes the material that is needed in a sentence is called *essential* (or *restrictive*), and the material that is not needed is called *nonessential* (or *nonrestrictive*).

Exercise 9 **Practice: Using Commas as Inserters (Two Commas)**

Add commas only where they are needed in the following sentences.

1. The man who identified the suspect was a witness to the crime.

2. One piece of furniture that I would love to own is a huge entertainment unit.

3. Catherine gave me a DVD of <u>The Incredibles</u> one of my favorite movies to cheer me up.

4. Anyone who can speak a second language has an advantage in this job market.

5. Snickers bars which I first tasted as a child remain my favorite candy.

6. My brother's apology which came a year too late did not change my mind about his character.

7. Professor Gilman taking pity on the class postponed the test for a week.

8. The woman it appears is trying to make friends in a new town.

9. Jason McNeill from my old high school has just been elected to the city council.

10. The stuffed teddy bear that Alan gave me is sitting on my bed.

Exercise 10 **Practice: Punctuating with Commas: The Four Main Ways**

Add commas only where they are needed in the following sentences.

1. While Alex played video games Bobby made some popcorn.

2. After we eat dinner we'll have some time to look at the old photograph albums and talk about old times.

3. Karen had candles on her coffee table in the kitchen and near her bathtub.

4. I would love to have a piece of coconut cake but I have to watch my weight.

5. It's my brother's birthday tomorrow so I have to find a funny card for him.

6. Isabel found a denim jacket some leather gloves and a red cap at the thrift shop.

7. Sizzling Seafood which is near my apartment offers weekday specials on shrimp dinners.

8. The speeding car slid across the icy road but managed to stop on the hilltop.

9. Only Gregory with all his charm and sincerity could have talked the officer out of issuing a traffic ticket.

10. Whether you like it or not you have to apologize to your friend.

Exercise 11 Practice: More on Punctuating with Commas: The Four Main Ways

Add commas only where they are needed in the following sentences.

1. Until Neal took me out to dinner I had never tasted sushi.

2. Most of my friends don't like to gossip nor do they enjoy constant complaining.

3. Mom can you lend me ten dollars?

4. Sarah didn't know anyone at the party yet she quickly made friends with two engineering students.

5. Penelope Greenberg who started a chain of clothing stores is going to speak to our Introduction to Business class next week.

6. Nelson will of course want to spend the long weekend with his family.

7. The house that I wanted was a fishing cabin near a beautiful lake.

8. The girl who won the spelling bee will receive a $10,000 college scholarship.

9. My sister spends most of her time putting on her makeup touching up her makeup and removing her makeup.

10. In my mother's big kitchen we have long conversations about everything from family to French toast and we have leisurely meals.

Exercise 12 Collaborate: The Four Main Ways to Use Commas: Create Your Own Examples

Collaborate

Do this exercise with a partner or group. Below are the rules for the four main ways to use commas. For each rule, write two sentences that are examples. The first one is done for you.

Rule 1: Use a comma as a lister.

example 1: _I have old photos stashed in my attic, in my closet, and in the garage._

example 2: <u>The movie was long, dull, and pointless.</u>

_____

Rule 2: Use a comma as a linker.

example 1: _____

_____

example 2: _____

_____

Rule 3: Use a comma as an introducer.

example 1: _____

_____

example 2: _____

_____

Rule 4: Use a comma as an inserter (two commas).

example 1: _____

_____

example 2: _____

_____

Connect

Exercise 13 **Connect: The Four Main Ways to Use Commas**

Add commas where they are needed in the following paragraph. Do not add or change any other punctuation; just add commas.

When I have achieved some goal I have a secret way of celebrating. Believe it or not I reward myself by making brownies. Last week for example I passed a really difficult chemistry test that had kept me awake for many nights. I had reviewed for the test joined a study group and even worked with a tutor but I was still uncertain about the test. As soon as I saw my passing score I rushed out and bought the ingredients for a pan of brownies. I spent some happy moments in my kitchen for I loved mixing the gooey batter licking the bowl watching the brownies bake and frosting the moist squares of chocolate heaven. Naturally I had to taste a large portion of the frosting and the warm brownies while I prepared them. The chemistry test which had caused me so much misery seemed a distant memory once I enjoyed my reward.

Connect

Exercise 14 **Connect: The Four Main Ways to Use a Comma**

Add commas where they are needed in the following paragraph. Do not add or change any other punctuation; just add commas.

Richie Scott my boyfriend was killed last week on a sunny street in our town, and his death was his own fault. Richie was street racing. He and another driver were weaving though rush-hour traffic on a busy avenue bordered by apartments and strip malls. According to eyewitness reports Richie driving at high speed bolted into oncoming traffic and the other racer followed. Richie's Mustang was torn in half; he died at the scene. Three other cars were involved in the crash. The other street racer was taken to the hospital but he is expected to survive his injuries. However, a young mother in an SUV died. Her four-year-old son is in critical condition. In addition, the driver of an old Toyota has several broken bones. Many people are grieving today asking questions and confronting some terrible guilt. I am one of them. To please Richie I used to attend regular street races late at night on lonely stretches of highway. I cheered his victories and found his driving exciting daring and heroic. I never dreamed that his love of speed would lead him to a busy street in rush hour. I never dreamed that his daring would lead to so much death and destruction.

Other Ways to Use a Comma

Besides the four main ways, there are other ways to use a comma. Reviewing these uses will help you feel more confident as a writer.

1. **Use commas with quotations.** Use a comma to set off direct quotations from the rest of the sentence.

    examples:
    Sylvia warned me, "Don't swim there."
    "I can give you a ride," Alan said.

    Note that the comma that introduces the quotation goes before the quotation marks. But once the quotation has begun, commas (or periods) go inside the quotation marks.

2. **Use commas with dates and addresses.** Put commas between the items in dates and addresses.

    examples:
    August 29, 1981, is the day we were married.
    I had an apartment at 2323 Clover Avenue, Houston, Texas, until I was
       transferred to California.

    Notice the comma after the year in the date, and the comma after the state in the address. These commas are needed when you write a date or an address within a sentence.

3. **Use commas in numbers.** Use commas in numbers of one thousand or larger.

examples:
He owed me $1,307.
That wall contains 235,991 bricks.

4. **Use commas for clarity.** Use a comma when you need to make something clear.

examples:
She waltzed in, in a stunning silk gown.
Whatever you did, did the trick.
I don't have to apologize, but I want to, to make things right between us.
Not long after, the party ended.

Exercise 15 **Practice: Other Ways to Use a Comma**

Add commas where they are needed in the following sentences.

1. When Nathan lived in Topeka Kansas he worked at a furniture warehouse.

2. "Money isn't everything" my grandmother used to say.

3. We lived at 307 Orchard Avenue Jackson Mississippi when my father was in the army.

4. A spokesperson from the police department said "We have no suspects at this time."

5. When you meet her her expensive jewelry will be the first thing you notice.

6. In Chicago Illinois you would pay rent of $2500 a month for this apartment.

7. Shortly before a man had been seen entering the building.

8. Priscilla paid $1279 for her living room furniture, but I got similar furniture on sale for $960.

9. "Someone took the last piece of pizza" my roommate complained.

10. Richard encouraged me to visit the flea market but said "If you go go early."

Exercise 16 **Practice: Punctuating with Commas: A Comprehensive Exercise**

Add commas where they are needed in the following sentences.

1. "Don't walk on the wet floor" my mother warned Joel but he paid no attention.

2. Sergei met Gina at a party and was instantly attracted to her.

3. After all we've dealt with plenty of bad luck over the years.

4. Amy who would be sending us a package from 770 Taft Boulevard Tulsa Oklahoma?

5. Todd met Dina's brother he spent time with her best friends he visited her cousins yet he never met her parents.

6. Teenagers who have nothing to do are likely to find dangerous ways to pass the time.

7. My parents got engaged on December 25 1979 but didn't get married until June 15 1981 because they waited until my mother had finished school.

8. Michelle Rodriguez who rides the bus with me always has a joke for me in the morning.

9. No one likes to hurt another person's feelings but you need to to clear up a misunderstanding.

10. The little dog never barked nor did it chew on the furniture.

Exercise 17 **Practice: Punctuating with Commas: Another Comprehensive Exercise**

Add commas where they are needed in the following sentences.

1. Since Ron got his own apartment he's learned to do his own laundry and shop for groceries.

2. Once Tamika got her phone bill she swore "I will never again stay on the phone for more than ten minutes."

3. Jon and Barbara spent $2700 on their trip to Cancun for they wanted a vacation that would remain in their minds forever.

4. Whenever I get tired of studying I think of the opportunities an education will bring and I feel better.

5. After Andrew tasted my homemade barbecue sauce he wanted the recipe.

6. The person who taught me how to swim is my uncle.

7. Sammy likes training to be a chef although he has a hard time dealing with the steaming kitchens the long hours and the hectic pace that are part of the job.

8. The Coffee Corner which is open all night is a favorite with college students who want to study with friends.

9. People are attracted to you Josh by your sense of fun.

10. Red white and blue streamers flew from the fence posts and the street lamps.

Exercise 18 **Collaborate: Punctuating with Commas**

Collaborate

Working alone, write a paragraph that is at least six sentences long. The paragraph should require at least five commas, but leave the commas out. Then give your paragraph to a partner; let your partner add the necessary commas. Meanwhile, you punctuate your partner's paragraph. When you are both finished, check each other's answers.

Write your paragraph in the lines below, using the sentence given to you as the topic sentence.

Of all the places I remember from my childhood, one place stands out.

_____

_____

_____

_____

_____

_____

_____

_____

_____

Connect

Exercise 19 **Connect: Punctuating with Commas: A Comprehensive Exercise**

Add commas where they are needed in the following paragraph. Do not add or change any other punctuation; just add commas.

Everyone seems to be short on cash these days and many people are looking for ways to save a few dollars. My cousin Sam, for instance, found a way to save money while he also made some money. Sam is a coffee lover and his weakness is a fancy coffee drink made with cream, foam, special flavors, and a price tag of five dollars. Because his daily trip to a coffee shop was cutting into his budget Sam reluctantly decided to sacrifice his high-priced coffee. After three bad days without his latte, Sam searched for another solution. He applied for and was offered a part-time job at a coffee shop that serves his favorite beverage. Although Sam already had one part-time job he decided the offer was extremely inviting. His decision was based on some new information about the coffee shop. Employees at the place he learned, are permitted free coffee during their working hours. If Sam works at the shop for two years and drinks one latte each day of his three-day work week, he will save $1560 in coffee expenses. Best of all, Sam says "Not many jobs pay a salary and give free drinks, too!"

THE APOSTROPHE

Use the apostrophe in the following ways:

1. Use an apostrophe in contractions to show that letters have been omitted.

    examples:

do not	=	don't
she will	=	she'll
he would	=	he'd
is not	=	isn't
will not	=	won't

    Use an apostrophe to show that numbers have been omitted, too.

    the winter of 1999 = the winter of '99,

    > **Note:** Your instructor may want you to avoid contractions in formal assignments. Be sure to follow his or her instructions.

2. Use an apostrophe to show possession. If a word does not end in *s*, show ownership by adding an apostrophe and *s*.

    examples:

the car belongs to Maria	=	Maria's car
the toy is owned by my cousin	=	my cousin's toy
the hat belongs to somebody	=	somebody's hat

    If two people own something, put the *'s* on the last person's name.

    Jack and Joe own a dog = Jack and Joe's dog

    If a word already ends in *s* and you want to show ownership, just add an apostrophe.

    examples:

The doll belongs to Dolores	=	Dolores' doll
two girls own a cat	=	the girls' cat
Mr. Ross owns a house	=	Mr. Ross' house

3. Use an apostrophe for special uses of time and to create a plural of numbers mentioned as numbers, letters mentioned as letters, and words that normally do not have plurals.

    special use of time: It took a *month's* work.
    numbers mentioned as numbers: Add the *7's*.
    letters mentioned as letters: Dot your *i's*.
    words that normally do not have plurals: Give me some more *thank you's*.

    > **Caution:** Be careful with apostrophes. Possessive pronouns like *his*, *hers*, *theirs*, *ours*, *yours*, and *its* do not take apostrophes.

    not this: I was sure the dress was ~~her's~~.
    but this: I was sure the dress was hers.

    not this: The movie has ~~it's~~ flaws.
    but this: The movie has its flaws.

Do not add an apostrophe to a simple plural.

not this: The pudding comes in three ~~flavor's~~.
but this: The pudding comes in three flavors.

Exercise 20 **Practice: Punctuating with Apostrophes**

Add apostrophes where they are needed in the following sentences.

1. One mans lifelong dream of helping others came true when a mens counseling center opened at the hospital.

2. Wed never interfere in other peoples private quarrels.

3. Its silly to buy an expensive hair product just because its advertising is glamorous.

4. The winter of 98 was so cold that my parents thought about moving to Nevada.

5. Frances little boy has trouble writing his *p*s.

6. My sisters knew that theyd have a long ride ahead of them before they got to Manny and Franks house.

7. You shouldnt have asked Jessica about her job; thats a subject she doesnt want to discuss.

8. Theres a pile of books on the table; you can take the ones that are yours.

9. Mrs. Rivera is planning for her grandchildrens education; she is saving money in a special bank account.

10. You never listen to anybodys advice, and I think youd better start paying attention to your friends.

Exercise 21 **Practice: More on Punctuating with Apostrophes**

Add apostrophes where they are needed in the following sentences.

1. On Saturday, Jareds taking me to see the monkeys at the Animal Sanctuary for Apes in Trentwood.

2. You still print your *t*s instead of writing them, but that habit doesnt make your writing difficult to read.

3. Ernie and Annabella both drive 2007 Mustangs, but his is a sportier model than hers.

4. Molly is taking care of Luke and Lucys cat over the weekend.

5. Im going to need everybodys help clearing out the weeds behind the house and planting flowers.

6. Patrick apologizes so often that his *sorry*s are starting to sound insincere.

7. Texas huge expanses of open land and its cowboys impressed the visitors from Japan.

8. If Desmond comes with us on our trip to Memphis, hell pay for our gas, but he wont let us take his car.

9. Jane and Catalina have years of experience in carpentry; theyll help you build a simple bookcase.

10. Tyler spent a months salary on a diamond ring for Julie, so it's unfortunate that Julie doesnt care for the rings style.

Exercise 22   **Connect: Punctuating with Apostrophes**

Connect

Edit the following paragraph, correcting the errors related to apostrophes. You need to add some apostrophes and eliminate the unnecessary apostrophes.

In a time when everybodys complaining about doctors, I was lucky enough to find a great doctor. Since I am rarely sick, I didnt know any doctor's to call when I got a bad case of bronchitis. I asked all my friends about their doctors, but all I heard were horror stories about long hours spent in the waiting room, days spent trying to get an appointment, and one or two minutes spent with a hurried and distracted doctor. Feeling worse, I turned to my mother. "Go to Dr. Morano," she said. "Dr. Moranos wonderful." Within ten minutes, I had reached the doctors office and made an appointment for the next day. The voice on the phone was warm and kind. Still, I was prepared for an hours wait in a room packed with unhappy patients. Thats not what I got. My time in the waiting room was about thirty minutes, for I had to fill out a form for new patient's. Then I prepared myself to sit alone in an examining room while the doctor tended to two or three other patients stacked up in other rooms. Dr. Morano appeared within ten minutes, and she actually sat down to talk. Id never met a doctor like Dr. Morano, and she left only after she had explored my medical history, checked me carefully, and prescribed some medication for my cough. I realized that its possible to find a kind and human atmosphere inside a doctor's office.

Exercise 23   **Connect: Punctuating with Apostrophes**

Connect

Punctuate the following paragraph, correcting the errors related to apostrophes. You need to add some apostrophes and eliminate the unnecessary apostrophes.

When I was a child, my grandparents had some old sayings that were a mystery to me. For instance, when a stressful incident occurred, my grandfather would say,

"Well, its all in a days work." Year's later, I began to understand that the saying was his way of accepting the stress and moving past it. My grandmother had several sayings about food. One that I have never been able to understand is "You cant make an omelet without breaking a few eggs." It seems obvious to me that egg's get broken when someone makes an omelet, but I don't see how the saying applies to work, or sports, or love, or anything else. Another egg saying became easier for me to comprehend as I grew up. I learned that "Don't put all your eggs in one basket" was a warning about counting too much on one solution to a problem or investing too much of one's resources in one area such as a quest for fame. The strangest effect of my grandparents proverbs is the way they linger in my brain. Even today, when I am twenty-five year's old, I become startled when a saying such as "The early bird catches the worm" pop's into my head. At that moment, I am back in my childhood again, safe in my grandmother and grandfathers wise and loving company.

THE COLON

A colon is used at the end of a complete statement. It introduces a list or explanation.

> **colon introducing a list:**
> When my father went to the Bahamas, he brought me back some lovely gifts: a straw bag, a shell necklace, and some Bahamian perfume.

> **colon introducing an explanation:**
> The salesperson was very helpful: he told us about special discounted items and the free gift-wrap service.

Remember that the colon comes after a complete statement. What comes after the colon explains or describes what came before the colon. Look once more at the two examples, and you'll see the point.

> When my father went to the Bahamas, he brought me back some lovely gifts: a straw bag, a shell necklace, and some Bahamian perfume. (The words after the colon, *a straw bag*, a *shell necklace*, *and some Bahamian perfume*, describe the lovely gifts.)

> The salesperson was very helpful: he told us about special discounted items and the free gift-wrap service. (The words after the colon, *he told us about special discounted items and the free gift-wrap service*, explain what the salesperson did to be helpful.)

Some people use a colon every time they put a list in a sentence, but this is not a good rule to follow. Instead, remember that a colon, even one that introduces a list, must come after a complete statement.

not this: ~~If you are going to the drug store, remember to pick up:~~
~~toothpaste, dental floss, and mouthwash.~~

but this: If you are going to the drug store, remember to pick up
these items: toothpaste, dental floss, and mouthwash.

A colon may also introduce a long quotation.

colon introducing a long quotation:
In a speech to the alumni at Columbia University, Will Rogers joked
about what a big university it was and said: "There are 3,200
courses. You spend your first two years in deciding what course to
take, the next two years in finding the building that these courses
are given in, and the rest of your life in wishing you had taken
another course."

Exercise 24 **Practice: Punctuating with Colons**

Add colons where they are needed in the following sentences.

1. After my first day of class at the college, I felt bewildered by the
crowds of students, the fast pace of the instructors' lectures, and
the long lines at the bookstore.

2. After my first day of class at the college, I felt bewildered by three
experiences the crowds of students, the fast pace of the instructors'
lectures, and the long lines at the bookstore.

3. My niece's bed is piled with bears teddy bears, bears dressed
in bride and groom outfits, bears in football jerseys, and even
talking bears.

4. To be sure I had enough clothes for the weekend at the Water
Adventure amusement park, I packed everything sweaters,
swimsuits, jeans, fancy dresses, t-shirts, sweatshirts, sneakers,
and high heels.

5. When my mother told my brother to clean out his closet, he stuffed
shoes, socks, empty soda cans, ancient bags of cookies, old magazines, and a broken light bulb under his bed.

6. With a big grin on his face, my boyfriend said he had won fifty dollars in a radio contest.

7. My supervisor's desk was always immaculate all the paper
stacked neatly, the pencils placed in a china mug, the computer
lined up with the mouse pad, and one personal photograph framed
in shiny metal.

8. Since Wednesday is a long day for me at the college, I always bring
snacks an apple, a candy bar, and a large bottle of water.

9. If you have more party guests than you expected, you can
always send Phil out to get tortilla chips, salsa, crackers, and
cheese.

10. The student who spoke at the student government meeting seemed
nervous he kept looking at the floor and forgetting what he wanted
to say.

Connect

Exercise 25   Connect: Punctuating with Colons

Edit the following paragraph, correcting the errors related to colons. You need to add some colons and eliminate any unnecessary colons.

Buying furniture can be tricky because so-called bargains can turn out to be deceptive. The other day I saw a newspaper advertisement for a bedroom set that looked like a good deal. It offered a five-piece set for a sale price of $900. The photograph showed an attractive group of furniture a large, queen-sized bed, two nightstands, a large dresser with a mirror, and a tall bureau. Because I desperately needed some new bedroom furniture, I visited the furniture showroom during the sale. The bedroom set was quite impressive the bed was large and sturdy, the dresser and bureau seemed solid, and the nightstands were a good size. I quickly found a salesperson and told him that I wanted to get: the bed, two nightstands, the bureau, and the dresser for the sale price. I was shocked by his reply: the sale price applied to five pieces of furniture, but the pieces were not the ones I had expected. I had failed to read the small print in the advertisement. It said that the five pieces were: the bed, the bed rails, the headboard, the dresser, and its mirror. The other pieces, the bureau and the nightstands, were sold separately and cost between $250 and $400 apiece. Feeling tricked and disappointed, I went home to my decrepit bedroom furniture.

THE EXCLAMATION MARK

The exclamation mark is used at the ends of sentences that express strong emotion.

appropriate:	Mr. Zimmerman, you've just become the father of triplets!
inappropriate:	The dance was fabulous! (*Fabulous* already implies excitement and enthusiasm, so you don't need the exclamation mark.)

Be careful not to overuse the exclamation mark. If your choice of words is descriptive, you should not have to rely on the exclamation mark for emphasis. Use it sparingly, for it is easy to rely on exclamation marks instead of using better vocabulary.

THE DASH

Use a dash to interrupt a sentence; use two dashes to set off words in a sentence. The dash is somewhat dramatic, so be careful not to overuse it.

examples:
Helena's frustration at her job made her an angry woman—a mean, angry woman.
My cousins Celia and Rick—the silly fools—fell off the dock when they were clowning around.

PARENTHESES

Use parentheses to set off words in a sentence.

examples:
The movies he rented (<u>Kung Fu Panda</u>, <u>Blades of Glory</u>, and <u>The Happening</u>) were all too silly for me.

Note: In student essays, movie titles are underlined.

Simon nominated Justin Lewis (his best friend) as club treasurer.

Note: Commas in pairs, dashes in pairs, and parentheses are all used as inserters. They set off inserted material that interrupts the flow of the sentence. The least dramatic and smoothest way to insert material is to use commas.

THE HYPHEN

A hyphen joins two or more descriptive words that act as a single word.

examples:
Mr. Handlesman was wearing a custom-made suit.
My great aunt's hair is a salt-and-pepper color.

Exercise 26 **Practice: Punctuating with Exclamation Marks, Dashes, Parentheses, and Hyphens**

In the following sentences, add exclamation marks, dashes, parentheses, or hyphens where they are needed. Answers may vary because some writers may use dashes instead of parentheses.

1. Artie used to be a good ballplayer one of the best at our college.

2. My old car once known as the Broken Beast has been running fairly well recently.

3. My parents encouraged me to spend the summer at a workshop for student leaders; they called it a once in a lifetime opportunity.

4. Rebecca Richman my former best friend is spreading a nasty rumor about me.

5. The Kennerly Lodge a first rate hotel is hiring extra staff for the summer season.

6. I've just seen a ghost

7. If you are self conscious, you may have a hard time speaking in public.

8. Patrice Green who was once a homeless mother of two has just completed her second year of work as a paralegal at a large law firm.

9. There's an alligator in your swimming pool

10. Eric put on some old clothes a ratty looking sweater and filthy jeans to clean the trash out of the cellar.

Connect

Exercise 27   **Connect: Punctutating with Exclamation Marks, Dashes, Parentheses, and Hyphens**

Edit the following paragraph, correcting the errors related to exclamation marks, dashes, parentheses, and hyphens. You can add, change, or eliminate punctuation. Answers may vary because dashes in pairs and parentheses are both used as inserters. Also, try to use only one exclamation mark in your edited version of the paragraph.

My visit to a fancy and expensive restaurant was not at all what I had expected. A new friend wanted to impress me and took me to Palm Breeze the most popular restaurant in town last Saturday night. We sat in a courtyard decorated with an elegant, bubbling fountain and lush foliage. Bright tropical flowers peeked from behind green palm fronds! The sights and sounds were enticing, but some unpleasant surprises followed! First, my friend ordered oysters for us both. I love seafood and expected a tasty dish of baked, broiled, or steamed shellfish. I recoiled in horror when I realized that the oysters were raw a gooey mess of gray, jelly like tissue. The main course was somewhat better, but the portions were tiny. Because Palm Breeze charges so much, I expected it to serve generous helpings that would cover the plate. Instead, my plate contained a tiny portion of roast pork, thin slivers of red, yellow, and green peppers, and a small spoonful of rice. Unfortunately, my biggest surprise was yet to come. For dessert, I ordered a Palm Breeze specialty a tropical fruit salad filled with guava, pineapple, mangoes, and berries. This dessert called Passion at Sunset was famous for the delicious orange sauce covering the fruit. However, one other item was also covered by that sauce. It was a large, green, scaly lizard. That lizard was a little more of the tropics than I wanted. Clearly, my first visit to Palm Breeze will also be my last.

QUOTATION MARKS

Use quotation marks for direct quotes, for the titles of short works, and for other, special uses.

1. Put quotation marks around direct quotations (a speaker or writer's exact words).

   quotation marks around direct quotations:
   Ernest always told me, "It is better to give than to receive."
   "Nobody goes to that club," said Ramon.
   "We could go to the movies," Christina offered, "but we'd better hurry."
   My mother warned me, "Save your money. You'll need it for a rainy day."

Look carefully at the preceding examples. Note that a comma is used to introduce a direct quotation, and that, at the end of the quotation, a comma or a period goes inside the quotation marks.

   Ernest always told me, "It is better to give than to receive."

Notice how direct quotations of more than one sentence are punctuated. If the quotation is written as one unit, quotation marks go before the first quoted word and after the last quoted word:

   My mother warned me, "Save your money. You'll need it for a rainy day."

But if the quote is not written as one unit, the punctuation changes:

   "Save your money," my mother warned me. "You'll need it for
      a rainy day."

> **Caution:** Do *not* put punctuation marks around indirect quotations.

   indirect quotation: Tyree asked if the water was cold.
   direct quotation: Tyree asked, "Is the water cold?"

   indirect quotation: She said that she needed a break from work.
   direct quotation: She said, "I need a break from work."

2. Put quotation marks around the titles of short works. If you are writing the title of a short work like a short story, an essay, a newspaper or magazine article, a poem, or a song, put quotation marks around the title.

   quotation marks around the titles of short works:
   My father's favorite poem is "The Raven" by Edgar Allan Poe.
   When I was little, I used to sing "Twinkle, Twinkle, Little Star."
   I couldn't think of a good title, so I just called my essay "How I Spent
      My Summer Vacation."

If you are writing the title of a longer work like a book, movie, magazine, play, television show, or music album, underline the title.

   underlining the titles of longer works:
   My favorite childhood movie was <u>Star Wars.</u>
   For homework, I have to read an article called "Children and Reading
      Skills" in <u>Education Today</u> magazine.

In printed publications such as books or magazines, titles of long works are put in italics. But when you are writing by hand, or typing, underline the titles of long works.

3. There are other, special uses of quotation marks. You use quotation marks around special words in a sentence.

quotation marks around special words:
When you say "sometimes," how often do you mean?
People from Boston say "frappe" when they mean "milkshake."

If you are using a quotation within a quotation, use single quotation marks.

a quotation within a quotation:
Janey said angrily, "You took my car without permission, and all you can say is, 'It's no big deal.' "
Aunt Mary said, "You need to teach that child to say 'please' and 'thank you' more often."

Exercise 28 **Practice: Punctuating with Quotation Marks**

Add quotation marks where they are needed in the following sentences.

1. There are so many meanings to the word love that it is hard to define.

2. Rena told her boyfriend, Unless you are willing to say I was wrong, we have no future together.

3. A British child may call his or her mother Mummy, but an American child is likely to say Mommy.

4. I have got to save some money, my sister said. I will have to cut back on expensive haircuts and manicures.

5. I have got to save some money. I will have to cut back on expensive haircuts and manicures, said my sister.

6. We were all shocked when Tara said she was quitting her job and moving out of the state.

7. The Wind beneath my Wings is a popular song at weddings and at banquets that honor a special person.

8. Did you remember to turn off the stove? Mrs. Bethel asked her husband as they left for work.

9. Yesterday, Linda called to ask if I knew anyone who wanted to work as a babysitter.

10. I can tell that you're not eating right, my Aunt Rita scolded, because you look like skin and bones.

Exercise 29 **Practice: More on Punctuating with Quotation Marks**

Add quotation marks where they are needed in the following sentences.

1. Sonya isn't sure whether she has to work late next weekend.

2. I've had enough of your nagging, she said. I'm not going to listen to it any longer, she added.

3. Stephanie once said, I wish my father had been able to say I love you to me at least once.

4. Groovy used to be a popular slang term in the 1960s; in fact, there was even a hit song called Feelin' Groovy about feeling happy.

5. My girlfriend sometimes says she loves a particular gift from me when I know she is just trying not to hurt my feelings.

6. Good idea, my roommate said when I asked him if he wanted to order a pizza.

7. I'm hungry, my five-year-old nephew complained. When can we get out of the car and get something to eat?

8. Sandra questioned why so many turning points in her life seemed to be the result of pure luck.

9. After I become a ballerina, my six-year-old daughter declared, I'm going to be a superhero.

10. The Legend of Sleepy Hollow is an old story about one man's encounter with a ghost called The Headless Horseman.

CAPITAL LETTERS

There are ten main situations when you capitalize.

1. Capitalize the first word of every sentence.

   examples:
   Sometimes we take a walk on the beach.
   An apple is a healthy snack.

2. Capitalize the first word in a direct quotation if the word begins a sentence.

   examples:
   Jensina said, "Here is the money I owe you and a little something extra."
   "Here is the money I owe you," Jensina said, "and a little something extra." (Notice that the second section of this quotation does not begin with a capital letter because it does not begin a sentence.)

3. Capitalize the names of people.

   examples:
   Ingrid Alvorsen and Sean Miller invited me to their wedding.
   I asked Father to visit me.

Do not capitalize words like *mother, father,* or *aunt* if you put a possessive in front of them.

   names with possessives:
   I asked my father to visit me.
   She disliked her aunt.

4. Capitalize the titles of people.

   examples:
   I worked for Dr. Mabala.
   She is interviewing Captain Richards.

Do not capitalize when the title is not connected to a name.

   a title not connected to a name:
   I worked for that doctor.
   She is interviewing the captain of the submarine.

5. Always capitalize nationalities, religions, races, months, days of the week, documents, organizations, holidays, and historical events or periods.

examples:
In eighth grade, I did a project on the American Revolution.
At my son's nursery school, the students presented a program to celebrate Thanksgiving.
Every Tuesday night, he goes to meetings at the African Heritage Club.

Use small letters for the seasons.

a season with a small letter:
I always look forward to the coming of winter.

6. Capitalize the names of particular places.

examples:
I used to attend Hawthorne Middle School.
My friends like to stroll through City Center Mall.

Use small letters if a particular place is not given.

small letter for no particular place:
My friends like to stroll through the mall.

7. Use capital letters for geographic locations.

examples:
Lisa wanted to attend a college in the South.
I love autumn in the Midwest.

But use small letters for geographic directions.

small letter for a geographic direction:
The easiest way to find the airport is to drive south on the freeway.

8. Capitalize the names of specific products.

examples:
I need some Tylenol for my headache.
Melanie eats a Snickers bar every day.

But use small letters for a general type of product.

small letter for a general product:
Melanie eats a candy bar every day.

9. Capitalize the names of specific school courses.

examples:
My favorite class is Ancient and Medieval History.
Alicia is taking Introduction to Computers this fall.

But use small letters for a general academic subject.

small letter for a general subject:
Before I graduate, I have to take a computer course.

10. Capitalize the first and last words in the titles of long or short works, and capitalize all other significant words in the title.

examples:
I loved the movie <u>Fifty First Dates.</u>
There is a beautiful song called "You Are the Sunshine of My Life."

> **Note:** Remember that, in writing or typing, the titles of long works, like movies, are underlined; the titles of short works, like songs, are placed in quotation marks.

Exercise 30   **Practice: Punctuating with Capital Letters**

Add capital letters where they are needed in the following sentences.

1. My cousin is a captain in the police department of a large city in the west.

2. I have recently become aunt Hannah to my sister's newborn baby, but I am not really sure what an aunt does.

3. In our introduction to american government class, we studied the parts of the constitution of the united states of america.

4. I have a bad cold, so I can't go anywhere without a box of kleenex and some cough drops.

5. The new professor who teaches education courses is not as friendly as professor Schaeffer.

6. On memorial day my family is going to a ceremony that will commemorate the American soldiers who died in the Vietnam war.

7. "you would make me very happy," my girlfriend said, "if you would wash my car."

8. The caribbean art center, north of Miami, is exhibiting a fine collection of haitian art.

9. Amanda got a job working at the john parker auditorium near chestnut street.

10. The manager at the service station is making me work on thanksgiving.

Exercise 31   **Collaborate: Punctuating with Capital Letters: Creating Your Own Examples**

Collaborate

Do this exercise with a partner or group. Below is a list giving situations when you should—or should not—use capital letters. Write a sentence at least five words long as an example for each item on the list.

1. Capitalize the names of particular places.

   example: _____

   _____

2. Use capital letters for geographic locations.

   example: _____

   _____

3. Use small letters for geographic directions.

   example: _____

   _____

4. Capitalize historic events or periods.

   example: _____

   _____

5. Capitalize nationalities.

   example: _____

   _____

6. Capitalize the names of persons.

   example: _____

   _____

7. Do not capitalize words like *mother*, *father*, or *uncle* if you put a possessive in front of them.

   example: _____

   _____

8. Capitalize the titles of persons.

   example: _____

   _____

9. Don't capitalize when the title is not connected to a name.

   example: _____

   _____

10. Capitalize the names of specific products.

    example: _____

    _____

Connect

Exercise 32 **Connect: Punctuating with Quotation Marks, Underlining, and Capital Letters**

Following is a paragraph with some blank spaces. Fill in the blanks, remembering the rules for using quotation marks, underlining, and capital letters. When you have completed the exercise, be ready to share your responses with members of the class.

When I think about last year, I remember some very specific details. I remember that one song I was always listening to was called _____ _____ , and the singer I admired most was _____ . The one movie I remember best is _____ , and a television show I recall watching is _____ . There are also several places I associate with last year. Among them is a store called _____ _____ , the school nearest to my home, called _____ , and a place I always wanted to go to, but never visited, called _____ . When I think of last year, I realize that I spent many hours eating or socializing at a fast-food restaurant named _____ . My favorite cold drink was _____ . Today, I realize that some of my habits and tastes have changed, yet I am still very much connected to the places and things of the past.

Exercise 33 **Connect: Punctuating with Quotation Marks, Underlining, and Capital Letters**

Connect

Edit the following paragraph, correcting the errors related to quotation marks, underlining, and capital letters. You need to add some quotation marks, underlining, and capital letters, and to eliminate the unnecessary or incorrect quotation marks, underlining, and capital letters.

I have recently become interested in ghosts. My interest began when I was flipping through the television channels and then stopped at a grainy black-and-white image of two men in a shadowy room. The men were walking quietly and carefully, and one held a light. The other had a camera. The scene was silent. When the image was replaced by a commercial break, I discovered the show I had been watching was "Ghost Hunters," and this episode was about ghosts in new england. After watching one or two more episodes of this show, I learned that the hunters were believers in ghosts or scientists trying to investigate the reality of ghosts. I have also learned some new vocabulary. The hunters focus on what they call sightings of spirits, or incidents of paranormal activity. Nobody on the show ever seems to wonder "if ghosts are real." I have an open mind on the subject but have become more curious. Recently, I went to my town's Library and asked a librarian "if she would help me search for books and articles about ghosts." I was surprised to find several books about hauntings in my area: "The Spirits Of Western Ghost Towns," "Mountain Mysteries," and "The haunted Mines of Colorado." In fact, I even discovered an article called <u>Paranormal Denver,</u> about the ghosts in my hometown. So far, my ghost-hunting has been limited to the library, and unless there is a spirit hiding among the bookshelves, I will never see a ghost.

NUMBERS

Spell out numbers that take one or two words to spell out.

> **examples:**
> The coat cost seventy dollars.
> Bridget sent two hundred invitations.

Use hyphens to spell out compound numbers from twenty-one to ninety-nine.

> **examples:**
> Clarissa, twenty-three, is the oldest daughter.
> I mailed sixty-two invitations.

Use numerals if it takes more than two words to spell out a number.

> **examples:**
> The company sold 367 toy trains.
> The price of the car was $15,629.

Also use numerals to write dates, times, and addresses.

> **examples:**
> You can visit him at 223 Sailboat Lane.
> I received my diploma on June 17, 2004.
> We woke up at 6:00 A.M., bright and early.

Use numbers with A.M. and P.M., but use words with *o'clock*.

> **example:**
> We woke up at six o'clock, bright and early.

ABBREVIATIONS

Although you should spell out most words rather than abbreviate them, you may use common abbreviations like *Mr.*, *Mrs.*, *Ms.*, *Jr.*, *Sr.*, and *Dr.* when they are used with a proper name. Abbreviations may also be used for references to time and for organizations widely known by initials.

> **examples:**
> I gave Dr. Lambert my medical records.
> The phone rang at 3:00 A.M. and scared me out of a sound sleep.
> Nancy got a job with the FBI.

Spell out the names of places, months, days of the week, courses of study, and words referring to parts of a book.

not this: I visited a friend in Philadelphia, ~~Penn~~.
but this: I visited a friend in Philadelphia, Pennsylvania.

not this: My brother skipped his ~~phys. ed.~~ class yesterday.
but this: My brother skipped his physical education class
    yesterday.

not this: Last week, our garbage was not picked up on ~~Weds.~~ or ~~Sat.,~~
    so I called the Dept. of Sanitation.
but this: Last week, our garbage was not picked up on Wednesday or
    Saturday, so I called the Department of Sanitation.

Exercise 34   **Practice: Punctuating with Numbers and Abbreviations**

Correct the errors in punctuating with numbers and abbreviations in the
following sentences.

1. Pres. Thurman closed Salton U. yesterday after heavy rains flooded

    parts of the campus.

2. I couldn't sleep last night, so I watched a movie about the CIA until

    one twenty-five A.M.

3. My sister got a scholarship to Penn. State U., and she leaves for her

    first semester on Weds.

4. You can find 5 or 6 topics for your psych. paper if you look on p. 323

    of the text.

5. I spent ninety five dollars on a blood test, but the doc. couldn't find

    anything wrong with me.

6. The last chapt. of our Intro. to Business textbook has a helpful sec-

    tion on writing a resume.

7. January 15, 2005, is the day I moved into Carlton Apts. in New Bed-

    ford, Mass.

8. Thomas started volunteering at the Red Cross during his sr. year in

    high school.

9. My father used to dream about becoming a scientist and working in

    one of the labs at NASA.

10. My neighbors had to wait 15 minutes for somebody from the police

    dept. to arrive.

Exercise 35 **Practice: Punctuation: A Comprehensive Exercise**

In the following sentences, add punctuation where it is needed and correct any punctuation errors.

1. After I pay off my college loans Sam said I can start saving for a house.

2. Macaroni and cheese which is my childrens favorite food is an easy meal to make when youre in a hurry.

3. Helena doesnt like to fly instead she drives long distances to see her son and daughter in law.

4. Lester had a hard time dealing with his puppies energy so he enrolled them in an obedience class for young dogs.

5. Prof. Marcus asked Does anyone want to do some work for extra credit

6. Prof. Marcus asked if anyone wanted to do some work for extra credit

7. After she moved to Los Angeles Sally considered a career in three fields computers health and education.

8. My boyfriend knows all about Jefferson community hospital because he spent two months there last Feb.

9. My father wants me to read a book called The purpose-driven life he loved it and wants to pass it on.

10. Boris used to call me from work then his supervisor warned him about making too many personal calls.

Exercise 36 **Practice: Punctuation: Another Comprehensive Exercise**

In the following sentences, add punctuation where it is needed and correct any punctuation errors.

1. Until Mitchell gets rid of that broken down truck I wont go anywhere with him.

2. My toddler dragged me out of bed at 7 A.M. consequently I got an early start on my chores on Sat. morning.

3. If you see Chelsea tell her to return my black dress gold sandals and hoop earrings before the weekend.

4. This summer, I found a box full of my grandparents old photographs their wedding pictures baby pictures and birthday celebrations.

5. No I don't have a boyfriend Mom but I don't want to meet Mrs. Youngs lovely nephew from Texas.

6. A movie that my two little boys love is The Wizard of Oz

7. I was born on Sept. 29 1985 in Boulder, Col. but spent most of my childhood with my grandmother in the east.

8. A few years ago aunt Marlene's favorite song was I hope you Dance.

9. After I saw dozens of cockroaches in my kitchen I spent one hundred and thirty-three dollars for pest control.

10. You like an active social life and Rick likes to stay home but both of you will be satisfied if you learn to compromise.

Exercise 37   **Connect: Editing a Paragraph for Errors in Punctuation**   Connect

Edit the following paragraph for errors in punctuation. You may have to add, omit, or change punctuation.

I am a receptionist in the office of a large Physical Therapy Center. My job has brought me many new friends; and each one has a special quality. Among these friends are Lynne Povitch, the manager of the center, Andrew Falzone, an experienced therapist specializing in back injuries, Kristin Wing, a therapist specializing in hand and wrist therapy, Alicia nardello, a therapy student training at the center, and Arthur Connolly, the office custodian. I know when Lynn Povitch has arrived at the office because she always sings the same song: You Had A Bad Day. Although her choice of song is a bit negative, Lynne sings it in a cheery voice. Andrew Falzone arrives each day in worn jeans and a hawaiian shirt; however, he carries a top of the line leather briefcase. He is a serious person dedicated to his work but he has a new joke for me every day. Kristin Wing loves to bake, and brings homemade cookies, muffins, or Banana bread to the office every Friday. Alicia Nardello, the trainee therapist spends most of her day assisting the other therapists. She runs from one piece of equipment to another. Sometimes she distributes fresh, hot towels or lotion at other times, she finds files or charts. Alicia is a tiny woman who scurries like a mouse and always smiles. Everyones favorite staff member is Arthur Connolly. he is respected because he can repair anything without losing his cheerful, calm personality. However, he is loved for his generosity. He has time to listen to every member of the office. I have confided in him many times. Arthur never proposes a solution to my problems but his willingness to listen to my stories allows me to think through my worries and find my own way to deal with them. When I think about the kindness, humor, and spirit of my office friends, I know that I am lucky to work in an environment, with so many special people.

CHAPTER 7

Quick Question

Does the following sentence contain a spelling error? Yes/No

Abandoning his lovely wife and adorable children was a shameful act on Tim's part, and everyone is hopeing that community support will help the family to survive.

(After you study this chapter, you will be confident of your answer.)

Chapter Objectives

Students will be able to (1) identify vowels and consonants, (2) apply basic spelling rules to determine proper word endings and variations, and (3) recognize when a one- or two-word spelling applies to certain terms.

No one is a perfect speller, but there are ways to become a better speller. If you can learn a few spelling rules, you can answer many of your spelling questions.

VOWELS AND CONSONANTS

To understand the spelling rules, you need to know the difference between vowels and consonants. **Vowels** are the letters *a, e, i, o, u,* and sometimes *y*. **Consonants** are all the other letters.

The letter *y* is a vowel when it has a vowel sound.

examples:
silly (The *y* sounds like *ee*, a vowel sound.)
cry (The *y* sounds like *i*, a vowel sound.)

The letter *y* is a consonant when it has a consonant sound.

examples:

yellow (The *y* has a consonant sound.)

yesterday (The *y* has a consonant sound.)

SPELLING RULE 1: DOUBLING A FINAL CONSONANT

Double the final consonant of a word if all three of the following are true:

1. The word is one syllable, or the accent is on the last syllable.
2. The word ends in a single consonant preceded by a single vowel.
3. The ending you are adding starts with a vowel.

examples:

begin	+	ing	=	beginning
shop	+	er	=	shopper
stir	+	ed	=	stirred
occur	+	ed	=	occurred
fat	+	est	=	fattest
pin	+	ing	=	pinning

Exercise 1 **Practice: Doubling a Final Consonant**

Add *-ed* to the following words by applying the rules for double consonants.

1. pad _____
2. scatter _____
3. scan _____
4. track _____
5. offer _____
6. defer _____
7. strand _____
8. wander _____
9. cover _____
10. repel _____

SPELLING RULE 2: DROPPING THE FINAL *E*

Drop the final *e* before you add an ending that starts with a vowel.

examples:

observe	+	ing	=	observing
excite	+	able	=	excitable
fame	+	ous	=	famous
create	+	ive	=	creative

Keep the final *e* before an ending that starts with a consonant.

examples:

love	+	ly	=	lovely
hope	+	ful	=	hopeful
excite	+	ment	=	excitement
life	+	less	=	lifeless

Exercise 2   Practice: Dropping the Final *e*

Combine the following words and endings by following the rule for dropping the final *e*.

1. adore   + able   _____
2. home   + less   _____
3. active   + ly   _____
4. name   + ing   _____
5. adore   + ing   _____
6. encourage + ment   _____
7. promote   + ion   _____
8. expense   + ive   _____
9. genuine   + ness   _____
10. inflate   + able   _____

SPELLING RULE 3: CHANGING THE FINAL *Y* TO *I*

When a word ends in a consonant plus *y*, change the *y* to *i* when you add an ending.

examples:

try   + es   = tries
silly + er   = sillier
rely   + ance = reliance
tardy + ness = tardiness

Note: When you add -*ing* to words ending in *y*, always keep the *y*.

examples:

cry   + ing = crying
rely + ing = relying

Exercise 3   Practice: Changing the Final *y* to *i*

Combine the following words and endings by applying the rule for changing the final *y* to *i*.

1. sloppy + er   _____
2. hardy   + ness _____
3. cry   + er   _____
4. pity   + less _____
5. try   + ing   _____
6. marry   + ed   _____
7. apply   + ance _____
8. plenty + ful   _____

9. apply   +   es   _____

10. convey   +   ed   _____

SPELLING RULE 4: ADDING -*S* OR -*ES*

Add -*es* instead of -*s* to a word if the word ends in *ch*, *sh*, *ss*, *x*, or *z*. The -*es* adds an extra syllable to the word.

examples:

box	+	es	=	boxes
witch	+	es	=	witches
class	+	es	=	classes
clash	+	es	=	clashes

Exercise 4   **Practice: Adding -*s* or -*es***

Add -*s* or -*es* to the following words by applying the rule for adding -*s* or -*es*.

1. astonish _____   6. fetch _____

2. perch _____   7. wonder _____

3. glass _____   8. block _____

4. bunch _____   9. fizz _____

5. fix _____   10. splash _____

SPELLING RULE 5: USING *IE* OR *EI*

Use *i* before *e* except after *c*, or when the sound is like *a*, as in *neighbor* and *weigh*.

examples of *i* before *e*:

relief   field   friend   piece

examples of *e* before *i*:

conceive   sleigh   weight   receive

Exercise 5   **Practice: Using *ie* or *ei***

Add *ie* or *ei* to the following words by applying the rules for using *ie* or *ei*.

1. bel _ _ ve   6. misch _ _ f

2. dec _ _ t   7. r _ _ ns

3. cr _ _ d   8. gr _ _ f

4. th _ _ f   9. perc _ _ ve

5. _ _ ght   10. n _ _ ce

Exercise 6   **Practice: Spelling Rules: A Comprehensive Exercise**

Combine the following words and endings by applying the spelling rules.

1. coax   +   s *or* es   _____
2. toy   +   s *or* es   _____
3. deny   +   s *or* es   _____
4. bounty   +   ful   _____
5. conserve +   ing   _____
6. shape   +   less   _____
7. force   +   ful   _____
8. force   +   ing   _____
9. confer   +   ed   _____
10. plan   +   er   _____

Exercise 7   **Practice: Spelling Rules: Another Comprehensive Exercise**

Combine the following words and endings by applying the spelling rules.

1. ready   +   ness   _____
2. commit   +   ment   _____
3. commit   +   ed   _____
4. forget   +   ing   _____
5. hatch   +   s *or* es   _____
6. harass   +   s *or* es   _____
7. filthy   +   er   _____
8. sleigh   +   s *or* es   _____
9. carry   +   ed   _____
10. rumor   +   ed   _____

Exercise 8   **Collaborate: Creating Examples for the Spelling Rules**

Collaborate

Working with a partner or group, write examples for the following rules.

Spelling Rule 1: Doubling the Final Consonant
Double the final consonant of a word if all three of the following are true:

1. The word is one syllable, or the accent is on the last syllable.
2. The word ends in a single consonant preceded by a single vowel.
3. The ending you added starts with a vowel.

example:

1. Write a word that is one syllable (or the accent is on the last syllable),
    and that ends in a consonant preceded by a single vowel: _____
2. Write an ending that starts with a vowel: _____
3. Combine the word and the ending: _____

Spelling Rule 2: Dropping the Final *e*

Drop the final *e* before you add an ending that starts with a vowel.

example:

1. Write a word that ends with an *e:* _____
2. Write an ending that starts with a vowel: _____
3. Combine the word and the ending: _____

Spelling Rule 3: Changing the Final *y* to *i*

When a word ends in a consonant plus *y*, change the *y* to *i* when you add an ending. (Note: When you add *-ing* to words ending in *y*, always keep the *y*.)

example:

1. Write a word that ends in a consonant plus *y:* _____
2. Write an ending (not an *-ing* ending): _____
3. Combine the word and the ending: _____

Spelling Rule 4: Adding *-s* or *-es*

Add *-es* instead of *-s* to a word if the word ends in *ch*, *sh*, *ss*, *x*, or *z*. The *-es* adds an extra syllable to the word.

example:

1. Write a word that ends in *ch*, *sh*, *ss*, *x*, or *z:* _____
2. Add *-es* to the word: _____

Spelling Rule 5: Using *ie* or *ei*

Use *i* before *e*, except after *c*, or when the sound is like *a*, as in *neighbor* and *weigh*.

example:

1. Write three words that use *i* before *e:* _____ , ____ , ____
2. Write one word that uses *ei:* _____

Connect

Exercise 9   **Connect: Editing a Paragraph for Spelling Errors**

Correct the ten spelling errors in the following paragraph. Write your corrections above each error.

Last night, when my neice Ella asked me to help her with her homework,

I suddenly realized how bad my spelling truly is. Here I was, triing hard to help a

nine-year-old child with an essay she had written about a beautyful day at the beach.

While I know something about beachs, I don't know much about puting a paper

together. In fact, I think my writing is hopless, and I will not be surprised if someday

soon Ella catchs me in a mistake or two, especially in spelling. I am almost ready

to spend some time learning to be a better speller. Not only would Ella respect me

more, but I also beleive that all my written work—business letters, job applications, reports, and forms—would be more convinceing if I could remove the sloppyness of bad spelling. In addition, learning to spell could be my first step to better writing.

| Exercise 10 | Connect: Editing a Paragraph for Spelling Errors |

Correct the eight spelling errors in the following paragraph. Write your corrections above each error.

Connect

I have had few experiences worse than the sudden suspicion of a problem with my car. The worrys may begin when I sense a slight hesitation as I begin a turn. At that moment, I fear that the car will stall and I will be hit by the car behind me. After I feel this hesitation once, I wait for it anxiously each time I turn. Another occurence that sends me into a panic is a strange sound that suddenly joins the usual car noises. The sound can be a clicking, wheezing, grinding, or spining noise. At first, I am likely to pretend that the noise was a one-time event, such as a pebble hiting the underside of the car or a sound completely unrelated to the car, such as the sound of a large truck comeing to a stop. Eventually, I percieve the reality of the situation and admit that the noise is now constant. It makes no difference what event causes me to expect a car problem, for each incident has that same effect on me. Any slight change in my car's behavior brings me the kind of excitment I don't need in my life.

HOW DO YOU SPELL IT? ONE WORD OR TWO?

Sometimes you can be confused about certain words. You are not sure whether to combine them to make one word or to spell them as two words. The lists below show some commonly confused words.

Words That Should Not Be Combined

a lot	even though	high school
all right	every time	good night
dining room	home run	living room
each other	in front	no one

Words That Should Be Combined

another	grandmother	southeast, northwest, etc.
bathroom	nearby	throughout
bedroom	nevertheless	worthwhile
bookkeeper	newspapers	yourself, myself, himself, etc.
cannot	playroom	
downstairs	roommate	
good-bye, goodbye, or good-by	schoolteacher	

Words Whose Spelling Depends on Their Meaning

one word: *Already* means "before."
He offered to do the dishes, but I had *already* done them.
two words: *All ready* means "ready."
My dog was *all ready* to play Frisbee.

one word: *Altogether* means "entirely."
That movie was *altogether* too confusing.
two words: *All together* means "in a group."
My sisters were *all together* in the kitchen.

one word: *Always* means "every time."
My grandfather is *always* right about baseball statistics.
two words: *All ways* means "every path" or "every aspect."
We tried *all ways* to get to the beach house.
He is a gentleman in *all ways*.

one word: *Anymore* means "any longer."
I do not want to exercise *anymore*.
two words: *Any more* means "additional."
Are there *any more* pickles?

one word: *Anyone* means "any person at all."
Is *anyone* home?
two words: *Any one* means "one person or thing in a special group."
I'll take *any one* of the chairs on sale.
He offered *any one* of the students a ride home.

one word: *Apart* means "separate."
Liam stood *apart* from his friends.
two words: *A part* is a piece or section.
I read *a part* of the chapter.

one word: *Everyday* means "ordinary."
Tim was wearing his *everyday* clothes.
two words: *Every day* means "each day."
Sam jogs *every day*.

one word: *Everyone* means "all the people."
Everyone has bad days.
two words: *Every one* means "all the people or things in a specific group."
My father asked *every one* of the neighbors for a donation to the Red Cross.

one word: *Maybe* means "perhaps."
Maybe you can go to a college near your home.
two words: *May be* means "might be."
Sam *may be* the right person for the job.

one word: *Thank-you* is an adjective that describes a certain kind of note or letter.
Heather wrote her grandfather a *thank-you* note.
two words: We state our gratitude by saying, "*Thank you.*"
"*Thank you* for lending me your car," Kyle said.

Exercise 11 **Practice: How Do You Spell It? One Word or Two?**

Underline the correct word in the following sentences.

1. It was an (everyday / every day) kind of luncheon; (nevertheless / never the less), I was glad to have been invited.

2. Steve saw (apart / a part) of the movie, but he left after ten minutes because the story didn't seem (worthwhile / worth while).

3. In my mother's apartment, the (livingroom / living room) is large and comfortable, but the (bedroom / bed room) is tiny and cramped.

4. I (cannot / can not) figure out how (everyone / every one) of my shirts got stained with blue ink.

5. My best friend lives (nearby / near by), and we see each other (a lot / alot).

6. My son was (already / all ready) to spend more time in the (play-room / play room) at the local mall.

7. Years after he graduated from college, Alonzo sent a (thank-you / thank you) letter to the (schoolteacher / school teacher) who had helped him learn to read.

8. You (always / all ways) nag me about putting gas in the car, (even-though / even though) you know I have never let the gauge get to "Empty."

9. I waited for a phone call (throughout / through out) the day, but (no one / noone) called with the results of my blood test.

10. Often my local (newspaper / news paper) is full of depressing stories of crime, natural disasters, and war, but yesterday the paper reported an (altogether / all together) inspiring story about a lost boy rescued by a search party of volunteers.

Exercise 12 **Connect: How Do You Spell It? One Word or Two?**

Connect

The following paragraph contains ten errors in word combinations. Correct the errors in the space above each line.

I have always been interested in numbers, and math has been my favorite sub-

ject for years, so a career in accounting has been my goal. My mother, who had only

a highschool education, has worked as a book keeper for many years. However, I

have a higher goal for my self and want to be an accountant. I have all ready applied

to several colleges near by and I hope that I will be accepted into one with a good

accounting program. Eventhough I would like to experience college life on my own,

I can not afford the cost of my own apartment, even if I shared with a room mate.

Living in a dormitory would also be expensive. As a person who likes to account for

every penny, I am all ways looking for the most economical way to reach my goal,

even if it means sleeping in my old bed room at home for a few more years.

A LIST OF COMMONLY MISSPELLED WORDS

Below is a list of words you use often in your writing. Study this list and use it as a reference.

1. absence
2. absent
3. accept
4. ache
5. achieve
6. acquire
7. across
8. actually
9. advertise
10. again
11. a lot
12. all right
13. almost
14. always
15. amateur
16. American
17. answer
18. anxious
19. apology
20. apparent
21. appetite
22. appreciate
23. argue
24. argument
25. asked
26. athlete
27. attempt
28. August
29. aunt
30. author
31. automobile
32. autumn
33. avenue
34. awful
35. awkward
36. balance
37. basically
38. because
39. becoming
40. beginning
41. behavior
42. belief
43. believe
44. benefit
45. bicycle
46. bought
47. breakfast
48. breathe

49. brilliant
50. brother
51. brought
52. bruise
53. build
54. bulletin
55. bureau
56. buried
57. business
58. busy
59. calendar
60. cannot
61. career
62. careful
63. catch
64. category
65. caught
66. cemetery
67. cereal
68. certain
69. chair
70. cheat
71. chicken
72. chief
73. children
74. cigarette
75. citizen
76. city
77. college
78. color
79. comfortable
80. committee
81. competition
82. conscience
83. convenient
84. conversation
85. copy
86. cough
87. cousin
88. criticism
89. criticize
90. crowded
91. daily
92. daughter
93. deceive
94. decide
95. definite
96. dentist

97. dependent
98. deposit
99. describe
100. desperate
101. development
102. different
103. dilemma
104. dining
105. direction
106. disappearance
107. disappoint
108. discipline
109. disease
110. divide
111. doctor
112. doesn't
113. don't
114. doubt
115. during
116. dying
117. early
118. earth
119. eighth
120. eligible
121. embarrass
122. encouragement
123. enough
124. environment
125. especially
126. etc.
127. every
128. exact
129. exaggeration
130. excellent
131. except
132. exercise
133. excite
134. existence
135. expect
136. experience
137. explanation
138. factory
139. familiar
140. family
141. fascinating
142. February
143. finally
144. forehead

145. foreign
146. forty
147. fourteen
148. friend
149. fundamental
150. general
151. generally
152. goes
153. going
154. government
155. grammar
156. grateful
157. grocery
158. guarantee
159. guard
160. guess
161. guidance
162. guide
163. half
164. handkerchief
165. happiness
166. heavy
167. height
168. heroes
169. holiday
170. hospital
171. humorous
172. identity
173. illegal
174. imaginary
175. immediately
176. important
177. independent
178. integration
179. intelligent
180. interest
181. interfere
182. interpretation
183. interrupt
184. iron
185. irrelevant
186. irritable
187. island
188. January
189. jewelry
190. judgment
191. kindergarten
192. kitchen
193. knowledge
194. laboratory
195. language

196. laugh
197. leisure
198. length
199. library
200. listen
201. loneliness
202. lying
203. maintain
204. maintenance
205. marriage
206. mathematics
207. meant
208. measure
209. medicine
210. million
211. miniature
212. minute
213. muscle
214. mysterious
215. naturally
216. necessary
217. neighbor
218. nervous
219. nickel
220. niece
221. ninety
222. ninth
223. occasion
224. o'clock
225. often
226. omission
227. once
228. operate
229. opinion
230. optimist
231. original
232. parallel
233. particular
234. peculiar
235. perform
236. perhaps
237. permanent
238. persevere
239. personnel
240. persuade
241. physically
242. pleasant
243. possess
244. possible
245. potato
246. practical

247. prefer
248. prejudice
249. prescription
250. presence
251. president
252. privilege
253. probably
254. professor
255. psychology
256. punctuation
257. pursue
258. quart
259. really
260. receipt
261. receive
262. recognize
263. recommend
264. reference
265. religious
266. reluctantly
267. remember
268. resource
269. restaurant
270. rhythm
271. ridiculous
272. right
273. sandwich
274. Saturday
275. scene
276. schedule
277. scissors
278. secretary
279. seize
280. several
281. severely
282. significant
283. similar
284. since
285. sincerely
286. soldier
287. sophomore
288. strength
289. studying
290. success
291. surely
292. surprise
293. taught
294. temperature
295. theater
296. thorough
297. thousand

continued

298. tied	**305.** unfortunately	**312.** Wednesday
299. tomorrow	**306.** unknown	**313.** weird
300. tongue	**307.** until	**314.** which
301. tragedy	**308.** unusual	**315.** writing
302. trouble	**309.** using	**316.** written
303. truly	**310.** variety	**317.** yesterday
304. twelfth	**311.** vegetable	

Connect

Exercise 13 **Connect: A Comprehensive Exercise on Spelling**

The following exercise contains ten spelling errors, including errors related to the spelling rules, one- or two-word errors, and errors related to commonly misspelled words. Correct the errors in the space above each line.

My brother is the only member of our family who reads for pleasure. I can

read, but I am more intrested in math than in English. I don't read books or maga-

zines for enjoyment. In addition, I never read the news paper becose I use the

Internet if I need to find information. My sister is not much of a reader, either.

She wants to be a graphic designer and spends more time looking at cartoons,

games, and videos than enjoying books. However, Adam, my older brother, reads

all the time. In fact, he will read anything, including the cerial box as he eats

breakfast. He is the happyest when he comes home from the library with an arm-

ful of books. On many weekends, I have seen him sit on his bed for hours, piles of

books stackked around him. Adam's favorite books are about the unknown or the

imaginery. He dreams of becomming an author who specializes in tales of fantasy

and the supernatural. If reading is good training for that type of writeing, then

Adam should be a tremendous sucess.

Words That Sound Alike/ Look Alike

Quick Question

Which sentence(s) is/ are correct?

A. I have looked all over town, and I can't find a decent apartment.

B. A series of small thefts began Leo's descent into criminal activity.

(After you study this chapter, you will be confident of your answer.)

Chapter Objectives

Students will be able to distinguish between common sound-alike and look-alike words and incorporate such distinctions in their writing.

WORDS THAT SOUND ALIKE/LOOK ALIKE

Words that sound alike or look alike can be confusing. Here is a list of some of the confusing words. Study this list, and make a note of any words that give you trouble.

a, an, and

A is used before a word beginning with a consonant or consonant sound.

> Jason bought *a* car.

An is used before a word beginning with a vowel or vowel sound.

> Nancy took *an* apple to work.

And joins words or ideas.

> Pudding *and* cake are my favorite desserts.
> Fresh vegetables taste delicious, *and* they are nutritious.

accept, except

Accept means "to receive."

> I *accept* your apology.

Except means "excluding."

> I'll give you all my books *except* my dictionary.

addition, edition

An *addition* is something that is added.

> My father built an *addition* to our house in the form of a porch.

An *edition* is an issue of a newspaper or one of a series of printings of a book.

> I checked the latest *edition* of the <u>Daily News</u> to see if my advertisement is in it.

advice, advise

Advice is an opinion offered as a guide; it is what you give someone.

> Betty asked for my *advice* about finding a job.

Advise is what you do when you give an opinion offered as a guide.

> I couldn't *advise* Betty about finding a job.

affect, effect

Affect means "to influence something."

> Getting a bad grade will *affect* my chances for a scholarship.

Effect means "a result" or "to cause something to happen."

> Your kindness had a great *effect* on me.
> The committee struggled to *effect* a compromise.

allowed, aloud

Allowed means "permitted."

> I'm not *allowed* to skateboard on those steps.

Aloud means "out loud."

> The teacher read the story *aloud*.

all ready, already

All ready means "ready."

> The dog was *all ready* to go for a walk.

Already means "before."

> David had *already* made the salad.

altar, alter

An *altar* is a table or place in a church.

> They were married in front of the *altar*.

Alter means "to change."

> My plane was delayed, so I had to *alter* my plans for the evening.

angel, angle

An *angel* is a heavenly being.

> That night, I felt an *angel* guiding me.

An *angle* is the shape formed by two intersecting lines.

> The road turned at a sharp *angle*.

are, our

Are is a verb, the plural of *is*.

> We *are* friends of the mayor.

Our means "belonging to us."

> We have *our* family quarrels.

beside, besides

Beside means "next to."

> He sat *beside* me at the concert.

Besides means "in addition."

> I would never lie to you; *besides*, I have no reason to lie.

brake, break

Brake means "to stop" or "a device for stopping."

> That truck *brakes* at railroad crossings.

> When he saw the animal on the road, he hit the *brakes*.

Break means "to come apart or "to make something come apart."

> The eggs are likely to *break*.

> I can *break* the seal on that package.

breath, breathe

Breath is the air you take in, and it rhymes with "death."

> I was running so fast that I lost my *breath*.

Breathe means "to take in air."

> He found it hard to *breathe* in high altitudes.

buy, by

Buy means "to purchase something."

> Sylvia wants to *buy* a shovel.

By means "near," "by means of," or "before."

> He sat *by* his sister.

> I learn *by* taking good notes in class.

> *By* ten o'clock, Nick was tired.

capital, capitol

Capital means "a city" or "wealth."

> Albany is the *capital* of New York.

> Jack invested his *capital* in real estate.

A *capitol* is a building.

> The city has a famous *capitol* building.

cereal, serial

Cereal is a breakfast food or type of grain.

> My favorite *cereal* is Cheerios.

Serial means "in a series."

> Look for the *serial* number on the appliance.

choose, chose

Choose means "to select." It rhymes with "snooze."

> Today I am going to *choose* a new sofa.

Chose is the past tense of *choose*.

> Yesterday I *chose* a new rug.

close, clothes, cloths

Close means "near" or "intimate." It can also mean "to end or shut something" when the *s* is pronounced as a *z*.

> We live *close* to the train station.

> James and Margie are *close* friends.

> Noreen wants to *close* her eyes for ten minutes.

Clothes are wearing apparel.

> Eduardo has new *clothes*.

Cloths are pieces of fabric.

> I clean the silver with damp *cloths* and a special polish.

coarse, course

Coarse means "rough" or "crude."

> The top of the table had a *coarse* texture.

> His language was *coarse*.

A *course* is a direction or path. It is also a subject in school.

> The hurricane took a northern *course*.

> In my freshman year, I took a *course* in drama.

complement, compliment

Complement means "complete" or "make better."

> The colors in that room *complement* the style of the furniture.

A *compliment* is praise.

> Trevor gave me a *compliment* about my cooking.

conscience, conscious

Your *conscience* is your inner, moral guide.

> His *conscience* bothered him when he told a lie.

Conscious means "aware" or "awake."

> The accident victim was not fully *conscious*.

council, counsel

A *council* is a group of people.

> The city *council* meets tonight.

Counsel means "advice" or "to give advice."

> I need your *counsel* about my investments.

> My father always *counsels* me about my career.

decent, descent

Decent means "suitable" or "proper."

> I hope Mike gets a *decent* job.

Descent means "the process of going down, falling, or sinking."

> The plane began its *descent* to the airport.

desert, dessert

A *desert* is a dry land. To *desert* means "to abandon."

> To survive a trip across the *desert*, people need water.

> He will never *desert* a friend.

Dessert is the sweet food we eat at the end of a meal.

> I want ice cream for *dessert*.

do, due

Do means "perform."

> I have to stop complaining; I *do* it constantly.

Due means "owing" or "because of."

> The rent is *due* tomorrow.

> The game was canceled *due* to rain.

does, dose

Does is a form of *do*.

> My father *does* the laundry.

A *dose* is a quantity of medicine.

> Whenever I had a cold, my mother gave me a *dose* of cough syrup.

fair, fare

Fair means "unbiased." It can also mean "promising" or "good."

> The judge's decision was *fair*.

> José has a *fair* chance of winning the title.

A *fare* is a fee for transportation.

My subway *fare* is going up.

farther, further

Farther means "at a greater physical distance."

His house is a few blocks *farther* down the street.

Further means greater or additional. Use it when you are not describing a physical distance.

My second French class gave me *further* training in French conversation.

flour, flower

Flour is ground-up grain, an ingredient used in cooking.

I use whole-wheat *flour* in my muffins.

A *flower* is a blossom.

She wore a *flower* in her hair.

forth, fourth

Forth means "forward."

The pendulum on the clock swung back and *forth*.

Fourth means "number four in a sequence."

I was *fourth* in line for the tickets.

hear, here

Hear means "to receive sounds in the ear."

I can *hear* the music.

Here is a place.

We can have the meeting *here*.

heard, herd

Heard is the past tense of *hear*.

I *heard* you talk in your sleep last night.

A *herd* is a group of animals.

The farmer has a fine *herd* of cows.

hole, whole

A *hole* is an empty place or opening.

I see a *hole* in the wall.

Whole means "complete" or "entire."

Silvio gave me the *whole* steak.

isle, aisle

An *isle* is an island.

We visited the *isle* of Capri.

An *aisle* is a passageway between sections of seats.

The flight attendant came down the *aisle* and offered us coffee.

its, it's

Its means "belonging to it."

The car lost *its* rear bumper.

It's is a shortened form of *it is* or *it has*.

It's a beautiful day.

It's been a pleasure to meet you.

knew, new

Knew is the past tense of *know*.

I *knew* Teresa in high school.

New means "fresh, recent, not old."

I want some *new* shoes.

know, no

Know means "to understand."

> They *know* how to play soccer.

No is a negative.

> Carla has *no* fear of heights.

Exercise 1 **Practice: Words That Sound Alike/Look Alike**

Circle the correct word in the following sentences.

1. When I first saw the (desert / dessert) in a Tucson sunset, the sight was so beautiful that I had to catch my (breath / breathe).

2. Ron and Sandy were (conscience / conscious) of the fact that they would need more (capital / capitol) to start their own business.

3. Marcy hoped that (buy / by) working extra hours, she would save enough money to (buy / by) her brother a special wedding present.

4. After graduation, the students felt that they could go (forth / fourth) into the world and face (knew / new) challenges.

5. I (heard / herd) that (hole / whole)-grain bread is better for people than white bread.

6. I hate to read (allowed / aloud); (beside / besides), I have a cold today, and my voice is weak.

7. Lee Anne had (all ready / already) eaten all the leftover macaroni and cheese by the time I got home; the only thing left in the cabinet was a box of (cereal / serial).

8. Martin (choose / chose) to make his (decent / descent) into a world of violence and despair instead of fighting for a better life.

9. The design of the building is all sharp (angles / angels); the (affect / effect) is cold and intimidating.

10. Let's stop this arguing; we (are / our) wasting (are / our) time over silly disagreements.

Collaborate

Exercise 2 **Collaborate: Words That Sound Alike/Look Alike**

With a partner or a group, write one sentence for each of the words below. When you have completed this exercise, exchange it with another group's completed exercise for evaluation.

1. a. its _____

   b. it's _____

2. a. addition _____

   b. edition _____

3. a. accept _____

   b. except _____

4. a. brake _____

   b. break _____

5. a. close _____

   b. clothes _____

   c. cloths _____

6. a. farther _____

   b. further _____

7. a. hear _____

   b. here _____

8. a. isle _____

   b. aisle _____

9. a. fair _____

   b. fare _____

10. a. its _____

    b. it's _____

Exercise 3 | **Connect: Correcting Errors in Words That Sound Alike/Look Alike**

Connect

The following paragraph has ten errors in words that sound alike or look alike. Correct the errors in the space above each error.

If someone asked me to chose a perfect day, I would not altar one moment of yesterday. Twenty-four hours ago, my brother returned from months of military duty in Iraq. Once I had been informed of his return, I spent the final days of his overseas service holding my breathe. I was conscience of the many stories of soldiers being wounded or killed days before their tours of duty were over. Every time I herd a knock at the door, I feared bad news. Yet the day came when Carleton was supposed to arrive, and my sisters and I were already to meet are hero at the airport. Seeing Carleton was better than I had expected. He looked strong, healthy, and happy. Being able to hug him was pure joy. I felt as if a whole in my heart had been filled with happiness. Fear had lost it's power over me, and I new real peace at last.

Exercise 4 | **Connect: Correcting Errors in Words That Sound Alike/Look Alike**

Connect

The following paragraph has eight errors in words that sound alike or look alike. Correct the errors in the space above each error.

Traveling by plane lost its appeal for me after a terrible experience last week. I and the two hundred other passengers on my flight boarded the aircraft on time. The weather seemed fine, but none of us new that we would be stuck on the ground for hours because of terrible storms at are destination. After we had been sitting on the runway with the engines running for about fifty minutes, the plane suddenly turned back to the terminal. Soon the pilot announced that we would be remaining at the airport until the blizzard-like weather cleared in Chicago, our destination. I could here the entire cabin begin to groan and moan. People realized that we could expect a long delay before we took off for Chicago. However, no one expected to spend seven hours on the grounded aircraft. We never returned to an airport building but sat in our seats. During that time, the air in the plane became stifling hot, it was difficult to breath, and the flight attendants ran out of snacks and beverages. In edition, the toilets overflowed. Most of the passengers complained and begged to be returned to the airline terminal. Although babies cried and older people felt weak, the airline choose to keep the passengers on the aircraft. Most of the passengers found it difficult to except this decision. They felt that the airline had desserted them. After two or three hours of thirst, hunger, and toxic air, I came to a bitter decision. I swore to limit my future flying to absolute necessities.

MORE WORDS THAT SOUND ALIKE/LOOK ALIKE

lead, led
When *lead* rhymes with *need*, it means "to give direction, to take charge."
When *lead* rhymes with *bed*, it is a metal.
> The marching band will *lead* the parade.
> Your bookbag is as heavy as *lead*.
Led is the past form of *lead* when it means "to take charge."
> The cheerleaders *led* the parade last year.

loan, lone
A *loan* is something you give on the condition that it be returned.
> When I was broke, I got a *loan* of fifty dollars from my aunt.
Lone means "solitary, alone."
> A *lone* shopper stood in the checkout line.

loose, lose
Loose means "not tight."
> In the summer, *loose* clothing keeps me cool.
To *lose* something means "to be unable to keep it."
> I'm afraid I will *lose* my car keys.

moral, morale

Moral means "upright, honorable, connected to ethical standards."

I have a *moral* obligation to care for my children.

Morale is confidence or spirit.

After the game, the team's *morale* was low.

pain, pane

Pain means "suffering."

I had very little *pain* after the surgery.

A *pane* is a piece of glass.

The girl's wild throw broke a window *pane*.

pair, pear

A *pair* is a set of two.

Mark has a *pair* of antique swords.

A *pear* is a fruit.

In the autumn, I like a *pear* for a snack.

passed, past

Passed means "went by." It can also mean "handed to."

The happy days *passed* too quickly.

Janice *passed* me the mustard.

Past means "a time before the present." It can also mean "beyond" or "by."

The family reunion was like a trip to the *past*.

Rick ran *past* the tennis courts.

patience, patients

Patience is calm endurance.

When I am caught in a traffic jam, I should have more *patience*.

Patients are people under medical care.

There are too many *patients* in the doctor's waiting room.

peace, piece

Peace is calmness.

Looking at the ocean brings me a sense of *peace*.

A *piece* is a part of something.

Norman took a *piece* of coconut cake.

personal, personnel

Personal means "connected to a person." It can also mean "intimate."

Whether to lease or own a car is a *personal* choice.

That information is too *personal* to share.

Personnel are the staff in an office.

The Digby Electronics Company is developing a new health plan for its *personnel*.

plain, plane

Plain means "simple," "clear," or "ordinary." It can also mean "flat land."

The restaurant serves *plain* but tasty food.

Her house was in the center of a windy *plain*.

A *plane* is an aircraft.

We took a small *plane* to the island.

presence, presents

Your *presence* is your attendance, your being somewhere.

We request your *presence* at our wedding.

Presents are gifts.

My daughter got too many birthday *presents*.

principal, principle

Principal means "most important." It also means "the head of a school."

My *principal* reason for quitting is the low salary.

The *principal* of Crestview Elementary School is popular with students.

A *principle* is a guiding rule.

Betraying a friend is against my *principles*.

quiet, quit, quite

Quiet means "without noise."

The library has many *quiet* corners.

Quit means "stop."

Will you *quit* complaining?

Quite means "truly" or "exactly."

Victor's speech was *quite* convincing.

rain, reign, rein

Rain is wet weather.

We have had a week of *rain*.

To *reign* is to rule; *reign* is royal rule.

King Arthur's *reign* in Camelot is the subject of many poems.

A *rein* is a leather strap in an animal's harness.

When Charlie got on the horse, he held the *reins* very tight.

right, rite, write

Right is a direction (the opposite of left). It can also mean "correct."

To get to the gas station, turn *right* at the corner.

On my sociology test, I got nineteen out of twenty questions *right*.

A *rite* is a ceremony.

I am interested in the funeral *rites* of other cultures.

To *write* is to set down words.

Brian has to *write* a book report.

sight, site, cite

A *sight* is something you can see.

The truck stop was a welcome *sight*.

A *site* is a location.

The city is building a courthouse on the *site* of my old school.

Cite means to quote an authority. It can also mean to give an example.

In her term paper, Christina wanted to *cite* several computer experts.

When my father lectured me on speeding, he *cited* the story of my best friend's car accident.

sole, soul

A *sole* is the bottom of a foot or shoe. *Sole* can also mean "only."

My left boot needs a new *sole*.

Lisa was the *sole* winner of the raffle.

A *soul* is the spiritual part of a person.

Some people say meditation is good for the *soul*.

stair, stare

A *stair* is a step.

The toddler carefully climbed each *stair*.

A *stare* is a long, fixed look.

I wish that woman wouldn't *stare* at me.

stake, steak

A *stake* is a stick driven into the ground. It can also mean "at risk" or "in question."

> The gardener put *stakes* around the tomato plants.

> Keith was nervous because his career was at *stake*.

A *steak* is a piece of meat or fish.

> I like my *steak* cooked medium rare.

stationary, stationery

Stationary means "standing still."

> As the speaker presented his speech, he remained *stationary*.

Stationery is writing paper.

> For my birthday, my uncle gave me some *stationery* with my name
>   printed on it.

than, then

Than is used to compare things.

> My dog is more intelligent *than* many people.

Then means "at that time."

> I lived in Buffalo for two years; *then* I moved to Albany.

their, there, they're

Their means "belonging to them."

> My grandparents donated *their* old television to a women's shelter.

There means "at that place." It can also be used as an introductory word.

> Sit *there*, next to Simone.

> *There* is a reason for his happiness.

They're is a short form of *they are*.

> Jaime and Sandra are visiting; *they're* my cousins.

thorough, through, threw

Thorough means "complete."

> I did a *thorough* cleaning of my closet.

Through means "from one side to the other." It can also mean "finished."

> We drove *through* Greenview on our way to Lake Western.

> I'm *through* with my studies.

Threw is the past form of *throw*.

> I *threw* the moldy bread into the garbage.

to, too, two

To means "in a direction toward." It is also a word that can go in front of a verb.

> I am driving *to* Miami.

> Selena loves *to* write poems.

Too means "also." It also means "very."

> Anita played great golf; Adam did well, *too*.

> It is *too* kind of you to visit.

Two is the number.

> Mr. Almeida owns *two* clothing stores.

vain, vane, vein

Vain means "conceited." It also means "unsuccessful."

> Victor is *vain* about his dark, curly hair.

> The doctor made a *vain* attempt to revive the patient.

A *vane* is a device that moves to indicate the direction of the wind.

> There was an old weather *vane* on the barn roof.

A *vein* is a blood vessel.

> I could see the *veins* in his hands.

waist, waste

The *waist* is the middle part of the body.

> He had a leather belt around his *waist*.

Waste means "to use carelessly." It also means "thrown away because it is useless."

> I can't *waste* my time watching trashy television shows.
>
> That manufacturing plant has many *waste* products.

wait, weight

Wait means "to hold oneself ready for something."

> I can't *wait* until my check arrives.

Weight means "heaviness."

> He tested the *weight* of the bat.

weather, whether

Weather refers to the conditions outside.

> If the *weather* is warm, I'll go swimming.

Whether means "if."

> *Whether* you help me or not, I'll paint the hallway.

were, we're, where

Were is the past form of *are*.

> Only last year, we *were* scared freshmen.

We're is the short form of *we are*.

> Today *we're* confident sophomores.

Where refers to a place.

> Show me *where* you used to play basketball.

whined, wind, wined

Whined means "complained."

> Paula *whined* about the weather because the rain kept her indoors.

Wind (if it rhymes with *find*) means "to coil or wrap something" or "to turn a key."

> *Wind* that extension cord or you'll trip on it.

Wind (if it rhymes with *sinned*) is air in motion.

> The *wind* blew my cap off.

If someone *wined* you, he or she treated you to some wine.

> My brother *wined* and dined his boss.

who's, whose

Who's is a short form of *who is* or *who has*.

> *Who's* driving?
>
> *Who's* been stealing my quarters?

Whose means "belonging to whom."

> I wonder *whose* dog this is.

woman, women

Woman means "one female person."

> A *woman* in the supermarket gave me her extra coupons.

Women means "more than one female person."

> Three *women* from Missouri joined the management team.

wood, would

Wood is the hard substance in the trunks and branches of trees.

> I have a table made of a polished *wood*.

Would is the past form of *will*.

> Albert said he *would* think about the offer.

your, you're

Your means "belonging to you."

I think you dropped *your* wallet.

You're is the short form of *you are*.

You're not telling the truth.

Exercise 5 **Practice: Words That Sound Alike/Look Alike**

Circle the correct word in the following sentences.

1. (Your / You're) not looking at the good parts of (your / you're) job.

2. Al (wood / would) like to know (weather / whether) Caitlin is selling her car.

3. (Were / We're / Where) at the spot (were / we're / where) that great seafood restaurant used to be.

4. King Henry VIII of England (rained / reigned / reined) for many years and (lead / led) his people during a time of great change.

5. I have to get some good (stationary / stationery) so I can (right / rite / write) letters of application to potential employers.

6. (Their / There / They're) house has a bright and cheerful kitchen, but (their / there / they're) is something gloomy about our small kitchen.

7. Every time Irving (whined / wind / wined) about the long (wait / weight) at the ticket line, Sheila wanted to shout at him.

8. I'm not sure (who's / whose) been making those prank phone calls, but I know (who's / whose) idea it was.

9. It seems as if my boss' (sole / soul) purpose in life is to get me to (quiet / quit / quite) my job.

10. If you find out that Damon is making more money (than / then) you are, (than / then) you should ask for a raise.

Exercise 6 **Collaborate: Words That Look Alike/Sound Alike**

Collaborate

With a partner or group, write one sentence for each of the words below. When you have completed this exercise, exchange it for another group's completed exercise for evaluation.

1. a. waist _____

   b. waste _____

2. a. principal _____

   b. principle _____

3. a. quiet _____

   b. quit _____

   c. quite _____

4. a. passed _____

   b. past _____

5. a. patience _____

   b. patients _____

6. a. stake _____

   b. steak _____

7. a. loan _____

   b. lone _____

8. a. pair _____

   b. pear _____

9. a. than _____

   b. then _____

10. a. loose _____

   b. lose _____

Connect

| Exercise 7 | **Connect: Correcting Errors in Words That Sound Alike/ Look Alike** |

The following paragraph has twelve errors in words that sound alike or look alike. Corect the errors in the space above each error.

Amanda is very self-conscious when people stair at her. Her first reaction is to assume that strangers are looking at her because something is wrong with her. She wonders if she's wearing to much makeup, or if her outfit is too plane, or if a peace of spinach is stuck to her teeth. Amanda is not a vane person; in fact, it's her insecurity that puts her thorough the pane of examining herself for her flaws. To try to improve her moral, I tell her that others are not staring because her presents is unattractive. I advise her that everyone enjoys the site of a women with personnel style.

Connect

| Exercise 8 | **Connect: Correcting Errors in Words that Sound Alike/ Look Alike** |

The following paragraph has eight errors in words that sound alike or look alike. Correct the errors in the space above each error.

A constant complainer can become a difficult companion. When I first met Andrew, he had a tendency to comment on every small annoyance in his day. He wined about the traffic, or the heat, or the cold, or his bad luck with women. Andrew interpreted even the slightest gesture, such as a waitress in a hurry to clear a table, as an insult specifically designed to injure his sole. At first I excused his perpetual misery as a small flaw in his personality, but eventually I lost

patients with Andrew. Instead of enjoying my time with him, I spent it weighting

for another complaint. I eventually concluded that he was to much of a pessimist

for me to tolerate. Instead of waisting my time with someone who seemed to

enjoy being in a bad mood, I ended the friendship. Once I was threw with Andrew,

I felt like a person who's life was suddenly brighter.

Exercise 9 Practice: Words That Sound Alike/Look Alike: A Comprehensive Exercise

Underline the correct word in the following sentences.

1. When I am trying to find the (right / rite / write) way to handle a big problem, my brother sometimes (councils / counsels) me.

2. I wonder if my warning had (a / an / and) (affect / effect) on Simon.

3. In my paper on the (rain / reign / rein) of Queen Victoria, I have to (sight / site / cite) at least three historians.

4. Hundreds of years ago, people wore (close / clothes / cloths) made of (coarse / course) wool (close / clothes / cloth).

5. Drive a little (farther / further) down the street, and you will see the (capital / capitol) building in the distance.

6. The doctor told the patient to increase her (does / dose) of the (pain / pane) medicine.

7. Train (fair / fare) has increased so much that (its / it's) forced many people to walk to work.

8. Above the (altar / alter) was a huge painting of an (angel / angle).

9. Whenever I go to the supermarket, I avoid the snack food (isle / aisle); all those Fritos, Doritos, salsa, and dips can add inches to my (waist / waste).

10. Every day, my grandfather rides his (stationary / stationery) bike; he gets many (complements / compliments) on his trim body.

Exercise 10 Practice: Words That Sound Alike/Look Alike: Another Comprehensive Exercise

Underline the correct word in the following sentences.

1. (Weather / Whether) we make it to class on time depends on you: you have to be (already / all ready) to leave when I pick you up.

2. I think a kitten (wood / would) be a welcome (addition / edition) to our family.

3. Every time I walk (passed / past) my old girlfriend's house, I find it hard to (accept / except) her decision to leave me.

4. We were wondering (who's / whose) (knew / new) car is parked in the driveway.

5. You should have a little more (patience / patients) when your father tries to give you (advice / advise).

6. Laurie is an understanding (woman / women); (beside / besides), she can keep a secret.

7. The chances for (peace / piece) in that part of the world can be improved by (farther / further) negotiations between the warring nations.

8. The amber beads you are wearing (compliment / complement) the color of (your / you're) eyes.

9. While Zack and I consumed a large pizza with three extra toppings, he (whined / wind / wined) about his struggle to (loose / lose) (wait / weight).

10. Yesterday was the (forth / fourth) time I tried to practice my speech (allowed / aloud).

Connect

Exercise 11 **Connect: Correcting Errors in Words That Sound Alike/Look Alike: A Comprehensive Exercise**

The following paragraph has eleven errors in words that sound alike or look alike. Correct the errors in the space above each line.

One big difference between me and my parents is in the role music plays

in there lives and in mine. I want music to be everywhere in my life. When I am

at home, music channels like MTV or VH1 are on constantly; they are the back-

ground music for my meals, my studies, my chores, and my free time. If I am not

listening to the music on television, I drown out the quite with CDs. In the car,

I have programmed the radio with the stations that are my favorites, and I blast

the music as I drive. My parents, on the other hand, may go threw an entire day

without music. My mother and father wood never think of turning on a music

channel like VH1, which appeals to older people. My mother sometimes listens

to music on the car radio, but my father tunes in to talk radio as he drives. To my

parents, the principle purpose of music seems to be to act as a background at

large gatherings like weddings or dances. Perhaps people our destined to brake

the habit of living with music as they grow older. Still, its hard for me to except

the idea that one day I, to, may loose my need for music in every part of the day

and night.

Exercise 12 **Connect: Correcting Errors in Words That Sound Alike/Look Alike: Another Comprehensive Exercise**

Connect

The following paragraph has twelve errors in words that sound alike or look alike. Correct the errors in the space above each line.

Color is a powerful element in our lives. Color effects our moods and behavior;

our choice of colors can also make a personnel statement about the image we want

to convey to others. Anyone who has ever been in a hospital remembers the muted

colors of beige, green, and gray-blue that cover the walls, floors, and fabrics. These

colors are supposed to be calming, but many people believe they create sadness

rather then piece. Bright neon colors and flashing bars of light create excitement

and invite people to video arcades, tattoo parlors, and nightclubs. Warm colors of

red, gold, and green attract diners to restaurants serving homestyle food such as

pizza, quesadillas, and barbecued ribs. Colors matter even more when a person's

identity is involved in a color choice. Women can spend hours debating the right

color for a special dress or a shade of makeup. Both men and women are very

conscience of the power of color in major purchases. No one wants to by a car in

an unpopular shade, and a cell phone in the rite color offers more status then one

in a dull color. Each season, the fashion industry introduces one or two colors that

will rein as the most important shades for anyone who longs to dress stylishly.

Meanwhile, home improvement stores and home design television channels advice

homeowners about the latest shades for walls, carpets, and tile. Because color has

a powerful influence on our mood, behavior, and self-image, choosing the rite color

for one's hair, house, or hot-dog stand can be quiet a challenge.

Quick Question

Which sentence(s) is/
are correct?

A. It's impossible to
reason with my
brother when he
is in a bad mood.

B. This psychology
class is different
than my last
psychology class.

(After you study this
chapter, you will be
confident of your
answer.)

Chapter Objectives

Students will be able to distinguish between proper and improper use of common prepositions and prepositional phrases.

Prepositions are usually short words that often signal a kind of position, possession, or other relationship. The words that come after the preposition are part of a **prepositional phrase.** You use prepositions often because there are many expressions that contain prepositions.

Sometimes it is difficult to decide on the correct preposition. The following pages explain kinds of prepositions and their uses, and list some common prepositions.

PREPOSITIONS THAT SHOW TIME

At a specific time means "then."
>I will meet you *at* three o'clock.
>*At* 7:00 P.M., he closes the store.

By a specific time means "no later than" that time.
>You have to finish your paper *by* noon.
>I'll be home *by* 9:30 P.M.

Until a specific time means "continuing up to" that time.
> I talked on the phone *until* midnight.
> I will wait for you *until* 7:00 P.M.

In a specific time period is used with hours, minutes, days, weeks, months, or years.
> *In* a week, I'll have my diploma.
> My family hopes to visit me *in* August.

> **Note:** Write *in* the morning, *in* the afternoon, *in* the evening, but *at* night.

For a period of time means "during" that time period.
> James took music lessons *for* five years.
> I studied *for* an hour.

Since means "from then until now."
> I haven't heard from you *since* December.
> Juanita has been my friend *since* our high school days.

On a specific date means "at that time."
> I'll see you *on* March 23.
> The restaurant will open *on* Saturday.

During means "within" or "throughout" a time period.
> The baby woke up *during* the night.
> Robert worked part time *during* the winter semester.

PREPOSITIONS TO INDICATE PLACE

On usually means "on the surface of," "on top of."
> Put the dishes *on* the table.
> They have a house *on* Second Avenue.

In usually means "within" or "inside of."
> Put the dishes *in* the cupboard.
> They have a house *in* Bolivia.

At usually means "in," "on," or "near to."
> I'll meet you *at* the market.
> The coffee shop is *at* the corner of Second Avenue and Hawthorne Road.
> Jill was standing *at* the door.

EXPRESSIONS WITH PREPOSITIONS

angry about: You are *angry about* a thing.
> Suzanne was *angry about* the dent in her car.

angry at: You are *angry at* a thing.
> Carl was *angry at* the cruel treatment of the refugees.

angry with: You are *angry with* a person.
> Richard became *angry with* his mother when she criticized him.

approve of, disapprove of: You *approve* or *disapprove of* a thing or a person or group's actions.
> I *approve of* the new gun law.
> I *disapprove of* smoking in public places.

argue about: You *argue about* some subject.
> We used to *argue about* money.

argue for: You *argue for* something you want.
> The Student Council *argued for* more student parking.

argue with: You *argue with* a person.
> When I was a child, I spent hours *arguing with* my little sister.

arrive at: You *arrive at* a place.
> We will *arrive at* your house tomorrow.

between, among: You use *between* with two. You use *among* with three or more.
> It will be a secret *between* you and me.
> We shared the secret *among* the three of us.

bored by, bored with: You are *bored by* or *bored with* something. Do *not* write *bored of.*
> The audience was *bored by* the long movie.
> The child became *bored with* her toys.
> **not this:** ~~I am bored of school.~~

call on: You *call on* someone socially or to request something of a person.
> My aunt *called on* her new neighbors.
> Our club will *call on* you to collect tickets at the door.

call to: You *call to* someone from a distance.
> I heard him *call to* me from the top of the hill.

call up: You *call up* someone on the telephone.
> When she heard the news, Susan *called up* all her friends.

differ from: You *differ from* someone, or something *differs from* something.
> Roberta *differs from* Cheri in hair color and height.
> A van *differs from* a light truck.

differ with: You *differ with* (disagree with) someone about something.
> Theresa *differs with* Mike on the subject of food stamps.

different from: You are *different from* someone; something is *different from* something else. Do *not* write *different than.*
> Carl is *different from* his older brother.
> The movie was *different from* the book.
> **not this:** ~~The movie was different than the book.~~

grateful for: You are *grateful for* something.
> I am *grateful for* my scholarship.

grateful to: You are *grateful to* someone.
> My brother was *grateful to* my aunt for her advice.

interested in: You are *interested in* something.
> The children were *interested in* playing computer games.

look at: You *look at* someone or something.
> My sister *looked at* my haircut and laughed.

look for: You *look for* someone or something.
> David needs to *look for* his lost key.

look up: You *look up* information.
> I can *look up* his address in the phone book.

made of: Something or someone is *made of* something.

    Do you think I'm *made of* money?

    The chair was *made of* plastic.

need for: You have a *need for* something.

    The committee expressed a *need for* better leadership.

object to: You *object to* something.

    Lisa *objected to* her husband's weekend plans.

obligation to: You have an *obligation to* someone.

    I feel an *obligation to* my parents, who supported me while I was in college.

opportunity for: You have an *opportunity for* something; an *opportunity* exists *for* someone.

    The new job gives her an *opportunity for* a career change.

    A trip to China is a wonderful *opportunity for* Mimi.

pay for: You *pay* someone *for* something.

    I have to *pay* the plumber *for* the repairs to my sink.

pay to: You *pay* something *to* someone.

    Brian *paid* fifty dollars *to* the woman who found his lost dog.

popular with: Something or someone is *popular with* someone.

    Jazz is not *popular with* my friends.

prefer . . . to: You *prefer* something *to* something.

    I *prefer* jazz *to* classical music.

prejudice against: You have a *prejudice against* someone or something.

    My father finally conquered his *prejudice against* women drivers.

    He is *prejudiced* against scientists.

> **Note:** Remember to add *-ed* when the word becomes an adjective.

protect against: Something or someone *protects against* something or someone.

    A good raincoat can *protect* you *against* heavy rain.

protect from: Something or someone *protects from* something or someone.

    A good lock on your door can *protect* you *from* break-ins.

qualification for: You have a *qualification for* a position.

    André is missing an important *qualification for* the job.

qualified to: You are *qualified to* do something.

    Tim isn't *qualified to* judge the paintings.

quote from: You *quote* something *from* someone else.

    The graduation speaker *quoted* some lines *from* Shakespeare.

reason for: You give a *reason for* something.

    He offered no *reason for* his rude behavior.

reason with: You *reason with* someone.

    Sonny tried to *reason with* the angry motorist.

responsible for: You are *responsible for* something.

    Luther is *responsible for* the mess in the kitchen.

responsible to: You are *responsible to* someone.
> At the restaurant, the waiters are *responsible to* the assistant manager.

rob of: You *rob* someone *of* something.
> His insult *robbed* me *of* my dignity.

similar to: Someone or something is *similar to* someone or something.
> Your dress is *similar to* a dress I had in high school.

succeed in: You *succeed in* something.
> I hope I can *succeed in* getting a job.

superior to: Someone or something is *superior to* someone or something.
> My final paper was *superior to* my first paper.

take advantage of: You *take advantage of* someone or something.
> Maria is going to *take advantage of* the fine weather and go to the beach.

take care of: You *take care of* someone or something.
> Rick will *take care of* my cat while I'm away.

talk about: You *talk about* something.
> We can *talk about* the trip tomorrow.

talk over: You *talk over* something.
> The cousins met to *talk over* the plans for the anniversary party.

talk to: You *talk to* someone.
> I'll *talk to* my father.

talk with: You *talk with* someone.
> Esther needs to *talk with* her boyfriend.

tired of: You are *tired of* something.
> Sylvia is *tired of* driving to work.

wait for: You *wait for* someone or something.
> Jessica must *wait for* Alan to arrive.

wait on: You use *wait on* only if you wait on customers.
> At the diner, I have to *wait on* too many people.

Exercise 1   Practice: Choosing the Correct Preposition

Underline the correct preposition in each of the following sentences.

1. With flowers or cookies in her hands, my aunt (calls on / calls to / calls up) lonely or housebound neighbors.

2. Paul likes shrimp, but he prefers a large steak (over / to) most seafood.

3. You have to be at work (by / during) 8:00 A.M. tomorrow.

4. Mark was never interested (at / in) going to college.

5. Hang your jacket (on / in) the closet.

6. Leo likes to work (in / at) night.

7. My boss said I had all the qualifications (for / to) a promotion to assistant manager.

8. A child who is abused is robbed (from / of) his or her innocence.

9. Emilio soon became bored (of / with) the silly game.

10. When it comes to the subject of teenage marriage, Kristin differs (from / with) me.

Exercise 2   **Practice: Choosing the Correct Preposition**

Underline the correct preposition in each of the following sentences.

1. If you go to the mall, be sure to look (up / for) a cheap raincoat.

2. My uncle works in a restaurant (in / at) the north end of Mill Road.

3. I have been waiting (on / for) you (since / for) twenty minutes.

4. Bruce was riding (in / on) a new pickup truck yesterday.

5. My college English class is different (from / than) my senior English class in high school.

6. At the school board meeting, several parents came to argue (with / for) smaller class sizes in the elementary grades.

7. After he saw the movie about starvation in Africa, John became angry (at / with) the hopeless situation of millions.

8. My grandmother wanted to divide her small collection of jewelry (between / among) her three daughters.

9. Yasar lived (on / in) Turkey before he came to the United States.

10. You are so angry that no one can reason (for / with) you.

Exercise 3   **Collaborate: Writing Sentences Using Expressions
with Prepositions**

Collaborate

Do this exercise with a partner or group. Below are pairs of expressions with prepositions. Write a sentence that contains each pair. The first one is done for you.

1. **a.** argue with   **b.** object to

   sentence: In college, I used to argue with my roommate whenever he would

   object to my loud music.

2. **a.** take advantage of   **b.** arrive at

   sentence: _____

   _____

3. **a.** grateful for   **b.** wait on

   sentence: _____

   _____

4. **a.** between   **b.** similar to

   sentence: _____

   _____

5. **a.** popular with   **b.** bored by

   sentence: _____

   _____

6. **a.** look for   **b.** qualified to

   sentence: _____

   _____

7. **a.** prejudice against   **b.** reason for

   sentence: _____

   _____

8. **a.** superior to   **b.** opportunity for

   sentence: _____

   _____

9. **a.** need for   **b.** made of

   sentence: _____

   _____

10. **a.** protect from   **b.** rob of

   sentence: _____

   _____

Collaborate

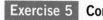

Exercise 4   **Collaborate: Writing Sentences Using Expressions with Prepositions**

Do this exercise with a partner. Review the list of expressions with prepositions in this chapter. Select five expressions that you think are troublesome for writers. Write the expressions below. Then exchange your list for a partner's list. Your partner will write a sentence for each expression on your list; you will write sentences for his or her list. When you have completed the exercises, check each other's sentences.

1. expression: _____

   sentence: _____

2. expression: _____

   sentence: _____

3. expression: _____

   sentence: _____

4. expression: _____

   sentence: _____

5. expression: _____

   sentence: _____

Connect

Exercise 5   **Connect: Using Prepositions Correctly**

The following paragraph has ten errors in prepositions. Correct the errors in the space above each error.

My roommate Bill has a habit of becoming angry with some minor incident,

and then it is impossible to reason for him. Last week, for example, he told me that he and I needed to talk with my careless behavior. Until the time I was able

to figure out what "behavior" Bill was describing, he had already turned into a

red-faced, shouting monster. He was ranting about my leaving the door unlocked

while I went down the hall to check our mailbox. "Someday, you'll be responsible

to a burglary when someone sees the unlocked door and walks right on!" he com-

plained. "You'll have to pay to the missing items when some criminal robs the

apartment!" Because our apartment door is about twenty feet from the mailboxes,

I refused to argue for Bill. I am getting tired by listening to Bill's tantrums. So,

instead of arguing, I am going to look on local "Roommate Wanted" ads online.

Maybe I'll find someone calmer than Bill.

Exercise 6 Connect: Using Prepositions Correctly

Connect

The following paragraph has eleven errors in prepositions. Correct the errors
in the space above each error.

    Our dog Annabelle was terrified of thunderstorms, and for a long time, we

couldn't do anything to help her. At the first distant rumble of thunder, Annabelle

looked up, with her ears raised, and listened. Then she would look at the fam-

ily (my father, my mother, and me) as if to beg us for some comfort. Annabelle

wanted the storm to go away. By the time the lightning and thunder had reached

our home, the dog was hiding under the bed or on a closet. Often she began to

wail. Since years, Annabelle suffered. We didn't know what to do. We couldn't

reason for a dog by explaining that the storm would be gone soon. Between the

three of us, we tried many remedies for Annabelle's pain. My mother sat near the

bed or closet, called up the dog, and, by holding a treat, tried to lure Annabelle

out of hiding. Using the Internet, my father looked on information about dogs

and thunderstorms, but he couldn't find much. I tried dragging the dog out of her

hiding place, but she shook so pitifully that I let her go back to her safe spot. We

felt extremely sorry for our dog and knew that we could not protect her about

inevitable summer storms. Eventually, we did succeed on helping, but not curing,

Annabelle. Our neighbor told us about an herb that helps to calm anxiety in pets.

We found the herb, in capsule form, at a local pet store. The next time we heard a faint roll of thunder, we slipped the herbal pill into a spoonful of canned dog food and fed the mixture to our dog. On that thunderstorm, Annabelle remained anxious, but she was not frightened enough to hide and cry. Until the day we first gave our dog the herbal remedy, we have continued to rely on it to calm Annabelle when a storm threatens. We will always be grateful for our neighbor for helping us to ease our dog's suffering.

Collaborate

| Exercise 7 | Collaborate: Recognizing Prepositional Phrases in a Famous Speech |

Do this exercise with a group. Following is part of a famous speech by Winston Churchill, prime minister of Great Britain during World War II. When Churchill gave this speech in 1940, the Nazis had just defeated the British troops at Dunkirk, France. In this speech, Churchill explained the events at Dunkirk and then rallied the nation to keep fighting.

To do this exercise, have one member of your group read the speech aloud while the other members listen. Then underline all the prepositional phrases in it. Be ready to share your answers with another group.

We shall not flag* nor fail. We shall go on to the end. We shall fight in France and on the seas and oceans; we shall fight with growing confidence and growing strength in the air.

We shall defend our island whatever the cost may be; we shall fight on beaches, on landing grounds, in fields, in streets and on the hills. We shall never surrender and even if, which I do not for a moment believe, this island or a large part of it were subjugated* and starving, then our empire beyond the seas, armed and guarded by the British Fleet,* would carry on the struggle until in God's good time the New World, with all its power and might, sets forth to the liberation and rescue of the Old.

*flag means to lose energy
*subjugated means conquered by the enemy
*the fleet is a group of warships

Writing in Stages:
The Process Approach

INTRODUCTION

Learning by Doing

Writing is a skill, and like any skill, writing improves with practice. This part of the book provides you with ample practice to improve your writing through a variety of individual and group activities. Whether you complete assignments at home or in the classroom, just remember that *good writing takes practice:* you can learn to write well by writing.

Steps Make Writing Easier

Writing is easier if you *do not try to do too much at once.* To make the task of writing easier, this section breaks the process into four major stages:

PREWRITING

In this stage, you think about your topic and you *gather ideas.* You *react* to your own ideas and add even more thoughts. You can also react to other people's ideas as a way of expanding your own writing.

PLANNING

In this stage, you examine your ideas and begin to *focus* them around one main idea or point. Planning involves combining, categorizing, and even eliminating some ideas. Placing your specific details in a logical order often involves *outlining.*

DRAFTING AND REVISING

In this stage, the thinking and planning begin to take shape as a piece of writing. You complete a draft of your work, a *rough version* of the finished product. Then you examine the draft and consider ways to *revise* it, a process that may require extensive editing and several versions of your original draft.

PROOFREADING

In this stage, you give the final draft of your writing one last, careful *review* when you are rested and alert. You *proofread* and concentrate on identifying and correcting any mistakes in spelling, mechanics, punctuation, or word choice you may have missed. This stage is the *final check* of your work to make your writing the best it can be.

These four stages in the writing process—**prewriting, planning, drafting and revising,** and **proofreading**—may overlap. You may be changing your plan even as you work on the draft of your paper. There is no rule that prevents you from returning to an earlier stage. In these writing chapters, you will have many opportunities to become familiar with the stages of effective writing. Working individually and with your classmates, you can become a better writer along *all* lines.

Contents   Page

Writing a Paragraph: Prewriting

CHAPTER 20

Jumping In

Where do you get your ideas for writing? Do they seem to come at you all at once? Working with a jumble of ideas is a natural part of the writing process. Fortunately, there are several ways to draw on your imagination, experiences, beliefs, and opinions as you sort through these ideas and begin a **paragraph** that focuses on one idea or point.

Chapter Objectives

Students will be able to (1) apply an effective prewriting strategy to determine a topic and narrow its focus, (2) generate specific details related to their topic, and (3) devise a topic sentence reflecting the main idea suggested by the details.

The paragraph is the basic building block of most writing. It is a group of sentences focusing on one idea or one point. Keep this concept in mind: *one idea for each paragraph.* Focusing on one idea or one point gives a paragraph *unity*. If you have a new point, start a new paragraph.

You may ask, "Doesn't this mean a paragraph will be short? How long should a paragraph be, anyway?" To convince a reader of one main point, you need to make it, support it, develop it, explain it, and describe it. There will be shorter and longer paragraphs, but for now, you can assume your paragraph will be between seven and twelve sentences long.

This chapter guides you through the first stage of the writing process, the **prewriting** stage, where you generate ideas for your paragraph.

BEGINNING THE PREWRITING

Suppose your instructor asks you to write a paragraph about family. To write effectively, you need to know your *purpose* and your *audience*. In this case, you already know your purpose: to write a paragraph that makes some point about family. You also know your audience, since you are writing this paragraph for your instructor and classmates. Often, your purpose is to write a specific type of paper for a class. However, you may have to write with a different purpose for a particular audience. Writing instructions for a new employee at your workplace, or writing a letter of complaint to a manufacturer, or composing a short autobiographical essay for a scholarship application are examples of different purposes and audiences.

Freewriting, Brainstorming, Keeping a Journal

Once you have identified your purpose and audience, you can begin by finding some way to *think* on paper. To gather ideas, you can use the techniques of freewriting, brainstorming, or keeping a journal.

Freewriting Give yourself ten minutes to write whatever comes into your mind on the subject. If you can't think of anything to write, just write, "I can't think of anything to write," over and over until you think of something else. The main goal of **freewriting** is to *write without stopping*. Don't stop to tell yourself, "This is stupid" or "I can't use any of this in a paper." Just write. Let your ideas flow. Write freely. Here's an example:

Freewriting About Family

Family. Family. Whose family? What is a family? What does she want me to write about? I'm not married. I don't have a family. Sure, my mother. I guess I have a big <u>other</u> family, too. Cousins, aunts, uncles. But my basic family is my mother and brother, Tito. Is that a family? She's a good mom. Always takes care of me. Family ties. Family matters. How a family treats children.

Brainstorming **Brainstorming** is like freewriting because you write whatever comes into your head, but it is a little different because you can *pause to ask yourself questions* that will lead to new ideas. When you brainstorm alone, you "interview" yourself about a subject. Or you can brainstorm within a group.

If you are brainstorming about family, alone or with a partner or group, you might begin by listing ideas and then add to the ideas by asking and answering questions. Here's an example:

Brainstorming About Family

Family.

Family members.

Who is your favorite family member?

I don't know. Uncle Ray, I guess.

Why is he your favorite?

He's funny. Especially at those family celebrations.

What celebrations?

Birthdays, anniversaries, dinners. I hated those dinners when I was little.

Why did you hate them?

I had to get all dressed up.

What else did you hate about them?

I had to sit still through the longest, most boring meals.

Why were they boring?

All these grown-ups talking. My mother made me sit there, politely.

Were you angry at your mother?

Yes. Well, no, not really. She's strict, but I love her.

If you feel like you are running out of ideas in brainstorming, try to form a question out of what you've just written. For example, if you write, "Families are changing," you could form these questions:

What families? How are they changing? Are the changes good? Why? Why not?

Forming questions helps you keep your thoughts flowing, and you will eventually arrive at a suitable focus for your paragraph.

Keeping a Journal A **journal** is a notebook of your personal writing, a notebook in which you write regularly and often. *It is not a diary, but it is a place to record your experiences, reactions, and observations.* In it, you can write about what you've done, heard, seen, read, or remembered. You can include sayings that you'd like to remember, news clippings, snapshots— anything that you'd like to recall or consider. Journals are a great way to practice your writing and a great source of ideas for writing.

If you were asked to write about family, for example, you might look through entries in your journal in search of ideas, and you might see something like this:

Journal Entry About Family

I was at Mike's house last night. We were just sitting around, talking and listening to CDs. Then we were bored, so we decided to go to the movies. When we left, we walked right past Mike's mother in the kitchen. Mike didn't even say goodbye or tell her where we were going. Mike is so rude to his mother. He can't stand her. Lots of my friends hate their parents. I'm lucky. I'm close to my mother.

Finding Specific Ideas

Whether you freewrite, brainstorm, or consult your journal, you end up with something on paper. Follow these first ideas; see where they can take you. You are looking for specific ideas, each of which can focus the general one you started with. At this point, you do not have to decide which specific idea you want to write about. You just want to narrow your range of ideas.

You might ask, "Why should I narrow my ideas? Won't I have more to say if I keep my topic big?" But remember that a paragraph has one idea. You want to say one thing clearly, and you want to use convincing details that support your main idea. If you write one paragraph on the broad topic of family, for example, you will probably make only general statements that say very little and that bore your reader.

General ideas are big, broad ones. Specific ideas are narrow. If you scanned the freewriting example on family, you might underline many specific ideas that could be topics.

> Family. Family. Whose family? What is a family? What does she want me to write about? I'm not married. I don't have a family. Sure, <u>my mother.</u> I guess I have a <u>big other family,</u> too. Cousins, aunts, uncles. But <u>my basic family</u> is my mother and brother, Tito. Is that a family? <u>She's a good mom.</u> <u>Always takes care of me.</u> Family ties. Family matters. How a family treats children.

Consider the underlined parts. Many of them are specific ideas about family. You could write a paragraph about one underlined item or about several related items.

Another way to find specific ideas is to make a list after brainstorming, underlining specific ideas. Here is an underlined list about family:

> Family.
>
> Family members.
>
> <u>Uncle Ray.</u>
>
> He's funny. Especially at those <u>family celebrations.</u>
>
> <u>Birthdays, anniversaries, dinners. I hated those dinners when I was little.</u>
>
> <u>I had to get all dressed up.</u>
>
> I had to sit still through the <u>longest, most boring meals.</u>
>
> All these grown-ups, talking. My mother made me sit there, politely.
>
> <u>She's strict, but I love her.</u>

These specific ideas could lead you to specific topics.

If you reviewed the journal entry on family, you would be able to underline many specific ideas:

> I was at Mike's house last night. We were just sitting around, talking and listening to CDs. Then we were bored, so we decided to go to the movies. When we left, we walked right past Mike's mother in the kitchen. <u>Mike didn't even say goodbye or tell her where we were going. Mike is so rude to his mother. He can't stand her. Lots of my friends hate their parents. I'm lucky. I'm close to my mother.</u>

Remember, following the steps can lead you to specific ideas. Once you have some specific ideas, you can pick one idea and develop it.

Exercise 1 Practice: Brainstorming Questions and Answers

Following are several general topics. For each one, brainstorm by writing three questions and answers related to the topic that could lead you to specific ideas. The first topic is done for you.

1. **general topic:** home computers

   Question 1: Do I need my home computer?

   Answer 1: Sure. I use it all the time.

   Question 2: But what do I use it for?

   Answer 2: Games. Going online to Facebook and YouTube. E-mail.

   Question 3: So I don't use it for anything serious, do I?

   Answer 3: It helps me do research and type my papers.

2. general topic: exercise

Question 1: _____

Answer 1: _____

Question 2: _____

Answer 2: _____

Question 3: _____

Answer 3: _____

3. general topic: memories

Question 1: _____

Answer 1: _____

Question 2: _____

Answer 2: _____

Question 3: _____

Answer 3: _____

4. general topic: promises

Question 1: _____

Answer 1: _____

Question 2: _____

Answer 2: _____

Question 3: _____

Answer 3: _____

5. general topic: nature

Question 1: _____

Answer 1: _____

Question 2: _____

Answer 2: _____

Question 3: _____

Answer 3: _____

Exercise 2 **Practice: Finding Specific Ideas in a List**

Following are general topics; each general topic is followed by a list of words
or phrases about the general topic. It is the kind of list you could make after
brainstorming. Underline the phrases that are specific and that could lead
you to a specific topic. The first list is done for you.

    1. general topic: sleeping habits
      how people sleep
      <u>snoring all night</u>
      everyone sleeps

<u>why people toss and turn</u>
ways of sleeping

2. **general topic:** sports
professional sports teams
baseball heroes through the years
my hockey injuries
sports energy drinks
televised soccer matches

3. **general topic:** employment
my terrible boss
bad jobs
office gossip
working the night shift
finding and keeping a suitable job

4. **general topic:** transportation
the hero of a train wreck
the future of transportation
big trucks
one motorcycling holiday
why I hate flying

5. **general topic:** money
financial problems
banking online
saving spare change
regular investing
people and finances

Exercise 3   Practice: Finding Specific Ideas in Freewriting

Following are two samples of freewriting. Each is a written response to a different topic. Read each sample, and then underline any words or phrases that could become the focus of a paragraph.

Freewriting on the Topic of Daydreaming

I never have time to daydream anymore. It's for kids. Kids have time. Maybe not. Maybe electronic toys have replaced daydreams. Best places to daydream. Not at work. Can get caught daydreaming. Think of blue skies. Sunny day. Can daydreams come true? Are daydreams worthless? There's a pleasure in emptying your mind. Letting dreams come in.

Freewriting on the Topic of Shoes

Comfortable shoes. Don't miss them until you get stuck in an uncomfortable shoe. A sandal pinches or cuts into your foot. Shoes are so important to style now. Outrageous prices of shoes. Shining your shoes. Boots. Are they shoes? Who cares about shoes? Everyone? How many pairs of shoes are too many?

Collaborate

Exercise 4   Collaborate: Finding Topics Through Freewriting

Begin this exercise alone; then complete it with a partner or group. First, pick one of the topics and freewrite on it for ten minutes. Then read your freewriting to your partner or group. Ask your listener(s) to jot down any words or phrases that lead to a specific subject for a paragraph.

Your listener(s) should read the jotted-down words or phrases to you. You will be hearing a collection of specific ideas that came from *your* writing. As you listen, underline the words in your freewriting.

Freewriting Topics (pick one):

a. adventures

b. arguments

c. promises

Freewriting on _____ (name of topic chosen)

_____

_____

_____

_____

_____

_____

Selecting an Idea

After you have a list of specific ideas, you must pick one and try to develop it by adding details. To pick an idea about family, you could survey the ideas you gathered through freewriting. Review the following freewriting in which the specific ideas are underlined:

Family. Family. Whose family? What is a family? What does she want me to write about? I'm not married. I don't have a family. Sure, my mother. I guess I have a big other family, too. Cousins, aunts, uncles. But my basic family is my mother and brother, Tito. Is that a family? She's a good mom. Always takes care of me. Family ties. Family matters. How a family treats children.

Here are the specific ideas (the underlined ones) in a list:

my mother	She's a good mom.
a big other family	Always takes care of me.
my basic family	

Looking at these ideas, you decide to write your paragraph on this topic: My Mother.

Now you can begin to add details.

Adding Details to an Idea

You can develop the one idea you picked a number of ways:

1. *Check your list* for other ideas that seem to fit the one you've picked.
2. *Brainstorm*—ask yourself more questions about your topic, and use the answers as details.
3. *List any new ideas* you have that may be connected to your first idea.

One way to add details is to go back and check your list for other ideas that seem to fit with the topic of My Mother. You find these entries:

> She's a good mom. Always takes care of me.

Another way to add details is to brainstorm some questions that will lead you to more details. These questions do not have to be connected to each other; they are just questions that could lead you to ideas and details.

> **Question: What makes your mom a good mom?**
>
> Answer: She works hard.
>
> **Question: What work does she do?**
>
> Answer: She cooks, cleans.
>
> **Question: What else?**
>
> Answer: She has a job.
>
> **Question: What job?**
>
> Answer: She's a nurse.
>
> **Question: How is your mother special?**
>
> Answer: She had a rough life.

Another way to add details is to list any ideas that may be connected to your first idea of writing about your mother. The list might give you more specific details:

> makes great chicken casserole
>
> good-looking for her age
>
> lost her husband
>
> went to school at night

If you tried all three ways of adding details, you would end up with this list of details connected to the topic of My Mother:

She's a good mom.	She had a rough life.
Always takes care of me.	makes great chicken casserole
She works hard.	good-looking for her age
She cooks, cleans.	lost her husband
She has a job.	went to school at night
She's a nurse.	

You now have details that you can work with as you move into the next stage of writing a paragraph.

This process may seem long, but once you have worked through it several times, it will become nearly automatic. When you think about ideas before you try to shape them, you are off to a good start.

INFO BOX:　Beginning the Prewriting: A Summary

The prewriting stage of writing a paragraph enables you to gather ideas. This process begins with four steps:

1. *Think on paper and write down any ideas that you have about a general topic.* You can do this by freewriting, brainstorming, or keeping a journal.

2. *Scan your writing for specific ideas that have come from your first efforts.* List these ideas.

3. *Pick one specific idea.* This idea will be the topic of your paragraph.

4. *Add details to your topic.* You can add details by reviewing your early writing, by questioning, and by thinking further.

FOCUSING THE PREWRITING

Once you have a topic and some ideas about the topic, your next step is to *focus* your topic and ideas around some point.

Two techniques that you can use are

- marking a list of related ideas
- mapping related ideas

Marking Related Ideas

To develop a marked list, take a look at the following marked list developed under the topic of My Mother. In this list, you'll notice some of the items have been marked with letters that represent categories for related items.

H	marks ideas about your mother *at home.*
J	marks ideas about your mother's *job.*
B	marks ideas about your mother's *background.*

Following is a marked list of ideas related to the topic of My Mother.

H	She's a good mom.	B	She had a rough life.
H	Always takes care of me.	H	makes great chicken casserole
H & J	She works hard.		good-looking for her age
H	She cooks and cleans.	B	lost her husband
H	She has a job.	B	went to school at night
J	She's a nurse.		

You have probably noticed that one item, *She works hard,* is marked with two letters, H and J, because your mother works hard both at home and on the job. One item on the list, *good-looking for her age,* isn't marked. Perhaps you can come back to this item later, or perhaps you will decide you don't need it in your paragraph.

To make it easier to see what ideas you have and how they are related, try *grouping related ideas,* giving each list a title, like this:

my mother at home

She's a good mom.	Always takes care of me.
She works hard.	She cooks, cleans.
makes great chicken casserole	

my mother at her job

She has a job.	She's a nurse.
She works hard.	

my mother's background

She had a rough life.   lost her husband

went to school at night

Mapping

Another way to focus your ideas is to mark your first list of ideas and then cluster the related ideas into separate lists. You can *map* your ideas like this:

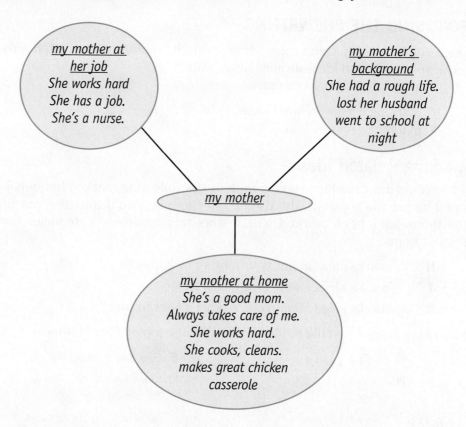

Whatever way you choose to examine and group your details, you are working toward a focus, a point. You are asking and beginning to answer the question, "Where do the details lead?" The answer will be the main idea of your paragraph, which will be stated in the topic sentence.

> **Exercise 5**   **Practice: Grouping Related Items in Lists of Details**

Following are lists of details. In each list, circle the items that seem to fit in one group; then underline the items that seem to belong to a second group. Some items may not belong in either group. The first list is done for you.

1. **topic:** my favorite aunt

   <u>always cheerful</u>   (unusual appearance)
   <u>tells jokes</u>   (wild hair)
   gives me compliments   an accountant
   <u>laughs at her troubles</u>   (outrageous hats)
   (dresses in wild colors)   drives a jeep

2. **topic:** snow

   airports close
   sledding   skiing
                               loss of electric power

first snowfall
winter clothes
weather reports

roads blocked
snowboarding
icicles

3. topic: accidents
carelessness
broken bones
fender-bender
faulty equipment
sirens blasting

plane crash
police investigation
bad weather
truck overturns
television news reports

4. topic: borrowing
home mortgage
overdue library book
bankruptcy
credit union
repossessed car

not returning clothes
student loan
foreclosure
car payments
banks

5. topic: breaking my ankle
bad pain for days
waiting in emergency room
strangers were kind
broke it slipping on a wet floor
trying to be patient

friend's gift of an ankle bracelet
hard to get to class with crutches
boring hours without any exercise
pain pills
lots of sympathy

Forming a Topic Sentence

To form a topic sentence, do the following:

1. Review your details and see if you can form some general idea that will summarize the details.
2. Write that general idea in one sentence.

The sentence that summarizes the details is the *topic sentence*. It makes a general point, and the more specific details you have gathered will support this point.

To form a topic sentence about your mother, you can ask yourself questions about the details. First, there are many details about your mother. You can ask yourself, "What kinds of details do I have?" You have details about your mother's background, about her job, and about her role as a mother. You might then ask, "Can I summarize those details?" You might then summarize those details to get the topic sentence:

My mother survived difficult times to become a good parent and worker.

Check the sentence against your details. Does it cover your mother's background? Yes, it mentions that she survived *difficult times*. Does it cover her job? Yes, it says she is a *good worker*. Does it cover her role as a mother? Yes, it says she is a *good parent*. The topic sentence is acceptable; it is a general idea that summarizes the details.

Hints About Topic Sentences

1. Be careful. *Topics are not the same as topic sentences. A topic is the subject you will write about. A topic sentence states the main idea you have developed on a topic.* Consider the differences between the following topics and topic sentences:

> **topic:**   my mother
> **topic sentence:**   My mother survived difficult times to become a good parent and worker.
>
> **topic:**   effects of drunk driving
> **topic sentence:**   Drunk driving hurts the victims, their families, and friends.

Collaborate

| Exercise 6 | **Collaborate: Turning Topics into Topic Sentences** |

Do this exercise with a partner or group. The following list contains some topics and some topic sentences. Have someone read the list aloud. As the list is read, decide which items are topics. Put an *X* by those items. On the lines following the list, rewrite the topics into topic sentences.

1. _____ A sound in the night

2. _____ Why you should drink water all day

3. _____ Family quarrels at the picnic

4. _____ How to write a thank-you note

5. _____ My father is my best friend

6. _____ I learned compassion at my job

7. _____ Atlanta is a wonderful place to live

8. _____ Speeding is foolish and selfish

9. _____ The misery and pain of a sore throat

10. _____ Getting lost in a strange place can be irritating

Rewrite the topics. Make each one into a topic sentence.

_____

_____

_____

_____

_____

_____

_____

2. *Topic sentences do not announce;* they make a point. Look at the following sentences and notice the differences between the sentences that announce and the topic sentences.

> **announcement:**   The subject of this paper will be my definition of a bargain.
> **topic sentence:**   A bargain is a necessary item that I bought at less than half the regular price.

announcement: I will discuss the causes of depression in my best friend.

topic sentence: My best friend's depression was caused by stress at home, work, and school.

Collaborate

Exercise 7 **Collaborate: Turning Announcements into Topic Sentences**

Do this exercise with a partner or group. The following list contains some topic sentences and some announcements. Have someone read this list aloud. As the list is read, decide which items are announcements. Put an *X* by those items. On the lines following the list, rewrite the announcements, making them topic sentences.

1. _____ My grandfather was the only role model in my childhood.

2. _____ How friendships grow is the subject of this paper.

3. _____ This essay will tell you why some people fly into rages.

4. _____ A true friend is supportive, loyal, and honest.

5. _____ The drawbacks to constantly changing jobs are the topic of this essay.

6. _____ Why Carson Elementary School needs a longer school day is the issue to be discussed.

7. _____ Riding a bike to work reduces auto emissions, improves the rider's health, and reduces traffic.

8. _____ I will explain the reasons for requiring frequent inspection of nail salons.

9. _____ Parents of a newborn need a 24-hour helpline to advise and reassure them.

10. _____ Imagination and empathy make a good nurse into a better nurse.

Rewrite the announcements. Make each one a topic sentence.

_____

_____

_____

_____

_____

_____

_____

_____

3. *Topic sentences should not be too broad to develop in one para-graph.* A topic sentence that is too broad may take many pages of writing to develop. Look at the following broad sentences and then notice how they can be narrowed.

too broad:	Television violence is bad for children. (This sentence is too broad because "television violence" could include anything from bloody movies to nightly news, and "children" could mean anyone under eighteen. Also, "is bad for children" could mean anything from "causes nightmares" to "provokes children to commit murder.")
a narrower topic sentence:	Violent cartoons teach preschoolers that hitting and hurting is fun.
too broad:	Education changed my life. (This sentence is so broad that you would have to talk about your whole education and your whole life to support it.)
a narrower topic sentence:	Studying for my high-school equivalency diploma gave me the confidence to try college.

Collaborate

Exercise 8 **Collaborate: Revising Topic Sentences That Are Too Broad**

Do this exercise with a partner or group. Following is a list of topic sentences. Some are too broad to support in one paragraph. Have someone read this list aloud. As the list is read, decide which sentences are too broad. Put an *X* by those sentences. On the lines following the list, rewrite those sentences, focusing on a limited idea—a topic sentence—that could be supported in one paragraph.

1. _____ When the economy is in trouble, people are reluctant to spend.

2. _____ Alicia found an outlet for her energy in rock climbing.

3. _____ A week at my sister's house introduced me to the challenges of cooking for a large family.

4. _____ My first year in college helped me to gain confidence.

5. _____ When I was sixteen, I believed that smoking cigarettes made me look sophisticated.

6. _____ Children can become spoiled by their parents.

7. _____ Videos waste too much of people's time.

8. _____ Education needs a complete overhaul.

9. _____ A trip to the local fresh market is a treat for me and my wife.

10. _____ Halloween has become too much of a theatrical production for me.

Rewrite the broad sentences. Make each one more limited.

_____

_____

_____

_____

_____

_____

_____

_____

4. *Topic sentences should not be too narrow* to develop in one paragraph. A topic sentence that is too narrow can't be supported by details. It may be a fact, which can't be developed. A topic sentence that is too narrow leaves you with nothing more to say.

too narrow:	We had fog yesterday.
a better, expanded topic sentence:	Yesterday's fog made driving difficult.
too narrow:	I moved to Nashville when I was twenty.
a better, expanded topic sentence:	When I moved to Nashville at age twenty, I learned to live on my own.

Exercise 9 **Collaborate: Revising Topic Sentences That Are Too Narrow**

Collaborate

Do this exercise with a partner or group. Following is a list of topic sentences. Some of them are too narrow to be developed in a paragraph. Have someone read the list aloud. As the list is read, decide which sentences are too narrow. Put an *X* by those sentences. On the lines following the list, rewrite those sentences as broader topic sentences that could be developed in a paragraph.

1. _____ My jacket cost ten dollars on sale, but it was a foolish purchase.

2. _____ Cameron borrowed $123 from his parents.

3. _____ When I ate two huge pieces of chocolate cake, I broke my promise to myself.

4. _____ My stepfather's call on my birthday was thoughtful and kind.

5. _____ Brendan offered me a ride to the train station.

6. _____ The dock at the rear of the motel was made of rotten wood.

7. _____ Living near the lake makes me happy in three ways.

8. _____ I have a new pickup truck.

9. _____ For me, sneakers are more sensible footwear than sandals.

10. _____ Jim threw away his leather necklace.

Rewrite the narrow sentences. Make each one broader.

_____

_____

_____

_____

_____

_____

_____

_____

_____

_____

Once you have a topic sentence, you have completed the prewriting stage of writing. This stage begins with free, unstructured thinking and writing. As you work through the prewriting process, your thinking and writing will become more focused.

INFO BOX: **Focusing the Prewriting: A Summary**

The prewriting stage of writing a paragraph enables you to develop an idea into a topic sentence and related details. You can focus your thinking by working in steps.

1. Try marking a list of related details or mapping to group your ideas.

2. Write a topic sentence that summarizes your details.

3. Check your topic sentence. Be sure that it makes a point and focuses the details you have developed. Be sure that it is a sentence (not a topic), is not too broad or too narrow, and is not an announcement.

Exercise 10 **Practice: Recognizing and Writing Good Topic Sentences**

Some of the following are good topic sentences. Others are not; they are topics (not topic sentences) or announcements, or they are too broad or too narrow. Put an *X* next to the ones that are not good topic sentences and rewrite them on the blank lines following the list.

1. _____ How you can make extra money in college.

2. _____ Movies about animals appeal to all of my nieces and nephews.

3. _____ Conflicts have always made me nervous.

4. _____ At dusk, I drive to work.

5. _____ Wearing wigs or hair pieces to cover hair loss.

6. _____ Many elderly people are fearful.

7. _____ Several dangers of traveling to parts of Africa will be the subject of this paper.

8. _____ Vitamin C can be found in many popular foods.

9. _____ This paper will discuss popular way to save money on groceries.

10. _____ An ATM can be a convenience or a danger.

Rewrite the faulty topic sentences:

_____

_____

_____

_____

_____

_____

_____

_____

Exercise 11 **Practice: Writing Topic Sentences for Lists of Details**

Following are lists of details that have no topic sentences. Write an appropriate topic sentence for each one.

1. topic sentence: _____

_____

Comforts me when I am sad.
Brings me small treats like brownies.
Always lets me choose the movie we watch.
Saves funny online videos to show me.
Appreciates all my cooking (even microwaved frozen dinners).
Walks the dog on rainy days.
Takes out the garbage.

2. topic sentence: _____

_____

It was a short walk to the beach.
I could open the windows and smell the sea air.
I could study and read on a blanket in the sand.
I could maintain a perfect tan.
It had one bedroom.
The bedroom had a bed and a dresser of fake wood.
The living room was furnished in plastic couches and a wire-legged coffee table.
The kitchen was big enough for one person.

3. topic sentence: _____

_____

high heels
low heels
spike heels
wedge heels

plastic heels
wooden heels
leather heels
clear heels
diamond-studded heels
platform heels

4. topic sentence: _____

_____

Ms. Chestnut was my kindergarten teacher.
She was a lively, smiling person.
She welcomed each child every morning.
She sang with us.
She danced in a circle with us.
She frowned only when we misbehaved.
If we didn't pay attention, she noticed and recaptured our attention.
If two or three of us fooled around, she gently brought us to the center of the group.

5. topic sentence: _____

_____

Chocolate tastes great.
It is full of fat and empty calories.
The sugar in chocolate is bad for a person's teeth.
Chocolate can also be bad for many people's complexions.
An apple tastes good.
It has no fat.
It is full of fiber, which is healthy for digestion.
Eating an apple is good for a person's skin and teeth.

Writing a Paragraph: Planning CHAPTER 21

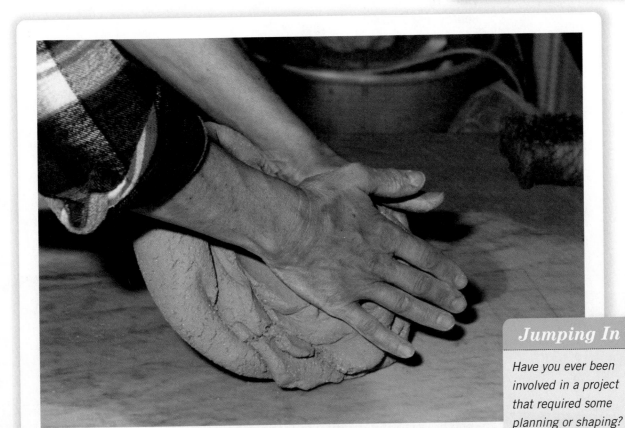

Jumping In

*Have you ever been involved in a project that required some planning or shaping? For example, have you ever painted a room? Worked with clay? Designed a Web page? Writers often begin with a range of ideas and details. Later, they find a way to sort, shape, and focus them. Part of the planning and shaping process involves devising a **topic sentence** and an **outline**.*

Chapter Objectives

Students will be able to devise a basic outline that incorporates (1) relevant details for *unity*, (2) a sufficient number of details for *support*, and (3) a logical sequence of points for *coherence*.

Once you have a topic sentence, you can begin working on an *outline* for your paragraph. The outline is a *plan* that helps you stay focused in your writing. The outline begins to form when you write your topic sentence and the details beneath it.

CHECKING YOUR DETAILS

You can now look at your list and ask yourself an important question: "Do I have enough details to support my topic sentence?" Remember, your goal is to write a paragraph of seven to twelve sentences.

Consider this topic sentence and list of details:

topic sentence:	Fresh fruit is a good dessert.
details:	tastes good
	healthy
	easy

Does the list contain enough details for a paragraph of seven to twelve sentences? Probably not.

Adding Details When There Are Not Enough

To add details, try brainstorming. Ask yourself some questions:

What fruit tastes good?
What makes fruit a healthy dessert?
Why is it easy? How can you serve it?

By brainstorming, you may come up with these details:

topic sentence:	Fresh fruit is a good dessert.
details:	tastes good
	a ripe peach or a juicy pineapple tastes delicious
	crunchy apples are always available and satisfying
	plump strawberries are great in summer
	healthy
	low in calories
	rich in vitamins and fiber
	easy
	served as it is
	in a fruit salad
	mixed with ice cream or sherbet
	no cooking necessary

Keep brainstorming until you feel you have enough details for a paragraph with seven to twelve sentences. Remember, it is better to have too many details than to have too few, for you can always edit the extra details later.

Collaborate

Exercise 1   **Collaborate: Adding Details to Support a Topic Sentence**

Do this exercise with a partner or group. The following topic sentences have some—but not enough—details. Write sentences to add details to each list.

1. **topic sentence:** A bad cold can make your life miserable.

    details: 1. A cold means you will have a runny nose.

    2. It means you will sneeze constantly.

    3. IT MEANS You WILL BLOW YOUR NOSE A LOT.

    4. IT MEANS YOUR NOSE WILL GET RAW FROM BLOWING IT SO MUCH.

    5. IT MEANS YOUR THROAT WILL HURT.

    6. IT MEANS IT WILL BE HARD TO SWALLOW.

2. topic sentence: When Patrick feels hungry in the middle of the night, he will eat nearly anything.

details: 1. He prefers leftover rice and beans.

2. However, he also enjoys cold meat such as ham.

3. HE ENJOYS JELLO

4. HE REALLY ENJOYS FRESH CAT.

5. HE WILL SETTLE FOR MAN FLESH.

6. HE PREFERS NOT TO EAT MEXICANS. THEY GIVE HIM HEART BURN.

3. topic sentence: People like to dance for a number of reasons.

details: 1. Dancing is good exercise.

2. They are good at dancing.

3. They like to show off their skills.

4. THEY ~~MIGHT~~ ARE DRUNK.

5. THEY ARE TRYING TO ATTRACT A SUITABLE MATE.

6. THEY MIGHT HAVE ANTS IN THEIR PANTS.

4. topic sentence: When my friends and I go out to eat, we always eat the same kinds of food.

details: 1. We go out for a burger and fries.

2. Sometimes we get fried chicken.

3. SOMETIMES WE KILL A HOBO AND MUNCH ON HIS/HER TOES.

4. USUALLY WE GO TO TIM HORTON'S.

5. SOMETIMES WE DON'T EAT, JUST GO AND GET DRUNK AT THE BAR

6. SOMETIMES WE TAKE A NAP.

5. topic sentence: Stress is hitting me from every part of my life.

details: 1. I am overwhelmed with coursework at school.

2. I need a better work schedule.

3. SOMETIMES ITS BECAUSE OF THE VOICES IN MY HEAD

4. SOMETIMS ITS NOT.

5. I DONT LIKE HOLDING IN A POOP.

6. KITTENS SCARE ME

Eliminating Details That Do Not Relate to the Topic Sentence

Sometimes, what you thought were good details don't relate to the topic sentence because they don't fit or support your point. Eliminate details that don't relate to the topic sentence. For example, the following list contains details that don't relate to the topic sentence. Those details are crossed out.

topic sentence: My neighbors are making my home life unbearable.
details: play their music loud at 3:00 A.M.
I can't sleep
leave garbage all over the sidewalk
~~come from Philadelphia~~
sidewalk is a mess
insects crawl all over their garbage
~~I carefully bag my garbage~~
they argue loudly and bang on the walls
my privacy is invaded
park their van in my parking space

Exercise 2   **Practice: Eliminating Details That Do Not Fit**

Following are topic sentences and lists of details. Cross out the details that do not fit the topic sentence.

1. topic sentence: Katherine's new apartment needs some work.
details: ~~The apartment complex is far from campus.~~
The toilet is leaking.
The paint in the kitchen is flaking off one wall.
The carpet in the bedroom needs cleaning.
~~There are no assigned parking spaces.~~
The closet door will not shut properly.
The baseboards are filthy.

2. topic sentence: I love city life for a number of reasons.
details: ~~I am a morning person.~~
I like the excitement of crowds.
In the city, I never run out of things to do or see.
I can meet all kinds of people in the city.
I rarely feel alone in the city.
City people tend to be accepting of nonconformists.
~~I was born in the suburbs.~~

3. topic sentence: A truly kind person has several defining traits.

details: A kind person doesn't enjoy gossip.

A kind person doesn't enjoy criticizing someone.

Most kind people do not want attention or praise for their good deeds.

Phony people criticize others and call it "constructive criticism."

A kind person is generous with his or her time and even money.

A kind person senses when someone needs emotional support.

Kind people can be found in most charitable organizations.

4. topic sentence: There are a number of reasons why many people fear thunderstorms..

details: Lightning might have struck near them in the past.

A flash of lightning is like fire to some people.

A thunderstorm is something fierce that humans cannot control.

The darkening sky and clouds are ominous to some people.

Some people enjoy the sounds of a battle in the sky.

It is not a good idea to seek shelter under a tree.

As the dark clouds move closer, the skies become magnificent.

5. topic sentence: Although we keep hearing about a paperless world, we still use paper in some critical parts of our daily life.

details: I need facial tissue.

It would be hard to find a substitute for toilet paper.

Paper creates problems with waste disposal.

Many of our financial transitions can already be paperless.

It would be difficult to find a substitute for the paper in disposable diapers.

Tissue paper protects fragile items when they are transported.

Boxes are generally made of cardboard, a form of paper.

From List to Outline

Take another look at the topic sentence and list of details on the topic of My Mother:

topic sentence: My mother survived difficult times to become a good parent and worker.

details: She's a good mom.

Always takes care of me.

She works hard.

She cooks, cleans.

makes a great chicken casserole

She has a job.

> She's a nurse.
> She had a rough life.
> lost her husband
> went to school at night

After you scan the list, you will be ready to develop the outline of a paragraph.

The outline is a plan for writing, and it can be a kind of draft in list form. It sketches what you want to write and the order in which you want to present it. An organized, logical list will make your writing unified because each item on the list will relate to your topic sentence.

When you plan, keep your topic sentence in mind:

My mother <u>survived difficult times</u> to become <u>a good parent</u> and <u>worker</u>.

Notice that the key words are underlined and lead to key phrases:

> survived difficult times
> a good parent
> a good worker

Can you put the details together so that they connect to one of these key phrases?

survived difficult times

She had a rough life, lost her husband, went to school at night

a good parent

She's a good mom, Always takes care of me, She cooks, cleans, makes a great chicken casserole

a good worker

She works hard, She has a job, She's a nurse

With this kind of grouping, you have a clearer idea of how to organize a paragraph. You may have noticed that the details grouped under each phrase explain or give examples that are connected to the topic sentence. You may also have noticed that the detail "She works hard" is placed under the phrase "a good worker." It could also be placed under "a good parent," so it would be your decision where to place it.

Now that you have grouped your ideas with key phrases and examples, you can write an outline:

An Outline for a Paragraph on My Mother

topic sentence:	My mother survived difficult times to become a good parent and worker.
details:	{ She had a rough life.
difficult times	{ She lost her husband.
	{ She went to school at night.
	{ She's a good mom and always takes care of me.
a good parent	{ She cooks and cleans.
	{ She makes a great chicken casserole.
a good worker	{ She works hard at her job.
	{ She's a nurse.

As you can see, the outline combines some details from the list. Even with these combinations, the details are very rough in style. As you reread the list of details, you may notice places that need more combining, places where ideas need more explaining, and places that are repetitive. Keep in mind that an outline is merely a rough organization of your paragraph.

As you work through the steps of devising an outline, you can check for the following:

Checklist for an Outline

✔ **Unity:** Do all the details relate to the topic sentence? If they do, the paragraph will be unified.

✔ **Support:** Do I have enough supporting ideas? Can I add to those ideas with more specific details?

✔ **Coherence:** Are the ideas listed in the right order? If the order of the points is logical, the paragraph will be coherent.

Coherence

Check the sample outline again, and you'll notice that the details are grouped in the same order as in the topic sentence: first, details about your mother's difficult life; next, details about your mother as a parent; finally, details about your mother as a worker. Putting details in an order that matches the topic sentence is a logical order for this paragraph. It makes the paragraph *coherent*.

Determining the Order of Details

Putting the details in a logical order makes the ideas in the paragraph easier to follow. The most logical order for a paragraph depends on the subject of the paragraph. If you are writing about an event, you might use **time order** (such as telling what happened first, second, and so forth); if you are arguing some point, you might use **emphatic order** (such as saving your most convincing idea for last); if you are describing a room, you might use **space order** (such as describing from left to right or from top to bottom).

Exercise 3 **Practice: Coherence: Putting Details in the Right Order**

These outlines have details that are in the wrong order. In the space provided, number the sentences so that they are in the proper order: 1 would be the number for the first sentence, and so on.

1. **topic sentence:** Christopher's apology was short, superficial, and hostile. (Put the sentences in the same order as in the topic sentence.)

___3___ Christopher's apology took approximately thirty seconds.

___2___ I was left to figure out his words: "I am sorry that you feel that I hurt you."

___1___ It was really no apology at all.

_____ I realized that he had not admitted that he had hurt me.

_____ Instead, he had maliciously focused on *my* problem (my feelings) rather than on his.

_____ Part of the reason that it was so short was that he spit out the words.

_____ After his thirty-second attempt at an apology, he disappeared.

2. topic sentence: Drinks that mix alcohol, a sickening sweet flavor, and a large jolt of caffeine are dangerous. (Put the sentences in emphatic order, from the least dangerous effect to the most.)

3 They make the drinker feel wide awake and energized.

2 The drinker feels capable of drinking more drinks (full of alcohol) than he or she would consume by drinking a traditional alcoholic beverage.

1 Consumers of these "energy drinks" do not sense the alcohol's effect on their brains.

6 Some of these drinkers kill themselves and/or others when they get behind the wheel.

4 Some of these drinkers believe they can drive home.

5 Some have car accidents.

3. topic sentence: Marguerite must have put on her makeup in the dark, for she was covered in an excess of makeup. (Put the sentences in space order, from the top of the head to the chin.)

4 Marguerite's cheeks were the cherry red of a clown face.

1 The space between the top of her forehead and her hairline showed a distinct, skin-toned line between her orange-colored foundation makeup and her brown hair.

2 Her eyebrows were penciled in as if a kindergartner had used a thick black crayon.

3 Mascara clotted her eyelashes and partially hid her sequined blue eyeshadow.

5 A wet pink lipstick was framed by a dramatic shade of red-brown lipliner.

4. topic sentence: Yoga class is not for the lazy. (Put the sentences in time order, from first to last.)

3 The instructor arrived and started us off with some simple stretching exercises.

6 The stretching exercises hurt me.

7 Then we moved on to what the instructor called simple yoga positions.

8 While most people enjoyed themselves in these "simple" positions, I kept falling over.

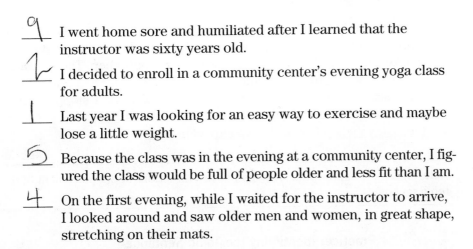

_9_ I went home sore and humiliated after I learned that the instructor was sixty years old.

_2_ I decided to enroll in a community center's evening yoga class for adults.

_1_ Last year I was looking for an easy way to exercise and maybe lose a little weight.

_5_ Because the class was in the evening at a community center, I figured the class would be full of people older and less fit than I am.

_4_ On the first evening, while I waited for the instructor to arrive, I looked around and saw older men and women, in great shape, stretching on their mats.

Where the Topic Sentence Goes

The outline format helps you organize your ideas. The topic sentence is written above the list of details. This position helps you remember that the topic sentence is the main idea and that the details that support it are written under it. You can easily check each detail on your list against your main idea. You can also check the unity (relevance) and coherence (logical order) of your details.

When you actually write a paragraph, the topic sentence does not necessarily have to be the first sentence in the paragraph. Read the following paragraphs, and notice where each topic sentence is placed.

Topic Sentence at the Beginning of the Paragraph

<u>Dr. Chen is the best doctor I have ever had.</u> Whenever I have to visit him, he gives me plenty of time. He does not rush me through a physical examination and quickly hand me a prescription. Instead, he takes time to chat with me and encourages me to describe my symptoms. He examines me carefully and allows me to ask as many questions as I want. After I am dressed, he discusses his diagnosis, explains what medicine he is prescribing, and tells me exactly how and when to take the medication. He tells me what results to expect from the medication and how long it should take for me to get well. Dr. Chen acts as if he cares about me. I believe that is the most important quality in a doctor.

Topic Sentence in the Middle of the Paragraph

The meal was delicious, from the appetizer of shrimp cocktail to the dessert of strawberry tarts. Marcel had even taken the time to make home-baked bread and fresh pasta. <u>Marcel had worked hard on this dinner, and his hard work showed.</u> Everything was served on gleaming china placed on an immaculate tablecloth. There were fresh flowers in a cut glass bowl at the center of the table, and there was a polished goblet at every place setting. The pale green napkins had been carefully ironed and folded into precise triangles.

Topic Sentence at the End of the Paragraph

I woke up at 5:00 A.M. when I heard the phone ringing. I rushed to the phone, thinking the call was some terrible emergency. Of course, it was just a wrong number. Then I couldn't get back to sleep because

I was shaken by being so suddenly awakened and irritated by the wrong number. The day got worse as it went along. My car stalled on the freeway, and I had to get it towed to a repair shop. The repair cost me $250. I was three hours late for work and missed an important training session with my boss. On my way out of work, I stepped into an enormous puddle and ruined a new pair of shoes. <u>Yesterday was one of those days when I should have stayed in bed.</u>

> **Note:** Be sure to follow your own instructor's directions about placement of the topic sentence.

Exercise 4 Practice: Identifying the Topic Sentence

Underline the topic sentence in each of the following paragraphs.

1. The autumn is my favorite season of the year. There is a huge sycamore tree outside the front window of my second-floor apartment, and it sheds huge, golden leaves for weeks. They are like a carpet of perfectly shaped, glowing pieces of art. I love the cool nights and the clear days when the sun keeps the wind from chilling me too much. In addition, I associate autumn with all the holidays to come. I dream of Halloween, Thanksgiving, and the long stretch of days for giving and celebration in December and January. To many people, autumn signals the decline of the old year, but to me it means a burst of nature's and human nature's goodness.

2. My friend Amanda got the call early one morning last month. Her boyfriend, Ryan, had been killed in what appeared to be a robbery at his family's home. The police investigators did not know much, but they knew that Ryan and his parents had been at home when it happened. The parents were asleep, and Ryan had gone into the kitchen at about 1:00 A.M. At or shortly after that time, Ryan's father and mother heard a noise, and the father went to the kitchen to investigate. Ryan lay on the floor, dead from a gunshot wound. The back door of the house was open. Amanda could not believe this account. Ryan was a good student and a popular one. He had no criminal record or gang affiliations. She could only speculate that Ryan, who liked to stay up late playing games on his computer, had gone to the kitchen for a snack. In a few minutes of unexplained violence, a beloved son and boyfriend had been taken from the earth.

3. If I stop at my mother's house to drop off a spare key or a borrowed hammer, I always leave with something. It could be a bottle of shampoo that she bought at a two-for-one sale. It might also be an extra lawn chair that she found at a garage sale. If I stay for a meal, I always leave with leftovers. There is no way for me to escape my mother's generosity. If I admire a plant on her patio, she cuts a shoot from it, sticks it in a plastic bag full of moist soil, and tells me to plant the shoot in a flower pot. If I tell her that I don't have any flower pots, she gives me one of hers. I can stay at my mother's house overnight on a cold night, and she will be likely to send me home the next day with a warm quilt that I loved when I was a child. Soon I will need a bigger apartment to hold all her gifts to me.

Writing a Paragraph: Drafting and Revising

Chapter Objectives

Students will realize that (1) multiple drafts are a natural part of the writing process, (2) careful revision often entails structural changes, and (3) effective editing includes changes in sentence patterns and word choice.

An outline is a draft of a paragraph in list form. Once you have an outline, you are ready to write the list in paragraph form, to create a first draft of your assignment.

DRAFTING

The drafting and revising stage of writing is the time to draft, revise, edit, and draft again. You may write several drafts or versions of the paragraph in this stage. Writing several drafts is not an unnecessary chore or a punishment.

Rather, it is a way of taking pressure off yourself. By revising several times, you are telling yourself, "The first try doesn't have to be perfect."

Review the outline on the topic of My Mother on page 294. You can create a first draft of this outline in the form of a paragraph. (Remember that the first line of each paragraph is indented.) In the draft of the following paragraph, the first sentence of the paragraph is the topic sentence.

A First Draft of a Paragraph on My Mother

My mother survived difficult times to become a good parent and worker. She had a rough life. She lost her husband. She went to school at night. She's a good mom and always takes care of me. She cooks and cleans. She makes a great chicken casserole. She works hard at her job. She's a nurse.

Revising the Draft

Once you have a first draft, you can begin to think about revising and editing it. *Revising* means rewriting the draft to change the structure, the order of the sentences, and the content. *Editing* includes making changes in the choice of words, in the selection of the details, in the punctuation, and in the patterns and kinds of sentences. It may also include adding transitions—words, phrases, or sentences that link ideas.

Below is a list of some common transitional words and phrases and the kind of connections they express.

INFO BOX: Common Transitions

To join two ideas

again	another	in addition	moreover
also	besides	likewise	similarly
and	furthermore		

To show a contrast or a different opinion

but	instead	on the other hand	still
however	nevertheless	or	yet
in contrast	on the contrary	otherwise	

To show a cause-and-effect connection

accordingly	because	for	therefore
as a result	consequently	so	thus

To give an example

for example	in the case of	such as	to illustrate
for instance	like		

To show time

after	first	recently	subsequently
at the same time	meanwhile	shortly	then
before	next	soon	until
finally			

One easy way to begin the revising and editing process is to read your work aloud to yourself. As you do so, listen carefully to your words and concentrate on their meaning. Each question in the following checklist will help you focus on a specific part of revising and editing. The name (or key term) for each part is in parentheses.

Checklist for Revising the Draft of a Paragraph (with key terms)

✔ Am I staying on my point? (unity)

✔ Should I eliminate any ideas that do not fit? (unity)

✔ Do I have enough to say about my point? (support)

✔ Should I add any details? (support)

✔ Should I change the order of my sentences? (coherence)

✔ Is my choice of words appropriate? (style)

✔ Is my choice of words repetitive? (style)

✔ Are my sentences too long? Too short? (style)

✔ Should I combine any sentences? (style)

✔ Am I running sentences together? (grammar)

✔ Am I using complete sentences? (grammar)

✔ Can I link my ideas more smoothly? (transitions)

If you apply the checklist to the draft of the paper on My Mother, you will probably find these rough spots:

- The sentences are very short and choppy.
- Some sentences could be combined.
- Some words are repeated often.
- Some ideas need more details for support.
- The paragraph needs transitions: words, phrases, or sentences that link ideas.

Consider the following revised draft of the paragraph, and notice the changes, underlined, that have been made in the draft:

A Revised Draft of a Paragraph on My Mother

topic sentence:

sentences combined

transition

details added,

transition

details added

details added

details added,

transition

details added

details added

> My mother survived difficult times to become a good parent and worker. <u>Her hard times began when she lost her husband. At his death, she was only nineteen and had a baby, me, to raise. She survived by</u> going to school at night <u>to train for a career. Even though she lives a stressful life,</u> she is a good mom. She always takes care of me. <u>She listens to my problems, encourages me to do my best, and praises all my efforts. She cleans our apartment until it shines, and she makes dinner every night.</u> She makes a great chicken casserole. <u>In addition,</u> she works hard at her job. She is a nurse <u>at a home for elderly people, where she is on her feet all day and is still kind and cheerful.</u>

When you are revising your own paragraph, you can use the checklist to help you. Read the checklist several times; then reread your draft, looking for answers to the questions on the list. If your instructor agrees, you can work with your classmates. You can read your draft to a partner or group. Your listener(s) can react to your draft by applying the questions on the checklist and by making notes about your draft as you read. When you are finished reading aloud, your partner(s) can discuss their notes about your work.

> **Note:** You can also revise a draft of your paragraph by working with a partner and using the Peer Review Form for a Paragraph at the end of Chapter 23.

Exercise 1   Practice: Revising a Draft for Unity

Some of the sentences in the following paragraph do not fit the topic sentence. (The topic sentence is the first sentence in the paragraph.) Cross out the sentences that do not fit.

My husband and I finally found a way to handle our child's nightmares. Our five-year-old son, Enrique, used to sleep peacefully through the night in his own room, but recently he has been waking up, screaming. He claims that there is a ghost in his room. Once he is awake, he cannot go back to sleep and instead becomes frightened at every ordinary sound. I remember when the sound of tree branches against the window used to terrify my little sister. At first we took Enrique into our bed, and he slept fairly well. However, he began to wake up, startled, and listen for "ghosts." Soon all three of us were awake for most of the night. The "ghosts" seemed to get worse. Comic books and cartoons often contain ghosts, but they don't always frighten small children. My husband realized that Enrique spent each night listening for ghosts, so our son might feel safer if he couldn't hear strange noises. Enrique returned to his own room where we played soft music all night. He sleeps much better now.

Exercise 2   Collaborate: Adding Support to a Draft

Collaborate

Do this exercise with a partner or group. The following paragraph needs more details to support its point. Add the details in the blank spaces provided.

Our weekend trip to a beach resort was nearly perfect. First of all, the weather really cooperated with our plans. (Add two sentences of details.)

_____

_____

The beach and the water could not have been better. (Add two sentences about

the beach and the water.) _____

_____

_____ In addition, our hotel was a pleasant surprise. (Add two sentences

about the unexpected pleasures of the hotel.) _____

_____

_____

Our only complaint was that we couldn't stay longer, but we will soon return.

Exercise 3   Practice: Revising a Draft for Coherence

In the following paragraph, one sentence is in the wrong place. Move it to the right place in the paragraph by drawing an arrow from the sentence to its proper place.

I thought I could get away with parking in a no-parking area for just a few min-

utes, but I could not escape one vigilant police officer. I had desperately searched the

parking lot at a local strip mall, but I couldn't find one empty spot. It was lunch hour,

and people were running errands, grabbing fast food, stopping at the bank, and pick-

ing up dry cleaning. All I needed was to dash into the pharmacy and pick up my pre-

scription medication. Unfortunately, a man in uniform caught me running back to my

illegally parked car. Desperate, I decided to snatch the only available—and tempting—

spot: a handicapped spot right in front of the pharmacy. I raced to the store and waited

impatiently until a clerk handed me my medication. By the time the electronic doors of

the pharmacy parted, I was feeling triumphant. A hefty fine and a well-deserved lecture

from the officer made me feel guilty about the nasty, selfish aspects of my behavior.

Collaborate

Exercise 4   Collaborate: Revising a Draft for Style

Do this exercise with a partner or a group. The following paragraph is repeti-tive in its word choice. Replace each underlined word with a word that is less repetitive. Write the new word above the underlined one.

My friend Isaac's tropical pets are all ugly. I expected some of them to be

pretty, but I was disappointed to find each one <u>uglier</u> than the next. For example,

Isaac has a pet iguana that lives in the yard, and I thought it would be a <u>pretty</u> lizard.

Instead, it was a large, <u>ugly</u> lizard with <u>ugly</u> scales on its back. Isaac also rescued

an abandoned parrot who had been left in a cage. People usually think of parrots

as <u>pretty</u> birds with <u>pretty</u> feathers, but Isaac's parrot is <u>ugly.</u> Isaac's tropical fish

were the worst disappointment. They were the <u>ugliest</u> tropical fish I had ever seen.

I know Isaac must love his pets, but I wish Isaac had found at least one <u>pretty</u> one.

Exercise 5   Practice: Revising a Draft by Combining Sentences

The following paragraph has many short, choppy sentences that are underlined. Wherever you see two or more underlined sentences clustered next
to each other, combine them into one clear, smooth sentence. Write your
revised version of the underlined sentences in the spaces above the lines.
To review ways to combine sentences, see Chapter 5.

Jessica is afraid of insects. <u>Even a line of tiny ants has been known to upset</u>

<u>her. Larger bugs can send her into a panic.</u> Cockroaches make her shudder. Their

shiny red-brown or gleaming black shells disgust her. <u>She has a specific fear. She</u>

<u>is afraid that she will wake up in the night. Then she will put out her hand and</u>

<u>touch a cockroach on her bed.</u> When Jessica sees a roach in her house, she uses

a can of insecticide spray to destroy the insect. Big, hairy spiders also make her

shudder. <u>These are the ones that stand tall. They are covered in hair. They move</u>

<u>fast. Then they hide.</u> When they hide, Jessica fears that these spiders are wait-

ing for her to relax so that they can come out again and bite her. Jessica's fear of

insects seems to have turned her daily life into one long horror movie.

Exercise 6   Practice: Revising a Draft by Correcting Run-Together
Sentences

The following paragraph has some run-together (run-on) sentences. Correct
the run-ons by writing in the spaces above the lines. To review ways to correct run-on sentences, see Chapter 3.

My brother Sam and I are identical twins, but we are not alike in personality.

I am outgoing and friendly he is shy. When people meet us, they expect us to act

like a stereotype of twins. Twins in movies and in commercials are expected to be

cute and clever. Whole film plots revolve around twins who change places to fool someone however we could never change places. Once we open our mouths, people can tell us apart our body language also gives us away. In addition, I am used to making eye contact when I meet strangers. Sam is wary of new people, and he takes his time in getting to know someone. Possibly Sam has a deeper nature than I do. However, we are both kind, caring, and loyal siblings.

Exercise 7 Practice: Editing a Paragraph for Complete Sentences

The following paragraph has some incomplete sentences (sentence fragments). Correct the fragments by writing in the spaces above the lines. To review ways to correct sentence fragments, see Chapter 6.

I love my father, but he has a few minor flaws. His clothes, for example. They show a lack of basic knowledge of what to wear. For instance, most men know that when they attend a formal wedding, they should not wear a polo shirt under a suit. He has been known to commit a few other fashion crimes. Such as wearing shoes with holes in them. He won't throw these shoes away because they are so comfortable. My father has also been known to sing in the shower. At 6:00 A.M. Anyone who is still asleep wakes up to his songs. His greatest flaw, however, has to do with corny jokes. He cannot stop. Telling them. Then he forgets which jokes he told you. I must have heard his joke about the elephant and the mouse twenty times. In spite of his jokes, his singing, and his lack of fashion sense, my father is loveable and loving. Lucky to have him.

Writing a Paragraph: Proofreading

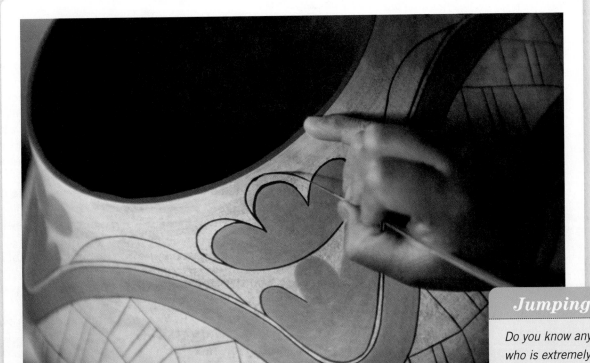

CHAPTER 23

Chapter Objectives

Students will be able to (1) recognize the importance of careful proofreading, (2) devise an appropriate title reflecting the main idea of the paragraph, and (3) understand the similarities between its topic sentence and concluding sentence.

The final version of your paragraph is the result of careful thinking, planning, and revising. After many drafts and much editing, and when you are satisfied with the result, read the final draft aloud to *proofread*. You can avoid too many last-minute corrections if you check your last draft carefully for the following:

- spelling errors
- punctuation errors
- grammar errors
- word choice
- a final statement

CORRECTING THE FINAL DRAFT OF A PARAGRAPH

Take a look at the following final draft of the paragraph on My Mother. The draft has been corrected directly above the crossed out material. You will notice corrections in spelling, punctuation, and word choice.

You'll notice that the slang term *mom* has been changed to *mother.* At the end, you'll notice that a final statement has been added to unify the paragraph.

A Corrected Final Draft of a Paragraph on My Mother

My mother survived difficult ~~time's~~ *times* to become a good ~~parrent~~ *parent* and worker. Her hard times began when she lost her husband. At his death, ~~She~~ *she* was only nineteen and had a baby, me, to raise. *She* she survived by going to school at ~~nite~~ *night* to train for a career. Even though she lives a stressful life, she is a good ~~mom~~ *mother.* She ~~allways take~~ *always takes* care of me. She listens to my ~~prolems~~ *problems,* ~~encourage~~ *encourages* me to do my best, and praises all my efforts. She cleans our apartment until it ~~shine~~ *shines,* and she makes dinner every night. She makes a ~~great~~ *delicious* chicken casserole. In addition, she works hard at her job. She is a nurse at a home for elderly people, where she is on her feet ~~allday~~ *all day* and is still kind and cheerful. At work or at home, my mother is an inspiration to me.

Exercise 1 **Practice: Correcting the Errors in the Final Draft of a Paragraph**

Proofread the following paragraph, looking for errors in word choice, spelling, punctuation, and grammar. Correct the ten errors by crossing out each mistake and writing the correction above it.

I'm not a great athlete, superior student, or son of wealthy parents, but I have 1 asset that makes me popular. I'm a good listener. For some reason, people like to tell me about themselfs. When I travel, strangers on a plane have told me there life stories. In high school, I new more secrets about my classmates then anyone would believe. At my job, my Coworkers and even my boss confide in me. When people confide in me, I don't do much talking but simply nod my head or make other appropriate responses. Maybe I have an honest-looking face. For some reason, people trust me and I have never enjoyed telling other peoples' secrets. Perhaps I should be studying for a career as a counselor. Because I have years of experience in listening.

Exercise 2   **Practice: More on Correcting the Errors in the Final Draft of a Paragraph**

Proofread the following paragraph, looking for errors in word choice, spelling, punctuation, and grammar. Correct the ten errors by crossing out each mistake and writing the correction above it.

Recently a friend was killed in a senseless crime, and onely one activity help me to cope. That activity was walking alone on a long road in the woods. When I began to feel overcome by greif, I would force my self to leave my house, and go to this place in the wood's. Something about using my energy to walk with a purpose helped me. The walking din't soothe me, but it gave me a focus. Instead of reliving the initial shock of this death, I was able to put the pane at a short distance. Once I made this walk into a habit, I grew stronger. The sun glittering above the tall trees made me think, about nature's Power. For a few minutes, I could be in peace.

Giving Your Paragraph a Title

When you prepare the final version of your paragraph, you may be asked to give it a title. The title should be short and should fit the subject of the paragraph. For example, an appropriate title for the paragraph on one's mother could be "My Wonderful Mother" or "An Inspiring Mother." Check with your instructor to see if your paragraph needs a title. (In this book, the sample paragraphs do not have titles.)

Exercise 3   **Collaborate: Creating a Title**

Collaborate

With a partner or group, create a title for the following paragraph.

Title: _____

My family left New Jersey when I was seven years old, and I am very happy living in Florida. However, sometimes I feel homesick for the North. At Christmas, especially, I wish I could see the snow fall and then run outdoors to make a snowman. In December, it feels strange to string outdoor lights on palm trees. I also miss the autumn when the leaves on the trees turn fiery red and gold. Sometimes my aunt in New Jersey sends me an envelope of autumn leaves, and I remember the crackle of leaves beneath my feet and the smell of the burning leaves in the fall bonfires. Life is different in Florida where we enjoy sunshine all year. We are spared the icy gray days of a Northern winter, the slush of melting snow, and the gloomy rain of early spring. I now live in a place that is always warm and bright, but sometimes I miss the changing seasons of my first home.

Reviewing the Writing Process

In four chapters, you have worked through *four important stages* in writing. As you become more familiar with the stages and with working through them, you will be able to work more quickly. For now, try to remember the four stages:

> ## INFO BOX: The Stages of the Writing Process
>
> **Prewriting:** gathering ideas, thinking on paper through freewriting, brain-storming, or keeping a journal
>
> **Planning:** planning the paragraph by grouping details, focusing the details with a topic sentence, listing the support, and devising an outline
>
> **Drafting and Revising:** drafting the paragraph, then revising and editing it
>
> **Proofreading:** preparing the final version of the paragraph, with one last proofreading check for errors in format, spelling, and punctuation

Following are an outline, revised draft, and final version of the paragraph on My Mother. Notice how the assignment evolved through the stages of the writing process.

An Outline for a Paragraph on My Mother

topic sentence:	My mother survived difficult times to become a good parent and worker.
details:	She had a rough life.
	She lost her husband.
	She went to school at night.
	She's a good mom and always takes care of me.
	She cooks and cleans.
	She makes a great chicken casserole.
	She works hard at her job.
	She's a nurse.

A Revised Draft of a Paragraph on My Mother

My mother survived difficult times to become a good parent and worker. Her hard times began when she lost her husband. At his death, she was only nineteen and had a baby, me, to raise. She survived by going to school at night to train for a career. Even though she lives a stressful life, she is a good mom. She always takes care of me. She listens to my problems, encourages me to do my best, and praises all my efforts. She cleans our apartment until it shines, and she makes dinner every night. She makes a great chicken casserole. In addition, she works hard at her job. She is a nurse at a home for elderly people, where she is on her feet all day and is still kind and cheerful.

Final Version of a Paragraph on My Mother

(Changes from the draft are underlined.)

My mother survived difficult times to become a good parent and worker. Her hard times began when she lost her husband. At his death, she was only nineteen and had a baby, me, to raise. She survived by going to school at night to train for a career. Even though she <u>still</u> lives a stressful life <u>today</u>, she is a good <u>mother.</u> She always takes care of me. She listens to my problems, encourages me to do my best, and praises all my efforts. She cleans our apartment until it shines, and she makes dinner every night. She makes a delicious chicken casserole. In addition, she works hard at her job. She is a nurse at a home for elderly people, where she is on her feet all day and is still kind and cheerful. <u>At work or at home, my mother is an inspiration to me.</u>

Critical Thinking and the Writing Process

As you know by now, one of the popular methods of prewriting is called *brainstorming*, the practice of asking yourself key questions that can lead you to new ideas and directions related to your writing topic. During your college career, you will find that such questioning can enable you to engage in **critical thinking,** a type of reasoning that has several meanings and practical uses. For now, just remember that any time you evaluate the relevance of supporting details, determine their order of importance, and attempt to justify their inclusion in your work, you are making judgments that are considered *critical.* Making such judgments will become more common for you as you undertake college writing assignments. You will soon appreciate the crucial role critical thinking plays in effective writing, whether you are recalling an order of events to include in a personal narrative, crafting vivid images for a descriptive paper, choosing the best supporting details for illustrating a point, or clearly explaining the key steps of a specific process.

At the end of this chapter and in subsequent writing chapters, you will find a variety of critical thinking and writing options. These topics may require you to defend a point of view, imagine a certain scenario, or examine a trend. Whether you discuss these topics with classmates, participate in a group assignment, or tackle an issue on your own, keeping an open mind will help you become a better writer and a stronger critical thinker.

Lines of Detail: A Walk-Through Assignment

Write a paragraph about a friend. To write this paragraph, follow these steps:

Step 1: For fifteen minutes, freewrite or brainstorm about a friend.

Step 2: Survey your freewriting or brainstorming and underline any specific ideas you can find. Put these ideas in a list.

Step 3: Pick one idea from your list; it will be your topic. Try to develop it by adding details. Get details by going back to your list for other ideas that fit your topic, by brainstorming for more ideas, and by listing new ideas.

Step 4: Put the ideas on your list into categories by marking them or by mapping them.

Step 5: Write a topic sentence and list your ideas below it.

Step 6: Draft your paragraph by writing the topic sentence and all the ideas on your list in paragraph form. Revise, draft, and edit until you are satisfied with your paragraph.

Step 7: Proofread your final draft; then prepare your good copy of your paragraph.

Topics for Writing Your Own Paragraph

When you write on any of these topics, be sure to work through the stages of the writing process in preparing your paragraph.

1. This assignment involves working with a group. First, pick a topic from the following list:

> bad drivers
> homesickness
> powerful music

Next, join a group of other students who picked the same topic you did. Brainstorm in a group. Discuss questions that could be asked to get ideas for your paragraph.

For the drivers topic, sample questions could include "What kind of driver is the worst?" or "How can you avoid being a bad driver?"

For the homesickness topic, sample questions could include "When were you homesick?" or "What did you miss most about your former home?"

For the music topic, sample questions could include "Is music most powerful at sad occasions or at happy ones?" or "Do the words or the rhythm make music powerful?"

As you brainstorm, write the questions down. Keep them flowing. Don't stop to answer the questions. Don't stop to say, "That's silly," or "I can't answer that." Try to generate at least twelve questions.

Twelve Brainstorming Questions

1. _____
2. _____
3. _____
4. _____
5. _____
6. _____
7. _____
8. _____
9. _____
10. _____
11. _____
12. _____

Once you have the questions, split up. Begin the prewriting step by answering as many questions as you can. You may also add more questions or freewrite. Then pick a specific topic, list the related details, and write a topic sentence.

Work through the planning stage by developing an outline with sufficient details.

After you've written a draft of your paragraph, read it to your writing group, the same people who met to brainstorm. Ask each member of your group to make one positive comment and one suggestion for revision.

Finally, revise and edit your draft, considering the group's ideas for improvement. When you are satisfied with your revised draft, prepare a final version of the paragraph.

2. Following are some topic sentences. Select one and use it to write a paragraph.

   The best way for me to relax is _____.

   Learning a new language is hard because _____.

   I still have two unanswered questions about college; they are _____ and _____.

   If I had a hundred extra dollars, I would spend it on _____.

   I am most suited for a career in _____.

3. This assignment requires you to interview a partner. Your final goal is to write a paragraph that will inform the class about your partner. Your paragraph should use this topic sentence:

   _____ (fill in your partner's name) has had three significant experiences.

   Collaborate

   Step 1: Before you write the paragraph, prepare to interview a classmate. Make a list of six questions you want to ask. They can be questions such as, "Have you ever had any interesting experiences?" or "Have you ever been in danger?" Write at least six questions *before* you begin the interview. List the questions below, leaving room to fill in short answers later.

Interview Form

1. Question: _____

   Answer: _____

2. Question: _____

   Answer: _____

3. Question: _____

   Answer: _____

4. Question: _____

   Answer: _____

5. Question: _____

   Answer: _____

6. Question: _____

Answer: _____

Additional questions and answers:

_____

_____

_____

Step 2: As you interview your partner, ask the questions on your list and jot down brief answers. Ask any additional questions you can think of as you are talking; write down the answers in the additional lines at the end of the interview form.

Step 3: Change places. Let your partner interview you.

Step 4: Split up. Use the list of questions and answers about your partner as the prewriting part of your assignment. Work on the outline and draft steps.

Step 5: Ask your partner to read the draft version of your paragraph, to write any comments or suggestions for improvement below the paragraph, and to mark any spelling or grammar errors in the paragraph itself.

Step 6: Revise your draft. When you have completed a final version of your paragraph, read the paragraph to the class.

4. Select one of the following topics. Then narrow it to one aspect of the topic and write a paragraph on that aspect. If you choose the topic of scary movies, for example, you might want to narrow it by writing about your favorite scary movie.

clothing styles	college rules	junk food
holidays	national heroes	habits
scary movies	viral videos	dreams
a dangerous sport	children	transportation

5. Study the photo of the silhouette as a prompt to write a paragraph about the most significant relationship in your life.

Topics for Critical Thinking and Writing

1. Consider how heavily you rely on technology either in school, at work, or with family and friends. Then imagine how your life would be different if you had no access to a cell phone, a computer, or a television. Write about how difficult or easy it would be for you to eliminate these technological devices from your daily life.

2. You have probably noticed several changes in your neighborhood or in your town over the years. Think about a significant change and describe the reactions of various residents to this change.

Name _____ Section _____

Peer Review Form for a Paragraph

After you have written a draft version of your paragraph, let a writing partner read it. When your partner has completed the following form, discuss it. Then repeat the same process for your partner's paragraph.

The topic sentence of this paragraph is _____

_____

_____

_____

The detail that I liked best begins with the words _____

_____

The paragraph has enough/too many/too few [circle one] details to support the topic sentence.

A particularly good part of the paragraph begins with the words _____

_____

I have questions about _____

_____

_____

_____

_____

Other comments on the paragraph _____

_____

_____

_____

_____

_____

_____

_____

Reviewer's Name _____

Jumping In

What do you think happened just before this dramatic scene? Can you imagine what led to the expressions of frustration? There must be a story behind this picture, and if you write the story, you will be writing a **narrative** paragraph.

Chapter Objectives

Students will be able to write a narrative paragraph that (1) has a narrow focus, (2) presents details in a clear order, and (3) uses effective transitional words and phrases.

Paragraphs use different methods to make their points. One kind of paragraph uses *narration*.

WHAT IS NARRATION?

Narration means telling a story. Everybody tells stories; some people are better storytellers than others. When you write a **narrative** paragraph, you can tell a story about something that happened to you or to someone else, or about something that you saw or read.

A narrative covers events in a time sequence because it is always about happenings: events, actions, incidents. However, interesting narratives do more than just tell what happened. They help the reader become involved in the story by providing vivid details. These details come from your memory, your observation, or your reading. Using good details, you don't just tell the story; you *show* it.

Give the Narrative a Point

We all know people who tell long stories that seem to lead nowhere. These people talk on and on; they recite an endless list of activities and soon become boring. Their narratives have no point.

The difficult part of writing a narrative is making sure that it has a point. That point will be included in the topic sentence. The point of a narrative is the meaning of the incident or incidents you are writing about. To get to the point of your narrative, ask yourself questions like these:

What did I learn?
What is the meaning of this story?
What is my attitude toward what happened?
Did it change me?
What emotion did it make me feel?
Was the experience a good example of something (like unfairness, or kindness, or generosity)?

The answers to such questions can lead you to a point. An effective topic sentence for a narrative is

not this: This paper will be about the time I found a wallet on the sidewalk. (This is an announcement; it does not make a point.)
but this: When I found a wallet on the sidewalk, my honesty was tested.

not this: Last week my car alarm wouldn't stop screeching. (This identifies the incident but does not make a point. It is also too narrow to be a good topic sentence.)
but this: I lost my faith in fancy gadgets when my car alarm wouldn't stop screeching.

Exercise 1 Practice: Recognizing Good Topic Sentences for Narrative Paragraphs

If a sentence is a good topic sentence for a narrative paragraph, write *OK* on the line provided.

1. _____ This is the story of an online rumor.

2. _____ Last week, someone was accused of a crime.

3. _____ When my brother stole my phone, he learned the force of my anger.

4. _____ The strength of a person's desire to win one important game will be discussed here.

5. _____ Raising money for a family who suffered in a fire made me feel useful and needed.

6. _____ Temporary employment in a department store gave me an understanding of sales techniques.

7. _____ Seeing a film about the Haitian earthquake horrified and motivated me.

8. _____ A few months ago, my fiancé lost his wallet with all his identification and credit cards.

9. _____ One night in jail will be the topic of this paragraph.

10. _____ I will tell you about my broken leg and the time I spent wearing a heavy cast.

Exercise 2   **Collaborate: Writing the Missing Topic Sentences in Narrative Paragraphs**

Collaborate

Below are three paragraphs. Working with a partner or group, write an appropriate topic sentence for each one. Be ready to share your answers with another group or with the class.

1. topic sentence: _____

_____

     Last month I had to renew my driver's license. I had recently moved to a new part of the state, and I was unsure of the procedure to follow. Had I brought sufficient identification? I was not sure. Would I have to pass any kind of test? I did not think so. After a series of long lines and stressful moments, I left the testing site with a new photo and my new address on my updated license. I felt triumphant. Later that afternoon, I returned to my, put my license in my pocket, and took a short walk. On the next morning, I couldn't find my license. In a panic, I searched my clothes, my house, and even the route where I had walked on the previous day. Furious at myself, I wound up back at the license bureau where I was ashamed to admit the truth: I had lost my new license within twenty-four hours. Later, my story had a somewhat happy ending. Ten days after I had lost the first license, an envelope addressed to me arrived in the mail. In it was my original "new" license. Someone had found it, and, using the address on the new license, mailed it to me. That person is a rare and kind human being.

2. topic sentence: _____

_____

     I met Jim at a party and was attracted to him at once. He was funny, handsome, and a little crazy. Jim seemed to have more spirit than the somewhat dull, highly focused, and ambitious students I had met at school. Soon we were seeing each other regularly. Unfortunately, I was also meeting his friends. I did not like them. They did not seem to like me, either. They seemed to resent me for pulling Jim out of his hard-drinking, hard-living pack. When they teased or taunted Jim into adventures such as shoplifting or shooting their guns in the woods, I had to make a choice. I could keep seeing Jim and accept his friends. If I could not tolerate these friends, I had to move on because Jim was too weak to risk losing their approval. I chose the only sane alternative and stopped seeing this funny, handsome, crazy, and pathetic boy.

3. topic sentence: _____

_____

     A huge music festival called Summer Fun was scheduled for the last weekend in August. Admission was inexpensive, and the park where the event would be held was nearby, so I agreed to go with two friends. Our first challenge was finding a parking space. We wound up parking in a dusty field transformed into an overflow parking lot. After a twenty-minute walk, we arrived at the crowded festival. Thousands of people were standing around three sound stages. Each stage had its own performers, and the noise of one band carried to the music on a second stage. It was hard to hear much. Smart people had brought their own lawn chairs or blankets, but we stood for a long time. The sun was baking our bodies, and we got thirsty. Unfortunately, a bottle of water cost $5.00 at one of the refreshment stands. Even if we had wanted to pay the price, we would have had to wait for twenty or thirty minutes to get to the head of the line. After an hour of trying to enjoy the festival, we left, sunburned, hot, and tired.

HINTS FOR WRITING A NARRATIVE PARAGRAPH

Everyone tells stories, but some people tell stories better than others. When you write a story, be sure to

- Be clear.
- Be interesting.
- Stay in order.
- Pick a topic that is not too big.

1. Be clear.   Put in all the information the reader needs in order to follow your story. Sometimes you need to explain the time, or place, or the relationships of the people in your story in order to make the story clear. Sometimes you need to explain how much time has elapsed between one action and another. This paragraph is not clear:

> Getting the right textbooks from the campus bookstore was a frustrating experience. First of all, I missed the first two days of classes, so José had to give me the list of books, and I really couldn't understand his writing. Then, when I got there, they didn't have all the books I needed. The book I needed the most, the workbook for my Intermediate Algebra class, wasn't on the shelves, and they said they had run out and wouldn't get more until next week. In addition, I couldn't use a Mastercard, only a Visa card, to pay, and I didn't have a Visa card. I left with only one of my required textbooks.

What is wrong with the paragraph? It lacks all kinds of information. Who is José? Is he a classmate? Someone who works in the bookstore? And what list is *the* list of books? The writer talks about getting "there," but is "there" the campus bookstore or another bookstore, and who are "they"?

2. Be interesting.   A boring narrative can make the greatest adventure sound dull. Here is a dull narrative:

> Volunteering with the homebuilders club was great. Last weekend I helped the club members fix up an old house. First, we did some things outside. Then we worked on the inside and cleaned up the kitchen. We did a little painting, too. I particularly liked the end of the project, when the family who owned the house saw the improvements. They were happy.

Good specific details are the difference between an interesting story and a dull one.

3. Stay in order.   Put the details in a clear order so that the reader can follow your story. Usually, time order is the order you follow in narration. This narrative has a confusing order:

> Celia was really upset with me yesterday. But that was before I explained about the car accident. Then she forgave me and felt guilty about being so mean. She was angry because I had promised to take her to the movies last night. When I didn't show up, she started calling me on my

cell phone. She claims she called seven times and never got an answer. What Celia didn't know was that, on my way to her house, I had skidded on a wet road and hit a tree. I wasn't badly hurt, but the paramedics insisted on taking me to the emergency room. My cell phone was in my car while I rode in an ambulance. By the time I left the hospital and made it to Celia's house, it was midnight, and Celia was not in a good mood.

There's something wrong with the order of events here. Tell the story in the order it happened: First, I promised to take Celia to the movies. Second, I had a car accident. Third, Celia tried to call many times. Fourth, I was taken to the emergency room and then released. Fifth, I went to Celia's house, where she was angry. Sixth, I told my story and she forgave me. A clear time sequence helps the reader follow your narrative.

4. Pick a topic that is not too big. If you try to write about too many events in a short space, you risk being superficial. You cannot describe anything well if you cover too much. This paragraph covers too much:

Visiting New York City was like exploring a new world for me. It started with a ride on the subway, which was both frightening and exciting. Then my cousin, a native New Yorker, introduced me to Times Square, where I saw people dressed like aliens in a science fiction movie and I learned to navigate through thousands of people all trying to cross the street. After that, we went to a famous New York deli where I ate Greek, Korean, and Italian food. The next day, we walked to Central Park and heard a free concert. That night, we went to a club where the music was loud and wild.

This paragraph would be better if it discussed one shorter time period in greater depth and detail. For example, it could cover one incident—the subway ride, the visit to Times Square, the deli meal, the concert, or the club—more fully.

Using a Speaker's Exact Words in Narrative

Narratives often include the exact words someone said. You may want to include part of a conversation in your narrative. To do so, you need to know how to punctuate speech.

A person's exact words get quotation marks around them. If you change the words, you do not use quotation marks.

exact words: "You're acting strangely," he told me.
not exact words: He told me that I was acting strangely.

exact words: My father said, "I can get tickets to the soccer match."
not exact words: My father said he could get tickets to the soccer match.

There are a few other points to remember about punctuating a person's exact words. Once you've started quoting a person's exact words, periods and commas generally go inside the quotation marks. Here are two examples:

Marcelline said, "My car needs new tires."
"Eat your breakfast," my grandmother told me.

When you introduce a person's exact words with phrases like "She said," or "The police officer told us," put a comma before the quotation marks. Here are two examples:

She said, "Take your umbrella."

The police officer told us, "This road is closed."

If you are using a person's exact words and have other questions about punctuation, check the section on quotation marks in Chapter 16.

WRITING THE NARRATIVE PARAGRAPH IN STEPS

PREWRITING NARRATION

Suppose your instructor asks you to write a narrative paragraph on this topic:

My Last _____

You might begin by *freewriting:*

Freewriting on My Last _____

My last _____. My last what? Last chance? Last dance? My last chance at passing Algebra. My last cup of coffee. My last day of high school. That was wild. Seniors are crazy sometimes. Coffee—I love coffee. Quit it suddenly. Last cup of morning coffee. Needed my morning coffee.

You scan your freewriting and realize that you have three possible topics: My Last Day of High School, My Last Chance at Passing Algebra, and My Last Cup of Coffee. Since you do not have any details on passing algebra, and the last day of high school seems like a topic that many students might write about, you decide to be original and work with My Last Cup of Coffee.

Exercise 3 Practice: Finding Topics in Freewriting

Each of the freewriting examples that follow contains more than one possible topic for a paragraph. In the spaces below each freewriting, write the possible topics, and write the one that you think would be the best topic for a narrative paragraph. Briefly explain why it would be the best topic: Is it the one with the most details? Is it the most original topic? Or is it the one that would be the easiest to develop with specific details?

1. Freewriting on this Topic: My First _____

My first what? My first kiss. How dumb is that? And I can't remember anything anyway. My first day in college. Maybe. Pretty confusing and intimidating. Will everyone write about college? My first taste of Mexican food. Wow. I wasn't ready for the hot sauce. Now I love it. All kinds of Mexican food. My first bike. Riding it on the sidewalk.

possible topics: _____

_____

your choice of the best topic: _____

reason for your choice: _____

2. Freewriting on This Topic: The Silliest _____

> The silliest thing I ever did? Lots of things to choose from. Driving all night to see my girlfriend and running out of gas on a deserted road. Quitting a good job because of an argument. But my boss was wrong. I had to tell my side of the story. Silly pranks. Some were dangerous, not silly. One silly prank at the beach stands out. Sharks in the water at night. Don't go in.

possible topics: _____

_____

your choice of the best topic: _____

reason for your choice: _____

Listing Ideas

Now that you have a specific topic, you can scan your freewriting for all your ideas on that topic. You put all those ideas into a list:

My Last Cup of Coffee

I love coffee.
Quit it suddenly.
Last cup of morning coffee.
Needed my morning coffee.

Adding Specific Details by Brainstorming

To add ideas to your list, try brainstorming. Add questions that will lead you to more details. You can start with questions that are based on the details you already have. See where the questions—and their answers—lead you.

Question: Why do you love coffee?

Answer: I love the taste.

Question: Is that the only reason?

Answer: It picks me up. Gives me energy.

Question: Why did you quit it suddenly?

Answer: I figured quitting suddenly would be the best way. Don't drag it out.

Question: Why was your last cup drunk in the morning? Why not the afternoon or evening?

Answer: My first cup in the morning was the one I needed the most. To wake up.

Question: Were there any other times you needed it?

Answer: I needed it all day.

Question: Can you be more specific?

Answer: I craved coffee around 10:00 a.m., and then again around 3:00 or 4:00 p.m., and also after dinner.

Question: How did you feel after you quit?

Answer: I felt terrible at first. The next day I felt better.

Question: What do you mean by saying you felt terrible?

Answer: I was irritable. Shaky. I had bad headaches.

As you can see, questions can lead you to more details and can help you to decide whether you will have enough details to develop a paragraph on your topic or whether you need to choose another topic. In this case, the details in the answers are sufficient for writing a paragraph.

Collaborate

Exercise 4 Collaborate: Brainstorming for Details

Following are topics and lists of details. With a partner or group, brainstorm at least five questions and answers, based on the existing details, that could add more details. The first one is partly done for you.

1. topic: Getting Lost at the University

It was our first visit.
We were going to a big football game.
We had no air conditioning or fans.
We felt grown up.
Three of us were driving around.
We had no idea the place was so big.

Brainstorming Questions and Answers:

Question 1: Who were the three of you? _____

Answer 1: Me (Ryan), Jack, and Marty _____

Question 2: How old were you? _____

Answer 2: We were seventeen. _____

Question 3: _____

Answer 3: _____

Question 4: _____

Answer 4: _____

Question 5: _____

Answer 5: _____

2. topic: Learning to Ride a Bicycle

I got my first two-wheeler.
I had wanted it so badly.
My mother was worried.
It was a surprise gift.
I got a used bike.
I loved it anyway.

Brainstorming Questions and Answers:

Question 1: _____

Answer 1: _____

Question 2: _____

Answer 2: _____

Question 3: _____

Answer 3: _____

Question 4: _____

    Answer 4: _____

Question 5: _____

    Answer 5: _____

3. topic: Saying Goodbye

> I had to say goodbye to a place.
> It was the city where I had lived all my life.
> I was twenty-five.
> I was afraid to start over in a new place.
> But I had to do it.

Brainstorming Questions and Answers:

Question 1: _____

    Answer 1: _____

Question 2: _____

    Answer 2: _____

Question 3: _____

    Answer 3: _____

Question 4: _____

    Answer 4: _____

Question 5: _____

    Answer 5: _____

Focusing the Prewriting

To begin focusing your topic and details around some point, list your topic and all the details you have gathered so far. The list that follows includes all of the details gathered from freewriting and brainstorming.

My Last Cup of Coffee

I love coffee.
Quit it suddenly.
Last cup of morning coffee.
Needed my morning coffee.
I love the taste of coffee.
It picks me up.
Gives me energy.
I figured quitting suddenly would be the best way.
Don't drag it out.
My first cup in the morning was the one I needed the most.
To wake up.
I needed it all day.
I craved coffee around 10:00 A.M., and then again around 3:00 or 4:00 P.M., and also after dinner.
I felt terrible at first.
The next day I felt better.
First I was irritable. Shaky. I had bad headaches.

Coherence: Grouping the Details and Selecting a Logical Order

If you survey the list, you can begin to group the details:

List of Details on My Last Cup of Coffee

Why I Love Coffee

I love the taste.
It picks me up.
Gives me energy.

The Morning I Quit

I quit it suddenly.
I figured quitting suddenly would be the best way.
Don't drag it out.
Drank my last cup in the morning.
My first cup in the morning was the one I needed most.
To wake up.

The Afternoon

I needed it all day.
Around 3:00 or 4:00 P.M., I craved coffee.
I felt terrible at first.
I was irritable and shaky.

The Evening

I craved coffee after dinner.
I was more irritable.
I had a bad headache.

The Next Day

I felt better.

Looking at these groups, you notice one, Why I Love Coffee, is background for your narrative. Three groups, The Morning I Quit, The Afternoon, and The Evening, tell about the *stages* of your quitting. And the last group tells how you felt *after* you had your last cup. These groups seem to lead to a *logical order* for the paragraph: a *time order.* A logical order will give your paragraph coherence.

Unity: Selecting a Topic Sentence

To give the paragraph unity, you need a point, a topic sentence. Surveying your topic and detail, you might decide on this topic sentence:

My last cup of coffee was in the morning.

To be sure that your paragraph has *unity,* check your topic sentence. It should (1) make a point and (2) relate to all your details.

Does it make a point? No. It says your last cup of coffee was in the morning. That isn't much of a point. It is too narrow to develop into a paragraph. Does the topic sentence relate to all your details? No. You have details about why you love coffee, when you needed it, how you quit, and how you felt afterward. But with your topic sentence, you can talk only about the morning you quit.

You need a better topic sentence. To find it, ask yourself questions like:

Did I learn anything from this experience?
Did the experience hurt me?
Did it help me?
Was it a sad experience?
Was it a joyful one?
Were the results good or bad?
Is there a lesson in this experience?

Surveying your details, you might realize that they tell of someone who drank a great deal of coffee and who feels better after he or she quit. You might decide on a better topic sentence:

My last cup of coffee was the beginning of better health.

This topic sentence relates to many of the details you have. You can mention why you love coffee and when you drank it so that you can give some background on how hard it was to quit. You can explain quitting and discuss how you felt afterward. This topic sentence will give your paragraph unity.

To check your topic sentence for unity, ask the following questions:

Checklist for Unity and the Topic Sentence

✔   Does the topic sentence make a point?

✔   Is the point broad enough to cover all the details?

✔   Do the details relate to the topic sentence?

If the answer to these questions is yes, you are helping to unify your paragraph.

Now that you have a topic sentence and a list of details, you are ready to begin the planning stage of writing.

Exercise 5   Practice: Grouping Details

Below are topics and lists of details. Group the details of each list, writing them under the appropriate headings. Some details may not fit under any of the headings.

1.   **topic:**   Starting Over

     details: After one semester, I quit college to find a job.

     I didn't see my old friends much because I had dropped out.

     I got promoted at my job once in five years.

     When I returned to college, I was more of an adult.

     Working had taught me a few things about getting stuck in a rut.

     I was a bored and restless nineteen-year-old sitting in a lecture hall.

     Returning to school, the first thing I did was take a deep breath.

     Once I had a job, I felt fairly satisfied at first.

On my first day back at college, I sat in the front row of the lecture hall.

At nineteen, I had no idea what I wanted in life—except some money.

Gradually, I felt stuck, lonely, and bored in my job.

This time, I looked at college as a way to test my limits.

I enjoyed my first day of being an older student.

I knew what I wanted on my second try.

After high school, all my friends were going to college, so I did, too.

List details about the writer's first try at college: _____

_____

_____

_____

List details about the time after his first try at college: _____

_____

_____

_____

List details about his different attitude on his return to college: _____

_____

_____

_____

List details about his first day back in college: _____

_____

_____

_____

_____

2. **topic:** Choices

    details: My parents and I came to America when I was two years old.

    My parents could not hold on to their business.

    Shortly after they arrived in the United States, my father and mother used all their savings to open a small business.

    They worked long, hard hours at their business.

    I considered returning to Taiwan because otherwise I would be all alone, without any family.

    I wanted to be a loyal son.

    The business did fairly well, but then bad times hit my parents hard.

    I've never understood the economics of small family businesses.

    They had no more money to invest.

They decided to ask me, an adult now, to return to Taiwan with them.

They decided to return to Taiwan where our extended family would help them.

I would be left without my parents' encouragement and care.

I knew no other life than my American life.

I had a steady job in America.

I knew that America was my real home, even without my family.

I chose to stay in America.

List details about the writer's family background in America: _____

_____

_____

_____

_____

_____

List details about the parents' decision: _____

_____

_____

_____

List details about the writer's dilemma: _____

_____

_____

_____

List details about the writer's choice: _____

_____

_____

_____

3. **topic:** A Surprise

    details: Cato was nowhere to be found, indoors or out.

    My dog always wants to be in the room that I am in.

    One busy Saturday, I began by running from room to room, taking out the trash and doing other chores.

    I dumped some clothes in my tiny laundry room on my way to make the bed.

    In my bedroom, I noticed that Cato wasn't with me.

    I checked all the rooms in my house, but it was no use.

    Panicked, I feared that he might haven gotten outside.

    I checked the back yard.

I ran to the front yard and called his name.

Feeling guilty and stupid, I hugged my dog tight.

I checked the dark garage in the back yard.

Few experiences are as bad as losing a pet.

Just as I was about to give up hope, I had an idea.

My idea was to check the one place I had forgotten: my tiny laundry room.

There was Cato, waiting quietly to be freed from the small space.

My dog Cato loves to be with people.

List details about Cato's personality: _____

_____

_____

_____

List details about what the narrator was doing before Cato disappeared

on Saturday: _____

_____

_____

List details about the realization that Cato was missing and the search

indoors: _____

_____

_____

List details about the search outdoors: _____

_____

_____

_____

List details about finding Cato: _____

_____

_____

_____

_____

Exercise 6   **Collaborate: Creating Topic Sentences**

Do this exercise with a partner or a group. Following are lists of details. For each list, write two appropriate topic sentences.

1. topic sentence 1: _____

   _____

   topic sentence 2: _____

   _____

details: On Saturday afternoon, I was returning to my house after a trip to the supermarket.

I felt proud of myself because I had planned for the week ahead.

I had stocked up on supplies for breakfast, dinner, and snacks.

As I approached my garage, I couldn't find the garage door opener.

Quickly, I bent down to check the floor of the car.

Suddenly, there was a loud sound of metal crumbling and glass breaking.

I had taken my foot off the brake just as my car had slowly hit the garage door.

The door had crumpled when my car bumped it.

I was horrified.

Then I was more horrified and ashamed when I thought about the cost of a new garage door.

2. topic sentence 1: _____

_____

topic sentence 2: _____

_____

details: My sister and her husband recently moved out of their old, two-story townhouse into a newer but smaller one.

My sister Abigail is an efficient and organized person.

Her husband Bill is a more spontaneous one.

My sister cleaned her clothes closet, sorting items into boxes labeled "keep," "give away," and "toss."

Then she began on her husband's closet.

Unfortunately, Bill appeared just as she was dumping his favorite t-shirt (full of holes) into the "toss" box.

Bill snatched the shirt and stuffed it in the "keep" box.

He commandeered his closet, grabbing faded jeans and ragged sweaters.

He found beloved shoes he had not seen in years.

Everything went into the "keep" box.

Abigail was unhappy.

Out of desperation, she tried to sneak a pair of Bill's sweatpants into the "give away" box.

At that moment, she found her old college sweatshirt in a corner of Bill's closet.

She decided to put her sweatshirt in the "keep" box.

3. topic sentence 1: _____

_____

topic sentence 2: _____

_____

details: I am always in a hurry, and yesterday was particularly hectic for me.

I was on my way home after a long day at work and school.

I realized that I had nothing to eat in my house.

Driving past a local supermarket, I swung into the parking lot to pick up something from the deli.

I left my cell phone on the front passenger seat.

I locked my car doors.

I raced into the market and went straight to the deli.

Within ten minutes, I left with a huge sandwich, some chips, and a bottle of lemonade.

I walked purposefully to my car.

The front passenger window was in pieces on the ground.

My cell phone was gone.

PLANNING **NARRATION**

Once you have a topic sentence and a list of details, you can write them in outline form. Below is an outline for a paragraph on My Last Cup of Coffee. As you read the outline, you will notice that some of the items on the earlier list have been combined and the details have been grouped into logical categories.

Outline on My Last Cup of Coffee

topic sentence: **details:**	My last cup of coffee was the beginning of better health.
why I love coffee	I love the taste of coffee. Coffee picks me up and gives me energy.
the morning I quit	I quit it suddenly. I figured quitting suddenly would be the best way. Don't drag it out. Drank my last cup in the morning. My first cup in the morning was the one I needed most. I needed it to wake up.
the afternoon	I needed it all day. Around 3:00 or 4:00 P.M., I craved coffee. I felt terrible at first. I was irritable and shaky.

the evening
$\left\{\begin{array}{l}\text{I craved coffee after dinner.}\\\text{I was more irritable.}\\\text{I had a bad headache.}\end{array}\right.$

the next day $\left\{\text{I felt better.}\right.$

Once you prepare your outline, check it for these qualities, using the following checklist.

Checklist for a Narrative Outline

✔ Do all the details connect to the topic sentence?

✔ Are the details in a clear order?

✔ Does the outline need more details?

✔ Are the details specific enough?

With a good outline, you are ready to write a rough draft of a narrative paragraph.

Exercise 7   **Practice: Finding Details That Do Not Fit**

Following are outlines. In each outline, there are details that do not relate to the topic sentence. Cross out the details that do not fit.

1. **topic sentence:** One of the most embarrassing incidents in my life started with a sneeze.

    details: I was sitting in my sociology class.

    Our instructor was giving a PowerPoint lecture and, aside from her words, the room was quiet.

    I have a hard time taking notes during a PowerPoint presentation.

    Suddenly I sneezed an enormous, loud sneeze.

    I was embarrassed.

    I looked around to see if anyone had noticed.

    Then I sneezed again, loudly.

    Five more enormous sneezes followed quickly.

    Now even my professor was looking at me.

    "Are you all right?" she asked.

    I felt an entire lecture room full of students staring at me in horror.

    Before I could answer, I sneezed again.

    I am not usually a big sneezer and don't have allergies.

    I slinked out of my seat, clutching a ragged tissue to my face, and sneezed all the way to the exit.

2. **topic sentence:** One evening, we had an unexpected visitor from the natural world.

     details: My husband and I live in a first-floor apartment.

                Although it is a large modern complex, it is close to a nature preserve.

                The complex has a large pool and patio area.

                One night after dinner, we were sitting outdoors on our small, screened porch.

                We like to relax as the sun goes down.

                Suddenly, we saw a small creature about fifteen feet away.

                "It's a cat," I said.

                The creature came closer.

                It was a small fox.

                We were thrilled to see the wild fox so close to us.

                We've seen many squirrels, but never a fox.

3.   **topic sentence:** When our plans for Friday night did not work out, we found a great alternative.

     details: A great new movie opened on Friday night.

                We arrived at our local theater where about a hundred people were already in line for the show.

                It was hot and humid in the line.

                The line didn't seem to be moving.

                Everyone wants to be the first to see a certain film so he or she can talk about the film at work.

                Finally, my girlfriend went up to the box office.

                She returned with bad news.

                The movie was already sold out for the current showing.

                The line was for tickets for the midnight show, and that show was nearly sold out.

                We decided to leave.

                On the way home, we devised a plan.

                We stopped at a Mexican restaurant and ordered take-out fajitas.

                There are two Mexican restaurants near our apartment.

                We went home, browsed through our DVDs, and found one comedy that we love.

                Comedies are good when people need to lift their moods.

                We turned down the air conditioner, lit candles, ate our fajitas, and laughed through the video.

Exercise 8   **Practice: Recognizing Details That Are Out of Order**

Each outline below has one detail that is out of order. Indicate where it belongs by drawing an arrow from it to the place where it should go.

1.   **topic sentence:**   In the future, I will eat only take-out pizza.

     details: Yesterday I was feeling both lazy and hungry.

     I decided to eat whatever I could find at home.

     Given a choice between wilted lettuce and pizza, I picked the pizza.

     My refrigerator held only a bag of wilted salad, a bottle of Diet Sprite, and a frozen pizza.

     I checked the required baking temperature on the pizza box.

     Then I set the oven for the correct temperature.

     When the oven had reached the correct temperature, I took the pizza out of the freezer.

     I ripped open the pizza box and tore off the plastic covering.

     I placed the pizza on a metal pan, set the oven timer, and popped the pizza in the oven.

     When the timer sounded, I pulled the pizza from the oven, set my meal on a plate, and cut the pizza into slices.

     Hungrily I bit into the first slice.

     It had a burnt flavor, and the texture was a bit strange.

     Examining the slice more carefully, I studied the bottom of the piece.

     I had baked the pizza without removing the cardboard that separates the bottom of the pizza from the box.

2.   **topic sentence:**   Two children made my long wait at the doctor's office into an amusing afternoon.

     details: I arrived on time for my 2:00 P.M. doctor's appointment.

     When I arrived, there were four other people in the waiting room.

     "The doctor is running a little late," said the receptionist a few minutes later when a sixth person arrived.

     At 2:30 P.M., a mother with a little girl arrived.

     The little girl sat next to her mother but soon began to fidget.

     By 2:45, the mother had warned the little girl, scolded, and even grabbed the child when the little girl began to wander.

The receptionist replied that the doctor had been handling an emergency.

At about ten minutes past three, a little boy and his mother entered the waiting room.

For the little boy, one look at the little girl led to instant love.

He ran to the little girl and kissed her.

Everyone in the room laughed.

After an hour of waiting, I asked the receptionist why no one had been called in to see the doctor.

For a few minutes, all of us in the waiting room forgot to be impatient as we watched the toddlers play together.

3. **topic sentence:** Every dog has its day, and my dog had a good day last weekend.

details: My dog Buster is a confusing mix of Labrador, German shepherd, and bull terrier.

He is hard to classify but easy to love.

I love him enough to take him on long walks every weekend.

Last Sunday, we were hiking in a wooded area south of our town.

Buster was sniffing in the brush, looking for treasures like bones and the remnants of other hikers' snacks.

I reached to take the paper before he began to chew it.

Once I had the paper in my hand, I realized it was a ten-dollar bill.

My first thought was to search the ground for a lost wallet or some other form of identification.

Soon I realized that there was nothing to find.

What should I do with the money? I wondered.

Then I looked down; Buster was panting, smiling, and waiting for some praise.

Suddenly I saw him with some paper in his mouth.

Later on Sunday, Buster got the largest bag of dog treats that he had ever dreamed of.

Collaborate

Exercise 9 **Collaborate: Putting Details in the Correct Order**

Do this exercise with a partner or a group. In each of the outlines below, the list of details is in the wrong order. Number the details in the correct order, writing *1* next to the detail that should be listed first, and so on.

1. **topic sentence:** My dream of a quiet evening at home turned into a nightmare.

details: _____ During a busy week at work, I promised myself a quiet, luxurious Saturday night at home alone.

_____ Once I stashed my goodies in the kitchen, I prepared for a long, hot bath.

_____ I was about to sink into a warm, bubble-filled bathtub when the phone rang.

_____ My former boyfriend was calling, was back in town, and wanted to know if he could stop by.

_____ Even though I knew I was being stupid, I agreed that he could come over.

_____ I was shocked to see him arrive with friends: two beautiful girls and a man.

_____ I rushed to dress, do my hair, and put on makeup before he arrived.

_____ I arrived home with all the necessities: two DVDs, fresh French bread from the bakery, cheese, a bottle of wine, and chocolates.

_____ The visitors sipped my wine, ate the bread, and savored my chocolate.

_____ As they feasted, I fumed and tried to determine the relationships among these visitors.

2. topic sentence: Getting my four-year-old ready for preschool yesterday became a mission I swore to accomplish.

details: _____ Miranda woke up in a bad mood.

_____ As I coaxed her out of bed, she grumbled.

_____ She resisted as I tried to wash her.

_____ After the battle of the bathroom, she could not decide what to eat.

_____ Dressing her proved to be worse than feeding her.

_____ She rejected her princess outfit, her pink dress and leggings, and all her other favorite styles.

_____ We left the house with Miranda still sulking but feeling somewhat victorious in her choice of clothes: a flowered hat, a fleece pajama top, sparkly jeans, and bunny slippers.

_____ I offered hot cereal, cold cereal, sliced bananas, sliced and diced peaches, milk, and two kinds of juice.

_____ She refused all my offerings.

_____ Desperate, I whipped up a smoothie in the blender.

_____ She agreed to drink a little but slipped most of the smoothie to our dog.

3. **topic sentence:** Yesterday, I began learning how to stand up for myself.

   details: _____ The supervisor said that one staff member was going to take two days of sick leave.

   _____ Mr. Ricci asked all of the remaining staff to pick up a few extra hours to cover for the missing person.

   _____ The remaining block of time was the late Saturday night time slot.

   _____ On Friday, my supervisor, Mr. Ricci, called a meeting to set the schedule for next week's work.

   _____ Everyone cooperated until only one block of time remained empty.

   _____ "Dan will take it," my coworker said. "Dan's a good guy."

   _____ After those kind words, I was about to accept the time slot when suddenly I changed my mind.

   _____ Everyone was silent when Mr. Ricci asked for a volunteer for Saturday night.

   _____ Then the silence was broken by one of my coworkers.

   _____ Instead of accepting the Saturday night hours, I said, "I've filled that slot too often; it's time for someone else to pitch in."

   _____ The silence in the group was astonishment at my assertiveness.

DRAFTING AND REVISING NARRATION

Once you have a good outline, you can write a draft of your paragraph. Once you have a first draft, you can begin to think about revising and editing. The checklist below may help you revise your draft.

Checklist for Revising the Draft of a Narrative Paragraph

✔ Is my narrative vivid?

✔ Are the details clear and specific?

✔ Does the topic sentence fit all the details?

✔ Are the details written in a clear order?

✔ Do the transitions make the narrative easy to follow?

✔ Have I made my point?

Transitions

Transitions are *words*, *phrases*, or even *sentences* that link ideas. Sometimes they tell the reader what he or she has just read and what is coming next. Every kind of writing has its own transitions. When you tell a story, you have to be sure that your reader can follow you as you move through the steps of your story. Most of the transitions in narration have to do with time. Below is a list of transitions writers often use in writing narratives.

INFO BOX: **Transitions for a Narrative Paragraph**

after	at the same time	immediately	now	until
again	before	in the meantime	soon	when
always	during	later	soon after	while
at first	finally	later on	still	
at last	first (second, etc.)	meanwhile	suddenly	
at once	frequently	next	then	

Following is a draft created from the outline on My Last Cup of Coffee. As you read it, you will notice that it combines some of the short sentences from the outline, adds some details, and adds transitions.

A Revised Draft of a Paragraph on My Last Cup of Coffee

My last cup of coffee was the beginning of better health. It was hard for me to stop drinking coffee because I love the taste of coffee. In addition, coffee picks me up and gives me energy. I quit it suddenly because I figured that a sharp break would be better than dragging out the process. I drank my last cup in the morning. It was the cup I needed most, to wake up, so I decided to allow myself that cup. By afternoon, I saw how much I needed coffee all day. Around 3:00 or 4:00 p.m., I craved it. I felt terrible. I was shaky and irritable. After dinner, my coffee craving was worse. I was more irritable, and I had a pounding headache. The next day, I felt better.

margin annotations:
sentences combined, added details
sentences combined, added details, transition added
details added

details added, transition added

Exercise 10   **Practice: Recognizing Transitions**

Underline all the transitions—words and phrases—in the paragraphs below.

1. Trying to amuse my two-year-old niece proved costly for me. On Saturday, my sister, desperate for someone to watch her daughter Sarah, begged me for help. Soon after, Sarah arrived with a bag full of toys. When her mother waved goodbye in a cheery voice, Sarah stared. Tears followed. Next, I offered Sarah every toy in her toy sack. First, she simply shook her head. Then she began to cry. Growing desperate, I surveyed my options. I turned the television on and found a cartoon channel. She was not interested, nor did she smile when I tried to dance with her to an old children's song. Soon after, I made my big mistake. I reached for an old plush toy from my own childhood. Sarah saw the green and blue frog in my hands and stopped sobbing. Then I brought it close to her eyes and danced the frog back and forth. She reached out, gurgling with pleasure. I had no idea a toddler could be so strong until Sarah grabbed the frog. At once, she put one of the little frog's legs in her mouth and drooled. While I watched in horror, Sarah bit off the frog's leg. I immediately grabbed the frog's leg, now coated in Sarah's saliva. Suddenly, I realized that my beloved frog would never be the same.

2. Desperation led to humiliation for Andrew. We had an important exam in our Introduction to Business class, and we were both nervous. In fact, we had spent most of the previous night studying for that test. I went to Andrew's house, and we crammed for hours. First, we skimmed the assigned reading and asked each other questions. Then we reviewed our lecture notes. Meanwhile, we drank plenty of coffee. When I couldn't stuff another piece of information into my head, I went home and caught a few hours of sleep. Next morning, I made it to the classroom just before the exam was to begin. Soon after, Andrew stumbled in, bleary-eyed. "I'd better do well on this exam," he whispered as he passed me. "I stayed up after you left and kept reviewing." He found a seat near the front and fell into it. I finished the test ahead of time and took a breath before I submitted my test

booklet and answer sheet. While I sat calmly, I looked around. Andrew had his head in his hands. Then his head began to fall toward the desk. His head fell softly into his folded arms. At once, Andrew began to snore. It was a loud snore, and at the same time that I heard it, the other students heard it, too. When our professor walked quietly to Andrew's seat, Andrew was still snoring over his test booklet.

Exercise 11 Practice: Adding the Appropriate Transitions

In the paragraphs below, transitions are shown in parentheses. Underline the appropriate transitions.

1. Getting to college and getting home again are complicated processes for me. I don't have a car, and my house is too far from college for me to walk or ride a bike. (After/While) I eat breakfast and pack my book bag, I walk about a mile to the nearest bus stop. There is a bench at the bus stop but no covered area. (Until/When) it rains, I get wet unless I remember to carry a small umbrella. The bus gets me to school an hour and a half (before/while) my classes start. The campus is not very crowded (during/next) this time so I can find a quiet place to read or study. (Later/When) my classes begin, they are scheduled one after the other. If the last class runs a few minutes overtime, I have to run to catch a bus home. If I miss that bus, I have to wait another hour (soon/until) another bus appears. Someday I will be rewarded for my long journeys to and from campus, but (at first/in the meantime), I just accept these trips as part of my education.

2. I have two wishes. (First/Always), I'd like to be taller; (suddenly/second), I'd like to be thinner. I'm below average in height, and I'm tired of being called "Shorty" and having tall people look down at me. If my first wish came true, I would (next/before) ask to be thin as well. I'm not fat, but I am a little overweight. If I could be taller and thinner, my life might improve. (While/Then) I might feel more comfortable about meeting strangers or speaking in public. Of course, my wishes are shallow and self-centered, but they are honest. (Later on/always) I may be more mature and have more substantial wishes, but (now/finally) I am very conscious of the flaws in my appearance.

Collaborate

Exercise 12 **Collaborate: Using Transitions**

Do this exercise with a partner or a group. Write a sentence for each item below. Be ready to share your answers with another group or with the entire class.

1. Write a sentence with *frequently* in the middle of the sentence

   _____

2. Write a sentence that begins with *Before.*

   _____

3. Write a sentence with *at last* in the middle of the sentence.

   _____

4. Write a sentence that begins with *At first.*

   _____

5. Write a sentence with *later on* in the middle of the sentence.

   _____

6. Write a sentence with *when* in the middle of the sentence.

   _____

7. Write a sentence with *always* in the middle of the sentence.

   _____

8. Write a sentence that begins with *Then.*

   _____

9. Write a sentence that begins with *Suddenly.*

   _____

10. Write a sentence with *in the meantime* in the middle of the sentence.

    _____

PROOFREADING **NARRATION**

The draft of the paragraph on My Last Cup of Coffee has some rough spots:

- One idea is missing from the paragraph: Why did you decide to give up coffee? How was it hurting your health?
- Added details could make it more vivid.
- The paragraph needs transitions to link ideas.
- To make its point, the paragraph needs a final sentence about better health.

Following is the final version of the paragraph on My Last Cup of Coffee. As you review the final version, you will notice several changes:

- A new idea, about why you wanted to stop drinking coffee, has been added.
- To avoid repetition, one use of the word *coffee* has been replaced with *it.*
- More transitions have been added, including words, phrases, and clauses.

- Some vivid details have been added.
- The verbs in the first few sentences of the paragraph have been changed to the past tense because those sentences talk about the time when you drank coffee.
- A final sentence about better health has been added.

Final Version of a Paragraph on My Last Cup of Coffee

(Changes from the draft are underlined.)

My last cup of coffee was the beginning of better health. It was hard for me to stop drinking coffee because I <u>loved</u> the taste of <u>it.</u> In addition, I <u>thought that</u> coffee <u>picked</u> me up and <u>gave</u> me energy. <u>However, I decided to quit drinking coffee when I realized how much I needed it to keep going and to keep from feeling low.</u> I quit it suddenly because I figured that a sharp break from my habit would be better than dragging out the process. I drank my last cup in the morning. It was the cup I needed most, to wake up, so I decided to allow myself that <u>final</u> cup. By afternoon, I saw how much I needed coffee all day. Around 3:00 or 4:00 P.M., I craved it. I felt terrible. I was shaky, <u>nervous,</u> and irritable. After dinner, <u>when I used to have two or three cups of strong coffee,</u> my craving was worse. I was more irritable, <u>I was ready to snap at anyone who asked me a question,</u> and I had a pounding headache. <u>Soon, the worst was over, and</u> by the next day, I felt better. <u>Now, free of my coffee-drinking habit, I have a steady flow of energy, few crashing lows, and pride in my achievement.</u>

Before you prepare your final copy of your paragraph, check it for any places where grammar, word choice, and style need revision. Check also for any errors in spelling and punctuation.

Exercise 13 **Connect: Correcting Errors in the Final Draft
of a Narrative Paragraph**

Connect

Proofread the following paragraphs. Correct any errors in spelling, punctuation, or word choice. There are eight errors in the first paragraph and eight in the second paragraph. Write your corrections in the space above each error.

1. Last Saturday, I tried and failed to convince my father to change his diet.

My effort's began when my Father and I went shopping together. After we had

finished looking for a good used car to replace his old Nissan, he offered to take

me to lunch. I agreed and suggest a nearby restaurant that is known for it's fresh

salads and homemade soup's. My father laughed and insisted that we go to his

favorite barbecue place. As soon as we arrived, my father was ready to order. He

always eats the same meal of steak fries, ribs covered with a thick, sugary barbe-

cue sauce, and a tub of cole slaw swimming in mayonnaise. Of course, flaky bis-

cuits shiny with grease come with this meal. My father teased me when I choose

to eat a few items from the salad bar. He warned me that the salad dressings were as unhealthy as butter or grease. My only response was to show him the raw vegetables and low-fat dressing I had on my plate. After he had gobbled his meal, I gave him a lecture about heart disease and stroke. Then I scolded him about high blood pressure. he did not become annoyed. Instead, he said I had made some good points. Then he ordered a piece, of key lime pie.

2. My parents' have discovered a new hobby, and their choice shocked the hole family. The story of this hobby began when my brother Cameron became engaged to Emma, his girlfriend. Everyone was very happy, until the news of Emma's background began to spread within the family. Emma, we learned, had wealthy parents, and those parents wanted to give her a magnificent wedding. This wedding would include a band and dancing. One of the dance's would begin with the bride and groom dancing alone, and then both the bride and the groom's parents would join the newlyweds. My parents were terrified. They had not danced since they were teenagers, and the dances of there teen year's were hardly graceful, or formal. How ever, they could not spoil the wedding or disgrace our family. Instead, my parents took dancing lessons. They planned to take the lessons long enough to learn the basics of dancing at an elegant gathering. The wedding went well, and my parents performed admirably. However, they did not stop there. After the wedding, my parents continued their dancing lessons. Two years later, they still go dancing at a dance studio every Friday night. They have graduated to a level of dancers that enjoys everything from tango to waltzes.

Lines of Detail: A Walk-Through Assignment

For this assignment, write a paragraph on My First _____. (You fill in the blank. Your topic will be based on how you complete Step 1 below.)

> **Step 1:** To begin the prewriting part of writing this paragraph, complete the following questionnaire. It will help you think of possible topics and details.

Collaborative Questionnaire for Gathering Topics and Details Answer the following questions as well as you can. Then read your answers to a group. The members of the group should then ask you follow-up questions, based on your answers. For example, if your answer is "I felt nervous," a group member might ask, "Why were you nervous?" or "What made you nervous?" Write your answers on the lines provided; the answers will add details to your list.

Finally, tear out the page and ask each member of your group to circle one topic or detail that could be developed into a paragraph. Discuss the suggestions.

Repeat this process for each member of the group.

Questionnaire

1. Have you ever been interviewed for a job? When? _____

   _____

   Write four details you remember about the interview:

   a. _____

   b. _____

   c. _____

   d. _____

   Additional details to add after working with the group:

   _____

   _____

   _____

2. Do you remember your first day of school (in elementary school, middle school, high school, or college)? Write four details about that day.

   a. _____

   b. _____

   c. _____

   d. _____

   Additional details to add after working with the group:

   _____

   _____

   _____

3. Do you remember your first visit to a special place? Write four details about that place.

   a. _____

   b. _____

   c. _____

   d. _____

   Additional details to add after working with the group:

   _____

   _____

   _____

Step 2: Select a topic from the details and ideas on the questionnaire. Brainstorm and list ideas about the topic.

Step 3: Group your ideas in time order.

Step 4: Survey your grouped ideas and write a topic sentence. Check that your topic sentence makes a point and is broad enough to relate to all the details.

Step 5: Write an outline of your paragraph, putting the grouped details below the topic sentence. Check your outline. Be sure that all the details relate to the topic sentence and that the details are in a clear and logical order.

Step 6: Write a first draft of your paragraph. Then revise and edit; check that you are sticking to your point, that all your details relate to your point, that your ideas are easy to follow, and that you are using effective transitions.

Step 7: Before you prepare the final copy of your paragraph, check your last draft for errors in punctuation, spelling, and word choice.

Topics for Writing Your Own Narrative Paragraph

When you write on any of the following topics, be sure to follow the stages of the writing process in preparing your paragraph.

Collaborate

1. Write about the most stressful day of your life. Begin by freewriting. Then read your freewriting, looking for both the details and the focus of your paragraph.

   If your instructor agrees, ask a writing partner or a group to (a) listen to your freewriting, (b) help you focus it, and (c) help you add details by asking you questions.

2. Interview a family member or friend who is older than you. Ask the person about a significant event in his or her childhood. Ask questions as the person speaks. You can ask questions like, "Why do you think you remember this incident?" or "How did you feel at the time?" Take notes. If you have a recording device, you can record the interview, but take notes as well.

   When you have finished the interview, review the information with the person you've interviewed. Would he or she like to add anything? If you wish, ask follow-up questions.

   Next, on your own, find a point to the story. Use that point in your topic sentence. In this paragraph, you will be writing about another person, not about yourself.

3. Write about a time when you were afraid. Begin by brainstorming questions about what frightened you, why you were afraid, how you dealt with the situation, and so forth. In the planning stage, focus on some point about the incident: Did you learn from it? Did it change you? Did it hurt or help you? Answering such questions can help you come to a point.

Computer

4. Visit the Web site of your local newspaper and find a news story about an unusual crime. Summarize the details of the story in time order and focus your summary with a topic sentence that states what type of crime was committed as well as the most unusual aspect of the crime.

Be aware that newspaper accounts of a crime are not always written in time order, so you may have to determine the sequence of events.

5. Following are some topic sentences. Complete one of them and use it to write a paragraph.
When _____, I was thrilled because _____.
Apologizing to _____ was one of the hardest things I have ever done.
One encounter _____ taught me _____.
The biggest surprise in my life came when _____.
The longest day of my life was the day I _____.
My best day at my first job was the day I _____.

6. To write on this topic, begin with a partner. Ask your partner to tell you about a day that turned out unexpectedly. It can be a day that included a good or bad surprise.
As your partner speaks, take notes. Ask questions. When your partner has finished speaking, review your notes. Ask your partner if he or she has anything to add.
On your own, outline and draft a paragraph on your partner's day. Read your draft to your partner, adding comments and suggestions. Check the final draft of your paragraph for errors in punctuation, spelling, and word choice.
Your partner can work through this same process to write a paragraph about a day that turned out unexpectedly for you.

Collaborate

7. Write a paragraph that tells a story based on the photograph of the couple who appear to be arguing. Create an incident from this photo. To develop your narrative, consider what they may be arguing about, why they are so angry, what the children are thinking, and what will happen next.

Topics for Critical Thinking and Writing

1. Think of a recent frustrating incident with a family member or friend. Write a narrative paragraph detailing what happened, but imagine that you are the family member or friend relating what happened. You will be writing what happened strictly from his or her perspective.

   Note: Critical thinking often involves examining an encounter or issue from perspectives other than your own.

2. Write a paragraph that tells a story based on the mysterious figure in the photograph of a dark alley. To get started, imagine who the hooded person is, where he or she has been, what he or she may have done, what he or she is thinking, and where he or she is headed.

Name _____   Section _____

Peer Review Form for a Narrative Paragraph

After you have written a draft of your paragraph, let a writing partner read it. When your partner has completed the following form, discuss the responses. Then repeat the same process for your partner's paragraph.

The topic sentence for this paragraph is _____

_____

I think the topic sentence (a) states the point well or (b) could be revised.

The part of the narrative I liked best begins with the words _____

_____

The part that could use more or better details begins with the words _____

_____

One effective transition is _____

(Write the words of a good transition.)

I would like to see something added about _____

_____

I would like to take out the part about _____

_____

I think this paragraph is (a) easy to follow or (b) a little confusing [choose one].

Other comments _____

_____

_____

_____

_____

_____

_____

_____

_____

_____

Reviewer's name _____

Jumping In

*What is your strongest impression of this scene? Does the scene stir up feelings of power? Excitement? Fear? Examining the scene carefully, along with your reactions, will help you **describe** it effectively.*

Chapter Objectives

Students will be able to write a descriptive paragraph that (1) supports a dominant impression and (2) contains effective sense details.

WHAT IS DESCRIPTION?

Description *shows, not tells,* a reader what a person, place, thing, or situation is like. When you write description, you want your reader to have a vivid picture of what you are describing. Your description may even make your reader think about or act upon what you have shown.

HINTS FOR WRITING A DESCRIPTIVE PARAGRAPH

Using Specific Words and Phrases

Your description will help the reader see if it uses specific words and phrases. If a word or phrase is *specific*, it is *exact and precise*. The opposite of specific language is language that is vague, general, or fuzzy. Think of the difference between specific and general in this way:

> Imagine that your mother asks you what gift you want for your birthday.
> "Something nice," you say.
> "What do you mean by 'nice'?" your mother asks.

"You know," you say. "Not the usual stuff."

"What stuff?" she asks.

"Like the usual things you always give me," you reply. "Don't give me that kind of stuff."

"Well, what would you like instead?" she asks.

The conversation could go on and on. You are being very general in saying that you want "something nice." Your mother is looking for specific details: What do you mean by "nice"? What is "the usual stuff"? What are "the usual things"?

In writing, if you use words like "nice" or "the usual stuff," you will not have a specific description or a very effective piece of writing. Whenever you can, try to use a more precise word instead of a general term. To find a more explicit term, ask yourself such questions as "What type?" or "How?" The examples below show how a general term can be replaced by a more specific one.

general word: sweater (Ask "What type?")
more specific words: pullover, vest, cardigan

general word: vegetables (Ask "What type?")
more specific words: broccoli, carrots, peas

general word: walked (Ask "How?")
more specific words: stumbled, strutted, strode

general word: funny (Ask "How?")
more specific words: strange, comical, entertaining

Exercise 1 **Practice: Identifying General and Specific Words**

Below are lists of words. Put an *X* by the one term in each list that is a more general term than the others. The first one is done for you.

List 1

_X_ silverware

_____ knife

_____ soup spoon

_____ teaspoon

_____ fork

List 2

_____ suitcase

_____ garment bag

_____ trunk

_____ overnight bag

_____ luggage

List 3

_____ cousin

_____ uncle

_____ relative

_____ brother

_____ grandmother

List 4

_____ aspirin

_____ cough syrup

_____ medicine

_____ antacid

_____ cold pills

List 5

_____ beans

_____ carrots

_____ peas

_____ vegetables

_____ celery

List 6

_____ broiled

_____ cooked

_____ roasted

_____ fried

_____ baked

Exercise 2   **Practice: Ranking General and Specific Items**

Below are lists of items. In each list, rank the items from the most general *1* to the most specific *4*.

List 1

_____ dogs

_____ trained dogs

_____ dogs in police work

_____ search and rescue dogs

List 2

_____ money

_____ United States dollars

_____ United States currency

_____ $250 U.S. currency

List 3

_____ law enforcement

_____ local law enforcement

_____ sheriff's deputy

_____ local law enforcement officer

List 4

_____ cookies

_____ cookies with chocolate

_____ baked goods

_____ chocolate chip macadamia cookies

Collaborate

Exercise 3   **Collaborate: Interviewing for Specific Answers**

To practice being specific, interview a partner. Ask your partner to answer the questions below. Write his or her answers in the spaces provided. When you have finished, change places. In both interviews, your goal is to find specific answers, so both you and your partner should be as explicit as you can in your answers.

Interview Questions

1. What is your favorite kind of pet? _____

_____

2. Name three objects that are in your wallet or purse right now. _____

_____

3. What is your favorite television commercial? _____

_____

4. What actor or actress do you most dislike? _____

_____

5. If you were buying a car, what color would you choose? _____

_____

6. What sound do you think is the most irritating? _____

_____

7. When you think of a beautiful woman or man, who comes to mind? _____

_____

8. When you think of a vacation getaway, what place do you picture?

_____

9. When you are at home and want to relax, what kind of chair do you sit on? _____

Exercise 4   **Practice: Finding Specific Words or Phrases**

List four specific words or phrases beneath each general one. You may use brand names where they are appropriate. The first word on List 1 is done for you.

List 1:

general word: green

specific word or phrase: _olive green_ _____

_____

_____

_____

List 2:

general word: student

specific word or phrase: _____

_____

_____

_____

List 3:

general word: car

specific word or phrase: _____

_____

_____

_____

List 4:

general word: sad

specific word or phrase: _____

_____

_____

_____

List 5:

general word: house

specific word or phrase: _____

_____

_____

_____

Exercise 5   **Practice: Identifying Sentences That Are Too General**

Below are lists of sentences. In each group put an *X* by one sentence that is general and vague.

1. a. _____ Jimmy is too full of himself.

   b. _____ Jimmy constantly brags about his expensive new truck.

   c. _____ Jimmy constantly checks his image as he passes store windows.

2. **a.** _____ She is afraid to go out at night.

   b. _____ She can't fall asleep until she has checked every door and window twice.

   c. _____ She is a nervous person.

3. **a.** _____ Michael is a great guy.

   b. _____ Michael lends me money often.

   c. _____ Michael volunteers at a homeless shelter.

4. **a.** _____ Charlie adores his newborn son.

   b. _____ Charlie loves everything about his life.

   c. _____ Charlie just got a great job.

5. **a.** _____ One of the stars on the awards show looked silly.

   b. _____ She wore a short dress covered in feathers.

   c. _____ Her hair was sprayed into a tall tower.

Using Sense Words in Your Descriptions

One way to make your description specific and vivid is to use **sense words**. As you plan a description, ask yourself,

What does it **look** like?
What does it **sound** like?
What does it **smell** like?
What does it **taste** like?
What does it **feel** like?

The sense details can make the description vivid. Try to include details about the five senses in your descriptions. Often you can brainstorm sense details more easily if you focus your thinking.

INFO BOX: Devising Sense Details

For the sense of	Think about
sight	colors, light and dark, shadows, or brightness.
hearing	noise, silence, or the kinds of sounds you hear.
smell	fragrance, odors, scents, aromas, or perfume.
taste	bitter, sour, sweet, or compare the taste of one thing to another.
touch	the feel of things: texture, hardness, softness, roughness, smoothness.

Collaborate

Exercise 6   **Collaborate: Brainstorming Sense Details for a Description Paragraph**

With a partner or a group, brainstorm the following ideas for a paragraph. That is, for each topic, list at least six questions and answers that could help you find sense details. Be prepared to read your completed exercise to another group or to the class.

1. topic: The fire fascinated and horrified the crowd.
Brainstorm questions and answers:

Question: _____

Answer: _____

Question: _____

Answer: _____

Question: _____

Answer: _____

Question: _____

Answer: _____

Question: _____

Answer: _____

Question: _____

Answer: _____

2. topic: The kitchen in my first apartment needed a major renovation.
Brainstorm questions and answers:

Question: _____

Answer: _____

Question: _____

Answer: _____

Question: _____

Answer: _____

Question: _____

Answer: _____

Question: _____

Answer: _____

Question: _____

Answer: _____

3. topic: The Halloween party turned into a nightmare.
Brainstorm questions and answers:

Question: _____

Answer: _____

Question: _____

Answer: _____

Question: _____

Answer: _____

Question: _____

Answer: _____

Question: _____

Answer: _____

Question: _____

Answer: _____

Exercise 7 **Practice: Writing Sense Words**

Write sense descriptions for the items below.

1. Write four words or phrases to describe what a new pair of sneakers feels like:

   _____

   _____

2. Write four words or phrases to describe what a sleeping kitten looks like:

   _____

   _____

3. Write four words or phrases to describe the sounds of a traffic jam:

   _____

   _____

4. Write four words or phrases to describe the taste of a slice of lemon:

   _____

   _____

WRITING THE DESCRIPTIVE PARAGRAPH IN STEPS

PREWRITING DESCRIPTION

Suppose your instructor asks you to write about this topic: An Outdoor Place. You might begin by *brainstorming*.

Sample Brainstorming on an Outdoor Place

Question: What place?

Answer: Outside somewhere.

Question: Like the outside of a building?

Answer: Maybe.

Question: The beach?

Answer: That would be OK. But everybody will write on that.

Question: How about a park?

Answer: Yes. A park would be good.

Question: How about the park near your workplace—the city park?

Answer: I could do that. I go there at lunchtime.

You scan your brainstorming and realize you have three possible topics: the outside of a building, the beach, or a city park. You decide that you can write the most about the city park, so you brainstorm further:

Brainstorming on a Specific Topic: A City Park

Question: What does the park look like?

Answer: It's small.

Question: How small?

Answer: Just the size of an empty lot.

Question: What's in it?

Answer: Some trees. Benches.

Question: What else is in it?

Answer: A fountain. In the middle.

Question: Any swing sets or jungle gyms?

Answer: No, it's not that kind of park. Just a green space.

Question: Why do you like this park?

Answer: I just like it. It's near the store where I work. I go there at lunchtime.

Question: But why do you go there?

Answer: It's nice and green. It's not like the rest of the city.

Question: What's the rest of the city like?

Answer: The rest of the city is dirty, gray, and noisy.

By asking and answering questions, you can (1) choose a topic and (2) begin to develop ideas on that topic. Each answer can lead you to more questions and thus to more ideas.

Exercise 8 Practice: Identifying Topics in Brainstorming

Following are examples of early brainstorming. In each case, the brainstorming is focused on selecting a narrow topic from a broad one. Imagine that the broad topic is one assigned by your instructor. Survey each example of brainstorming and list all the possible narrower topics within it.

1. **broad topic:** Describe a place that made you feel uncomfortable.

   brainstorming:

   Question: What does "uncomfortable" mean? Physically uncomfortable?

   Answer: It could be. It could mean emotionally out of place.

   Question: What about being crowded in an elevator with too many people?

   Answer: That would be physically uncomfortable.

   Question: Couldn't it be emotionally stressful, too?

   Answer: If it made me feel trapped, and once, when I got stuck in an elevator, it did.

Question:	Did you ever feel emotionally uncomfortable in another place?
Answer:	The first prom I attended made me feel nervous and foolish.
Question:	Why did you feel uncomfortable?
Answer:	I barely knew the girl I took to the prom.
Question:	Did you feel physically crowded in another space?
Answer:	Once. On a subway in a big city.

possible topics: _____

_____

_____

2. **broad topic:** Write about a powerful person.

brainstorming:

Question:	Who is powerful?
Answer:	The president. A sports star. A rich person.
Question:	Can it be a different kind of power?
Answer:	Somebody with a powerful personality.
Question:	What's a powerful personality?
Answer:	A strength that can change lives. Or maybe someone who just changed his or her life.
Question:	What do you mean when you say "changed"?
Answer:	Changed attitudes, changed bad habits, or maybe just improved life for one or more people.

possible topics: _____

_____

_____

Collaborate

Exercise 9 **Collaborate: Developing Ideas Through Further Brainstorming**

Following are examples of brainstorming. Each example brainstorms a single, narrow topic. Working with a group, write four more questions and answers based on the ideas already listed.

1. **topic:** My Favorite Cap

brainstorming:

Question:	What can you say about your favorite cap?
Answer:	It's comfortable.
Question:	Why is it comfortable?
Answer:	It's broken in.
Question:	What does that mean?
Answer:	It's old and soft.

Question: How did it get soft?

Answer: I sat on it, threw it on the floor.

Question: Deliberately?

Answer: No, I'm just very careless.

Four additional questions and answers:

Question: _____

Answer: _____

Question: _____

Answer: _____

Question: _____

Answer: _____

Question: _____

Answer: _____

2. topic: My Favorite Family Member: My Little Sister

brainstorming:

Question: How old is your little sister?

Answer: She's ten.

Question: Is she funny?

Answer: Sometimes. But she doesn't mean to be funny.

Question: What does she do that amuses you?

Answer: She dances to music from the latest videos.

Question: Does she ask you to dance, too?

Answer: Sometimes.

Four additional questions and answers:

Question: _____

Answer: _____

Question: _____

Answer: _____

Question: _____

Answer: _____

Question: _____

Answer: _____

Focusing the Prewriting

To begin focusing your topic and details around some point, list the topic and all the details you've gathered so far. The following list includes all the details you've gathered from both sessions of brainstorming on a city park.

topic: A City Park

park near my workplace
I go there at lunchtime.
It's small.
just the size of an empty lot
Some trees. Benches.
A fountain. In the middle.
a green space
I like it.
It's near the store where I work.
It's nice and green.
It's not like the rest of the city.
The rest of the city is dirty, gray, and noisy.

Grouping the Details

If you survey the list, you can begin to group the details:

What It Looks Like
It's small.
just the size of an empty lot
it's nice and green.
a green space
Some trees. Benches.
A fountain.
In the middle.

Where It Is
park near my workplace
It's near the store where I work.

How I Feel About It

I like it.
I go there at lunchtime.
It's not like the rest of the city.
The rest of the city is dirty, gray, and noisy.

Surveying the details, you notice that they focus on the look and location of a place you like. You decide on this topic sentence:

A small city park is a nice place for me because it is not like the rest of the city.

You check your topic sentence to decide whether it covers all your details. Does it cover what the park looks like and its location? Yes, the words *small* and *city* relate to what it looks like and its location. Does it cover how you feel about the park? Yes, it says the park is "a nice place for me because it is not like the rest of the city."

Now that you have a topic sentence and a list of details, you are ready to begin the planning stage of writing.

Exercise 10 Practice: Grouping Details

Following are topics and lists of details. Group the details of each list, writing them under the appropriate headings. Some details may not fit under any of the headings.

1. **topic:** A Great Front Porch

   details: It got a constant breeze from the nearby river.

   The wood floor and railings were painted white.

Oak trees shaded it on three sides.

Flower pots of fragrant jasmine lined the edges of the railings.

White wicker chairs sat on the porch.

Hanging plants smelled fresh and clean.

Each chair had a soft pillow for a seat.

List details about the temperature: _____

_____

_____

_____

List details about the colors related to the porch: _____

_____

_____

_____

List details about the scents and smells related to the porch: _____

_____

_____

_____

2. topic: A Cheap Motel Room

details: There were cracks in the bathroom sink.

The bedroom smelled moldy.

The hairdryer didn't work.

Two small holes in the drapes allowed light to penetrate into the bedroom.

The coffeemaker was missing the carafe.

The bedroom carpet was worn and shiny.

The people in the next room were noisy.

The bathtub was stained.

List details about the bathroom: _____

_____

_____

_____

List details about the appliances: _____

_____

_____

_____

List details about the bedroom: _____

_____

_____

_____

3. topic: A Cluttered Desk

details: It is an old, scratched, and dented desk.

One of the drawers has an old packet of microwave popcorn peeping out.

The floor beneath the desk is covered in dust bunnies.

The top of the desk is stacked with folders and papers.

The drawers overflow with manila envelopes, notebooks, and crumpled documents.

Ballpoint pens without tops and stubs of pencils lie under the desk.

Two pages had stains.

A box crammed with markers, pens, pencils, and erasers has been pushed to the edge of the desktop.

The desk drawers are always open; they are too full to shut.

List details about what is on the desk: _____

_____

_____

_____

List details about what is inside the desk drawers: _____

_____

_____

_____

List details about what is under the desk: _____

_____

_____

_____

Collaborate

Exercise 11 **Collaborate: Writing Appropriate Topic Sentences**

Do this exercise with a partner or a group. Following are lists of details. For each list, write two appropriate topic sentences.

1. topic sentence 1: _____

_____

_____

topic sentence 2: _____

_____

_____

details: The abandoned factory had once employed most of the
townspeople.

The impressive entrance showed traces of white trim on
gray stone.

Inside, debris covered the floors.

Large stone counters, now cracked, ran in parallel lines.

Long, high windows cast the only light.

Dust shimmered in the beams of light.

An elaborate molding at the top of the walls still survived.

A high ceiling gave a touch of style.

2. topic sentence 1: _____

_____

_____

topic sentence 2: _____

_____

_____

details: The young couple in front of me at the movies sat stiffly.

Neither made body contact with the other.

Both looked straight ahead at the movie screen.

When he offered her some popcorn, she ignored him.

He laughed a very small laugh at a comic moment in the film.

She pulled farther away from him.

He made a few sideways glances at her.

She pulled a tissue out of her purse and wiped her eyes.

3. topic sentence 1: _____

_____

_____

topic sentence 2: _____

_____

_____

details: I had always resisted my friends' attempts to get me to try
frozen yogurt.

I imagined the sour taste of regular yogurt with an ice
cream texture.

One day, my cousin dragged me to a frozen yogurt store.

"Try the white chocolate mousse," she said.

I gave in to her urging.

The taste was not at all sour.

It hinted at white chocolate but also at vanilla.

The yogurt was softer than ice cream.

It was more like the ice cream products that are swirled onto a cone.

The light texture felt smooth on my tongue.

I wanted more of this tasty treat.

4. **topic sentence 1:** _____

_____

_____

topic sentence 2: _____

_____

_____

details: After the blizzard, most of the residents of our town had no power for nearly a week.

Snow had piled up so high that residents could not open their doors.

The snow plows could not reach all the areas that needed help.

Abandoned cars blocked the main highway.

Trees had fallen into the streets and onto the roofs of homes and stores.

Heavy snow had also caused the stadium's roof to collapse inward.

Pedestrians ran for cover.

PLANNING **DESCRIPTION**

Once you have a topic sentence, a list of details, and some grouping of the details, you can write them in outline form. Before you write your details in outline form, check their order. Remember, when you write a description, you are trying to make the reader *see*. It will be easier for the reader to imagine what you see if you put your description in a simple, logical order. You might want to put descriptions in order by **time sequence** (first to last), by **spatial position** (e.g., top to bottom, right to left, or outside to inside), or by **similar types** (e.g., all about the flowers, then all about the trees in a garden).

If you are describing a house, for instance, you may want to start with the outside of the house and then describe the inside. You do not want the details to shift back and forth, from outside to inside and back to outside.

If you are describing a person, you might want to group all the details about his or her face before you describe the person's body. You might want to describe a meal from the first course to dessert.

Look again at the grouped list of details on a city park. To help make the reader see the park, you decide to arrange your details in *spatial order*: First, describe where the park is located; second, describe the edges and the middle of the park. The final lines of your paragraph can describe your feelings about the park. The following outline follows this order.

Outline for a Paragraph on A City Park

topic sentence: A small city park is a nice place for me because it is not like the rest of the city.

details:

location   { It is near the store where I work.

appearance   ⎧ It is just the size of an empty lot.
from edges   ⎪ It is nice.
to the middle   ⎨ It is a green space.
                  ⎪ It has some trees and benches.
                  ⎩ It has a fountain in the middle.

how I feel   ⎧ I like it.
about it   ⎪ I go there at lunchtime.
                  ⎨ It is not like the rest of the city.
                  ⎩ The rest of the city is dirty, gray, and noisy.

Once you have an outline, you can begin writing a description paragraph.

Exercise 12   **Practice: Putting Details in Order**

Following are lists that start with a topic sentence. The details under each topic sentence are not in the right order. Put the details in the right order by labeling them, with *1* being the first detail, *2* the second, and so forth.

1. **topic sentence:** The children's choir quickly found its rhythm.
   (Arrange the details in time order.)

   details: _____   By their second selection, they and their audience were having fun.

   _____   As they entered the stage, the children awkwardly stumbled into their places.

   _____   The music director calmly extended his hands to the children as they stood waiting to sing.

   _____   Family and friends waited eagerly for the children to appear.

   _____   They began their first number a little hesitantly.

   _____   The children's power grew until they left the stage with a standing ovation.

2. topic sentence: When I was young, the attic in my grandmother's old house was my fantasy land.
(Arrange the details from outside to deeper and deeper inside the attic.)

details: _____ I could reach the attic by climbing a set of narrow, creaking stairs.

_____ Once I had entered the attic, I could see an old mirror covered in cobwebs.

_____ At the top of the stairs was a door.

_____ The door opened to the attic itself, a wide area with a sloping roof.

_____ Beyond the mirror were countless boxes full of treasures such as old toys, tools, and clothes.

3. topic sentence: The painting of the old man's face showed an angry person. (Arrange the details from forehead to chin.)

details: _____ The wrinkles on the forehead led to scowling eyebrows.

_____ The chin jutted out defiantly.

_____ The old man's eyes were dark slits.

_____ There were deep lines around the sides of his nose.

_____ These lines extended below his mouth, pulling downward.

Collaborate

Exercise 13 **Collaborate: Creating Details Using a Logical Order**

The following lists include a topic sentence and indicate a required order. With a partner or group, write five sentences of details in the required order.

1. topic sentence: I tried to imagine what breeds of dogs had mated to create my beautiful, adopted dog.
(Describe the appearance of the dog from head to tail.)

a. _____

b. _____

c. _____

d. _____

e. _____

2. topic sentence: By the time he had finished talking, the guest speaker had put nearly everyone to sleep.
(Describe his speech from the beginning to the end.)

a. _____

b. _____

c. _____

d. _____

e. _____

3. **topic sentence:** My girlfriend embarrassed me at my family's celebration.
(First describe the girlfriend's behavior; then describe the writer's reaction.)

a. _____

b. _____

c. _____

d. _____

e. _____

4. **topic sentence:** My little sister looked like a model.
(Describe the person from head to foot.)

a. _____

b. _____

c. _____

d. _____

e. _____

DRAFTING AND REVISING DESCRIPTION

After you have an outline, the next step is creating a rough draft of the paragraph. Once you have the first draft, look it over, using the following checklist:

Checklist for Revising a Descriptive Paragraph

✔ Are there enough details?

✔ Are the details specific?

✔ Do the details use sense words?

✔ Are the details in order?

✔ Is the description easy to follow?

✔ Have I made my point?

If you look at the outline about a city park, you'll notice that it has some problems:

- The details are not very specific. Words like *nice* do not say much, and *nice* is used twice, in the topic sentence and in the details.

- Some parts of the outline need more support. The description of the inside of the park needs more details.

- The description would also be easier to follow if it had some effective transitions.

These weak areas can be improved in the drafting and revising stage of the writing process.

Transitions

As you revise your description paragraph, you may notice places in the paragraph that seem choppy or abrupt. That is, one sentence may end and another may start, but the two sentences don't seem to be connected. Reading your paragraph aloud, you may sense that it is not very smooth. Good transitions can help to make smooth connections between your ideas. Here are some transitions you may want to use in writing a description:

INFO BOX: **Transitions for a Descriptive Paragraph**

To show ideas brought together

and	also	in addition	next

To show a contrast

although	however	on the contrary	unlike
but	in contrast	on the other hand	yet

To show a similarity

all	each	like	similarly
both			

To show a time sequence

after	first	next	then
always	second (etc.)	often	when
before	meanwhile	soon	while

To show a position in space

above	beside	in front of	over
ahead of	between	inside	there
alongside	beyond	near	toward
among	by	nearby	under
around	close	next to	underneath
away	down	on	up
below	far	on top of	where
beneath	here	outside	

> **Note:** There are many other transitions you can use, depending on what you need to link your ideas.

Below is a revised draft of the paragraph on A City Park. When you read it, you will notice the added details and more precise words. You will also notice that some short, choppy sentences have been combined and that transitions have been added. In addition, a final sentence of details has been added to the end of the paragraph.

A Revised Draft of a Paragraph on a City Park

specific detail:	A small city park is a <u>pleasant</u> place for me because it is not like the rest of the city. The park
added details,	is near the store where I work; <u>in fact, it is only a</u>
sentences combined,	<u>ten-minute walk. It is just the size of an empty lot,</u>
specific detail, transition	<u>yet it is an attractive green space.</u> <u>Under</u> the trees
added detail, transition	are <u>weathered wooden</u> benches <u>where people of</u>
sense details,	<u>every age sit and enjoy the calm.</u> The only sound is
sentences combined	the <u>splash</u> of the fountain at the center of the park. <u>I</u>
	<u>enjoy the park and visit it at lunchtime.</u> It is not like
sense words and	the rest of the city, which is dirty, gray, and <u>filled</u>
specific details	<u>with the noise of screeching brakes, rumbling trucks,</u>
final sentence, transition,	<u>and blaring horns. The park is a quiet, clean spot</u>
and sense words	<u>where the sun filters through the leaves of trees.</u>

Although it is important to work on specific details and sense words in each stage of your writing, it is easiest to focus on revising for details in the drafting stage, when you have a framework for what you want to say. With that framework, you can concentrate on the most vivid way to express your ideas.

Exercise 14 **Practice: Recognizing Transitions**

Underline the transitions in the paragraph below.

My first visit to a yoga class was not what I had expected. The class was

an adult education class held once a week at the local high school. My only

knowledge of yoga came from television commercials where dozens of slim,

fit people dressed in black leotards posed gracefully. Most of the people in

the commercials are young, and most are female. When I entered the yoga

class, I saw people of all ages, wearing loose clothing from sweatpants to

shorts. Most were talking, standing, sitting, or stretching on the floor. Close to me, a woman was casually striking a pose that would have turned me into a pretzel. Alongside her, an elderly man was effortlessly stretching his legs. People in their twenties chatted near a lady who seemed middle-aged and fit. As that lady moved to the front of the group, she challenged us to spread our yoga mats. Next, she led us in a beginner's exercise. As she effortlessly performed a stretch that challenged me, I saw the elderly man and two gray-haired ladies gracefully follow the instructor's moves. Meanwhile, someone behind me said, "Isn't our yoga teacher wonderful? Who would believe that she is 63 years old?"

Exercise 15 Practice: Adding the Appropriate Transitions

In the paragraph below, transitions are shown in parentheses. Underline the appropriate transitions.

Mrs. Gallagher served me and her son an unforgettable breakfast. (First / Before) she gave each of us a huge glass of fresh-squeezed orange juice. (After / While) we were enjoying the juice, she was whisking a huge bowl of raw eggs, milk, and spices into a frothy mix for scrambled eggs. (Soon / Often,) the egg mixture was slowly cooking in a buttered pan. As it cooked, Mrs. Gallagher focused on popping some homemade cinnamon buns into the oven. (Always / When) the scrambled eggs began to gel, Mrs. Gallagher stirred them softly with a wooden spoon. (Then / Second) the scent of cinnamon filled the room. With perfect timing, Mrs. Gallagher pulled the buns from the oven and spooned the scrambled eggs onto our plates. The eggs were the creamiest I had ever tasted. (Until / In addition,) the cinnamon buns were the softest, sweetest, and most cinnamon-infused of my life. (After / Before) my first taste of Mrs. Gallagher's breakfast, I had no idea how good breakfast could be.

Exercise 16 Practice: Revising for Specific Details or Sense Words

In the following paragraph, replace each underlined word or phrase with more specific details or sense words. Write your changes in the space above the underlined items.

I had a difficult time selecting a special shirt for Calvin, my boyfriend. I wanted him to look <u>nice</u> at his cousin's graduation party, but I couldn't find a shirt that <u>would look right on Calvin</u>. I looked at <u>lots of</u> shirts in <u>a bunch of</u> stores, but most of the shirts were either <u>funny-looking</u> or <u>wrong</u>. One came in <u>a weird color</u>, another had a <u>stupid</u> stripe, and another <u>wouldn't fit him right</u>. I became <u>fed up with</u> looking at <u>stuff</u> that I would never want Calvin to wear. Just as I was leaving the mall, I saw one <u>nice</u> shirt on a sale rack. I grabbed the shirt, paid for it, and left the mall, feeling <u>good</u>.

PROOFREADING **DESCRIPTION**

Focus on Support and Details

Before you prepare the final version of your paragraph, check it again for any problems in support and details, and for any places where grammar, word choice, and style need revision. Check also for any errors in spelling and punctuation.

Following is the final version of the paragraph on A City Park. As you review it, you'll notice several changes:

- The name of the park has been added to make the details more specific.
- More sense details have been added.
- There were too many repetitions of "it" in the paragraph, so "it" has frequently been changed to "the park," "Sheridan Park," and so forth.
- An introductory sentence has been added to make the beginning of the paragraph smoother.

Final Version of a Paragraph on a City Park

(Changes from the draft are underlined.)

<u>Everyone has a place where he or she can relax.</u> A small city park is a pleasant place for me because it is not like the rest of the city. <u>Sheridan Park</u> is near the store where I work; in fact, it is only a ten-minute walk. <u>The park</u> is just the size of an empty lot, yet it is an attractive green space <u>ringed with maple trees.</u> Under the trees are weathered wooden benches where people of every age sit and enjoy the calm. The only sound is the splash of the fountain at the center of the park. I enjoy the park and visit it at lunchtime. <u>This special place</u> is not like the rest of the city, which is dirty, gray, and filled with the noise of screeching brakes, rumbling trucks, and blaring horns. The park is a clean, quiet spot where the sun filters through the leaves of trees.

Connect

Exercise 17 **Connect: Correcting Errors in the Final Draft of a Descriptive Paragraph**

Proofread the following paragraphs. Correct any errors in spelling, punctuation, or word choice. There are ten errors in the first paragraph and eleven in the second paragraph. Write your corrections in the space above the errors.

1. My dentist's office is not the kind of madman's den that you see in a horrer movie, but it is not a version of Disney World's Magic Kingdom, either. The patient's chair is quiet comfortable, and includes a soothing headrest and a relaxing seat. Soft, music plays as I am push in to place for the dentist. She moves an overhead light in my direction, and I clothes my eye's. I hear the music play as she surveys my teeth for problems. Soon I hear a whirring noise, I open my eyes, and I see the dental assistant. The assistant than hands a pointed tool to the dentist. The whirring sound enters my mouth; next I sense the buzzing is deeper in my mouth. Then I feel a burn. Soon I am choking on water as the assistant rinses my mouth. The buzz, burn, and rinse continues as tears form in my eyes. Finally, the dentist has finished her work, and I relax for the last rinse and cleaning with a cinnamon-flavored dental floss. As I enjoy the smell of the cinnamon, I celebrate the end of another trip, to my dentist.

2. My first steady boyfriend had a decrepit car, and I am surprised that it didnot fall into pieces as we drove around town. The car was so old that I never really knew the make, or model of the automobile. We called it the Green Beast, for it had a faded hint of mint green paint on its battered body. On the passenger's side of the front seat, parts of the floor had rusted thru two the pavement. As a result, I had to be carful where I put my feet when my boyfriend drove me to class the mall, and the movies. The car radio could find only two stations within a three-mile area, so we usually gave up on music. The back seat area of the car had lost it's cushions long ago but the empty space was good for storage. The catch on the car's trunk was holded together by rope. With all it's faults, the car gave us a chance to explore and to escape the restrictions of depending on some one else for transportation. It made us feel grown up and free.

Lines of Detail: A Walk-Through Assignment

For this assignment, write a paragraph about your classroom, the one in which you take this class.

Step 1: To begin, freewrite about your classroom for ten minutes. In your freewriting, focus on how you would *describe* your classroom.

Step 2: Next, read your freewriting to a partner or a group. Ask your listener(s) to write down any ideas in your freewriting that could lead to a specific topic for your paragraph. (For example, maybe your freewriting has several ideas about how you feel when you are in the classroom, how others behave, or how the furniture and decor of the room create a mood.)

Step 3: With a specific topic in mind, list all the ideas in your freewriting that might fit that main topic.

Step 4: Now, brainstorm. Write at least ten questions and answers based on your list of ideas.

Step 5: Group all the ideas you've found in freewriting and brainstorming. Survey them and write a topic sentence for your paragraph. Your topic sentence may focus on the atmosphere of the classroom, the look of the classroom, how you feel in the classroom, the activity in the classroom, and so forth.

Step 6: Write an outline. Be sure that your outline has enough supporting points for you to write a paragraph of seven to twelve sentences.

Step 7: Write and revise your paragraph. Check each draft for support, and work on using specific details and sense words.

Step 8: Share your best draft with a partner or the group. Ask for suggestions or comments. Revise once more.

Step 9: Prepare the final copy of your paragraph, checking for errors in punctuation, spelling, or word choice.

Topics for Writing Your Own Descriptive Paragraph

When you write on any of the following topics, be sure to follow the stages of the writing process in preparing your paragraph.

1. Write about your most comfortable piece of clothing. In your topic sentence, focus on what makes it so comfortable.

2. Interview a partner so that you and your partner can gather details and write separate paragraphs with the title "My Dream Vacation."

   First, prepare a list of at least six questions to ask your partner. Write down your partner's answers and use these answers to ask more questions. For example, if your partner says she wants a trip to the Caribbean, ask her what part of the Caribbean she would like to visit. If your partner says he would like to go to the Super Bowl, ask him what teams he would like to see.

   When you have finished the interview, switch roles. Let your partner interview you.

   Finally, give your partner his or her interview responses; take your own responses and use them as the basis for gathering as many details as you can. In this way, you are working through the prewriting stage of your paragraph. Then go on to the other stages. Be prepared to read your completed paragraph to your partner.

3. Write a paragraph that describes one of the following:
   the place where you work
   the contents of your refrigerator
   people running through a sudden rain storm
   people in the express lane at the supermarket
   children riding the school bus
   a toddler in a car seat or stroller
   the contents of the glove box of your car
   what you ate for breakfast
   Be sure to focus your paragraph with a good topic sentence.

4. Write a paragraph about the messiest storeroom, office, or closet you've ever seen.

5. Imagine a place that would bring you a sense of peace. In a paragraph, describe that place.

6. Following are some topic sentences. Complete one of them and use it to write a paragraph.
   The happiest place I know is _____.
   _____ is the most comfortable place in my home.
   Whenever I visit _____, I feel a sense of _____.
   Between classes, the halls of the college seem _____.
   I like to spend time alone at _____ because _____.

7. Write about the sensations of riding in a crowded elevator. You might begin by brainstorming all the details you recall.

8. Look carefully at the two photographs below. In a paragraph, describe the face in either photograph. To write this description, consider how you can use specific details and sense descriptions to express what you see and what impression it conveys.

Topics for Critical Thinking and Writing

1. Visit your school's home page and describe its appearance. Consider what you feel is attractive about the page, whether the descriptions of your schools are accurate, and whether the page would attract a potential student. Pay close attention to such details as the use of color, size and style of print, and use of space as you make your judgments.

2. Write a paragraph about the photograph below. Describe the scene; be sure to include a description of the weather, the body language, the man in profile, and what you imagine to be the circumstances of the competition.

Name _____   Section _____

Peer Review Form for a Descriptive Paragraph

After you have written a draft version of your paragraph, let a writing partner read it. When your partner has completed the following form, discuss the responses. Then repeat the same process for your partner's paragraph.

The part of this paragraph that I like best begins with the words _____

_____

This paragraph uses some sense words and phrases. Among these sense words and phrases are _____

_____

_____

The part of the paragraph that could use more specific details or sense words begins with the words _____

_____

The topic sentence of this paragraph is _____

_____

_____

I think there is (enough/too little) [circle one] support for the topic sentence.

I have questions about _____

_____

_____

Other comments on the paragraph _____

_____

_____

_____

_____

_____

_____

_____

_____

Reviewer's name _____

Writing an Illustration Paragraph

CHAPTER 26

Jumping In

Love of one's country can be exhibited in a number of ways, including parades and celebrations of national holidays. Are there other ways to express a love of one's country? Are they public or personal? Do some involve a long-term commitment? By answering such questions, you will be *illustrating* ways that people express love of their country.

Chapter Objectives

Students will be able to (1) distinguish between general statements and specific details and (2) write an illustration paragraph containing a clear topic sentence and sufficient supporting details.

WHAT IS ILLUSTRATION?

Illustration uses specific examples to support a general point. In your writing, you often use *illustration* because you frequently want to explain a point with a specific example.

HINTS FOR WRITING AN ILLUSTRATION PARAGRAPH

Knowing What Is Specific and What Is General

A *general* statement is a broad point. The following statements are general:

> College students are constantly short of money.
> Bronson Avenue is in a bad neighborhood.
> Pictures can brighten up a room.

You can support a general statement with specific examples:

general statement:	College students are constantly short of money.
specific examples:	They need gas money, or bus or subway fare.
	They need cash for snacks, lunch, or dinner.

general statement:	Bronson Avenue is in a bad neighborhood.
specific examples:	It has burned-out and abandoned buildings.
	There are drug dealers on the corners.

general statement:	Pictures can brighten up a room.
specific examples:	I love to look at my grandmother's family photos, which cover a whole living room wall.
	My dentist has framed cartoons on the walls of his waiting room.

When you write an illustration paragraph, be careful to support a general statement with specific examples, not with more general statements:

not this: general statement:	Essay tests are difficult.
more general statements:	~~I find essay tests to be hard.~~
	~~Essay tests present the most challenges.~~

but this: general statement:	Essay tests are difficult.
specific examples:	They test organizational skills.
	They demand a true understanding of the subject.

If you remember to illustrate a broad statement with specific examples, you will have the key to this kind of paragraph.

Exercise 1 **Practice: Recognizing Broad Statements**

Each list below contains one broad statement and three specific examples. Underline the broad statement.

1. A quilt is filled with warm material but feels light.

   On a cold night, nothing is more comfortable than a quilt.

   A quilt will conform to any person's size and shape.

   A blanket can be itchy, but a quilt is always smooth.

2. Toddlers like to explore, not to sit in one place.

   Small children have short attention spans.

   Kindergartners don't like to play any game for an hour.

   Five-year-olds can't listen to music for long unless they can sing or dance.

3. Some teens film their crimes of violence and put the videos online.

   Most stores have cameras that record all in-store activity.

   Today many crimes are solved because of videos.

   Some cities have installed cameras on all their streets.

4. Eating spaghetti is fun but tricky.

   Many people have childhood memories of playing with spaghetti strands.

   In a room full of adults, there is no polite way to suck up a spaghetti strand.

   Spaghetti sauce can drip on a person's chin or clothing.

5. Dogs have to be walked even if it is raining or snowing.

   Most dogs have "accidents" that have to be cleaned up.

   Loving and caring for a dog means taking on some unpleasant chores.

   A smart dog owner has to keep items such as shoes and socks out of the reach of dogs seeking toys.

Exercise 2   **Practice: Distinguishing the General Statement from the Specific Example**

Each general statement below is supported by three items of support. Two of these items are specific examples; one is too general to be effective. Underline the one that is too general.

1. **general statement:** Most television reality programs focus on contests.
   support: Contestants often compete to be the best model.
   Competition is at the heart of most television reality shows.
   Some contestants fight to become the most outstanding chef.

2. **general statement:** Trying to wear only the latest styles is foolish.
   support: Overspending on the newest clothing can break any budget.
   Respect doesn't come to a person because of what he or she wears.
   Many styles in shirts, shoes, jackets, and caps change within months, so a person can never be truly in style.

3. **general statement:** Staying up all night to study doesn't work very well.
   support: People who try to cram too much material into one evening can panic and lose their ability to concentrate.
   It is not a good idea to rely on one desperate study session.
   The all-night study technique substitutes a few desperate hours for a calm, regular regimen of reading and reviewing.

4. **general statement:** I never drink chocolate milk.
   support: Chocolate milk is fine for some people, but not for me.
   I don't want a chocolate flavor to mix with a meal of meat, gravy, and mashed potatoes.
   To me, chocolate milk is a parent's trick to get a child to drink milk.

5. general statement: Other people's music can be irritating.
support: Teens tend to hate their parents' favorite songs.
Neighbors will complain about the loud music nest door.
Only our kind of music pleases us.

Collaborate

Exercise 3 **Collaborate: Adding Specific Examples to a General Statement**

With a partner or group, add four specific examples to each general statement below.

1. general statement: We associate certain types of candy with specific occasions.
examples: _____
_____
_____
_____

2. general statement: People can fall asleep almost anywhere.
examples: _____
_____
_____
_____

3. general statement: Babies are used in many television commercials.
examples: _____
_____
_____
_____

4. general statement: In any home, we use water for more than just drinking.
examples: _____
_____
_____
_____

WRITING THE ILLUSTRATION PARAGRAPH IN STEPS

PREWRITING ILLUSTRATION

Suppose your instructor asks you to write a paragraph about some aspect of **cars.** You can begin by listing ideas about your subject to find a focus for your paragraph. Your first list might look like the following:

Listing Ideas About Cars
cars in my neighborhood
my brother's car
car prices
drag racing
cars in the college parking lot
parking at college
car insurance

This list includes many specific ideas about cars. You could write a paragraph about one item or about two related items on the list. Reviewing the list, you decide to write your paragraph on cars in the college parking lot.

Adding Details to an Idea

Now that you have a narrowed topic for your paragraph, you decide to write a list of ideas about cars in the college parking lot:

Cars in the College Parking Lot: Some Ideas
vans
cars with strollers and baby seats
beat-up old cars, some with no bumpers
a few new sports cars, gifts from rich parents
some SUVs
older people's cars, Volvos and Cadillacs
racing cars, modified, brightly striped
elaborate sound systems
bumper stickers
some stickers have a message
some brag

Creating a Topic Sentence

If you examine this list and look for *related ideas*, you can create a topic sentence. The ideas on the list include (1) details about the kinds of cars, (2) details about what is inside the cars, and (3) details about the bumper stickers. Not all the details fit into these categories, but many do.

Grouping the related ideas into the three categories can help you focus your ideas into a topic sentence.

Kinds of Cars
beat-up old cars, some with no bumpers
vans
few new sports cars, gifts from rich parents
some SUVs
older people's cars, Volvos and Cadillacs
racing cars, modified, brightly striped

Inside the Cars
elaborate sound systems
strollers and baby seats

Bumper Stickers
some stickers have a message
some brag

You can summarize these related ideas in a topic sentence:

Cars in the college parking lot reflect the diversity of people at the school.

Check the sentence against your details. Does it cover the topic? Yes. The topic sentence begins with "Cars in the college parking lot." Does it make some point about the cars? Yes. It says the cars "reflect the diversity of people at the school."

Because your details are about old and new cars, what is inside the cars, and what is written on the bumper stickers, you have many details about differences in cars and some hints about the people who drive them.

<hr>

Exercise 4   **Practice: Finding Specific Ideas in Lists**

Following are two lists. Each is a response to a broad topic. Read each list, and then underline any phrases that could become a more specific topic for a paragraph.

topic: crime
criminals in our state
prison guards in danger
a local rape crisis center
bullies at Lincoln High School
the death penalty in the
United States

probation and parole
safety precautions at student
apartments
drug dealing
an effective burglar alarm
an inefficient court system

topic: health
getting a flu shot
health insurance
nursing around the world
staying healthy
mental illness

home remedies for a cold
heart attacks
healthy snacks for children
a silly high-school health class
medical school

<hr>

Exercise 5   **Practice: Grouping Related Ideas in Lists of Details**

Following are lists of details. In each list, circle the items that seem to fit into one group; then underline the items that seem to fit into a second group. Some items may not fit into either group.

1. **topic:** healthy and unhealthy distrust

creates a hole in a close marriage
can become paranoia in a
friendship

open communication

healthy to distrust "miracle"
cures

can cause parents to spy on
their children

distrust in the population

becoming trustworthy

good to doubt sleazy bargain deals

trust funds

beware of investments that seem too good

2. **topic:** appropriate times to be good to yourself

you've achieved a difficult goal

a loved one has died

financial losses are hurting

happy memories of an old friend

satisfying an urge to overeat

shopping sprees

you have an unexpected holiday at work or school

a distant cousin calls for a long talk

giving small gifts to yourself

depression hits you

3. **topic:** marrying young: pros and cons

sharing new adventures

increased responsibilities

constant source of support

role of friends

emotional closeness

freedom from parental control

wedding anniversaries

coping with another person's needs

new demands on each other's time

financial stresses

4. **topic:** losing weight through exercise and diet

mail-order devices for losing weight

replace soft drinks with water

going to a gym

avoid desserts, unhealthy snacks

a walk every day

the struggle to lose weight

eating fresh fruits and vegetables

realistic goals

a regular bike ride

weight-loss contests on television

Exercise 6 Practice: Writing Topic Sentences for Lists of Details

Following are lists of details that have no topic sentences. Write an appropriate topic sentence for each one.

1. **topic sentence:** _____

   _____

   details: Four people live in our two-bedroom house.

   There is only one bathroom.

   It is difficult for two people to fit into our kitchen.

   We have a well-kept front porch.

   Many windows fill the house with light.

   Large trees surround the house and keep it cool in the summer.

2. **topic sentence:** _____

   _____

details: At the age of four, my brother used his plastic blocks to build little forts.

By six, he could tell long, exciting stories about the friendly monsters in his room.

In fourth grade, he wrote a long story about space travel.

That year, he drew intricate maps of a planet he created.

At ten, he won a school contest for the best-designed robot.

3. topic sentence: _____

_____

details: A young family owns the Pine Tree Café.

The panels behind the counter are covered with children's art.

Sometimes the owners' children, ages six and eight, help their parents.

The children get to push the buttons on the cash register.

The children hand bags of takeout food to the customers.

Families with small children like to come to the café for weekend breakfasts.

The restaurant gives a free cookie to each child.

4. topic sentence: _____

_____

details: He can talk his mother out of a bad mood by teasing her.

Leonard always avoided punishment in school because he made his teachers laugh.

He once convinced me to look at the bright side of paying a parking ticket.

Leonard has an uncle who never smiles except when Leonard visits him.

My sister is always worrying about something, but a call from Leonard can make her forget her worries.

After Leonard broke his leg, he made the emergency room physician laugh.

Exercise 7 **Practice: Choosing the Better Topic Sentence**

Following are lists of details. Each list has two possible topic sentences. Underline the better topic sentence for each list.

1. possible topic sentences:

a. Laura and Tyler don't get along.

b. Laura is bullying Tyler, her boyfriend.

details: Laura constantly teases her boyfriend Tyler about his weight.

She criticizes him for eating dessert or fattening snacks.

Tyler looks miserable when Laura scolds him.

He tries to please her by giving her small gifts.

Laura doesn't seem impressed by his efforts.

She makes him return many of the gifts.

As a result, Tyler tries harder.

He often asks Laura what would make her happy.

She says that he ought to know.

2. **possible topic sentences:**

a. Rodney and Sean are bad for each other.

b. Sean pushes Rodney into foolish and dangerous behavior.

details: Rodney and Sean are brothers.

They are only two years apart in age.

Rodney, the older brother, is outgoing and confident.

Sean is more shy and uncertain.

Both young men have been in trouble.

Rodney was arrested for disturbing the peace at a large party in his neighborhood.

He has also been cautioned about aggressive behavior toward an ex-girlfriend.

Once, he was accused of vandalism to several cars.

Sean is usually quiet and peace-loving.

However, he was present at the site of the vandalized cars.

Sean also convinced Rodney to go to the neighborhood party where trouble started.

Sean, however, was not arrested.

3. **possible topic sentences:**

a. Trying to fit in can be a way of losing yourself.

b. Starting at a new school in one's senior year can be difficult.

details: Lewis entered McFarlane High School in his senior year.

He felt lucky when Craig, a popular senior, introduced him to a group of other seniors.

The group was at the peak of popularity because of the members' looks, style, and confidence.

Lewis soon realized that he would have to try hard in order to fit in.

He got the right haircut, wore the right clothes, and socialized with the most popular women.

Then he met a junior named Lisa, who didn't care much about style, clothes, or status.

She had a casual hairstyle and ordinary clothes.

Lisa liked Lewis for himself.

He liked her because she seemed genuine.

Lewis took a chance and began seeing less of his clique and more of Lisa.

Soon Craig and his friends teased Lewis.

Then, using fear tactics, they mocked and scorned him.

Lewis realized what he wanted and made the right choice for him: Lisa.

PLANNING   ILLUSTRATION

When you plan your outline, keep your topic sentence in mind:

Cars in the college parking lot reflect the diversity of people at the school.

Remember the three categories of related details:

Kinds of Cars
Inside the Cars
Bumper Stickers

These three categories can give you an idea for how to organize the outline.
Below is an outline for a paragraph about cars in the college parking lot. As you read the outline, you will notice that details about the insides of the cars and about bumper stickers and license plates have been added. Adding details can be part of the outlining stage.

Outline on Cars in the College Parking Lot

topic sentence: Cars in the college parking lot reflect the diversity of people at the school.

details:

kinds of cars
{
There are beat-up old cars.
Some have no bumpers.
There are vans.
There are a few new sports cars.
Maybe these are gifts from rich parents.
There are some SUVs.
Older people's cars, like Volvos and Cadillacs, are there.
There are a few racing cars, modified and brightly striped.
}

inside the cars
{
Some cars have elaborate sound systems.
Some have a baby stroller or baby seat.
Some have empty paper cups and food wrappers.
}

bumper stickers
{
Some have stickers for a club.
There are stickers with a message.
There are stickers that brag.
}

As you can see, the outline used the details from the list and included other details. You can add more details, combine some details to eliminate repetition, or even eliminate some details as you draft your essay.

Exercise 8   **Collaborate: Adding Details to an Outline**

Below are three partial outlines. Each has a topic sentence and some details. Working with a partner or group, add more details that support the topic sentence.

1. **topic sentence:** Many people suffer from allergies to certain plants, animals, or food.

   details:
   a. Some people sneeze when ragweed blooms.
   b. Pollen from flowers or trees provoke other people's allergic reactions.
   c. Cats can cause allergies in people who react to cat hair or dander.
   d. _____
      _____
   e. _____
      _____
   f. _____
      _____
   g. _____
      _____

2. **topic sentence:** For a number of reasons, parents may give their child an unusual first name.

   details:
   a. Some parents choose an old family name.
   b. Some parents pick the name of a celebrity.
   c. Other parents name their child after a wealthy relative.
   d. _____
      _____
   e. _____
      _____
   f. _____
      _____
   g. _____
      _____

3. **topic sentence:** Many college students have similar hopes.

   details:
   a. They hope to finish their college courses according to their timeline.
   b. They hope for good grades.
   c. They hope they will find a good job after college.

d. _____

_____

e. _____

_____

f. _____

_____

g. _____

_____

Exercise 9 **Practice: Eliminating Details That Are Repetitive**

In the following outlines, some details use different words to repeat an example given earlier on the list. Cross out the repetitive details.

1. topic sentence: Many hungry students on a budget rely on a few inexpensive foods.

details: Toaster pastries are popular at any time of day.

Microwave popcorn can fill an empty stomach.

Cereal makes up a large part of many students' diet.

Frozen pizzas fill many students' freezers.

Frozen dinners, such as chicken pot pies and beef with rice, satisfy student appetites.

If a product such as popcorn can be microwaved, it is attractive.

Students also buy ramen noodles.

Some students resort to the sugary cereals they enjoyed as children.

No student can resist potato chips.

Dinners that can be reheated are often stacked in students' freezers.

2. topic sentence: I am picky about the kind of pen or pencil that I use.

details: Pencils with sharpened points please me.

I dislike pencils with rounded points because they lead to blurry writing.

I hate pencils whose points break every time I write more than three words.

I love rolling-ball pens with medium points.

Rolling-ball pens with fine points irritate me because my writing becomes pale and scratchy.

Felt-tip pens can be too wide, as if I am writing with a magic marker.

A rolling-ball pen with a medium point is my favorite.

A fine-point felt pen can help to produce clear, easily read writing.

Pencils with points that break every two minutes are awful.

3. topic sentence: Mrs. Galliano saved my college career.

details: I met with Mrs. Galliano when I needed to choose the classes for my third semester of college.

She was cheerful, welcoming, and patient.

She quickly surveyed my transcript, and then we talked.

I knew I had some bad grades and dropped classes on my records.

I expected a lecture.

Mrs. Galliano did not lecture me.

Instead of making me feel ashamed, she asked about my plans.

I told her that I wanted to be a nurse.

I also told her about my problems in math classes.

We talked about my options.

Mrs. Galliano was patient with me.

She and I designed a class schedule that included one attractive class and one challenging one.

We focused on my options.

I waited for her to lecture me about my responsibilities, but she never did.

I left with a sense that I would have to work hard but had someone in my corner.

DRAFTING AND REVISING ILLUSTRATION

Review the outline about cars in the college parking lot on page 386. You can create a first draft of this outline in the form of a paragraph. At this point, you can combine some of the short, choppy sentences of the outline, add details, and add transitions to link your ideas. You can revise your draft using the following checklist.

Checklist for Revising an Illustration Paragraph
✔ Should some of the sentences be combined?
✔ Do I need more or better transitions?
✔ Should I add more details to support my points?
✔ Should some of the details be more specific?

Transitions

As you revise your illustration paragraph, you may find places where one idea ends and another begins abruptly. This problem occurs when you forget to add **transitions,** the words, phrases, or sentences that connect one idea to another. When you write an illustration paragraph, you will need (1) some transitions that link one example to another and (2) other transitions to link one section of your paragraph to another section. Below are some transitions you may want to use in writing an illustration paragraph.

INFO BOX: **Transitions for an Illustration Paragraph**

a second example	in addition	other examples
another example	in the case of	other kinds
another instance	like	such as
for example	one example	the first instance
for instance	one instance	to illustrate

Look carefully at the following draft of the paragraph about cars in the college parking lot, and note how it combines sentences, adds details, and uses transitions to transform the outline into a clear and developed paragraph.

Revised Draft of a Paragraph on Cars in the College Parking Lot

	Cars in the college parking lot reflect the
details added,	diversity of people at the school. <u>There are beat-up</u>
sentences combined	<u>old cars, some with no bumpers, and several vans.</u>
sentences combined	<u>There are one or two sports cars like BMWs; they</u>
details added,	<u>might belong to the few lucky students with rich</u>
transition added	<u>and generous parents.</u> <u>Other kinds</u> include SUVs
transition added	and older people's cars <u>such as</u> Volvos and Cadillacs.
transition added	<u>In addition,</u> the parking lot holds a few racing
	cars, modified and brightly striped. Some cars have
details added	elaborate sound systems for <u>music lovers.</u> <u>Others</u>
details added	<u>must belong to parents</u> because they have a baby
	stroller or baby seat inside. Many are filled with
details added	empty paper cups or food wrappers <u>since busy</u>
transition,	<u>students have to eat on the run.</u> <u>Many cars also</u>
details added	<u>have bumper stickers;</u> some are for clubs, <u>like</u>
details, transition added	<u>Morristown Athletic Club,</u> while others have a mes-
details added	sage <u>such as "Give Blood, Save Lives" or "Animals:</u>
details added	<u>It's Their World, Too."</u> Some stickers brag that <u>the</u>
details added	<u>driver is the "Proud Parent of an Honor Roll Student</u>
	<u>at Grove Elementary" or is "Single—and Loving It."</u>

Exercise 10   Practice: Revising a Draft by Combining Sentences

The paragraph below has many short, choppy sentences, which are underlined. Wherever you see two or more underlined sentences clustered next to each other, combine them into one clear, smooth sentence. Write your revised version of the paragraph in the spaces above the lines.

In the summer, I want to enjoy every minute of sunshine. I live in an area with a cold climate. <u>Winter starts early. Also, winter lasts a long time.</u> Although we do have spring ahead of us, spring is generally cold. <u>People cannot put away their coats during the spring. Jackets are also necessary.</u> As a result of all this bad weather, I celebrate summer. When I am at my job, I spend every minute of each break sitting in the sun. <u>At college, I study between classes. I find a sunny bench. Sitting on the grass is also a possibility.</u> Instead of spending my time off at a mall or at the movies, I choose outdoor activities. <u>I run in my neighborhood. Barbecuing on my tiny balcony before sunset also offers the benefit of sunshine.</u> I am not obsessed with sunbathing or looking good in summer clothes. I crave sun for other reasons. Sunny days are actually brighter days. <u>Sunny days improve my mood. People look better in sunlight. Even buildings and trees are more attractive when the sky is clear and the air warm.</u> In sunshine, I like my life better.

Exercise 11 Practice: Revising a Draft by Adding Transitions

The paragraph below needs some transitions. Add appropriate transitions (words or phrases) to the blanks.

I have a hard time understanding my boyfriend. Sometimes Charles emphasizes his need for freedom and takes off with his friends. Then he suddenly becomes a family man. _____ he will return from a weekend with the boys and spend two days taking me and my daughter to a water park. _____ he will treat my daughter like a princess at the park, snapping endless photographs and buying her expensive souvenirs. _____ he will say he loves me and, ten minutes later, will talk about an old girlfriend. Money is related to _____ of mixed signals. Charles sometime buys me expensive clothes. He has given me some valuable jewelry. However, he has also been known to ask me to split the bill for dinner at a drive-in burger place. Feeling close to Charles can also be difficult for me. _____ conversation, Charles will sometimes talk all night about his dreams for the future. Yet at other times, Charles does not want to talk at all. I am torn between hoping to know Charles better or giving up on his dual personality.

Collaborate

Exercise 12 **Collaborate: Adding Details to a Draft**

The paragraph below lacks the kind of details that would make it more interesting. Working with a partner or group, add details in the blank spaces provided. When you are finished, read the revised paragraph to the class.

Until a few weeks ago, I lived with my parents, but now I am learning

the costs of living independently. I expected the basic costs of rent, food, and

_____. However, I am suddenly responsible for kitchen items such as paper

towels, _____, and _____. At home, my parents paid for basic bath-

room products, including _____ and _____, but now I have to spend

money on these and other items like deodorant and razor blades. Even doing my

laundry means I have to pay for using the washer, dryer, and for _____

and _____. I am tempted to make a quick trip to my parents' house for two

more items: an old drain board for the sink and a doormat.

PROOFREADING **ILLUSTRATION**

As you prepare the final version of your illustration paragraph, make any changes in word choice or transitions that can refine your writing. Following is the final version of the paragraph about cars in the college parking lot. As you read it, you will notice a few more changes:

- Some details have been added.

- Several long transitions have been added. The paragraph needed to signal the shift in subject from the kinds of cars to what was inside the cars; then it needed to signal the shift from the interior of the cars to bumper stickers.

- A concluding sentence has been added to reinforce the point of the topic sentence: A diverse college population is reflected in its cars.

Final Version of a Paragraph on Cars in the College Parking Lot

(Changes from the draft are underlined.)

Cars in the college parking lot reflect the diversity of people at the school. There are beat-up old cars, some with no bumpers, near several vans. There are one or two new sports cars like BMWs; they might belong to the few lucky students with rich and generous parents. Other kinds include SUVs and older people's cars such as Volvos and Cadillacs. In addition, the parking lot holds a few racing cars, modified and brightly striped. <u>What is inside the cars is as revealing as the cars themselves.</u> Some cars have elaborate sound systems for music lovers <u>who can't drive without pounding sound.</u> Others must belong to parents because they have a baby stroller or baby seat inside. Many are filled with empty paper cups or food wrappers since busy students have to eat on the run. <u>Bumper stickers also tell a</u>

story. Many cars have stickers; some are for clubs, like Morristown Athletic Club, while others have a message, such as "Give Blood: Save Lives" or "Animals: It's Their World, Too." Some stickers brag that the driver is the "Proud Parent of an Honor Student at Grove Elementary School" or is "Single—and Loving It." <u>A walk through the parking lot hints that this college is a place for all ages, backgrounds, and interests.</u>

Note: Before you prepare the final version of your illustration paragraph, check your latest draft for errors in spelling or punctuation and for any errors made in typing and copying.

Exercise 13 **Practice: Correcting the Errors in the Final Draft of an Illustration Paragraph**

Following are two illustration paragraphs with the kind of errors it is easy to overlook when you prepare the final version of an assignment. Correct the errors by writing above the lines. There are ten errors in the first paragraph and ten errors in the second paragraph.

1. Growing up is full of dangers, and younger childs should be keeped from exposure to frightening situations or stories. Halloween can be a thrilling time for small children, but it can easily bring to many grotesque images or threatening moments. During that holiday, for example, the youngest children should not be confronted by masked adults or older children jumping out from a dark space. Haunted house attractions are fun for teens or grown-ups, and small children may beg to visit these places. How ever, the fear and shock can haunt a second-grader for a long time Similarly, children of seven or 8 do not belong in the audience at horror movies designed to scare teenagers At home, children may here more than adults my think. As a result, a five-year-old sitting on the floor and playing with an electronic toy may be absorbing adult tales of ghosts and monsters. Adults may enjoy seeing a young boy's eyes widen as he hears about Frankenstein. However, the child is not likely to enjoy replaying that story when he is alone in bed that night. Worst of all, boys and girls of preschool or kindergarten age will remember an overherd conversation about a local robbery or assault. A child who listens to such a frightening tale can develop long-lasting irrational fears.

2. Every student wants to make a good impression, on Campus. If a student does not or cannot make that impression, he or she may wish to be inconspicuous among the professors, students, librarians, deans, and others that fill the institution. I have thought about the situations that would fill me with embarrassment or even shame, and there are many. One situation has already occurrd, and I am afraid it will happen again. I dread the moment when the sole flips off another of my sandals. When I experienced this calamity as I walked up the steps to a classroom, I felt a sudden flopping of the paper lineing of my sandal and heard a noise. The noise sounded like a flat tire rolling around on the wheel of a car. Everyone stared. Another of my fears has never become a reality, but it could. I can also imagine spilling a can of cola allover my jeans as I head for a conference with a professor. The smell, the sight, the stickness would be terrible and noticeble. Other embarrassing moments that I fear include bringing the wrong textbook to a small class. As we sat in a small circle, everyone would notice that I was carrying a a botany book with plants on the cover instead of a psychology book with a head on the cover. A second academic disaster involve my book bag. In this scenario, everything in my bag suddenly falls to the floor. My secrets such as my addiction to tic-tacs and my ragged notebook, are revealed. All these fears haunt me. However, they also make me laugh when I realize there foolishness.

Lines of Detail: A Walk-Through Assignment

Your assignment is to write an illustration paragraph about change.

Step 1: List all your ideas on this broad topic for ten minutes. You can list ideas on any aspect of change, such as a change of attitude, changing schools, a new job, a change in a daily routine, and so forth.

Step 2: Review your list. Underline any parts that are specific ideas related to the broad topic: change.

Step 3: List all the specific ideas. Choose one as the narrowed topic for your paragraph.

Step 4: Add related ideas to your chosen, narrowed topic. Do this by reviewing your list for related ideas and by brainstorming for more related ideas.

Step 5: List all your related ideas and review their connection to your narrowed topic. Then write a topic sentence and an outline for your paragraph.

Step 6: Write a first draft of your paragraph.

Step 7: Revise your first draft. Be sure it has enough details and clear transitions. Combine any choppy sentences.

Step 8: After a final check for any errors in punctuation, spelling, and word choice, prepare the final version of the paragraph.

Topics for Writing Your Own Illustration Paragraph

When you write on any of these topics, be sure to work through the stages of the writing process in preparing your paragraph.

1. Select one of the topics listed. Narrow the topic and write a paragraph on it. If you choose the topic of money, for example, you might narrow it by writing about credit cards for college students or about paying bills.

basketball	money	boredom
driving	exercise	sleep
songs	movies	children
photographs	gambling	rumors
crime	style	worrying
books	celebrities	boxing
time	lies	travel

2. Following are topic sentences. Select one and use it to write a paragraph.

The best advice I've ever been given is _____.

There are several parts of my daily routine that I dislike.

There are several parts of my daily routine that I enjoy.

The most hurtful word in the English language is _____.

The most overused word in the English language is _____.

The most frustrating part of relying on someone else for transportation is _____.

An empty classroom makes me think of _____.

Three teams represent the best in _____ (baseball, football, basketball, hockey, soccer—choose one).

Several people illustrate what it means to be a hero.

3. Look carefully at the photographs below, and use these photos to think about this topic sentence: *Tired people can fall asleep anywhere.* In a paragraph, support this topic sentence with your own examples.

4. Look carefully at the following photographs. Use them as a way to begin thinking about a paragraph with this topic sentence: The best kind of pet is a _____. Draw on your experience with any kind of pet (from a cat to an iguana) to write an illustration paragraph.

Topics for Critical Thinking and Writing

1. Imagine that you are at a job interview, and your interviewer asks you to think of a motto that guides your life. For example, would you state, "Treat other people the way you would like to be treated," "Always do your best," or some other motto? Write a paragraph that illustrates why a particular motto best describes your work ethic or your core values.

2. Assume that you are a member of a student advisory board at your college, and the administration has asked the board to identify potential safety hazards on campus. Make a list of potential dangers, and then identify what you believe to be the most severe hazard. For this assignment, illustrate why this safety hazard poses such a serious threat to the campus population.

MyWritingLab™ For support in meeting this chapter's objectives, log in to www.mywritinglab.com and select **Paragraph Development— Illustrating.**

Peer Review Form for an Illustration Paragraph

Name _____   Section_____

After you have written a draft version of your paragraph, let a writing partner read it. When your partner has completed the following form, discuss the responses. Then repeat the same process for your partner's paragraph.

The topic sentence of the paragraph is _____

_____

_____

The details that I liked best begin with the words _____

_____

The paragraph has _____ (enough, too many, too few) details to support the topic sentence.

A particularly good part of the paragraph begins with the words _____

_____

I have questions about _____

_____

_____

I noticed several transitions in the paragraph. They include the following _____

_____

Other comments on the paragraph _____

_____

_____

_____

_____

_____

_____

_____

_____

_____

Reviewer's Name_____

Writing a Process Paragraph

Chapter Objectives

Students will be able to (1) recognize the difference between directional and informational process papers and (2) write a process paragraph that contains a logical sequence, consistency in person, and effective transitional devices.

WHAT IS PROCESS?

Process writing explains how to do something or describes how something happens or is done. When you tell the reader how to do something (a **directional process**), you speak directly to the reader and give him or her clear, specific instructions about performing some activity. Your purpose is to explain an activity so that a reader can do it. For example, you may have to leave instructions telling a new employee how to close the cash register or use the copy machine.

When you describe how something happens or is done (an **informational process**), your purpose is to explain an activity without telling a reader how to do it. For example, you can explain how a boxer trains for a fight or how the special effects for a movie were created. Instead of speaking directly to the reader, an informational process speaks about *I, he, she, we, they,* or about a person by his or her name. A directional process uses *you* or, in the way it gives directions, the word *you* is understood.

A Process Involves Steps in Time Order

Whether a process is directional or informational, it describes something that is done in steps, and these steps are in a specific order: a **time order.** The process can involve steps that are followed in minutes, hours, days, weeks, months, or even years. For example, the steps in changing a tire may take minutes, whereas the steps taken to lose ten pounds may take months.

You should keep in mind that a process involves steps that *must follow a certain order*, not just a range of activities that can be placed in any order. This sentence *signals a process:*

Planting a rose garden takes planning and care. (Planting a rose garden involves following steps in order; that is, you cannot put a rose bush in the ground until you dig a hole.)

This sentence *does not signal a process:*

There are several ways to build your confidence. (Each way is separate; there is no time sequence here.)

Telling a person in a conversation how to do something or how something is done gives you the opportunity to add important points you may have overlooked or to throw in details you may have skipped at first. Your listener can ask questions if he or she does not understand you. Writing a process, however, is more difficult. Your reader is not there to stop you, to ask you to explain further, or to question you. In writing a process, you must be organized and very clear.

HINTS FOR WRITING A PROCESS PARAGRAPH

1. **In choosing a topic, find an activity you know well.** If you write about something familiar to you, you will have a clearer paragraph.

2. **Choose a topic that includes steps that must be done in a specific time sequence.**

not this: I find lots of things to do with old photographs.

but this: I have a plan for turning an old photograph into a special gift.

3. **Choose a topic that is fairly small.** A complicated process cannot be covered well in one paragraph. If your topic is too big, the paragraph can become vague, incomplete, or boring.

too big: There are many steps in the process of an immigrant becoming an American citizen.

smaller and manageable: Persistence and a positive attitude helped me through the stages of my job search.

4. **Write a topic sentence that makes a point.** Your topic sentence should do more than announce. Like the topic sentence for any paragraph, it should have a point. As you plan the steps of your process and gather details, ask yourself some questions: What point do I want to make about this process? Is the process hard? Is it easy? Does the process require certain tools? Does the process require certain skills, like organization, patience, or endurance?

an announcement: This paragraph is about how to change the oil in your car.

a topic sentence: You do not have to be a mechanic to change the oil in your car, but you do have to take a few simple precautions.

5. Include all of the steps. If you are explaining a process, you are writing for someone who does not know the process as well as you do. Keep in mind that what seems clear or simple to you may not be clear or simple to the reader, and be sure to tell what is needed before the process starts. For instance, what ingredients are needed to cook the dish? Or what tools are needed to assemble the toy?

6. Put the steps in the right order. Nothing is more irritating to a reader than trying to follow directions that skip back and forth. Careful planning, drafting, and revision can help you get the time sequence right.

7. Be specific in the details and steps. To be sure you have sufficient details and clear steps, keep your reader in mind. Put yourself in the reader's place. Could you follow your own directions or understand your steps?

If you remember that a process explains, you will focus on being clear. Now that you know the purpose and strategies of writing a process, you can begin the prewriting stage of writing one.

Exercise 1 **Practice: Recognizing Good Topic Sentences for Process Paragraphs**

If a sentence is a good topic sentence for a process paragraph, put *OK* on the line provided. If a sentence has a problem, label that sentence with one of these letters:

A This is an announcement; it makes no point.

B This sentence covers a topic that is too big for one paragraph.

S This sentence describes a topic that does not require steps.

1. _____ I've learned a better, shorter system for giving myself a manicure.

2. _____ The best way to clean bathroom tile will be the subject of this paragraph.

3. _____ There are several places to look for previously owned lamps.

4. _____ The steps required to set a person's broken leg are intricate.

5. _____ Finding a deal on a phone plan takes a little research.

6. _____ This paper shows a way to curl long, straight hair.

7. _____ The role of the governor in this state evolved in several stages.

8. _____ A few hints can help you make a good impression at a job interview.

9. _____ If you can remember how to avoid a few messy places, you can change the oil in your car.

10. _____ My father showed me how to repair a broken lawn chair.

Collaborate

Exercise 2   Collaborate: Including Necessary Materials in a Process

Below are three possible topics for a process paragraph. For each topic, work with a partner or a group and list the items (materials, ingredients, tools, utensils, supplies) the reader would have to gather before he or she began the process. When you've finished the exercise, check your lists with another group to see if you've missed any items.

1. **topic:** polishing a pair of leather shoes

    needed items: _____

    _____

2. **topic:** wrapping a box as a gift

    needed items: _____

    _____

3. **topic:** doing your laundry

    needed items: _____

    _____

WRITING THE PROCESS PARAGRAPH IN STEPS

PREWRITING   PROCESS

The easiest way to start writing a process paragraph is to pick a small topic, one that you can cover well in one paragraph. Then you can gather ideas by listing or freewriting or both.

If you decided to write about how to adopt a shelter dog, you might begin by freewriting.

Then you might check your freewriting, looking for details that have to do with the process of adopting a shelter dog. You can underline those details, as in the example that follows.

Freewriting for a Process Paragraph

Topic: How to Adopt a Shelter Dog

<u>What kind of dog do you want? It's difficult to walk through an animal shelter</u> and see all those dogs begging for a home. Be realistic. A purebred or a mixed breed? A puppy? <u>Can you afford it? There's a fee at the shelter. You have to be willing to take care of a dog for a long time.</u>

Next, you can put what you've underlined into a list, in correct time sequence:

before you decide on any dog

Can you afford it?
You have to be willing to take care of a dog for a long time.

considering the right dog

What kind of a dog do you want?
A purebred or a mixed breed? A puppy?
Be realistic.

at the shelter

It's difficult to walk through a shelter.
A fee at the shelter.

Check the list. Are some details missing? Yes. A reader might ask, "How do you decide what kind of dog is best for you?" or "What's so expensive about getting a dog at a shelter?" or "How much does it cost to own a dog, anyway?" Answers to questions like these can give you the details needed to write a clear and interesting informational process.

Writing a Topic Sentence for a Process Paragraph

Freewriting and a list can now help you focus your paragraph by identifying the point of your process. You already know that the subject of your paragraph is how to adopt a shelter dog. But what's the point? Is it easy to adopt a shelter dog? Is it difficult? What does it take to find the right dog?

Looking at your list of steps and details, you notice that most of the steps come before you actually select a dog. Maybe a topic sentence could be

> You have to do your homework if you want to find the shelter dog that's right for you.

Once you have a topic sentence, you can think about adding details that explain your topic sentence, and you can begin the planning stage of writing.

Exercise 3 **Practice: Finding the Steps of a Process in Freewriting**

Read the following freewriting, then reread it, looking for all the words, phrases, or sentences that have to do with steps. Underline all those items. Then once you've underlined the freewriting, put what you've underlined into a list in a correct time sequence.

How to Make Brewed Coffee: Freewriting

I love coffee in the morning. Especially brewed. Instant tastes awful once you've had brewed coffee. Don't forget to fill the glass carafe with the right amount of water for the number of cups. Start it all with a clean carafe. Use a spoon or plastic scoop to put the coffee in the brew basket. After you put a clean paper filter in the brew basket, get ready to add coffee. Don't turn on the coffeemaker until all the other steps have been completed. If you forget the paper filter, you'll have a mess. Make sure you measure out the right amount of coffee. The tempting smell of coffee brewing. Pour the water from the carafe into the water-heating compartment. Coffee tastes funny if it comes from a dirty carafe. Decide how many cups of coffee you want to make.

Your List of Steps in Time Sequence

_____

_____

_____

_____

_____

_____

_____

_____

_____

_____

_____

PLANNING **PROCESS**

Using the freewriting and topic sentence on how to adopt a shelter dog, you could make an outline. Then you could revise it, checking the topic sentence and improving the list of details where you think they could be better. A revised outline on adopting a shelter dog is shown below.

Outline for a Paragraph on How to Adopt a Shelter Dog

topic sentence: You have to do your homework if you want to find the shelter dog that's right for you.

details:

before you decide on any dog
- Decide whether you can afford a dog.
- Dogs cost money for food, regular veterinary care, and grooming.
- Decide if you are willing to take care of a dog for a long time.
- Dogs can live ten to fifteen years.
- They need exercise, attention, and training.

considering the right dog
- Think carefully about what kind of dog you want.
- You have to decide whether you want a purebred or mixed breed.
- You can get both types at a shelter.
- Puppies are adorable and fun.
- They need more training and attention.
- The size and temperament of the dog are important, too.
- Do some research and talk to friends who own dogs.

at the shelter
- It is difficult to walk through an animal shelter and see all the dogs begging for a home.
- But remember the kind of dog you've decided to adopt.
- Look around carefully.
- Make your selection, pay the adoption fee, and look forward to giving your dog the best years of its life.

You probably noticed that the outline follows the same stages as the list but has many new details. These details can be added as you create your plan.

The following checklist may help you revise an outline for your own process paragraph.

Checklist for Revising a Process Outline

✔ Is my topic sentence focused on some point about the process?

✔ Does it cover the whole process?

✔ Do I have all the steps?

✔ Are they in the right order?

✔ Have I explained clearly?

✔ Do I need better details?

Exercise 4 **Practice: Revising the Topic Sentence in a Process Outline**

The topic sentence below doesn't cover all the steps of the process. Read the outline several times; then write a topic sentence that covers all the steps of the process and has a point.

topic sentence: On a chilly autumn day, you can stay warm.

details: First, step outdoors and feel the temperature.

If the sun is shining and you are not shivering, you probably don't want to wear a heavy coat.

Instead, survey the contents of your closet.

Choose a t-shirt or other cotton shirt for the first layer of your clothing.

Finish this layer with a fairly heavy pair of jeans.

For the next layer, look for something warm such as a heavy pullover or sweatshirt.

Then cover it all with a jacket that is large enough to hold the layers in place.

As the day goes by and the temperature rises, you can shed the jacket.

Later in the day, you can remove the second layer of your clothing.

At each time of the day, the number of layers you wear will keep you as warm or as cool as you want to be.

In addition, you will not have to drag a heavy coat around when the weather becomes warm.

revised topic sentence: _____

_____

Exercise 5   **Practice: Revising the Order of Steps in a Process Outline**

The steps in each of these outlines are out of order. Put numbers in the spaces provided, indicating what step should be first, second, and so forth.

1.   topic sentence: From Monday through Friday, I follow the same morning schedule.

details: _____   Finally, I grab my coffee, lead my twins to the car, and I drive first to my boys' pre-school and second to my job.

_____   My alarm rings at 6:00 A.M. and I do not dare to linger in bed and fall back to sleep.

_____   In the kitchen, I give them juice, cereal, milk, and fruit while I make myself instant coffee.

_____   While they eat breakfast, they chatter and play.

_____   Soon I take them away from the remains of their breakfast.

_____   They resist getting dressed, but I finally manage to tug them into some wrinkled clothes.

_____   I force myself out of bed and stagger to my sons' room.

_____ Nagging my twin four-year-old sons, Zachary and Marshall, I manage to get them up.

_____ While they use the toilet and wash their sleepy faces, I dress.

2. **topic sentence:** In ten minutes, my brother Ryan can transform himself from a dirty mess into an attractive man.

      details: _____ Within ten minutes, Ryan has emerged from a cloud of dirt, sweat, and various odors and become a magnet for young women.

_____ He comes in after a vicious soccer game on a hot day, sweating and smeared with dirt.

_____ He zips into the shower and spends five minutes scrubbing away the dirt and sweat.

_____ Wrapping the damp towel around his waist, he brushes his teeth, rolls on some deodorant, and examines his damp hair.

_____ Grabbing a large towel, Ryan dries his hair and body.

_____ A few swipes of his hairbrush are all he needs to style his hair.

_____ After he completes the hairstyling, he puts on any pair of jeans and semi-clean shirt he can find.

Exercise 6 **Practice: Listing All of the Steps in an Outline**

Following are three topic sentences for process paragraphs. Write all of the steps needed to complete an outline for each sentence. After you've listed all of the steps, number them in the correct time order.

1. **topic sentence:** Anyone can cook spaghetti and tomato sauce.

     steps: _____

             _____

             _____

             _____

             _____

             _____

             _____

             _____

             _____

             _____

             _____

             _____

2.   **topic sentence:** When you have ten minutes between classes, you can find an easy way to make the most of your time.

   steps: _____

   _____

   _____

   _____

   _____

   _____

   _____

   _____

   _____

3.   **topic sentence:** In a few minutes, anyone can turn a dirty car interior into a fairly clean one.

   steps: _____

   _____

   _____

   _____

   _____

   _____

   _____

   _____

   _____

   _____

   _____

DRAFTING AND REVISING   PROCESS

You can take the outline and write it in paragraph form, and you'll have a first draft of the process paragraph. As you write the first draft, you can combine some of the short sentences from the outline. Then you can review your draft and revise it for organization, details, clarity, grammar, style, and word choice.

Using the Same Grammatical Person

Remember that the *directional* process speaks directly to the reader, calling him or her "you." Sentences in a directional process use the word *you*, or they imply *you*.

   directional: *You* need a good skillet to get started.
   Begin by cleaning the surface. ("You" is implied.)

Remember that the *informational* process involves somebody doing the process. Sentences in an informational process use words such as *I, we, he, she*, or *they* or a person's name.

   informational: Dave needed a good skillet to get started.
   First, I can clean the surface.

One problem in writing a process is shifting from describing how somebody did something to telling the reader how to do an activity. When that shift happens, the two kinds of processes get mixed. That shift is called a **shift in person.** In grammar, the words *I* and *we* are considered to be in the first person, *you* is in the second person, and *he, she, it,* and *they* are in the third person.

If these words refer to one, they are *singular;* if they refer to more than one, they are *plural.* The following list may help.

INFO BOX: **A List of Persons**

First person singular:	I
Second person singular:	you
Third person singular:	he, she, it, or a person's name
First person plural:	we
Second person plural:	you
Third person plural:	they, or the names of more than one person

---

In writing your process paragraph, decide whether your process will be directional or informational, and stay with one kind.

Below are two examples of a shift in person. Look at them carefully and study how the shift is corrected.

shift in person: After *I* preheat the oven to 350 degrees, *I* mix the egg whites and sugar with an electric mixer set at high speed. *Mix* until stiff peaks form. Then *I* put the mixture in small mounds on an ungreased cookie sheet. ("Mix until stiff peaks form" is a shift to the "you" person.)

shift corrected: After *I* preheat the oven to 350 degrees, *I* mix the egg whites and sugar with an electric mixer set at high speed. *I* mix until stiff peaks form. Then *I* put the mixture in small mounds on an ungreased cookie sheet.

shift in person: A *salesperson* has to be very careful when a customer tries on clothes. The *clerk* can't hint that a suit may be a size too small. *You* can insult a customer with a hint like that. (The sentences shifted from "salesperson" and "clerk" to "you.")

shift corrected: A *salesperson* has to be very careful when a customer tries on clothes. The *clerk* can't hint that a suit may be a size too small. *He or she* can insult a customer with a hint like that.

Using Transitions Effectively

As you revise your draft, you can add transitions. Transitions are particularly important in a process paragraph because you are trying to show the steps in a *specific sequence,* and you are trying to show the *connections* between steps. Good transitions will also keep your paragraph from sounding like a choppy, boring list.

Following is a list of some of the transitions you can use in writing a process paragraph. Be sure that you use transitional words and phrases only when logical to do so, and try not to overuse the same transitions in a paragraph.

> **INFO BOX:** **Transitions for a Process Paragraph**
>
> | | | | |
> |---|---|---|---|
> | after | during | later | then |
> | afterward | eventually | meanwhile | to begin |
> | as | finally | next | to start |
> | as he/she is | first, second, etc. | now | until |
> | as soon as | first of all | quickly | when |
> | as you are | gradually | sometimes | whenever |
> | at last | in the beginning | soon | while |
> | at the same time | immediately | suddenly | while I am |
> | before | initially | the first step | |
> | begin by | last | the second step, etc. | |

   When you write a process paragraph, you must pay particular attention to clarity. As you revise, keep thinking about your audience to be sure your steps are easy to follow. The following can help you revise your draft.

> **Checklist for Revising a Process Paragraph**
>
> ✔ Does the topic sentence cover the whole paragraph?
>
> ✔ Does the topic sentence make a point about the process?
>
> ✔ Is any important step left out?
>
> ✔ Should any step be explained further?
>
> ✔ Are the steps in the right order?
>
> ✔ Should any sentences be combined?
>
> ✔ Have I used the same person throughout the paragraph to describe the process?
>
> ✔ Have I used transitions effectively?

Exercise 7   **Practice: Correcting Shifts in Person in a Process Paragraph**

Below is a paragraph that shifts from being an informational to a directional process in several places. Those places are underlined. Rewrite the underlined parts, directly above the underlining, so that the whole paragraph is an informational process.

   Eddie has an efficient system for sorting and organizing his mail. As soon as he picks up his mail, he begins sorting it. Any junk mail, such as advertisements and offers for credit cards or phone plans, never reaches the kitchen table. <u>You</u> immediately <u>toss</u> it into the garbage. Then Eddie sits at the table and sorts the remaining mail. Eddie opens all the bills. He puts the ones that <u>you need</u> to pay right away in one stack; he places the ones he can pay later in another stack. Next, Eddie places each stack in its own compartment in a plastic tray. Finally, he looks at what mail is left: cards from friends, a reminder from the dentist about his next appointment, a bank statement. By sorting his mail every day, Eddie never has to face a mountain of old mail that can take <u>you</u> hours to sort.

> Exercise 8   **Practice: Revising Transitions in a Process Paragraph**

The transitions in this paragraph could be better. Rewrite the underlined transitions, directly above each one, so that the transitions are smoother.

Packing glassware for a move can be tricky, but a few steps can save you stress and broken glass. <u>First,</u> get a sturdy cardboard box that can be sealed across the top. <u>Second,</u> gather a stack of old newspapers or a pile of tissue paper. <u>Third,</u> place a roll of strong, wide packing tape and a pair of scissors near the box and the paper. <u>Fourth,</u> line the box with paper so that the glasses will be cushioned. <u>Fifth,</u> pick up one glass. Wrap it tightly in paper, making sure that the paper protects the inside, outside, and any stem or base on the glass. <u>Sixth,</u> place the first wrapped glass in the bottom of the box. <u>Seventh,</u> continue the packing process, using paper to separate each wrapped glass from the others. <u>Eighth,</u> close the box, cut large lengths of tape, and tape the top openings. <u>Ninth,</u> breathe deep, relax, and feel sure that your glasses will arrive intact at your destination.

> Exercise 9   **Practice: Combining Sentences in a Process Paragraph**

The paragraph below has many short, choppy sentences, which are underlined. Wherever you see two or more underlined sentences clustered next to each other, combine them into one clear, smooth sentence. Write your revised version of the paragraph in the spaces above the lines.

My uncle has come up with a smart way to avoid standing in line at popular restaurants. <u>His first step was to do</u> <u>a little research. He looked into which restau-</u> <u>rants issue pagers to their waiting customers.</u> Next, he drove around town and surveyed those restaurants. <u>He was looking for specific ones. He wanted ones near a</u> <u>bookstore. He also wanted ones near a discount store.</u> Once he was familiar with these restaurants, he began to put his plan into action. When he wants to eat at a restaurant, he always chooses one on his new list. <u>If there is a long wait at the restaurant, my uncle knows what to do. He takes the pager. He leaves for the nearby bookstore. Sometimes he leaves for the nearby discount store.</u> He browses in the bookstore or picks up a few items at the discount store. When his pager tells him his table is ready, he walks a few steps and has a good dinner.

A Draft of a Process Paragraph

Below is a draft of the process paragraph on adopting a shelter dog. This draft has more details than the outline on page 404. Some short sentences have been combined and transitions have been added.

Draft of a Paragraph on How to Adopt a Shelter Dog

transition added details added	You have to do your homework if you want to find the shelter dog that's best for you. <u>Begin by</u> deciding whether you can afford a dog. <u>Most shelters spay and neuter their animals,</u> but dogs cost money for food, regular veterinary care, and grooming.
transition added, sentences combined detail added transition added	<u>Then decide if you are willing to take care of a dog for the ten or fifteen years that is its likely lifespan.</u> Remember that dogs need <u>regular</u> exercise, attention, and training. <u>If you are ready to make the personal and financial commitment</u> of owning a pet, you can begin thinking carefully about the kind of dog you want.
sentences combined	<u>You have to decide whether you want a purebred or a mixed breed, for you can get both types at a shelter.</u>
transition sentence added sentences combined	<u>At the same time, think about the age of the dog you want. Puppies are adorable and fun, but they need more training and attention.</u> The size and temperament of the dog are important, too. Do some research and talk to friends who own dogs. It is difficult to walk through an animal shelter and see all the
transition added, sentences combined transition added	dogs begging for a home. <u>When you make your adoption visit, remember the kind of dog you've decided to adopt and look around carefully. Finally,</u> make you selection, pay the adoption fee, and look forward to giving your dog the best years of its life.

PROOFREADING PROCESS

Before you prepare the final copy of your process paragraph, you can check your latest draft for any places in grammar, word choice, and style that need revision.

Following is the final version of the process paragraph on adopting a shelter dog. You'll notice that it contains several changes from the draft above.

- A sentence of introduction has been added; it begins the paragraph and creates a smoother opening.

- Two more transitions have been added.
- "Look around" has been changed to "look" to emphasize that this is not a quick or casual glance but an examination.
- The second use of "carefully" has been changed to "thoroughly" to avoid repetition.

Final Version of Paragraph on How to Adopt a Shelter Dog

(Changes from the draft are underlined.)

<u>Most people who love animals and have big hearts have thought about adopting a dog with no home, a shelter dog.</u> <u>However,</u> you have to do your homework if you want to find the shelter dog that's best for you. Begin by deciding whether you can afford a dog. Most shelters spay and neuter their animals, but dogs cost money for food, regular veterinary care, and grooming. Then decide if you are willing to take care of a dog for the ten or fifteen years that is its likely lifespan. Remember that dogs need regular exercise, attention, and training. If you are ready to make the personal and financial commitment of owning a pet, you can begin thinking carefully about the kind of dog you want. You have to decide whether you want a purebred or a mixed breed, for you can get both types at a shelter. At the same time, think about the age of the dog you want. Puppies are adorable and fun, but they need more training and attention. The size and temperament of the dog are important, too. <u>To make all these decisions,</u> do some research and talk to friends who own dogs. <u>Later, as you prepare to go to the shelter,</u> be aware that it is difficult to walk through an animal shelter and see all the dogs begging for a home. When you make your adoption visit, remember the kind of dog you've decided to adopt and <u>look thoroughly.</u> Finally, make your selection, pay the adoption fee, and look forward to giving your dog the best years of its life.

Before you prepare the final copy of your process paragraph, check your latest draft for errors in spelling, punctuation, and formatting.

Exercise 10   **Practice: Correcting Errors in the Final Draft of a Process Paragraph**

Following are two process paragraphs with the kind of errors it is easy to overlook when you prepare the final version of an assignment. Correct the errors, writing above the lines. There are ten errors in the first paragraph and ten in the second paragraph.

1. Their is a right way to brush your teeth, and brushing correctly can save you many unpleasant moments in the dentists office. One of the first lessons I learned in the dental hygiene Program at my college is, that millions of people make mistakes during the simple process of brushing their teeth. You may be one of them. First of all, you need to brush with the proper toothbrush. Many

people think a hard toothbrush is the best because it will be tough on tooth decay. However, a soft toothbrush is better at massaging your gums and covering the surface of your teeth. Second, don't waste your money on fancy new toothpasts. Most toothpastes contain the same cavity-fighting ingredients so a inexpensive one will do. Once you have put a small amount of toothpaste on your brush, you should brush gently. Don't scrub your teeth as if they were a dirty pot or pan. Softly massage them near the gum line. Last, brush for a long time. A long time don't mean hours, but it does mean two minutes. You may think that you all ready brush for two minutes, but you probably don't. The next time you brush, time yourself. Two minutes feels like a long time. However, if you spend thirty seconds one each part of your teeth (the upper teeth on the inner surface, the upper teeth on the outer surface, and so forth), you will be on your way to healthier teeth.

2. I have taken some important steps to overcome my paneful shyness. When I started college, I was terfied of sitting in the cafeteria alone. I felt sure that everyone would be starring at me, wondering why I didnt have any friends. For months, I avoided the place. Then, slowly, I began to practice being more confident. I began by simply setting down, alone, at a table in a corner. For a few minute's I sat there, my heart racing. After about a dozen of these short stays, I took the next step. I actually bought a Coke and some chips and ate them, alone, at a table. Two weeks after I recovered from this frightening experience, I repeated it, but this time I am brave enough to scan the people at the other tables. Noone seemed to notice me at all! Feeling encouraged, I took a big step soon after. I choosed a table in the middle of the room, not one in a distance corner. After a few moments, I experienced a major victory. I made eye contact with another student sitting alone, and I said, "Hi. How are you doing?" My steps may be small ones for other people, but for me, they are big strides.

Lines of Detail: A Walk-Through Assignment

Your assignment is to write an informational process on how you found the perfect gift for your best friend or parent. Follow these steps:

Step 1: Decide whether to write about a gift for your friend or for your parent. Then think about a time when you found a gift that made that person very happy.

Step 2: Now freewrite. Write anything you can remember about the gift, how you decided what to give, how you found it and gave it.

Step 3: When you've completed the freewriting, read it. Underline all the details that refer to steps in finding the gift. List the underlined details in time order.

Step 4: Add to the list by brainstorming. Ask yourself questions that can lead to more details. For example, if an item on your list is, "I realized my mother likes colorful clothes," ask questions like, "What colors does she like?" "What is her favorite color?" or "What kind of clothes does she like to wear?"

Step 5: Survey your expanded list. Write a topic sentence that makes some point about your finding this gift. To reach a point, think of questions like, "What made the gift perfect?" or "What did I learn from planning, finding, and giving this gift?"

Step 6: Use the topic sentence to prepare an outline. Be sure that the steps in the outline are in the correct time order.

Step 7: Write a first draft of the paragraph, adding details and combining short sentences.

Step 8: Revise your draft. Be careful to use smooth transitions, and check that you have included all the necessary steps.

Step 9: Proofread and prepare the final copy of your paragraph.

Topics for Writing Your Own Process Paragraph

When you write on one of these topics, be sure to work through the stages of the writing process in preparing your process paragraph.

1. Write a **directional or informational process** about one of these topics:

cleaning out a closet	asking a professor for help in a college course
setting a fancy table	
painting a chair	getting children to eat vegetables
training for a marathon	remembering the name of a person you've met recently
coloring your hair	
choosing a roommate	fixing a leaky pipe
using coupons to save on groceries	installing speakers in a car
	buying airline tickets online
avoiding morning traffic jams	quitting a job gracefully
handling a customer's complaint	getting or giving a manicure
	fighting a traffic ticket
making a telemarketing call	getting ready for moving day
getting to school on time	sticking to an exercise program

2. Imagine that one of your relatives has never used a computer but wants to know how to use e-mail. Explain how to send an e-mail by describing the steps you use in sending one through your online service.

3. Interview someone who always seems to be organized at school or at work. Ask that person to tell you how he or she manages to be so efficient. Narrow the question by asking how the person always manages to get all his work done at the store or how she always submits her assignments on time. Ask whether the person has developed a system and what steps are involved in that system. Take notes or tape the interview.

   After the interview, write a paragraph about that system, explaining how to be organized for a particular task at college or at work. Your paragraph will explain the process to someone who needs to be more organized.

4. The children in the photograph below are playing tug-of-war. Use the photograph to think about a childhood game you used to play that was popular with boys and girls. Write a paragraph explaining how to play that game.

Topics for Critical Thinking and Writing

1. Imagine that a friend is about to register for classes at your college, but he cannot visit the campus during regular business hours to register in person. This will be your friend's first term at the college. Write a paragraph giving your friend clear directions for registering online. For each step, explain what is involved and emphasize its importance to the overall process.

2. Interview one of the counselors at your college. Ask him or her to tell you the steps in applying for a scholarship. Take notes or record the interview, obtain copies of any forms that may be included in the application process, and be sure to ask questions about these forms if they appear confusing to you. After the interview, write a paragraph explaining the application process, and assume that your audience is a current student who has never applied for any scholarship or financial aid.

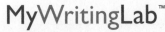 For support in meeting this chapter's objectives, log in to www.mywritinglab.com and select **Paragraph Development—Process.**

Name _____   Section _____

Peer Review Form for a Process Paragraph

After you've written a draft of your process paragraph, let a writing partner read it. When your partner has completed the form below, discuss. Repeat the same process for your partner's paragraph.

The steps that are most clearly described are _____

_____

_____

I'd like more explanation about this step _____

_____

This paragraph is a directional/information process (choose one).

Some details could be added to the part that begins with the words _____

_____

A transition could be added to the part that begins with the words _____

_____

I have questions about _____

_____

When I finished a careful reading of this paragraph, I found the explanation of the process (1) clear and simple, (2) a little confusing, (3) over my head (choose one). Explain your choice _____

_____

_____

Other comments on the paragraph

_____

_____

_____

_____

_____

_____

_____

Reviewer's Name_____

Title:_____

Aphorism in topic sentence.

Topic Sentence: _____

I._____

    A. _____

    B. _____

    C. _____

    D. _____

II._____

    A. _____

    B. _____

    C. _____

    D. _____

III. _____

    A._____

    B. _____

    C. _____

    D. _____

IV. _____

    A. _____

    B. _____

    C. _____

    D. _____

V. _____

    A. _____

    B. _____

    C. _____

    D. _____

And so on....

Concluding Sentence: _____

Aphorism: "When elephants fight, it is the grass that suffers"

Illustrations:

1. Big people rumble, little people get knocked around on accident.

2. Drop a bomb and there will be colateral damages.

3. Elephants shouldn't fight, just eat peanuts.

4. when Godzilla fights, chinese people panic.

5.

Aphorism:

Illustrations:

1.

2.

3.

4.

5.

Aphorisms and Illustration

Aphorism: "No pain, no gain"

Illustrations:

1. I could describe a specific student in English 050 I had last winter semester who wasn't willing to endure any intellectual pain to gain more writing and grammar knowledge.
2. Using narration, I could tell a story about what happened when an English 101 student I had in class over the summer wanted to gain an "A" without any pain.
3. I could describe a new teacher this semester who is currently enduring all kinds of pain but will gain so much knowledge about what works in class and what doesn't.
4. Using narration, I could show what happened yesterday when a student complained to the Dean about me (pain) and what that student gained.
5. This morning, I endured the pain of an uninformed staff member making a poor decision, but after discussing it with him, I believe both of us gained something.

Aphorism: "You can lead a horse to water, but you can't make him drink

Illustrations:

1. You could give somebody all the tools to do a job, but it doesnt mean they are going to do a good one.

2. Just because there is water does not mean the horse is thirsty.

3. You tell a kid not to touch the hot stove, he burns his hand anyway.

4. Horses don't like water if its contaminated.

5. Open note, open book test; fail.

Moving from Paragraphs to Essays

Jumping In

*A well-built house begins with proper framing and quality building blocks. Similarly, a well-constructed **essay** relies on logical organization as its frame and on effective paragraphs as its building blocks. Keep this analogy in mind as you move from the paragraph to the essay.*

Chapter Objectives

Students will be able to (1) identify the basic components of an essay, (2) recognize the differences between a topic sentence and a thesis statement, and (3) write a multiparagraph essay incorporating sufficient unity, support, and coherence.

WHAT IS AN ESSAY?

You write an essay when you have more to say than can be covered in one paragraph. An **essay** can consist of one paragraph, but in this book, we take it to mean a writing of more than one paragraph. An essay has a main point, called a *thesis*, supported by subpoints. The subpoints are the *topic sentences*. Each paragraph in the *body*, or main part, of the essay has a topic sentence. In fact, each paragraph in the body of the essay is like the paragraphs you've already written because each one makes a point and then supports it.

COMPARING THE SINGLE PARAGRAPH AND THE ESSAY

Read the paragraph and the essay that follow, both about sharing happy moments. You will notice many similarities.

A Single Paragraph

When I am happy, I want to share my happiness. When my wife gave birth to our son, for example, I couldn't wait to tell everyone. I started by calling my parents, my wife's parents, and every other relative I could think of. After I had run out of family members, I told friends, coworkers, and even a few total strangers. In another instance, I had to share the news about my dream of getting a college education. As soon as I opened the letter announcing my college loan, I wanted to spread the information. Just seeing the look on my wife's face increased my happiness. Later, telling my best friend, who had encouraged me to apply for the loan, was a pleasure. When good comes into my life, I figure, why not share it?

An Essay

Everybody has special moments of pure joy when a dream suddenly becomes a reality or a goal is finally in sight. These rare times mark the high points in life, and some people like to experience them alone. However, I am not one of these people. When I am happy, I want to share my happiness.

When my wife gave birth to our son, for example, I couldn't wait to tell everyone. I started by calling my parents, my wife's parents, and every other relative I could think of. By the time I found myself calling my second cousin in New Zealand, I realized I had run out of relatives. I prolonged my happiness by calling all my friends, the people at the bakery where I work, and even a few strangers. One poor man nearly tripped when I ran into him as he tried to get out of the hospital elevator. "Oh, I'm so sorry," I said, "but I've just had a baby boy." I even told the mail carrier on my street.

In another instance, I had to share the news about my dream of getting a college education. As soon as I opened the letter announcing my college loan, I wanted to spread the information. Just seeing the look on my wife's face increased my happiness. She knew what I was thinking: With the loan, I wouldn't have to take a second job in order to attend college. Later, telling my best friend, who had encouraged me to apply for the loan, was a pleasure. My getting the loan was his victory, too, for without him, I would have given up on going to college.

I suppose I could have told my friend about my financial aid a few days later, over lunch. As for the birth of my son, I could have saved hefty long-distance phone charges by sending birth announcements to aunts, uncles, and cousins who live far away. But I chose not to hold back. When good comes into my life, I figure, why not share it?

If you read the two selections carefully, you noticed that they make the same main point, and they support that point with two subpoints.

main point: When I am happy, I want to share my happiness.

subpoints: 1. When my wife gave birth to our son, I couldn't wait to tell everyone.
2. I had to share the news about my dream of getting a college education.

You noticed that the essay is longer because it has more details and examples to support the points.

ORGANIZING AN ESSAY

When you write an essay of more than one paragraph, the **thesis** is the focus of your entire essay; it is the major point of your essay. The other important points that relate to the thesis are in topic sentences.

> **thesis:** Working as a salesperson has changed my character.
>
> **topic sentence:** I have had to learn patience.
>
> **topic sentence:** I have developed the ability to listen.
>
> **topic sentence:** I have become more tactful.

Notice that the thesis expresses a bigger idea than the topic sentences below it, and it is supported by the topic sentences. The essay has an introduction, a body, and a conclusion.

1. **Introduction:** The first paragraph is usually the introduction. The thesis goes here.
2. **Body:** This central part of the essay is the part where you support your main point (the thesis). Each paragraph in the body of the essay has its own topic sentence.
3. **Conclusion:** Usually one paragraph long, the conclusion reminds the reader of the thesis. It can be shorter than a body paragraph.

WRITING THE THESIS

There are several characteristics of a thesis:

1. It is expressed in a sentence. A thesis is *not* the same as the topic of the essay or the title of the essay:

> **topic:** learning to ski
> **title:** Why I Learned to Ski
> **thesis:** I learned to ski because all my friends ski, I needed more exercise in the winter, and I wanted to meet girls.

2. A thesis **does not announce;** it makes a point about the subject.

> **announcement:** This essay will explain the reasons why street racing is popular with teens.
> **thesis:** Street racing is popular with teens because it gives them a sense of power and identity.

3. A thesis **is not too broad.** Some ideas are just too big to cover well in an essay. A thesis that tries to cover too much can lead to a superficial or boring essay.

> **too broad:** The world would be a better place if everyone would just be more tolerant.
> **acceptable thesis:** The diversity celebration at our school spread good feelings among many groups.

4. A thesis **is not too narrow.** Sometimes, writers start with a thesis that looks good because it seems specific and precise. Later, when they try to support such a thesis, they can't find anything to say.

> **too narrow:** Yesterday I spent five hours in a hospital emergency room, waiting for help.
> **acceptable thesis:** Because I have no health insurance, illness is always a crisis for me.

Hints for Writing a Thesis

1. Your thesis can **mention the specific subpoints** of your essay. For example, your thesis might be like the following:

> Boundaries are important because they make children feel safe, connected, and loved.

With this thesis, you have indicated the three subpoints of your essay: (1) Boundaries make children feel safe, (2) boundaries make children feel connected, and (3) boundaries make children feel loved.

2. Another way to write your thesis is to **make a point** without listing your subpoints. For example, you can write a thesis like the following:

> Children need boundaries in order to grow.

With this thesis, you can still use the subpoints stating that boundaries make children feel safe, boundaries make children feel connected, and boundaries make children feel loved. You just don't have to mention all your subpoints in the thesis.

Exercise 1 Practice: Recognizing Good Thesis Sentences

Review the entries below and determine which ones are suitable thesis sentences. Note that some entries are too broad or narrow, and one is not a sentence. Write a *G* next to the "good" thesis sentences.

1. _____ How rumors spread on college campuses will be discussed.

2. _____ On Saturday, a local police officer stopped my brother for speeding.

3. _____ Family support influences all future relationships.

4. _____ Cartoons with sophisticated humor appeal to many adults.

5. _____ Organized crime is an evil force spreading fear and corruption.

6. _____ A married college student with a job and family juggles many responsibilities.

7. _____ Discount stores do not always offer the best bargains.

8. _____ Brazil is a large South American nation with many natural resources.

9. _____ The advantages of working from a home office.

10. _____ Traffic congestion keeps many local people from visiting the city.

Exercise 2 Practice: Selecting a Good Thesis Sentence

In each pair of thesis statements below, put a *G* next to the good thesis sentence.

1. a. _____ The most stressful times for me.

   b. _____ My most stressful times come during final exams.

2. a. _____ Photographing red-light violations has positive and negative effects.

   b. _____ Something must be done to solve the growing problem of serious traffic accidents in our country.

3. a. _____ The difficulties of learning English as a second language will be discussed in this essay.

   b. _____ Students learning English as a second language have difficulties with fast-talking native speakers and confusing grammar rules.

4. a. _____ What to do if a tornado threatens your neighborhood

   b. _____ If a tornado threatens your neighborhood, act fast and sensibly.

5. a. _____ I quit my job because the working conditions were terrible.

   b. _____ The terrible working conditions and what I did about them will be the subject of this essay.

6. a. _____ Dancing is a great way to stay in shape.

   b. _____ What dancing can do for people.

7. a. _____ The differences between a convertible and a car with a sunroof.

   b. _____ A car with a sunroof is less likely to be vandalized or robbed than a convertible is.

8. a. _____ The public schools in our town need money for more teachers, smaller classes, and new technology.

   b. _____ Public schools are in trouble.

9. a. _____ The hidden story of bottled water and its origins.

   b. _____ Bottled water can have the same risks and come from the same sources as tap water.

10. a. _____ The Washington County Animal Shelter has a foster pet program.

    b. _____ Fostering shelter pets is a great way to give them comfort and hope.

Exercise 3 Practice: Writing a Thesis That Relates to the Subpoints

Following are lists of subpoints that could be discussed in an essay. Write a thesis for each list. Remember that there are two ways to write a thesis: you can write a thesis that includes the specific subpoints, or you can write one that makes a point without listing the subpoints. As an example, the first one is done for you, using both kinds of topic sentences.

1. **one kind of thesis:** Children need to leave their computers and televisions and play some outdoor sports.

   another kind of thesis: For children, playing sports outdoors burns more energy, creates more friendships, and stimulates more interest than playing indoors.

   subpoints: a. Sitting at a computer or in front of a television burns very little energy; playing sports burns more energy.
   b. Playing indoors is often solitary; sports involve other children and may lead to friendships.

    c. Children playing indoors can easily become bored, but outdoor sports require more involvement.

2. thesis: _____

_____

subpoints: **a.** Prospective buyers think a cluttered house is smaller than it really is.

            b. To potential buyers, a cluttered house appears messy or even dirty.

3. thesis: _____

_____

subpoints: **a.** Too great a need to win can take the pleasure out of friendly games.

            b. An obsessive need to win encourages some people to cheat.

            c. When winning becomes the only goal, people in professional sports may damage their bodies in order to win.

            d. Corporations that are competing for financial success have been known to break laws.

4. thesis: _____

_____

subpoints: **a.** People of retirement age should not be ridiculed for their physical challenges.

            b. The young and physically able can easily take a minute to hold open a door for an elderly woman.

            c. Young people can also accept an older driver's pace and habits without ridiculing or protesting them.

5. thesis: _____

_____

subpoints: **a.** A house surrounded by large trees will stay cooler in the summer.

            b. Large trees around a house offer more privacy.

            c. A house circled by large trees may be expensive to heat in the winter.

            d. Large trees surrounding a house may make the house dark and gloomy.

WRITING THE ESSAY IN STAGES

In an essay, you follow the same stages you learned in writing a paragraph—prewriting, planning, drafting and revising, and proofreading—but you adapt them to the longer essay form.

PREWRITING   AN ESSAY

Often you begin by *narrrowing a topic*. Your instructor may give you a large topic so you can find something smaller, within the broad one, that you would like to write about.

Some students think that because they have several paragraphs to write, they should pick a big topic, one that will give them enough to say. But big topics can lead to boring, superficial, general essays. A smaller topic can challenge you to find the specific, concrete examples and details that make an essay effective.

If your instructor asked you to write about student life, for instance, you might *freewrite* some ideas as you narrow the topic:

Narrowing the Topic of Student Life

Student activities—how boring!

Maybe how to meet people at college, except how <u>do</u> you meet people? I don't really know. I have my friends, but I'm not sure how I met them.

The food on campus. Everyone will do that topic.

The classrooms in college. The tiny chairs and the temperature.

Yes!

In your freewriting, you can consider your *purpose*—to write an essay about some aspect of student life—and *audience*—your instructor and classmates. Your narrowed topic will appeal to this audience because both college teachers and students spend a good part of their time in classrooms.

Listing Ideas

Once you have a narrow topic, you can use whatever process works for you. You can brainstorm by writing a series of questions and answers about your topic, you can freewrite on the topic, you can list ideas on the topic, or you can do any combination of these processes.

Following is a sample *listing of ideas* on the topic of classrooms.

College Classrooms: A List

the tiny chairs	the temperature
the awful desks	all the graffiti
the carvings in the desks	too hot in the room
freezing on some days	cramped rooms
blinds on windows don't close	the teacher's desk
no one cares	

By *clustering* related items on the list, you'll find it easier to see the connections between ideas. The following items have been clustered (grouped), and they are listed under subtitles.

College Classrooms: Ideas in Clusters

the furniture	**student damage**
the tiny chairs	the carvings in the desks
the awful desks	all the graffiti
the teacher's desk	

the temperature

freezing on some days

too hot in the room

blinds on windows don't close

When you surveyed the clusters, you probably noticed that some of the ideas from the original list were left out. These ideas on the cramped rooms and no one caring could fit into more than one place and might not fit anywhere. You might come back to them later.

When you name each cluster by giving it a subtitle, you move toward a focus for each body paragraph of your essay. And by beginning to focus the body paragraphs, you start thinking about the main point, the thesis of the essay. Concentrating on the thesis and on focused paragraphs helps you to *unify* your essay.

Reread the clustered ideas. When you do so, you'll notice that each cluster is about a different kind of problem in the college classroom. You can incorporate that concept into a thesis with a sentence like this:

The typical classroom at my college is unwelcoming because of its tiny furniture, uncomfortable temperature, and student damage.

Once you have a thesis and a list of details, you can begin working on the planning part of your essay.

Collaborate

Exercise 4 **Collaborate: Narrowing Topics**

Working with a partner or a group, narrow these topics so that the new topics are related but smaller and suitable for short essays between four and six paragraphs long. The first topic is narrowed for you.

1. **topic:** health
   smaller, related topics:
   a. *fighting a cold*
   b. *the right vitamins to take*
   c. *getting a good night's sleep*

2. **topic:** crime
   smaller, related topics:
   a. _____
   b. _____
   c. _____

3. **topic:** movies
   smaller, related topics:
   a. _____
   b. _____
   c. _____

4. **topic:** nature
   smaller, related topics:
   a. _____
   b. _____
   c. _____

5. **topic:** employment

   smaller, related topics: a. _____

   b. _____

   c. _____

Practice: Clustering Related Ideas

Below are two topics, each with a list of ideas. Mark all the related items on the list with the same number (1, 2, or 3). Some items might not get any number. When you've finished marking the list, write a title for each number that explains the cluster of ideas.

1. **topic:** why friendships end

   _____ one friend joins the army and is sent overseas

   _____ one friend betrays the other friend's secret

   _____ one friend works at two full-time jobs

   _____ one friend spends all his time trying to save the family business

   _____ one friend dies in a car accident

   _____ one friend borrows money and never repays it

   _____ the friends share mutual goals

   _____ family members accept and act kindly toward the friends

   _____ one is sent to prison and is unable to prove his innocence

   _____ one marries someone who hates the old group of friends

   The ideas marked 1 can be titled _____

   The ideas marked 2 can be titled _____

   The ideas marked 3 can be titled _____

2. **topic:** losing your wallet

   _____ desperately search your pockets or purse

   _____ call your credit card companies to cancel your cards

   _____ search every inch of your house in a panic

   _____ think about any stranger who bumped into you

   _____ your heart beats as you retrace your steps of the day

   _____ get a replacement driver's license

   _____ blame yourself for the loss of the wallet

   _____ consider the possibility of theft

   _____ get a new insurance card

   _____ frantically try to recall when and where you last handled your wallet

   The items marked 1 can be titled _____

   The items marked 2 can be titled _____

   The items marked 3 can be titled _____

PLANNING **AN ESSAY**

In the next stage of writing your essay, draft an outline. Use the thesis to focus your ideas. There are many kinds of outlines, but all are used to help a writer organize ideas. When you use a **formal outline,** you show the difference between a main idea and its supporting detail by *indenting* the supporting detail. In a formal outline, Roman numerals (numbers) and capital letters are used. Each Roman numeral represents a paragraph, and the letters beneath the numeral represent supporting details.

The Structure of a Formal Outline

first paragraph	I.	Thesis
second paragraph	II.	Topic sentence
details		A.
		B.
		C.
		D.
		E.
third paragraph	III.	Topic sentence
details		A.
		B.
		C.
		D.
		E.
fourth paragraph	IV.	Topic sentence
details		A.
		B.
		C.
		D.
		E.
fifth paragraph	V.	Conclusion

Hints for Outlining

Developing a good, clear outline now can save you hours of confused, disorganized writing later. The extra time you spend to make sure that your outline has sufficient details and that *each paragraph stays on one point* will pay off in the long run.

1. Check the topic sentences. Keep in mind that each topic sentence in each body paragraph should support the thesis sentence. If a topic sentence is not carefully connected to the thesis, the structure of the essay will be confusing. Here are a thesis and a list of topic sentences; the topic sentence that does not fit is crossed out:

thesis:	I. Designing a CD of a person's favorite songs is a creative act and a thoughtful gift.
topic sentences:	II. Selecting just the right songs takes insight.
	III. Assembling the CD requires imagination.
	IV. ~~CD players are getting cheaper all the time.~~
	V. Whoever receives the CD will be flattered that someone took the time to design such a personal gift.
	VI. A personally crafted CD challenges the mind of the giver and opens the heart of the receiver.

Because the thesis of this outline is about the creative challenge of designing a personal CD as a gift and the pleasure of receiving one, topic sentence IV doesn't fit: it isn't about making the gift or receiving it. It takes the essay off track. A careful check of the links between the thesis and the topic sentences will help keep your essay focused.

2. Include enough details. Some writers believe that they don't need many details in the outline. They feel they can fill in the details later, when they actually write the essay. Even though some writers do manage to add details later, others who are in a hurry or who run out of ideas run into problems.

For example, imagine that a writer has included very few details in an outline such as in this outline for a paragraph:

II. Vandalism of cars takes many forms.
   A. Most cars suffer external damage.
   B. Some are hit in their interiors.

The paragraph created from that outline might be too short and lack specific details, like this:

> Vandalism of cars takes many forms. First of all, most cars suffer external damage. However, some are hit in their interiors.

If you have difficulty thinking of ideas when you write, try to tackle the problem in the outline. The more details you put into your outline, the more detailed and effective your draft essay will be. For example, suppose the same outline on the vandalism topic had more details, like this:

II. Vandalism of cars takes many forms.

more details about exterior damage
   A. Most cars suffer external damage.
   B. The most common damage is breaking off the car antenna.
   C. "Keying" a car, scratching its surface with a key, is also widespread.
   D. Some vandals slash or take the air out of the tires.
   E. Others pour paint on the body of the car.

more details about interior damage
   F. Some are hit in their interiors.
   G. Interior damage ranges from ripped upholstery to torn carpet.

You will probably agree that the paragraph will be more detailed, too.

3. Stay on one point. It is a good idea to check the outline of each body paragraph to see if each paragraph stays on one point. Compare each topic sentence, which is at the top of the list for the paragraph, against the details indented under it. Staying on one point gives each paragraph unity.

Below is the outline for a paragraph that has problems staying on one point. See if you can spot the problem areas.

III. Charles is a fun-loving and cheerful person.

   A. Every morning at work, he has a new joke for me.
   B. He even makes our boss, who is very serious, smile.
   C. One day when a customer was extremely rude to him, he kept his temper.
   D. On weekends, when our job gets hectic, Charles never becomes irritable.

E. Most of our customers love him because he always greets them with, "How are you on this beautiful day?"

F. When we all took a pay cut, he looked on the positive side.

G. "At least we still have our jobs," he said.

The topic sentence of the paragraph is about Charles' love of fun and cheerfulness. But sentences C and D talk about Charles' ability to remain calm. When you have a problem staying on one point, you can solve the problem two ways:

1. Eliminate details that do not fit your main point.
2. Change the topic sentence to cover all the ideas in the paragraph.

For example, you could cut out sentences C and D about Charles' calm nature, getting rid of the details that do not fit. As an alternative, you could change the topic sentence in the paragraph so that it relates to all the ideas in the paragraph. A better topic sentence is "Charles is a fun-loving, even-tempered, and cheerful person."

Revisiting the Prewriting Stage

Writing an outline can help you identify skimpy places in your plan, places where your paragraphs will need more details. You can get these details in two ways:

1. Go back to the writing you did in the prewriting stage. Check whether items on a list or ideas from freewriting can lead you to more details for your outline.
2. Brainstorm for more details by using a question-and-answer approach. For example, if the outline includes "My little sister is greedy," you might ask, "When is she greedy? How greedy is she?" Or if the outline includes "There is nothing to do in this town," you might ask, "What do you mean? Sports? Clubs? Parties?"

The time you spend writing and revising your outline will make it easier for you to write an essay that is well developed, unified, and coherently structured. The checklist below may help you to revise.

Checklist for Revising the Outline of an Essay

✔ **Unity:** Do the thesis and topic sentences all lead to the same point? Does each paragraph make one, and only one, point? Do the details in each paragraph support the topic sentence? Does the conclusion unify the essay?

✔ **Support:** Do the body paragraphs have enough supporting details?

✔ **Coherence:** Are the paragraphs in the most effective order? Are the details in each paragraph arranged in the most effective order?

A sentence outline on college classrooms follows. It includes the thesis in the first paragraph. The topic sentences have been created from the titles of the ideas clustered earlier. The details have been drawn from ideas in the clusters and from further brainstorming. The conclusion has just one sentence that unifies the essay.

Outline for an Essay

paragraph 1:	I. Thesis: The typical classroom at my college is unwelcoming because of its tiny furniture, uncomfortable temperature, and student damage.

paragraph 2:
topic sentence
details

II. Child-size furniture makes it difficult to focus on adult-level classes.
   A. The student chairs are tiny.
   B. I am six feet tall, and I feel like I am crammed into a kindergarten chair.
   C. The chairs are attached to miniature desks, which are just slightly enlarged armrests.
   D. I cannot fit my legs under the desk.
   E. I cannot fit my textbook and a notebook on the surface of the desk.
   F. In some classrooms, the teacher has no desk and is forced to use one of the miniature student versions.

paragraph 3:
topic sentence
details

III. The temperature in the classrooms is anything but pleasant.
   A. I have been at the college for both the fall and winter terms.
   B. In the early fall, the rooms were too hot.
   C. The air conditioning feebly pumped hot air.
   D. The sun beat through the glass windows because the blinds were broken.
   E. On some days in the winter, we froze.
   F. Two of my teachers have reported the problems to maintenance, but nothing changed.
   G. It is hard to concentrate when you are sweating or shivering.

paragraph 4:
topic sentence
details

IV. Student damage to the classrooms makes them seedy and ugly.
   A. There is graffiti all over the desks.
   B. There are messages, slogans, and drawings.
   C. They are all childish.
   D. Half the desks and chairs have gum stuck to their undersides.
   E. Some students carve into the desks and chairs.
   F. Others have stained the carpet with spilled coffee or soft drinks.
   G. It's depressing to think that my fellow students enjoy damaging the place where they come to learn.

paragraph 5:
conclusion

V. When I started college, I knew I would face many challenges, but I didn't expect them to include squeezing into the chairs, dressing for a blizzard or a heat wave, and picking gum off my desk.

Exercise 6 **Practice: Completing an Outline for an Essay**

Following is part of an outline that has a thesis and topic sentences, but no details. Add the details and write them in complete sentences. Write one sentence for each capital letter. Be sure that the details are connected to the topic sentence.

I. **Thesis:** Money has a different meaning for different people.

II. When some people think of money, they think of the freedom to spend it on whatever they want for themselves.

A. _____

B. _____

C. _____

D. _____

E. _____

III. To others, money means security.

A. _____

B. _____

C. _____

D. _____

E. _____

IV. Some people think of money as something to share.

A. _____

B. _____

C. _____

D. _____

E. _____

V. The way people perceive money reveals what matters to them.

Exercise 7 **Practice: Focusing an Outline for an Essay**

The outline below has a thesis and details, but it has no topic sentences for the body paragraphs. Write the topic sentences.

I. **Thesis:** My girlfriend and I will never eat at the The Bridge Restaurant again.

II. _____

_____

A. We had to stand in line for a table.

B. The restaurant's hostess promised us the waiting time would be short.

C. The wait lasted half an hour.

D. The line of people grew longer as time passed.

    E. There was no place to sit as we all crowded into a small front room.

    F. No one seemed to be led from the line to the dining room.

III. _____

_____

    A. The shrimp salad that I ordered had tiny canned shrimp.

    B. Steak is supposed to be the specialty of the house.

    C. My steak was gristly and tough.

    D. An order of grilled vegetables was cold and mushy.

    E. My girlfriend's chicken was not thoroughly cooked.

    F. The key lime pie we both ordered for dessert appeared to be a pie crust filled with lime pudding.

IV. _____

_____

    A. My shrimp salad appetizer cost me ten dollars.

    B. The steak that The Bridge Restaurant features cost me more than my weekly food budget.

    C. I paid extra money for a side order of grilled vegetables.

    D. My girlfriend's request for an iced tea cost $2.50.

    E. For dessert, I ordered a "special" cup of coffee flavored with amaretto that cost five dollars.

    F. Worst of all, I could have bought an entire pie at the local bakery for the price of our two slices.

V. Our visit to The Bridge restaurant was our first—and last.

DRAFTING AND REVISING   AN ESSAY

When you are satisfied with your outline, you can begin your drafting and then revising of the essay. Start by writing a first draft of the essay, which includes these parts: introduction, body paragraphs, and conclusion.

WRITING THE INTRODUCTION

Where Does the Thesis Go?

The **thesis** should appear in the introduction of the essay, in the first paragraph. But most of the time it should not be the first sentence. In front of the thesis, write a few (three or more) sentences of introduction. Generally, the thesis is the *last sentence* in the introductory paragraph.

    Why put the thesis at the end of the first paragraph? First of all, writing several sentences in front of your main idea gives you a chance to lead into it, gradually and smoothly. This will help you build interest and gain the reader's attention. Also, by placing the thesis after a few sentences of introduction, you will not startle the reader with your main point.

Finally, if your thesis is at the end of the introduction, it states the main point of the essay just before that point is supported in the body paragraphs. Putting the thesis at the end of the introduction is like putting an arrow pointing to the supporting ideas in the essay.

Hints for Writing the Introduction

There are a number of ways to write an introduction.

1. You can **begin with some general statements** that gradually lead to your thesis:

| general statements | My mother has two framed pictures in the living room. They are sketches of a town square. In the pictures, people are sitting and talking, shopping in the small stores around the square, and strolling through the friendly streets. I envy the people in these scenes, for they seem to enjoy a calm, central gathering place, far from busy highways and enormous parking lots. Unfortunately, my community has no such place. |
| thesis at end | <u>My town needs a neighborly, accessible town center.</u> |

2. You can **begin with a quote** that leads smoothly to your thesis. The quote can be a quote from someone famous, or it can be an old saying. It can be something your mother always told you, a slogan from an advertisement, or the words of a song.

| quotation | A song tells us, "It's a small, small, small, small world." There are days when I wish my world were smaller. Sometimes I get sick of driving to a huge supermarket for my groceries, then dashing to a giant mall for new shoes, and finally making a quick stop at a drive-through restaurant for a hamburger. As I make this journey, I rarely meet anyone I know. At these times, I wish my life were different: I'd like to get off the highway, forget the fast food and the huge malls, and run into a few friends as I do my errands. Then |
| thesis at end | I realize that <u>my town needs a neighborly, accessible town center.</u> |

> **Note:** Remember that you can add transitional words or phrases that lead into your thesis, as in the sample above.

3. You can **tell a story** as a way of leading into your thesis. You can open with the story of something that happened to you or to someone you know, a story you read about or heard on the news.

| story | Yesterday my best friend called, and we got into a lengthy conversation. After we had talked for half an hour, we realized we wanted to continue our conversation face to face. "Let's meet for coffee," my friend said. He suggested a coffee shop near the interstate highway. I suggested another place, which he said was "in the middle of nowhere." Then we ran out of ideas. |
| thesis at end | There was no easy, central place. At that moment, it occurred to me that <u>my town needs a neighborly, accessible town center.</u> |

4. You can **explain why this topic is worth writing about.** Explaining could mean giving some background on the topic, or it could mean discussing why the topic is an important one.

explain   Almost everyone feels lonely at some time. Teens feel left out by the many cliques that make up high-school society. Older people, often suffering the loss of a spouse, need human contact. Singles try to find a comfortable place in what seems to be a world of married couples. As for couples, each partner needs to feel part of a world outside of marriage. In my community, there is no friendly place where all types **thesis at end**   of people can feel accepted. <u>My town needs a neighborly, accessible town center.</u>

5. You can **use one or more questions** to lead into your thesis. You can open with a question or questions that will be answered by your thesis. Or you can open with a question or questions that catch the reader's attention and move toward your thesis.

question   Have you ever seen an old movie called <u>It's a Wonderful Life?</u> It's about George Bailey, a small-town husband and father whose life changes on Christmas Eve when an angel visits to teach George a lesson. Although I enjoy the plot of the movie, what I like most about the film is the small town George lives in, where everyone seems to know everyone else and life centers on a few streets of stores, homes, and businesses. I sometimes wish that I had a little of **thesis at end**   that simple life. Then I conclude that <u>my town needs a neighborly, accessible town center.</u>

6. You can **open with a contradiction** of your main point as a way of attracting the reader's interest and leading to your thesis. You can begin with an idea that is the opposite of what you will say in your thesis. The opposition of your opening and your thesis creates interest.

contradiction   My town appears to have every shopping and entertainment attraction of an ideal community. It has two giant malls, a movie theater with sixteen screens and stadium seating, cafes, restaurants, popular clubs, a water park, a skating rink, and a bowling alley. However, it doesn't offer what people want most: the comfort of a small-town gathering place that invites shoppers, strollers, people with their dogs, and people **thesis at end**   who like to sit, talk, and drink coffee. <u>My town needs a neighborly, accessible town center.</u>

> **Note:** Always check with instructor regarding thesis sentence placement for your assignments.

Exercise 8 **Practice: Writing an Introduction**

Below are five thesis sentences. Pick one. Then write an introductory paragraph on the lines provided. Your last sentence should be the thesis sentence. If your instructor agrees, read your introduction to others in the class who wrote an introduction to the same thesis, or read your introduction to the entire class.

Thesis Sentences

1. What men wear makes a statement about the image they want to convey.

2. Technology has revolutionized the music industry.

3. Today's tattoos can be art, fashion, or personal statements.

4. Many parents try to give their children what the parents never had.

5. A million dollars would/would not change the way I live my life.

(Write an introduction) _____

_____

_____

_____

_____

_____

_____

WRITING THE BODY OF THE ESSAY

In the body of the essay, the paragraphs *explain*, *support*, and *develop* your thesis. In this part of the essay, each paragraph has its own topic sentence. The topic sentence in each paragraph does two things:

1. It focuses the sentences in the paragraph.
2. It makes a point connected to the thesis.

The thesis and the topic sentences are ideas that need to be supported by details, explanations, and examples. You can visualize the connections among the parts of an essay like this:

Introduction with Thesis

Body {
    Topic Sentence
      Details
    Topic Sentence
      Details
    Topic Sentence
      Details

Conclusion

When you write topic sentences, you can help to organize your essay by referring to the checklist at the top of the next page.

> ### Checklist for the Topic Sentences of an Essay
>
> ✔ Does the topic sentence give the point of the paragraph?
>
> ✔ Does the topic sentence connect to the thesis of the essay?

How Long Are the Body Paragraphs?

Remember that the body paragraphs of an essay are the places where you explain and develop your thesis. Those paragraphs should be long enough to explain, not just list, your points. To do this well, try to make your body paragraphs *at least seven sentences* long. As you develop your writing skills, you may find that you can support your ideas in fewer than seven sentences.

Developing the Body Paragraphs

You can write well-developed body paragraphs by following the same steps you used in writing single paragraphs for the earlier assignments in this course. By working through the stages of gathering ideas, outlining, drafting, revising, editing, and proofreading, you can create clear, effective paragraphs.

To focus and develop the body paragraphs, ask the questions below as you revise:

> ### Checklist for Developing Body Paragraphs for an Essay
>
> ✔ Does the topic sentence cover everything in the paragraph?
>
> ✔ Do I have enough details to explain the topic sentence?
>
> ✔ Do all the details in the paragraph support, develop, or illustrate the topic sentence?

Exercise 9   Practice: Creating Topic Sentences

Following are thesis sentences. For each thesis, write topic sentences (as many as indicated by the numbered blanks). The first one is done for you.

1. **thesis:** Many families have traditions for celebrating special occasions.

   topic sentence 1: Family birthdays can involve special rituals.

   _____

   topic sentence 2: At weddings, many family traditions appear.

   _____

   topic sentence 3: Some families have customs for celebrating New Year's Day.

   _____

2. **thesis:** Daytime college classes are different from evening college classes.

   topic sentence 1: _____

   _____

topic sentence 2: _____

_____

3. **thesis:** Many people share the same fears.

topic sentence 1: _____

_____

topic sentence 2: _____

_____

topic sentence 3: _____

_____

4. **thesis:** Best friends share many aspects of their lives.

topic sentence 1: _____

_____

topic sentence 2: _____

_____

topic sentence 3: _____

_____

5. **thesis:** Working at night has its good and bad points for college students.

topic sentence 1: _____

_____

topic sentence 2: _____

_____

topic sentence 3: _____

_____

topic sentence 4: _____

_____

WRITING THE CONCLUSION

The last paragraph in the essay is the **conclusion.** It does not have to be as long as a body paragraph, but it should be long enough to tie the essay together and remind the reader of the thesis. You can use any of these strategies in writing the conclusion:

1. You can **restate the thesis in new words.** Go back to the first paragraph of your essay and reread it. For example, this could be the first paragraph of an essay:

introduction   I recently moved to a city that is a thousand miles from my hometown. I drove the long distance with only one companion, my mixed-breed dog Casey. Casey was a wonderful passenger: he kept me company, never asked to stop or complained about my driving, and was happy to observe the

thesis at end　endless stretches of road. By the end of our trip, I loved Casey even more than I had when we started. Unfortunately, I found that landlords do not appreciate the bonds between dogs and their owners. In fact, <u>renting a decent apartment and keeping a dog is nearly impossible.</u>

The thesis, underlined above, is the sentence that you can restate in your conclusion. Your task is to *keep the point but put it in different words.* Then work that restatement into a short paragraph, like this:

restating the thesis　Most dogs can adapt to apartment living. They will not bark too much, destroy property, or threaten the neighbors. They can adjust to being alone indoors as long as their owners provide time for fun, exercise, and affection. But most landlords refuse to give dogs the benefit of the doubt. <u>The landlords pressure dog owners to make a choice between an apartment and a pet.</u>

2. You can make a judgment, valuation, or recommendation. Instead of simply restating your point, you can end by making some comment on the issue you've described or the problem you've illustrated. If you were looking for another way to end the essay on finding an apartment that allows pets, for example, you could end with a recommendation.

ending with a recommendation　I understand that landlords need to make a profit on their property and that some dogs and dog owners damage that property. However, not all dogs go wild, and not all dog owners let their pets destroy an apartment. <u>If landlords made an individual judgment about each applicant with a pet, instead of following a hard, cold, policy, they might realize that dogs can be model apartment dwellers.</u>

3. You can conclude by framing your essay. You can tie your essay together neatly by *using something from your introduction* as a way of concluding. When you take an example, a question, or even a quote from your first paragraph and refer to it in your last paragraph, you are "framing" the essay. Take another look at the sample introduction to the essay on finding an apartment that will allow a dog. The writer talks about driving a thousand miles away from home, about his or her dear companion, Casey. The writer also mentions the difficulties of finding a decent place to live when landlords will not allow dogs. Now consider how the ideas of the introduction are used in this conclusion:

frame
frame　When <u>I drove into this city a thousand miles from my home, I brought my dear friend and loyal companion with me.</u> That
frame　friend, <u>my dog Casey,</u> made me smile as he sat in the passenger seat, a tall, proud

frame
frame
frame

traveler. He fell asleep on my feet when I stopped at a lonely rest stop. <u>Many cruel landlords told me I would have to give Casey up if I wanted a comfortable place to live.</u> But I refused, for Casey brings me more comfort than any fancy apartment ever could.

Exercise 10 **Practice: Choosing a Better Way to Restate the Thesis**

Following are five clusters. Each cluster consists of a thesis sentence and two sentences that try to restate the thesis. Each restated sentence could be used as part of the conclusion to an essay. Put *B* next to the sentence in each pair that is a better restatement. Remember that the better choice repeats the same idea as the thesis but does not rely on too many of the same words.

1. **thesis:** When you are upset about a problem, take a long walk.

   restatement 1: ___ A long walk can help you when you are upset about a problem.

   restatement 2: ___ When something is troubling you, a long walk can bring you some relief.

2. **thesis:** The way a man treats his mother is a good indication of the way he will treat his wife.

   restatement 1: ___ A clue to how a man will relate to his wife is his relationship to his mother.

   restatement 2: ___ A good indication of the way a man will treat his wife is the way he treats his mother.

3. **thesis:** Alexandra has a talent for buying low-cost groceries, combining them in unusual ways, and producing delicious meals.

   restatement 1: ___ Alexandra produces delicious meals after she buys low-cost groceries and combines the food in unusual ways.

   restatement 2: ___ Alexandra can find bargain groceries, mix them creatively, and serve tasty meals.

4. **thesis:** Leo quit his job because the pay was awful, the workplace was depressing, and the manager was dishonest.

   restatement 1: ___ Low pay, a dreary work environment, and an unethical manager drove Leo to leave his job.

   restatement 2: ___ Leo quit his job because of awful pay, a depressing workplace, and a dishonest manager.

5. **thesis:** Schoolchildren dream of summer vacation but can become bored or lonely in the long, unstructured days.

   restatement 1: ___ While every schoolboy or girl fantasizes about summer vacation, the reality may be more boring and empty than the fantasy.

   restatement 2: ___ Although many young students dream of summer vacation, they may become bored when the vacation days are long and unstructured.

Revising Your Draft

Once you have a rough draft of your essay, you can begin revising it. The following checklist may help you to make the necessary changes in your draft.

Checklist for Revising the Draft of an Essay

✔ Does the essay have a clear, unifying thesis?

✔ Does the thesis make a point?

✔ Does each body paragraph have a topic sentence?

✔ Is each body paragraph focused on its topic sentence?

✔ Are the body paragraphs roughly the same size?

✔ Do any of the sentences need combining?

✔ Do any of the words need to be changed?

✔ Do the ideas seem to be smoothly linked?

✔ Does the introduction catch the reader's interest?

✔ Is there a definite conclusion?

✔ Does the conclusion remind the reader of the thesis?

Transitions Within Paragraphs

In an essay, you can use two kinds of transitions: those within a paragraph and those between paragraphs.

Transitions that link ideas **within a paragraph** are the same kinds you've used earlier. Your choice of words, phrases, or even sentences depends on the kind of connection you want to make. Here is a list of some common transitions and the kind of connection they express.

INFO BOX: Common Transitions Within a Paragraph

To join two ideas

again	another	in addition	moreover
also	besides	likewise	similarly
and	furthermore		

To show a contrast or a different opinion

but	instead	on the other hand	still
however	nevertheless	or	yet
in contrast	on the contrary	otherwise	

To show a cause-and-effect connection

accordingly	because	for	therefore
as a result	consequently	so	thus

---

continued

To give an example			
for example	in the case of	such as	to illustrate
for instance	like		

To show time			
after	first	recently	subsequently
at the same time	meanwhile	shortly	then
before	next	soon	until
finally			

Transitions Between Paragraphs

When you write something that is more than one paragraph long, you need transitions that link each paragraph to the others. There are several effective ways to link paragraphs and remind the reader of your main idea and of how the smaller points connect to it. Here are two ways:

1. Restate an idea from the preceding paragraph at the start of a new paragraph. Look closely at the following two paragraphs and notice how the second paragraph repeats an idea from the first paragraph and provides a link.

Buying clothes for their designer labels is expensive. A t-shirt marked with the name of a popular designer can cost twenty or thirty dollars more than a similar t-shirt without the name. More expensive items like fleece jackets can be as much as seventy or eighty dollars higher if they carry a trendy name. For each designer jacket a person buys, he or she could probably buy two without a trendy logo or label. If a person decides to go all the way with fashion, he or she can spend a hundred dollars on designer socks and underwear.

transition restating an idea

Creating a wardrobe of designer clothes is not only expensive; it is also silly. While designers want buyers to think the designer label means quality, many trendy clothes are made in the same factories as less fashionable clothes. And after all, how much "design" can go into a pair of socks to make them worth four times what an ordinary pair costs? The worst part of spending money on designer labels has to do with style. The hot designer of today can be out of style tomorrow, and no one wants to wear that name across a shirt, a jacket, or a pair of socks.

2. Use synonyms and repetition as a way of reminding the reader of an important point. For example, in the two paragraphs below, notice how certain repeated words, phrases, and synonyms all remind the reader of a point about kindness and generosity. The repeated words and synonyms are underlined.

Often the <u>kindest</u> and most <u>generous</u> people are the ones who don't have much themselves. When I was evicted from my apartment, my Aunt Natalie, who has three children under ten, took me into her two-room apartment. Her <u>heart was too big</u> for her to leave me homeless. Another <u>giving</u> person is my best friend. He is a security guard trying to pay for college, but he <u>regularly donates his time and money</u> to the local Police Athletic League. One of the most <u>compassionate</u> people I know is a grandmother living on Social Security. Every day, she gets up at 5:00 A.M. to make sandwiches at the local food bank. She swears she isn't doing anything special, that she gets more than she <u>gives</u> by <u>taking care of others.</u>

Not everyone can be a hero working in a food bank at 5:00 A.M. But everyone can perform small acts of <u>generosity</u> and <u>humanity,</u> and most people do. Many are <u>thoughtful</u> and <u>caring</u> enough to leave a large tip for the server who lives on tips. Most people are <u>decent</u> on the highways; they let desperate drivers merge lanes. In the mall, shoppers routinely help lost children, hold the door for the shoppers behind them, and give directions to strangers. Without feeling at all heroic, people give blood at a blood drive, walk in a walk-a-thon, take in lost pets, and sell candy bars for their children's school. But even if they are not thinking about it, these people are <u>acting for others</u> and <u>giving to others.</u>

A Draft Essay

Below is a draft of the essay on college classrooms. As you read it, you'll notice many changes from the outline on page 429

- An introduction has been added, phrased in the first person, "I," to unify the essay.
- Transitions have been added within and between paragraphs.
- Sentences have been combined.
- Details have been added.
- General statements have been replaced by more specific ones.
- Word choice has been improved.
- A conclusion has been added. The conclusion uses one of the ideas from the lead-in, the idea that the outside and inside of National College are different. In addition, one of the other ideas in the conclusion, the point that no one seems to care about the condition of the classrooms, comes from the original list of ideas about the topic of college classrooms. It did not fit in the body paragraphs, but it works in the conclusion.

A Draft of an Essay

(Thesis and topic sentences are underlined.)

National College, which I attend, has impressive buildings of glass and concrete. It has covered walkways, paved patios, and large clusters of trees and flowers. From the outside, the college looks great. However, on the inside, National

College has some problems. The most important rooms in the institution do not attract the most important people in the institution, the students. <u>The typical classroom at my college is unwelcoming because of its tiny furniture, uncomfortable temperature, and student damage.</u>

First of all, <u>child-size furniture makes it difficult to focus on adult-level classes.</u> The student chairs are tiny. They are too small for anyone over ten years old, but for large or tall people, they are torture. For example, I am six feet tall, and when I sit on one of the classroom chairs, I feel like I am crammed into a kindergarten chair. They are attached to miniature desks, which are the size of slightly enlarged armrests. As I sit in class, I cannot fit my legs under the desk. I cannot fit my textbook and a notebook on the surface of the desk. Something always slips off and makes a noise that disrupts the class. In some classrooms, the instructor has no desk and is forced to use one of the miniature student versions.

As students twist and fidget in their tiny desks, they face another problem. <u>The temperature in the classroom is anything but pleasant.</u> I have been at the college for both fall and winter terms, and I have seen both extremes of temperature. In the early fall, the rooms were hot. The air conditioner feebly pumped hot air, which, of course, made the heat worse. Meanwhile, the sun beat through the glass windows because the blinds were broken. Winter did not bring any relief because in winter we froze. On some days, we wore our winter coats during class. Two of my teachers reported the problems to the maintenance department, but nothing changed. I wish the maintenance manager understood how hard it is for students to concentrate when they are sweating or shivering.

Heat and cold create an uncomfortable learning place, but students create a shabby one. <u>Student damage to the classrooms makes them seedy and ugly.</u> Graffiti covers the desks with childish messages, slogans, and drawings. In addition, half the desks have gum stuck to their undersides. Some students even carve their initials and artwork into the plastic and wood of the desks and chairs. Others have stained the carpet with spilled coffee or soft drinks. Sometimes I have to be careful where I walk so that my shoes don't stick to the mess. It's depressing to think that my fellow students enjoy damaging the place where they come to learn.

National College is impressive outside, but no one seems to care about the problems inside. The classrooms seem to be designed without a thought for adult learners who need to sit in adult-size seats and take lecture notes at adult-size desks. The maintenance department does not maintain a comfortable temperature so that students can learn, and students do not respect their learning environment. These problems surprise me. <u>When I started college, I knew I would face many challenges, but I didn't expect them to include squeezing into the chairs, dressing for a blizzard or heat wave, and picking gum off my desk.</u>

Exercise 11   **Practice: Identifying the Main Points in the Draft of an Essay**

Below is the draft of a four-paragraph essay. Read it, then reread it and underline the thesis and the topic sentences in each body paragraph and in the conclusion.

During my high school years, I held several part-time jobs that involved dealing with the public. I once worked as an activities director for an after-school program where ten-year-olds started giving me orders. In my senior year, I worked at a local sandwich shop and learned how to smile at hungry, impatient customers waiting for their twelve-inch submarine orders. I am now a sophomore in college and work at Cook's Place, a small but popular family restaurant. I have learned much while working at this family establishment, first as a waiter and now as the restaurant's first night manager.

The restaurant's owner, Dan Cook, hired me a year ago to be a waiter for what he humorously calls "the dinner crowd shift." I learned several essential business skills in a short time. Although the restaurant has only ten tables (each seating four), I quickly learned how to keep track of multiple orders, how to work the computerized cash register, how to verify active credit card numbers, and how to use certain abbreviations while taking orders. Dan also showed me how to fill out weekly orders for our food and beverage suppliers. Many of our customers are regulars, and I also learned that maintaining a positive attitude and friendly manner can make my job enjoyable, even on slow nights. After a few weeks, I felt confident about my skills as a waiter and looked forward to going to work.

After I had been a waiter for five months, Dan told me he'd like to start spending more time visiting his grown children who live in another state. He asked me if I would like to become the restaurant's "first official night manager." I accepted his offer immediately, and I have acquired even more business skills in this position. I now manage the restaurant three nights each week and one Saturday evening each month. I plan the dinner specials with the cook, negotiate with suppliers to get the best bulk-order prices, and make calls to customers who fill out an evaluation form Dan and I devised. I have learned that if I treat people respectfully, they will usually treat me professionally. Over the past year, I've had to interview applicants whenever a server position became available, and I've learned how important it is to be tactful and encouraging even when I've had to turn someone down. Finally, I've even met with Dan's accountant several times. She showed me the forms various business owners have to fill out, and I've learned about the importance of accurate records for tax purposes. Dan says he's proud of my progress and jokes that I "work well with people and work the numbers well."

At Cook's Place, I was fortunate to have on-the-job training that was both educational and enjoyable. I've gained many business skills, but most importantly, I've learned the value of encouragement, teamwork, respect, and friendship. They are my ingredients for success in any relationship.

Exercise 12 **Practice: Adding Transitions to an Essay**

The essay below needs transitions. Add the transitions where indicated, and add the kind of transition—word, phrase, or sentence—indicated.

When I registered for my college classes at the beginning of the term, I was a

little upset by a new problem. Because I had waited so long to sign up for classes,

I had few choices of time slots. One problem particularly troubled me. In order to

get into one required course, I had to take it as an evening class. _____

(add a word or phrase) while the time of the class is not my first choice, I have found some advantages to taking an evening class.

_____ (add a word) I began the class, I was certain that I would not be able to absorb all the information of a three-hour session. I had never had to focus on that much material in one long session instead of in shorter classes that met two or three times a week. _____ (add a word or a phrase) three hours just seemed too long to sit. _____ (add a word) I began the class, I learned to adjust to the differences in a long session. _____ (add a word or phrase) My instructor varied the pace of the class by using several teaching methods _____ lecture, discussion, and small group work. _____ (add a word or phrase) she allowed us a short break halfway through class time.

The length of each class session became manageable because of my instructor's ability to change the pace, and she shifted the pace by mixing methods of instruction. Another benefit of the class is related to the students. Although a few students, including me, signed up for the evening class because the time slot was the only one left for the course they needed, others had other motives. Some of the students worked full time during the day; _____ (add a word or phrase) they needed to take evening classes. Many of these students came to class directly from their workplace or from their hectic roles as mothers and fathers. Other students had taken this teacher before and enjoyed her organized, energetic teaching style. Both types of students had chosen this class at this time. I felt that this evening class had a larger percentage of lively, committed students than many daytime classes, and _____ (add a word or phrase) those students made the class lively for everyone.

_____

_____ After a few weeks, I learned to appreciate having seven days to complete a long reading assignment. Writing assignments also were easier when I had more time to plan, draft, revise, and proofread them. Best of all, I discovered the benefits of doing a little each day instead of racing to prepare for a test or scratch together an essay, This method of starting early and breaking my assignments into small steps can also work in my other classes.

I now recognize that the benefits of my evening class outweigh its disadvantages. Several hours is a long time to spend in one place _____ (add a word or a phrase) the time is not as dull or as deadly as I expected it to be. _____ (add a word or a phrase), the atmosphere in the class is lively because of the students enrolled in it. _____ I have realized that the method of breaking assignments into small steps can work in many of my classes. My night class has introduced me to a good teacher, motivated students, and a better way to learn.

<table>
<tr><td>Exercise 13</td><td>**Practice: Recognizing Synonyms and Repetition Used to Link Ideas in an Essay**</td></tr>
</table>

In the following essay, underline all the synonyms and repetition (of words or phrases) that help remind the reader of the thesis sentence. (To help you, the thesis is underlined.)

Some people have artistic talent. They become famous painters, musicians, or actors. Others are known for their athletic abilities, and they are seen on television in tournaments, matches, games, or other sports contests. My brother will never be on stage or in a tournament, yet he has a special talent. <u>My brother Eddie has a gift for making friends.</u>

Our family has moved six times in the past ten years, and every time, Eddie was the first to get acquainted with the neighbors. There is something about his smile and cheerful attitude that draws strangers to him. On one of our moves, Eddie had met our neighbors on both sides of the house and directly across the street by the time we unloaded the van. Within a week, Eddie had made the acquaintance of almost every family on the block. Eddie's ability to connect with others helped our whole family to feel comfortable in a new place. As Eddie formed links within the area, he introduced us to the community. Thanks to my brother, we all got to know Mrs. Lopez next door, the teenagers down the street, and even the mail carrier. Soon familiarity turned into deeper friendships.

One of the most amazing examples of Eddie's talent occurred when he and I took a long bus trip. Twenty-four hours on a bus can be exhausting and depressing, but Eddie made the trip fun. He began by talking to the man seated across from us. Soon the couple behind us joined in. When Eddie passed around a bag of potato chips, he drew four more passengers into this cluster of newfound buddies. Eddie and I didn't sleep during the entire trip. We were too busy talking, laughing, and swapping life stories with the other travelers. Some of the toughest-looking passengers turned out to be the kindest, warmest companions.

Only Eddie could transform a dreary bus ride into a cheerful trip with new friends. And thanks to Eddie, our family's many moves became opportunities to meet new people. If I am with my brother, I know we will never be lonely, for Eddie's real talent is his ability to draw others to him.

PROOFREADING AN ESSAY

Creating a Title

When you are satisfied with the final draft of your essay, you can begin preparing a good copy. Your essay will need a title. Try to think of a short title that is connected to your thesis. Because the title is the reader's first contact with your essay, an imaginative title can create a good first impression. If you can't think of anything clever, try using a key phrase from your essay.

The title is placed at the top of your essay, about an inch above the first paragraph. Always capitalize the first word of the title and all other words except *the, an, a*, prepositions (like *of, in, with*), and coordinating conjunctions (*for, and, nor, but, or, yet, so*). *Do not* underline or put quotation marks around your title.

The Final Version of an Essay

Following is the final version of the essay on college classrooms. When you compare it to the draft on pages 441–442, you will notice some changes:

- A title has been added.
- Transitions have been added; one is a phrase and one is a sentence.
- The word choice has been changed so that descriptions are more precise and repetition (of the word "problems") is avoided.
- Specific details have been added.

Final Version of an Essay

(Changes from the draft are underlined.)

A Look Inside One College's Classrooms

National College, which I attend, has impressive buildings of glass and concrete. It has covered walkways, paved patios, and large clusters of trees and flowers. From the outside, the college looks <u>distinguished.</u> However, on the inside, National College has some problems. The most important rooms in the institution do not <u>appeal to</u> the most important people in the institution, the students. The typical classroom at my college is unwelcoming because of its tiny furniture, uncomfortable temperature, and student damage.

First of all, child-size furniture makes it difficult to focus on adult-level classes. The student chairs are tiny. They are too small for anyone over ten years old, but for large or tall people, they are torture. For example, I am six feet tall, and when I sit on one of the classroom chairs, I feel like I am crammed into a kindergarten chair. They are attached to miniature desks, which are the size of slightly enlarged armrests. As I sit in class, I cannot fit my legs under the desk. I cannot fit my textbook and a notebook on the surface of the desk. Something always slips off and makes a noise that disrupts the class. <u>The child-friendly atmosphere even affects the instructors.</u> In some classrooms, the instructor has no desk and is forced to use one of the miniature student versions.

As students twist and fidget in their tiny desks, they face another problem. The temperature in the classrooms is anything but pleasant. I have been at the college for both fall and winter terms, and I have seen both extremes of temperature. In the early fall, the rooms were <u>sweltering.</u> The air conditioner feebly pumped hot air, which, of course, made the heat worse. Meanwhile, the sun beat through the glass windows because the blinds were broken. Winter did not bring any relief because in winter we froze. On some days, we wore our winter coats during class. <u>At different times during the semester,</u> two of my teachers reported the problems to the maintenance department, but nothing changed. I wish the maintenance manager understood how hard it is for students to concentrate when they are sweating or shivering.

Heat and cold create an uncomfortable learning place, but students create a shabby one. Student damage to the classrooms makes them seedy and ugly. Graffiti covers the desks with childish messages, slogans, and drawings. In addition, half the desks have gum stuck to their undersides. Some students even carve their initials and artwork into the plastic and wood of the desks and chairs. Others have stained the carpet with spilled coffee or soft drinks <u>and left crumbs and ground-in food behind.</u> Sometimes I have to be careful where I walk so that my shoes don't stick to the mess. It's depressing to think that my fellow students enjoy damaging the place where they come to learn.

National College is impressive outside, but no one seems to care about the <u>flaws</u> inside. The classrooms seem to be designed without a thought for adult learners who need to sit in adult-size seats and take lecture notes at adult-size desks. The maintenance department does not maintain a comfortable temperature so that students can learn, and students do not respect their learning environment. These problems surprise me. When I started college, I knew I would face many challenges, but I didn't expect them to include squeezing into the chairs, dressing for a blizzard or heat wave, and picking gum off my desk.

Before you prepare the final copy of your essay, check your latest draft for errors in spelling and punctuation, and for any errors made in typing or recopying.

Exercise 14 **Practice: Proofreading to Prepare the Final Version**

Following are two essays with the kinds of errors it is easy to overlook when you prepare the final version of an assignment. Correct the errors, writing above the lines. There are sixteen errors in the first essay and fifteen in the second.

"Why Tina Upsets Me"

1. I have a cousin who is about my age. Tina is an attractive young women

with an interesting job, a good education, and a loving family. Because the mem-

bers of my family meet often for meal's and celebrations, I see Tina frequently.

Everytime Tina and I meet, I leave the gathering frustrated and angry. Tina has ways of coping and negative attitudes that make me want to avoid her. Tina's most common state of mind is misery. On the outside, Tina appears to be surrounded by love, happiness, and success. her parent's are proud of her. She has a loving, thoughtful, faithful partner. Her years at collage enabled her to find a good job as a pediatric nurse. Yet Tina cannot focus on her advantages. Instead, she concentrates on the sorrows and disappointments in her life. If her parents praise her for getting a promotion at work, Tina wonders why they expect so much of her? Her boyfriend is a constant source of support in her life. Unfortunately, Tina worries whether he may be sticking with her only because he feels pity for her Even her beautiful and pampered pet, a Siamese cat that her boyfriend gave her, makes her sad. She cannot forget that the cat came from an animal shelter, and she dwells on the cat's previous life of misery.

Worrying is Tina's hobby. Each morning, she worries about traffic jams on the way to work. At work, Tina worries that her job may be in jeopardy if a day goes by without some praise from her supervisor. On the other hand, if her supervisor or the parents of one of Tina's patients note Tina's patience or skill, Tina prepares for a problem. She is sure that anyone who expresses appreciation is secretly feeling sorry for her. When she leaves work and head's for home, she worries about making dinner. She obsesses about what to make and whether she has time to cook it. At night, Tina lays awake, worrying about the problems of the next day.

Tina's toughest challenge is coping with her fear. In her life, fear is almost as natural as breathing. She have always been afraid of the dark. Driving at night, hearing a strange sound in the night, and loosing electric power in an evening thunderstorm, all terrify her. Tina rarely travels because she dreads a plane crash. Even through she is a nurse, she is nervous before every visit to her own doctor. Unfortunately, her training as a nurse has made her too conscious of many symptoms that could mean danger to her health, and she dwells on these possibilities.

I pity Tina, and I would like, to help her. Unfortunately, I do not have enough insight or patience to deal with her misery. perhaps I have one significant fear myself: I may be afraid that Tina's anxiety is contagious, and I do not want to be infected by her fears and miseries.

The Partially broken Television

2. I live at home with my mother and my ten-year-old sister. We manage to get along farely well, but sometimes I am drawn into problem-solving situations that have little connection to me. The problem of the partially broken television was not exactly mine, but my sister pushed me into helping her to handle it.

My sister loves to dance. Very often, she dances to loud music in a small space in front of the television. One day, she was dancing with extra, enthusiasm and knocked our light but large television off it's stand. At the time, the television had been turned to my sister's favorite music channle. Once the television fell behind the television stand and hit the floor, the room was silent and the television screen went blank.

Fortunately, my mother was not home, so my sister relied on me to fix the problem before our mother got home. We both cringed at the sight of a fairly, new television propped up only by a wall. Than, more out of despair then hope, I placed the silent screen back on its stand. I plugged in the unit and turned on the television. No picture appeared on the screen. However, we heard a terrible sound like a thousand buzzing bees swarming in the room. We were sure our television had died.

After about two minutes of mechanical buzzing and human misery, a strange change took place. The buzzing stopped, the television screen filled with a picture, and dialogue blasted into the room. Our source of entertainment had repaired itself! We changed channels adjusted the sound, and holded our breath. The set continued to perform as if it had never fallen. We tested our good luck by turning off the television and then turning it on again. Immediately after we turned it on, the buzz greeted us. However, the buzz soon stopped; and was replaced by the usual transmission of sound and picture.

Because our mother was about to return home, we collaborated on an explanation for the sudden change in our television. When she turned on the tube to watch her favorite show, she was greeted by the opening moments of screeching sound and a blank screen. Before she could scream, I jumped into action. Yes, I said, the noise was terrible. It had started in the afternoon during a terrible storm with lightning and thunder. My sister quickly added that at the time she had been watching an educational program. Then something, perhaps a bold of lightning, had struck the television. By the time we had finished our tale of lightning and storms, the buzzing in the room had stopped and my Mother got to see her favorite show.

The three of us got used to the introductory buzzing noise and the blank screen We decided that we could live with the annoyance of a partially broken television and save the expense of a new and perfect unit. Although my sister had dragged me into this crisis, she and I (and a few fibs) were able to save the day.

Lines of Detail: A Walk-Through Assignment

Write a five-paragraph essay about three things in your life you would like to get rid of. These things must be tangible objects like an old car, a bicycle, a uniform, and so forth. They cannot be people or personal qualities like fear or insecurity. To write the essay, follow these steps:

Step 1: Freewrite a list of all the things you would like to get rid of in your life. To get started, think about what is in your room, car, purse, wallet, house, apartment, garage, basement, and so forth.

Step 2: Select the three items you would most like to toss out. Then prepare a list of questions you can ask yourself about these three items. You can ask questions such as the following:

Why do I want to get rid of the following?
Is it useless to me?
Does it remind me of an unpleasant part of my life?
Is it ugly? Broken? Out of style?
Does it remind me of a habit I'd like to break?
Can I get rid of it? If so, why don't I get rid of it? If not, why can't I get rid of it?

Answer the questions. The answers can lead you to details and topic sentences for your essay. For instance, you might hate the uniform you have to wear because it represents a job you would like to leave. However, you might not be able to get rid of the uniform because you need the job. Or maybe you'd like to toss out your cigarettes because you want to stop smoking.

Step 3: Survey your answers. Begin by listing the three things you would like to get rid of. Then list the details (the answers to your questions) beneath the item they relate to. For example, under the item "uniform," you could list the reason you hate it and the reason you cannot get rid of it.

Step 4: Once you have clustered the three items and the details related to each, you have the beginnings of a five-paragraph essay. Each item will be the focus of one of the body paragraphs, and its details will develop the paragraph.

Step 5: Focus all your clusters around one point. To find a focus, ask yourself whether the things you want to throw away have anything in common. If so, you can make that point in your thesis. For instance, you could write a thesis like one of these:

> The things I would like to get rid of in my life are all related to a _____ part of my life.

> My weaknesses are reflected in three items I would like to get rid of in my life.

> If I could get rid of _____, _____, and _____, I would be _____

If the things you would like to be rid of are not related, then you can use a thesis like one of the following:

> Three items I'd like to throw out reflect different aspects of my life.

> I'd like to get rid of _____, _____, and _____ for three different reasons.

Step 6: Once you have a thesis and clustered details, draft your outline. Then revise your outline until it is unified, expresses the ideas in a clear order, and has enough supporting details.

Step 7: Write a draft of your essay. Revise the draft, checking it for a smooth lead-in, balanced paragraphs, relevant and specific details, a strong conclusion, and smooth transitions.

Step 8: Before you prepare the final version of your essay, check for spelling, word choice, punctuation, and formatting errors.

Topics for Writing Your Own Essay

When you write on any of these topics, be sure to work through the stages of the writing process in preparing your essay.

1. Take any paragraph you wrote for this class and develop it into an essay of four or five paragraphs. If your instructor agrees, read the paragraph to a partner or group, and ask your listener(s) to suggest points inside the paragraph that can be developed into paragraphs of their own.

2. Narrow down one of the following topics, and then write an essay on it.

parents	heroes	crime	cities
small towns	war	success	country life
pleasures	relationships	childhood	unemployment
fitting in	accidents	apologies	responsibilities

3. Write an essay on any one of the following topics:

My Three Favorite Places
Three People Who Changed My Life
Three Mistakes in Using the Internet
Three Songs I Will Always Remember
Three Memories That I Cherish
My Three Best/Worst Experiences Playing _____
(name a sport)

4. Write a four-paragraph essay about a dream you had. In your first body paragraph, describe the dream in detail. In your second body paragraph, explain what you think the dream means: Does it connect to one of your fears or hopes? Is it related to a current problem in your life? Does it suggest an answer to a problem? What does the dream tell you about yourself?

5. Study Photographs A, B, C, and D. Use them to think about this topic for an essay: The three best part-time jobs for college students.

Photograph A

Photograph B

Photograph C

Photograph D

6. Write a five-paragraph essay about Photograph E. In the first body paragraph, describe one of the people in the photo. Describe what the person looks like, the expression on his or her face, and what the person is doing. In the second body paragraph, describe the other person in the photograph. In the third body paragraph, write about the relationship of the two people. Are they married? Friends? In love? Use specific details from the photograph to support your ideas about their relationship.

Photograph E

7. The cat in Photograph F seems determined to get the fish, even if it means snorkeling in a fish tank. Write an essay about three pets or people who were willing to do ridiculous things to get what they wanted.

Photograph F

Topics for Critical Thinking and Writing: Essay Options

1. Examine your place in your family. Are you an only child? The oldest child? The middle child? Do you have brothers? Sisters? Both? Think about how your position in the family has affected your self-image and the roles you play within the family. Then write an essay about the way you and other family members interact.

2. Find an advertisement (in print or online). It should be one that you find effective and attention-getting. Study it carefully. Then write an essay about what the advertisement depicts, what product it advertises, and what makes this advertisement powerful.

Topics for a Narrative Essay

1. Write about a time when you were surprised. It can be a good or bad experience.

2. Write about how you met your current boyfriend, girlfriend, partner, or spouse.

3. Write about the time you lost something or someone.

4. Write about your first day in a new home, at a new job, or in a new town.

Topics for Critical Thinking and Writing: Narrative Essay

1. Write about the most frustrating experience of your life. As you tell the story of this incident, analyze what parts of the incident annoyed, upset, or infuriated you, and why.

2. Tell the story of an incident in which you were involved and which you regret today. Be sure to discuss what particular parts of this incident and its consequences seem humiliating, foolish, reckless, or unkind today.

Topics for a Descriptive Essay

1. Describe the best social event you ever attended. It can be a wedding, a dance, a holiday party, a graduation celebration, or any other special event. Describe the people at the event, the place where it happened, the food and refreshments served, and the activity (dance, music, awards ceremony) connected to the event.

2. Write an essay describing any of the following:

   your two favorite childhood toys
   your two (or three) favorite places to relax
   three beautiful animals
   any scene at sunset

3. Go to a place you visit regularly, but on this visit, study the place carefully. You may choose to visit a supermarket, service station, coffee shop, convenience store, and so forth. As soon as you leave, take notes about what you noticed. Then write an essay describing that place.

4. Imagine that someone who has never seen you (a distant relative, someone you've been corresponding with) is coming to visit. You will be meeting this person at the airport or train station. In an essay, describe yourself to this person. You can describe your face, body, clothes, walk, voice, or any other distinguishing characteristic.

Topic for Critical Thinking and Writing: Descriptive Essay

1. Imagine your ideal home or apartment. In a five-paragraph essay, describe the three rooms that would be most important to you. As you describe each room's appearance and contents (such as furniture, accessories, equipment, and appliances), explain why the room itself also holds special significance for you.

2. Describe a place or situation that frightened you when you were young. The source of your fear could be a dark cellar (place) or a visit to a relative (situation). In your description, explain what the experience felt like to the child you were. Then describe how the place or situation affects you today.

Topics for an Illustration Essay

1. Make a statement about yourself and illustrate it with examples. You can use a thesis like one of the following:

   When faced with a problem, I am a person who _____.
   Everyone who knows me thinks I am too _____.
   I have always felt satisfied with my _____.
   My greatest strength is _____.
   My greatest weakness is _____.

2. Write about a person who has been kind to you. In the body paragraphs, give examples of this person's kindness to you.

3. Here are some general statements that you may have heard:

   Teenage marriages never work out.
   Hard work will get you where you want to be.
   Children these days are too spoiled.
   Old people have an easy life; all they do is sit around all day.

Pick one of these statements and, in an essay, give examples (from your own experience and observation) of the truth or falseness of the statement.

4. Complete this statement: The best part of living in _____ (name your city, town, or neighborhood) is its _____. Then write an essay supporting this statement with examples.

Topics for Critical Thinking and Writing: Illustration

1. Think about a famous person (a political or spiritual leader, celebrity, performer, athlete, and so forth) whom you believe is misunderstood. Illustrate the ways in which he or she is misunderstood. Include examples of incidents in which the person has been misjudged, and arrange your examples in emphatic order. You may want to do some research into this person's background to support your thesis.

2. Have you ever received criticism that you felt was unfair? In an essay, give examples of this criticism and then challenge the criticism with your own specific examples of your behavior.

Topics for a Process Essay

1. Think of some process you perform often. It could be something as simple as doing the laundry or setting your DVR to record a program while you are not home. Now, pretend that you must explain this process to someone who has no idea how to perform it. Write an essay explaining the process to that person.

2. Observe someone perform a task you've never looked at closely. You can watch your boss close up the store, for instance, or watch a friend braid hair. Then write an essay on how the person works through the steps of that process.

3. Interview a law enforcement officer, asking him or her what steps a person should take to protect a home from crime. Use the information you learned from the interview to write an essay on how to protect a home from crime.

Topics for Critical Thinking and Writing: Process

1. Think of a routine in your life. It could be something as simple as getting ready for work or cleaning out the inside of your car. List the steps of this process and the necessary materials. Next, write about a quicker, easier way to complete the same process.

2. Imagine that you need a big favor from a friend or family member. This favor will involve either money, a written recommendation of your character to a prospective employer, or another important form of generosity or support. In an essay, describe that steps you would take to ask for, and receive, this favor.

MyWritingLab™ For support in meeting this chapter's objectives, log in to www.mywritinglab.com and select **Recognizing the Essay, Essay Organization, The Thesis Statement, Essay Introductions, Conclusions, and Titles,** and **The Writing Process.**

Name _____   Section _____

Peer Review Form for an Essay

After you have completed a draft of your essay, let a writing partner read it. When your partner has completed the form below, discuss the comments. Then repeat the same process for your partner's paragraph.

The thesis of this essay is _____

_____

_____

The topic sentences for the body paragraphs are _____

_____

_____

_____

_____

The topic sentence in the conclusion is _____

_____

_____

The best part of the essay is the _____ (first, second, third, etc.) paragraph.

I would like to see details added to the part about _____

_____

I would take out the part about _____

_____

Additional comments _____

_____

_____

_____

_____

_____

_____

Reviewer's Name _____

CHAPTER 29

Writing from Reading

Chapter Objectives

Students will be able to (1) apply prereading strategies to assigned readings, (2) write an effective summary of a reading selection by working through the stages of the writing process, and (3) engage in critical thinking by agreeing or disagreeing with the premise or key points of an article.

WHAT IS WRITING FROM READING?

One way to find topics for writing is to draw from your ideas, memories, and observations. Another way is to write from reading you've done. You can react to something you've read; you can agree or disagree with it. You can summarize what you've read. Many college assignments ask you to write about an assigned reading such as an essay, a chapter in a textbook, or an article in a journal. This kind of writing requires an active, involved attitude toward your reading. Such reading is done in steps:

1. Preread.
2. Read.
3. Reread with a pen or pencil.

Attitude

Before you begin the first step of this reading process, you have to have a certain attitude. That attitude involves thinking of what you read as half of a conversation. The writer has opinions and ideas; he or she makes points just as you do when you write or speak. The writer supports his or her points with specific details. If the writer were speaking to you in conversation, you would respond to his or her opinions or ideas. You would agree, disagree, or question. You would jump into the conversation, linking or contrasting your ideas with those of the other speaker.

The right attitude toward reading demands that you read the same way you converse: you become involved. In doing this, you talk back as you read, and later, you may react in your own writing. Reacting as you read will keep you focused on what you are reading. If you are focused, you will remember more of what you read. With an active, involved attitude, you can begin the step of prereading.

Prereading

Before you actually read an assigned essay, a chapter in a textbook, or an article in a journal, magazine, or newspaper, take a few minutes to look it over, and be ready to answer the following questions.

Checklist for Prereading

✔ How long is this reading?

✔ Will I be able to read it in one sitting, or will I have to schedule several time periods to finish it?

✔ Are there any subheadings in the reading? Do they give any hints about the reading?

✔ Are there any charts? Graphs? Is there boxed information? Are there any photographs or illustrations with captions? Do the photos or captions give any hints about the reading?

✔ Is there any introductory material about the reading or the author? Does the introductory material give me any hints about the reading?

✔ What is the title of the reading? Does the title hint at the point of the reading?

✔ Are there any parts of the reading underlined or emphasized in some other way?

✔ Do the emphasized parts hint at the point of the reading?

Why Preread?

Prereading takes very little time, but it helps you immensely. Some students believe it's a waste of time to scan an assignment; they think they should just jump right in and get the reading over with. However, spending just a few minutes on preliminaries can save hours later. And most important, prereading helps you become a focused reader.

If you scan the length of an assignment, you can pace yourself. And if you know how long a reading is, you can alert yourself to its plan. For example, a short reading has to come to its point soon. A longer essay may take more time to develop its point and may use more details and examples.

Subheadings, charts, graphs, and boxed or other highlighted materials are important enough that the author wants to emphasize them. Looking over that material before you read gives you an overview of the important points the reading will contain.

Introductory material or introductory questions also help you know what to look for as you read. Background on the author or on the subject may hint at ideas that will come up in the reading. Sometimes the title of the reading will give you the main idea.

You should preread so that you can start reading the entire assignment with as much knowledge about the writer and the subject as you can get. When you then read the entire assignment, you will be reading actively, for more knowledge.

Forming Questions Before You Read

If you want to read with a focus, it helps to ask questions before you read. Form questions by using the information you gained from prereading.

Start by noting the title and turning it into a question. If the title of your assigned reading is, "Causes of the Civil War," ask, "What were the causes of the Civil War?"

You can turn subheadings into questions. If you are reading an article about self-esteem, and one subheading is "Influence of Parents," you can ask, "How do parents influence a person's self-esteem?"

You can also form questions from graphics and illustrations. If a chapter in your economics textbook includes a photograph of Wall Street, you can ask, "What is Wall Street?" or "What is Wall Street's role in economics?" or "What happens on Wall Street?"

You can write down these questions, but it's not necessary. Just forming questions and keeping them in the back of your mind helps you read actively and stay focused.

An Example of the Prereading Step

Take a look at the article that follows. Don't read it; *preread* it.

Part-Time Job May Do Teenagers More Harm Than Good

Gary Klott

Gary Klott is a personal finance consultant for the National Newspaper Syndicate. In this article, he explores the effects of part-time jobs on high school students.

Words You May Need to Know (Corresponding paragraph numbers are in parentheses.)

extracurricular activities (2): activities outside the regular academic course, like clubs and sports

assume (3): suppose, take for granted

menial (4): of a low level, degrading

instant gratification (4): immediate satisfaction

1   Given today's high cost of auto insurance, dating, video games, music CDs and designer clothing, it shouldn't come as any surprise that a growing number of high school students are taking part-time jobs during the school year. Most parents have done little to discourage their children from working after school. In fact, many parents figure that part-time

jobs can help teach their children about responsibility and the value of a dollar and better prepare them for life in the adult workaday world. But there is growing evidence to suggest that parents ought to sharply restrict the number of hours their children work during the school year.

Academic studies over the past decade have found that high school students who work—particularly those who work long hours during the school week—tend to do less well in school, miss out on the benefits of extra-curricular activities and have more behavioral problems. Most recently, a study of 12th-graders by Linda P. Worley, a high school counselor in Marietta, Georgia, indicated that grades suffer when students work more than ten hours during the school week. The highest grade-point averages were found for students who worked only on weekends, 3.07, and for those who baby-sat or did yard work, 3.13. Students who didn't work at all had an average GPA of 3.02, while those who worked up to ten hours a week earned an average GPA of 2.95. Students working ten to twenty hours a week averaged 2.77, twenty to thirty hours per week 2.53 and thirty or more hours 2.10.

Even if a student manages to maintain good grades, parents shouldn't automatically assume that long work hours aren't harming their child's education. Several studies found that many students kept up their grades by choosing easier courses. A 1993 study of 1,800 high-school sophomores by researchers at Temple University and Stanford University found that students who worked more than twenty hours a week spent less time on homework, cut class more often, cheated more on tests and assignments, had less interest in formal education, had a higher rate of drug and alcohol use and had lower self-esteem.

Researchers also note that some of the perceived benefits of after-school jobs are often overrated. For example, many of the jobs high school students take on are menial and provide few skills that will prove useful after high school. And many students learn the wrong lessons about the value of a dollar since they tend to spend all of their job earnings on cars, clothes, and other purchases that provide instant gratification without saving a penny.

By prereading the article, you might notice the following:

- The title of the article is "Part-Time Job May Do Teenagers More Harm Than Good."
- The article is short and can be read in one sitting.
- The author writes about money, and he writes for newspapers.
- The introductory material says the article is about teenagers with part-time jobs.
- There are several vocabulary words you may need to know.

You might begin reading the article with these questions in mind:

- Why are part-time jobs harmful to teens?
- What are the harmful effects?

- Why is a writer who writes about money arguing that it is bad for teens to make money?
- Should teens have full-time jobs instead of part-time ones?

Reading

The first time you read, try to *get a sense of the whole piece* you are reading. Reading with questions in mind can help you do this. If you find that you are confused by a certain part of the reading selection, go back and reread that part. If you do not know the meaning of a word, check the vocabulary list to see if the word is defined for you. If it isn't defined, try to figure out the meaning from the way the word is used in the sentence.

If you find that you have to read more slowly than usual, don't worry. People vary their reading speed according to what they read and why they are reading it. If you are reading for entertainment, for example, you can read quickly; if you are reading a chapter in a textbook, you must read more slowly. The more complicated the reading selection is, the more slowly you will read it.

An Example of the Reading Step

Now read "Part-Time Job May Do Teenagers More Harm Than Good." When you've completed your first reading, you will probably have some answers to the prereading questions that you formed.

Answers to Prereading Questions:

Part-time jobs can hurt teens' grades and other areas of their lives such as their behavior and attitudes.
The writer, who writes about money, says part-time jobs give students bad spending habits.
Full-time work would be worse than part-time work.

Rereading with Pen or Pencil

The second reading is the crucial one. At this point, you begin to think on paper as you read. In this step, you make notes or write about what you read. Some students are reluctant to do this because they are not sure what to note or write. *Think of making these notes as a way of learning, thinking, reviewing, and reacting.* Reading with a pen or pencil in your hand keeps you alert. With that pen or pencil, you can

- mark the main point of the reading,
- mark other points,
- define words you don't know,
- question parts of the reading that seem confusing,
- evaluate the writer's ideas,
- react to the writer's opinions or examples, and
- add ideas, opinions, or examples of your own.

There is no single system for marking or writing as you read. Some readers like to underline the main idea with two lines and to underline other important ideas with one line. Some students like to put an asterisk (a star) next to important ideas, while others like to circle key words.

Some people use the margins to write comments like "I agree!" or "Not true!" or "That's happened to me." Sometimes readers put questions in the margin; sometimes they summarize a point in the margin, next to its location in the essay. Some people list important points in the white space above the reading, while others use the space at the end of the reading.

Every reader who writes as he or she reads has a personal system; what these systems share is an attitude. *If you write as you read, you concentrate on the reading selection, get to know the writer's ideas, and develop ideas of your own.*

As you reread and write notes, don't worry too much about noticing the "right" ideas. Instead, think of rereading as the time to jump into a *conversation* with the writer.

An Example of Rereading with Pen or Pencil

For "Part-Time Job May Do Teenagers More Harm Than Good," your marked article might look like the following:

Part-Time Job May Do Teenagers More Harm Than Good

Gary Klott

Given today's high cost of auto insurance, dating, video games, music CDs and designer clothing, it shouldn't come as any surprise that a growing number of high school students are taking part-time jobs during the school year. Most parents have done little to discourage their children from working after school. In fact, many parents figure that part-time jobs can help teach their children about responsibility and the value of a dollar and better prepare them for life in the adult workaday world. But there is growing evidence to suggest that parents ought to sharply restrict the number of hours their children work during the school year.

I agree!

What parents believe

What parents should do

Academic studies over the past decade have found that high school students who work—particularly those who work long hours during the school week—tend to do less well in school, miss out on the benefits of extracurricular activities and have more behavioral problems. Most recently, a study of 12th-graders by Linda P. Worley, a high school counselor in Marietta, Georgia, indicated that grades suffer when students work more than ten hours during the school week. The highest grade-point averages were found for students who worked only on weekends, 3.07, and for those who baby-sat or did yard work, 3.13. Students who didn't work at all had an average GPA of 3.02, while those who worked up to ten hours a week earned an average GPA of 2.95. Students working ten to twenty hours a week averaged 2.77, twenty to thirty hours per week 2.53 and thirty or more hours 2.10.

*

example
The more you work, the lower the grades

Even if a student manages to maintain good grades, parents shouldn't automatically assume that long work hours aren't harming their child's education. Several studies found that many students kept up their grades by choosing easier courses. A 1993 study of 1,800 high-school sophomores by researchers at Temple University and Stanford University found that students who worked more than twenty hours a week spent less time on

other harm to education

self-respect, pride

homework, <u>cut class</u> more often, <u>cheated</u> more on tests and assignments, had <u>less interest</u> in formal education, <u>had a higher rate of drug and alcohol use</u> and had lower (self-esteem.)

Researchers also note that <u>some of the perceived benefits of after-school jobs are often overrated.</u> For example, many of the jobs high school students take on are menial and provide few skills that will prove useful after high school. <u>And many students learn the wrong lessons about the value of a dollar since they tend to spend all of their job earnings on cars, clothes, and other purchases that provide instant gratification without saving a penny.</u>

What the Notes Mean

In the sample above, much of the underlining indicates sentences or phrases that seem important. The words in the margin are often summaries of what is underlined. In the first paragraph, for example, the words "what parents believe" and "what parents should do" are like subtitles in the margin.

An asterisk in the margin signals an important idea. When "example" is written in the margin, it notes that a point is being supported by a specific example. Sometimes, what is in the margin is the reader's reaction, like "I agree!" One item in the margin is a definition. The word "self-esteem" is circled and defined in the margin as "self-respect, pride."

The marked-up article is a flexible tool. You can go back and mark it further. You may change your mind about your notes and comments and find other, better, or more important points in the article.

You write as you read to involve yourself in the reading process. Marking what you read can help you in other ways, too. If you are to be tested on the reading selection or are asked to discuss it, you can scan your markings and notations at a later time for a quick review.

> **Exercise 1** **Practice: Reading and Making Notes for a Selection**

Following is a paragraph from "Part-Time Job May Do Teenagers More Harm Than Good." First, read it. Then reread it and make notes on the following:

1. Underline the first eight words of the most specific example in the paragraph.

2. Circle the phrase "formal education" and define it in the margin.

3. At the end of the paragraph, summarize its main point.

Paragraph from "Part-Time Job May Do Teenagers More Harm Than Good"

Even if a student manages to maintain good grades, parents shouldn't automatically assume that long work hours aren't harming their child's education. Several studies found that many students kept up their grades by choosing easier courses. A 1993 study of 1,800 high-school sophomores and juniors by researchers at Temple University and Stanford University found that students who worked more than twenty hours a week spent less time on homework, cut class more often, cheated more on tests and assignments, had less interest in formal education, had a higher rate of drug and alcohol use and had lower self-esteem.

Main point of the paragraph (in your own words): _____

_____

_____

WRITING A SUMMARY OF A READING

One way to write about a reading is to write a summary. A *summary* of a reading tells the important ideas in brief form and in your own words. It includes (1) the writer's main idea, (2) the ideas used to explain the main idea, and (3) some examples or details.

PREWRITING   MARKING A LIST OF IDEAS: SUMMARY

When you preread, read, and make notes on the reading selection, you have already begun the prewriting stage for a summary. You can think further, on paper, *by listing the points* (words, phrases, sentences) you've already marked on the reading selection.

To find the main idea for your summary and the ideas and examples connected to the main idea, you can *mark related ideas* on your list. For example, the list below was made from "Part-Time Job May Do Teenagers More Harm Than Good." Three symbols are used to mark the following:

S   the effects of part-time jobs on **schoolwork**

O   **other** effects of part-time jobs

P   what **parents** think about part-time jobs

Some items on the list don't have a mark because they do not relate to any of the categories.

A Marked List of Ideas for a Summary of "Part-Time Job May Do Teenagers More Harm Than Good"

     high cost of car insurance, dating, video games, music CDs, and designer clothing

P   parents think part-time jobs teach responsibility, money, and job skills
     parents should restrict teens' work hours

S   working students do less well in school

S   study of 12th-graders by Linda P. Worley said grades suffer if students work more than ten hours in school week

S   students who work long hours choose easier courses

S   they spend less time on homework

S   they cut class more

S   they cheat

S   they are less interested in school

O   they use drugs and alcohol more

O   they have lower self-esteem
     some perceived benefits are overrated

O   students spend money foolishly

The marked list could then be reorganized, like this:

the effects of part-time jobs on schoolwork

- working students do less well in school
- study of 12th-graders by Linda P. Worley said grades suffer if students work more than ten hours in the school week
- students who work long hours choose easier classes
- they spend less time on homework
- they cut class more
- they cheat
- they are less interested in school

other effects of part-time jobs

- if they work over twenty hours, they use drugs and alcohol more
- they have lower self-esteem
- working students spend money foolishly

what many parents think about part-time jobs

- parents think part-time jobs teach responsibility and money and job skills

Selecting a Main Idea

The next step in the process is to select the idea you think is the writer's main point. If you look again at the list of ideas, you see one category that has only one item: what many parents think about part-time jobs. In this category, the only item is that parents think part-time jobs teach responsibility and money and job skills.

Is this item the main idea of the article? If it is, then all the other ideas support it. But the other ideas contradict this point.

It is not the main idea, but it *is* connected to the main idea. The author is saying that parents *think* part-time jobs are good for high school students, but they may not be, especially if students work long hours.

You can write a simpler version of this main idea:

Parents should know that working long hours at part-time jobs is not good for teens.

Once you have a main idea, check it to see if it fits with the other ideas in your organized list. *Do the ideas in the list connect to the main idea?* Yes. The ideas about the effects of jobs on schoolwork show the negative impact of part-time work. So do the ideas about the other effects. And even the part about what some parents think can be used to contrast what jobs *really* do to teens.

Now that you have a main point that fits an organized list, you can move to the *planning* stage of a summary.

Exercise 2 **Practice: Marking a List and Finding the Main Idea for a Summary**

Following is a list of ideas from an article called "Binge Nights: The Emergency on Campus" by Michael Winerip. It tells the true story of Ryan Dabbieri, a senior at the University of Virginia, who nearly died from binge drinking at a tailgating party before a football game. Read the list, and then mark each item with one of these symbols:

L	**lessons learned** from the experience
P	**personal background** on the binge drinker
S	**steps** leading to the emergency
E	the life-and-death **emergency**

After you've marked all the ideas, survey them and think of one main idea. Try to focus on a point that connects to what Ryan Dabbieri, the binge drinker, learned.

_____ Ryan Dabbieri was a 22-year-old senior at the University of Virginia.

_____ Ryan did not think he was a binge drinker.

_____ About once a week, he would drink five to seven drinks in two hours.

_____ Before one big football game, he drank five or six very big shots of bourbon in fifteen minutes at a party.

_____ At the stadium, he straightened up to get by security.

_____ Inside, he passed out.

_____ His friends carried him outside.

_____ They couldn't revive him.

_____ In the emergency room, he stopped breathing for four minutes.

_____ His friends were terrified.

_____ The doctors did a scan for brain damage.

_____ Ryan's father flew in from Atlanta.

_____ Ryan awoke the next day in intensive care.

_____ Ryan says he won't drink again.

_____ He says he is lucky to be alive.

main idea: _____

_____

_____

PLANNING **SUMMARY**

Following is an outline for a summary of "Part-Time Job May Do Teenagers More Harm Than Good." As you read it, you'll notice that the main idea of the prewriting stage has become the topic sentence of the outline, and most of the other ideas have become details.

Outline for a Summary of "Part-Time Job May Do Teenagers More Harm Than Good"

topic sentence:	Parents should know that working long hours at part-time jobs is not good for teens.
details:	

effects on schoolwork
- Working students do less well in school.
- A study of 12th-graders by Linda P. Worley showed this.
- It showed that grades suffer if students worked more than ten hours in the school week.
- Students who work long hours choose easier classes.
- They spend less time on homework.
- They cut class more.
- They are less interested in school.

other effects
- They use drugs and alcohol more.
- They have lower self-esteem.
- They spend money foolishly.

In the outline, the part about what many parents think about part-time jobs has been left out. Since it was an idea that contrasted with the topic sentence, it didn't seem to fit. That kind of selecting is what you do in the planning stage of writing a summary. In the drafting and revising stage, you may change your mind and decide to use the idea later.

DRAFTING AND REVISING   ATTRIBUTING IDEAS IN A SUMMARY

The first draft of your summary paragraph is your first try at *combining* all the material into one paragraph. The draft is much like the draft of any other paragraph, with one exception: *When you summarize another person's ideas, be sure to say whose ideas you are writing.* That is, *attribute* the ideas to the writer. Let the reader of your paragraph know the following:

1. The author of the selection you are summarizing
2. The title of the selection you are summarizing

You may want to *attribute ideas by giving your summary paragraph a title*, such as

A Summary of Gary Klott's "Part-Time Job May Do Teenagers More Harm Than Good"

Note that you put the title of Klott's article in quotation marks.

Or you may want to *put the title and author into the paragraph itself.* Below is a draft version of a summary of "Part-Time Job May Do Teenagers More Harm Than Good" with the title and the author incorporated into the paragraph.

Draft of a Summary of "Part-Time Job May Do Teenagers More Harm Than Good"

"Part-Time Job May Do Teenagers More Harm Than Good" by Gary Klott says that parents should know that working long hours at part-time jobs is not good for teens. Working students do less well in school. A study of 12th-graders by Linda P. Worley showed that grades suffer if students work more than ten hours during the school week. Students who work long hours choose easier courses, spend less time on homework, cut class more often, and cheat. They are less interested in school. They use drugs and alcohol more and have lower self-esteem. They spend money foolishly.

When you look this draft over and read it aloud, you may notice a few problems:

- The draft is very choppy; it needs transitions.
- In some places, the word choice could be better.
- The beginning of the paragraph could use an introduction.
- Linda P. Worley did a study about grades and working students. But the other information about effects on schoolwork came from other studies. This difference should be made clear.
- The paragraph ends abruptly.

PROOFREADING **SUMMARY**

Look carefully at the final version of the summary. Notice how the idea about what parents think has been added to an introduction and how transitions and word choice have improved the summary. Also notice how one phrase, "Other studies indicate that," clarifies the ideas in the summary and how an added conclusion clinches the paragraph.

Final Version of a Summary of "Part-Time Job May Do Teenagers More Harm Than Good"

(Changes from the draft are underlined.)

<u>Many parents think part-time jobs teach their children responsibility and money and job skills, but they may be wrong.</u> <u>An article called</u> "Part-Time Job May Do Teenagers More Harm Than Good" by Gary Klott says that parents should know that working long hours at part-time jobs is not good for teens. <u>First of all,</u> working students do less well in school. A study of 12th-graders by Linda P. Worley showed that grades suffer if students work more than ten hours during the school week. <u>Other studies indicate that</u> students who work long hours choose easier courses, spend less time on their homework, <u>and are likely to cheat and cut classes.</u> <u>In addition, such students</u> are less interested in school. <u>Their problems extend outside of school, too, where</u> they use drugs and alcohol <u>more than other students</u> and have lower self-esteem. <u>Finally,</u> they <u>do not learn financial responsibility from their jobs since</u> they spend money foolishly. <u>Parents must consider all these drawbacks before they allow their teens to work long hours.</u>

Writing summaries is good writing practice, and it also helps you develop your reading skills. Even if your instructor does not require you to turn in a polished summary of an assigned reading, you may find it helpful to summarize what you have read. In many classes, midterms or other exams cover many assigned readings. If you make short summaries of each reading as it is assigned, you will have a helpful collection of focused, organized material to review.

THE ROLE OF CRITICAL THINKING AS YOU READ

When you start forming opinions based on what you observe, hear, read, or discuss, you are applying **critical thinking skills**. Thinking critically as you read involves examining an issue from different sides as well as evaluating the validity, or truthfulness, of the information presented. Applying the critical thinking process to evaluate what you are reading requires that you ask yourself the following questions:

- What is the writer's main idea or proposal?
- Is the main idea supported by facts? Personal experience? Expert opinion(s)?
- Does the writer reach logical conclusions based on his or her evidence?

Sharpening critical thinking skills by using this type of questioning as you read can enable you to form reasonable opinions and express them confidently. Reading critically can help you succeed in all of your college classes, and it will be especially beneficial in your future composition classes.

WRITING A REACTION TO A READING SELECTION

A summary is one kind of writing you can do after reading, but there are other kinds. Your instructor might ask you to *react* by writing about some idea you got from your reading. If you read "Part-Time Job May Do Teenagers More Harm Than Good," your instructor might have asked you to react by writing about this topic:

> Gary Klott says that parents may have the wrong idea about their children's jobs. Write about another part of teen life that parents may not understand.

You may begin to gather ideas by freewriting.

PREWRITING   **REACTION TO A READING: FREEWRITING**

You can freewrite in a reading journal, if you wish. This kind of journal is a special journal in which you write about selections that you've read. To freewrite, you can

- write key points made by the author,
- write about whatever you remember from the reading selection,
- write down any of the author's ideas that you think you might want to write about someday,
- list questions raised by what you've read, and
- connect the reading selection to other things you've read, heard, or experienced.

A freewriting that reacts to "Part-Time Job May Do Teenagers More Harm Than Good" might look like this:

Freewriting for a Reaction to a Reading

"Part-Time Job May Do Teenagers More Harm Than Good"—Gary Klott

Jobs can be bad for teens. Author says parents should stop teens from working too many hours. But how? Most parents are afraid of their teens. Or they don't want to interfere.

They figure teens want to be independent. I know wanted to be independent when I was in high school. Did I? I'm not so sure. I think I wanted some attention from my folks. Maybe parents don't know this. Why didn't I say anything?

Selecting a Topic, Listing, and Developing Ideas

Once you have your freewriting, you can survey it for a topic. You might survey the freewriting above and decide you can write about how parents don't know that their teens want attention. To gather ideas, you begin a list:

teens want attention and parents don't know

sometimes teens look independent

they act smart

no real self-confidence

friends aren't enough

I wanted my father's approval

teens can't say what they need

to get attention, they break rules

I would have liked some praise

Next, you organize, expand, and develop this list until you have a main point, the topic sentence, and a list of details. You decide on this topic sentence:

Some parents are unaware that their teenage children need attention.

With a topic sentence and a list of details, you are ready to begin the planning stage of writing.

PLANNING   REACTION TO A READING

An outline might look like the one following. As you read it, notice that the topic sentence and ideas are *your* opinions, not the ideas of the author of "Part-Time Job May Do Teenagers More Harm Than Good." You used his ideas to come up with your own. Also notice how it builds on the ideas on the list and organizes them in a clear order.

Outline of a Reaction to a Reading

topic sentence:	Some parents are unaware that their teenage children need attention.
details: **what parents see**	Teens act independent. They act smart. They break rules. Parents think that rule-breaking means teens want to be left alone. Teens do it to get attention.
what teens want	Teens can't say what they need. They have no real self-confidence. Their friends aren't enough.
personal example	I wanted my father's approval. I would have liked some praise.

DRAFTING AND REVISING **REACTION TO A READING**

If your outline gives you enough good ideas to develop, you are on your way to a paragraph. If you started with the outline points from the previous page, for example, you could develop them into a draft much like the following:

Draft of a Reaction to a Reading

Some parents are unaware that their teenage children need attention. Teens act independent and smart. They break their parents' rules, so their parents think teenage rule-breaking is a sign the children want to be left alone. Teens break rules to get attention. They can't say what they need; therefore, they act out their needs. Teens have no real self-confidence. Friends aren't enough. I wanted my father's approval. I would have liked some praise.

PROOFREADING **REACTION TO A READING**

When you read the draft version of the paragraph, you probably noticed some places where it could be revised:

- The word choice could be better.
- There is too much repetition of words like *need*, *needs*, *their parents*, and *children*.
- The paragraph needs many transitions.
- Since the ideas are reactions related to a point by Gary Klott, he needs to be mentioned.
- The ending is a little abrupt.

Following is the final version of the same paragraph. As you read it, notice how the changes make it a clearer, smoother, more developed paragraph.

> **Note:** Remember that a final version is often the result of *several* drafts.

Final Version of a Reaction to a Reading

(Changes from the draft are underlined.)

<u>Gary Klott says that many parents do not understand the impact of their teenagers' part-time jobs. There is another part of teen life that parents may not understand.</u> Some parents are unaware that their teenage children need attention. Teens act independent and <u>self-assured.</u> They will break their parents' rules, so their parents think the rule-breaking is a sign the children want to be left alone. However, <u>adolescents</u> break rules to get attention. They can't say what they <u>crave;</u> therefore, they act out their needs. Teens have no real self-confidence. <u>While friends help adolescents develop self-confidence,</u> friends aren't enough. <u>My own experience is a good example of what adolescents desire.</u> I wanted my father's approval. I would have liked some praise, <u>but I couldn't ask for what I needed. My father was a parent who was unaware.</u>

WRITING ABOUT AGREEMENT OR DISAGREEMENT

PREWRITING   AGREE OR DISAGREE PARAGRAPH

Another way to write about a reading selection is to find a point in it and *agree or disagree with that point.* To begin writing about agreement or disagreement, you can review the selection and jot down any statements that provoke a strong reaction in you. You are looking for statements with which you can agree or disagree. If you reviewed "Part-Time Job May Do Teenagers More Harm Than Good," you might list these statements as points of agreement or disagreement:

Points of Agreement or Disagreement from a Reading

Grades suffer when students work more than ten hours during the school week.—agree

High school students who work many hours "have less interest in formal education"—disagree

---

Then you might *pick one of the statements and react to it in writing.* If you disagreed with the statement that high school students who work many hours "have less interest in formal education," you might begin by brainstorming.

Brainstorming for an Agree or Disagree Paragraph

Question: Why do you disagree that high school students who work long hours "have less interest in formal education"?

Answer: I worked long hours. I was interested in getting a <u>good</u> education.

Question: If you were interested in school, why were you so focused on your job?

Answer: To make money.

Question: Then wasn't money more important than school?

Answer: No. I was working to make money to pay for college. Working was the only way I could afford college.

Question: Do you think it <u>looked</u> as if you didn't care about education?

Answer: Yes, sure.

Question: Why?

Answer: I used to be so tired from working I would fall asleep in class.

Once you have some ideas from brainstorming, you can list them, group them, and add to them by more brainstorming. Your topic sentence can be a way of stating your disagreement with the original point, like this:

> Although Gary Klott says that high school students who work long hours tend to lose interest in school, my experience shows the opposite.

With a topic sentence and details, you can work on the planning stage of your paragraph.

PLANNING **AGREE OR DISAGREE PARAGRAPH**

An outline might look like the following. Notice that the topic sentence is your opinion and that the details are from your experience.

Outline for an Agree or Disagree Paragraph

topic sentence:	Although Gary Klott says that high school students who work long hours may lose interest in school, my experience shows the opposite.

details:	While I was in high school, I worked long hours.
my experience	I was very interested in getting a good education.
	I wanted to graduate from college.
	To save money for college, I was working long hours.
	Working was the only way I could pay for college.

why I appeared uninterested	I probably looked as if I didn't care about school.
	I fell asleep in class.
	I was tired from working.

DRAFTING AND REVISING **AGREE OR DISAGREE PARAGRAPH**

Once you have a good outline, you can develop it into a paragraph:

Draft of an Agree or Disagree Paragraph

Although Gary Klott says that high school students who work long hours lose interest in school, my experience shows the opposite. When I was in high school, I worked long hours. I endured my job and even increased my hours because I was interested in getting a good education. I wanted to graduate from college. I was working long hours to save money for college. Working was the only way I could pay tuition. I know that, to my teachers, I probably looked like I didn't care about school. I was tired from working. I fell asleep in class.

PROOFREADING **AGREE OR DISAGREE PARAGRAPH**

When you surveyed the draft of the paragraph, you probably noticed some places that need revision:

- The paragraph could use more specific details.
- Some sentences could be combined.
- It needs a last sentence, reinforcing the point that students who work long hours may be very interested in school.

As you read the final version of the paragraph, notice how the revisions improve the paragraph.

<u>Final Version of an Agree or Disagree Paragraph</u>

(Changes from the draft are underlined.)

> Although Gary Klott says that high school students who work long hours lose interest in school, my experience shows the opposite. When I was in high school, I worked long hours. <u>Sometimes I worked twenty-five hours a week at a fast-food restaurant.</u> I endured my job and even increased my hours because I was interested in getting a good education. I wanted to graduate from college. <u>I was working long hours to save money for college since working was the only way I could pay tuition.</u> I know that, to my teachers, I probably looked like I didn't care about school. I was so tired from working that <u>I came to school in a daze.</u> I fell asleep in class. <u>But my long, hard hours at work made me determined to change my life through education.</u>

WRITING FOR AN ESSAY TEST

Another kind of writing from reading involves the essay test. Most essay questions require you to write about an assigned reading. Usually, an essay test requires you to write from memory, not from an open book or notes. Such writing can be stressful, but breaking the task into steps can eliminate much of the stress.

Before the Test: The Steps of Reading

If you work through the steps of reading days before the test, you are half-way to your goal. Prereading helps to keep you focused, and your first reading gives you a sense of the whole selection. The third step, rereading with a pen or pencil, can be particularly helpful when you are preparing for a test. Most essay questions will ask you either to summarize or react to a reading selection. In either case, you must be familiar with the reading's main idea, supporting ideas, examples, and details. If you note these by marking the selection, you are teaching yourself about the main point, supporting ideas, and structure of the reading selection.

Shortly before the test, review the marked reading assignment. Your notes will help you focus on the main point and the supporting ideas.

During the Test: The Stages of Writing

Answering an essay test question may seem very different from writing at home. After all, on a test, you must rely on your memory and write within a time limit, and these restrictions can make you feel anxious. However, by following the stages of the writing process, you can meet that challenge calmly and confidently.

PREWRITING   ESSAY TEST

Before you begin to write, think about these questions: Is the instructor asking for a summary of a reading selection? Or is he or she asking you to react to a specific idea with examples or by agreeing or disagreeing? For example, in an essay question about the article, "Part-Time Job May Do Teenagers More Harm Than Good," by Gary Klott, you might be asked to (1) explain why Klott thinks a part-time job can be bad for a teenager (a summary), (2) explain what Klott means when he says that students who work long hours may keep their grades up but still miss out on the best education (a reaction, in which you develop and explain one part of the reading), or (3) agree or disagree that after-school jobs teach the wrong lesson about the value of money (a reaction, so you have to be aware of what Klott said on this point).

Once you have thought about the question, list or freewrite your first ideas. At this time, do not worry about how "right" or "wrong" your writing is; just write your first thoughts.

PLANNING   ESSAY TEST

Your writing will be clear if you follow a plan. Remember that the audience for this writing is your instructor and that he or she will be evaluating how well you stick to the subject, make a point, and support it. Your plan for making a point about the subject and supporting it can be written in a brief outline.

First, reread the question. Next, survey your list or freewriting. Does it contain a main point that answers the question? Does it contain supporting ideas and details?

Next, write a main point and then list supporting ideas and details under the main point. Your main point will be the topic sentence of your answer. If you need more support, try brainstorming.

DRAFTING AND REVISING   ESSAY TEST

Write your point and supporting ideas in paragraph form. If you have time to revise, remember to use effective transitions and to combine short sentences.

PROOFREADING   ESSAY TEST

You will probably not have time to copy your answer, but you can review it, proofread it, and correct any errors in spelling, punctuation, or word choice. The final check can produce a more polished answer.

Organize Your Time

Some students skip important stages of the writing process. Without thinking or planning, they immediately begin writing their answer to an essay question. Sometimes they find themselves stuck in the middle of a paragraph, panicked because they have no more ideas. At other times, they find themselves writing in a circle, repeating the same point over and over. Occasionally, they even forget to include a main idea.

You can avoid these hazards by spending time on each of the stages. Planning is as important as writing. For example, if you have half an hour to write an essay, you can divide your time like this:

> 5 minutes thinking, freewriting, listing
> 10 minutes planning, outlining
> 10 minutes drafting
> 5 minutes reviewing, proofreading

Writing from Reading: A Summary of Options

Reading can give you many opportunities for your own writing. You can summarize a writer's work, use it as a springboard for your own related writing, or agree or disagree with it. However you decide to write from reading, you must still work through the same writing process. Following the stages of prewriting, planning, drafting and revising, and proofreading will help you develop your work into a successful paragraph.

Lines of Detail: A Walk-Through Assignment

Here are three ideas from "Part-Time Job May Do Teenagers More Harm Than Good":

a. Students who work long hours miss out on extracurricular activities at school.
b. Parents should prevent their teenage children from working long hours.
c. Teens who work spend their money foolishly.

Pick *one* of these ideas with which you agree or disagree. Write a paragraph explaining why you agree or disagree. To write your paragraph, follow these steps:

Step 1: Begin by listing at least three reasons or examples why you agree or disagree. Make your reasons or examples as specific as you can, using your experiences or the experiences of friends and family.

Step 2: Read your list to a partner or group. With the help of your listener(s), add reasons, examples, and details.

Step 3: Once you have enough ideas, transform the statement you agreed or disagreed with into a topic sentence.

Step 4: Write an outline by listing your reasons, examples, and details below the topic sentence. Check that your list is in a clear and logical order.

Step 5: Write a draft of your paragraph. Check that you have attributed Gary Klott's statement, you have enough specific details, you have combined any choppy sentences, and you have used good transitions. Revise your draft until the paragraph is smooth and clear.

Step 6: Before you prepare the final copy, check your draft for errors in spelling, punctuation, and word choice.

WRITING YOUR OWN PARAGRAPH

Writing from Reading "Part-Time Job May Do Teenagers More Harm Than Good"

When you write on any of these topics, be sure to work through the stages of the writing process in preparing your paragraph.

1. Klott talks about high school students who work to pay for car insurance, dates, video games, music, and designer clothes. However, students might not have to work so hard if they learned to do without things they don't really need: the latest clothes, the newest CD, their own car, and so on. Write a paragraph about the many things high school students buy that they don't really need.

2. Work can interfere with high school. Write about some thing else that interferes with high school. You can write about social life, extracurricular activities, sports, family responsibilities, or any other part of a student's life that can prevent him or her from focusing on school.

As you plan this paragraph, think about details that could fit these categories:

Why students choose this activity/responsibility over school

The effects on students' schoolwork

How to balance school and other activities or responsibilities

Collaborate

3. Many parents believe that a part-time job is good for high school students, but the job can be harmful. Write a one-paragraph letter to parents, warning them about some other part of teen life (not jobs) that parents may think is good but that may be harmful. You can write about the dangers of their child being popular, or having a steady boyfriend or girlfriend, or always being number one in academics.

Once you've chosen the topic, brainstorm with a partner or group: ask questions, answer them, add details. After you've brainstormed, work by yourself and proceed through the stages of preparing your letter to parents.

4. Some parents have misconceptions (incorrect ideas) about their teenage children; for instance, they may believe the teen with a part-time job is automatically learning how to handle money. On the other hand, teenage children have misconceptions about their parents. Write about some misconception that teens have about their parents. You might, for instance, write about some teens' mistaken belief that (1) the best parents are the ones who give their children the most freedom, or (2) parents who love you give you everything you want, or (3) parents do not remember what it is like to be young.

To begin, freewrite on one mistaken idea that teens might have about their parents. Focus on your own experiences, memories, and so forth—as a teen or as a parent of teenagers. Use your freewriting to find details and a focus for your paragraph.

5. Klott writes about parents' need to restrict teens' work hours. This restriction might be a difficult rule for some working students to accept. Write about a family rule that you hated when you were a child or teen. Include your feelings about that rule today.

Writing from Reading

To practice the skills you've learned in this chapter, follow the steps of prereading, reading, and rereading with a pencil as you read the following selection.

New Directions

Maya Angelou

Maya Angelou was born Marguerite Johnson in St. Louis, Missouri, in 1928. She survived many hardships to become one of the most famous and beloved writers in America. Although she is best known for her autobiographical books, Angelou is also a political activist, singer, and performer on stage and screen. Her achievements include bestselling books, literary awards, and the reciting of her poetry at the inauguration of President William Jefferson Clinton. In this essay, Angelou tells the story of a woman who cut a new path for her life.

Words You May Need to Know (Corresponding paragraph numbers are in parentheses.)

burdensome (1): troublesome, heavy

conceded (2): admitted

domestic (3): a household worker

meticulously (4): very carefully

cotton gin (4): a factory with a machine for separating cotton fibers from seeds

brazier (6): a container that holds live coals covered by a grill, used for cooking

savors (6): food that smells and tastes good

lint (6): cotton fibers

specters (6): ghosts

balmy (9): mild and soothing

hives of industry (9): places swarming with busy workers

looms (11): rises in front of us

ominous (11): threatening

resolve (11): determination

unpalatable (11): not acceptable

1   In 1903 the late Mrs. Annie Johnson of Arkansas found herself with two toddling sons, very little money, a slight ability to read and add simple numbers. To this picture add a disastrous marriage and the burdensome fact that Mrs. Johnson was a Negro.

2   When she told her husband, Mr. William Johnson, of her dissatisfaction with their marriage, he conceded that he too found it to be less than he expected, and had been secretly hoping to leave and study religion. He added that he thought God was calling him not only to preach but to do so in Enid, Oklahoma. He did not tell her that he knew a minister in Enid with whom he could study and who had a friendly, unmarried daughter. They parted amicably, Annie keeping the one-room house and William taking most of the cash to carry himself to Oklahoma.

3   Annie, over six feet tall, big-boned, decided that she would not go to work as a domestic and leave her "precious babes" to anyone else's care. There was no possibility of being hired at the town's cotton gin or lumber mill, but maybe there was a way to make the two factories work for her. In other words, "I looked up the road I was going and back the way I come, and since I wasn't satisfied, I decided to step off the road and cut me a new path." She told herself that she wasn't a fancy cook but that she could "mix groceries well enough to scare hungry away from starving a man."

4   She made her plans meticulously and in secret. One early evening to see if she was ready, she placed stones in two five-gallon pails and carried them three miles to the cotton gin. She rested a little, and then, discarding some rocks, she walked to the sawmill five miles farther along the dirt road. On her way back to her house and her babies, she dumped the remaining rocks along the path.

5   That same night she worked into the early hours boiling chicken and frying ham. She made dough and filled the rolled-out pastry with meat. At last she went to sleep.

6   The next morning she left her house carrying the meat pies, lard, an iron brazier, and coal for a fire. Just before lunch she appeared in an empty lot behind the cotton gin. As the dinner noon bell rang, she dropped the savors into boiling fat, and the aroma rose and floated over the workers who spilled out of the gin, covered with white lint, looking like specters.

7   Most workers had brought their lunches of pinto beans and biscuits or crackers, onions, and cans of sardines, but they were tempted by the hot meat pies which Annie ladled out of the fat. She wrapped them in newspapers, which soaked up the grease, and offered them for sale at a nickel each. Although business was slow, those first days Annie was determined. She balanced her appearances between the two hours of activity.

8   So, on Monday if she offered hot fresh pies at the cotton gin and sold the remaining cooled-down pies at the lumber mill for three cents, then on Tuesday she went first to the lumber mill presenting fresh, just-cooked pies as the lumbermen covered in sawdust emerged from the mill.

9   For the next few years, on balmy spring days, blistering summer noons, and cold, wet, and wintry middays, Annie never disappointed her customers, who could count on seeing the tall, brown-skin woman bent over her brazier, carefully turning the meat pies. When she felt certain the workers had become dependent on her, she built a stall between the two hives of industry and let the men run to her for their lunchtime provisions.

10   She had indeed stepped from the road which seemed to have been chosen for her and cut herself a brand-new path. In years that stall became a store where customers could buy cheese, meat, syrup, cookies, candy, writing tablets, pickles, canned goods, fresh fruit, soft drinks, coal, oil, and leather soles for worn-out shoes.

11   Each of us has the right and responsibility to assess the roads which lie ahead, and those over which we have traveled, and if the future road looms ominous or unpromising, and the roads back uninviting, then we need to gather our resolve and, carrying only the necessary baggage, step off that road into another direction. If the new choice is also unpalatable, without embarrassment, we must be ready to change that as well.

Topics for Writing from Reading: "New Directions"

When you write on any of the following topics, be sure to work through the stages of the writing process in preparing your paragraph.

1. Using the ideas and examples you gathered by prereading, reading, and, with a pen or pencil, rereading "New Directions," write a summary of Maya Angelou's essay.

2. Write about someone who had many strikes against him or her but who succeeded. Be sure that you include some of the difficulties this person faced.

3. Maya Angelou says, "Each of us has the right and responsibility to assess the roads which lie ahead, and those over which we have traveled," and if an old road or a future road looks dark, we must "step off that road into another direction."

    Write a paragraph that agrees or disagrees with that statement.

    Begin by working with a group. First, discuss what you think the statement means. Then ask at least six questions about the statement. You may ask such questions as, "Does everyone have the courage or talent to choose a new road?" or "What keeps some people from choosing a new direction?" or "Do you know anyone who has done what Angelou advises?"

    Use the questions and answers to decide whether you want to agree or disagree with Angelou's statement.

4. There is an old saying, "When the going gets tough, the tough get going," and Mrs. Annie Johnson's story seems to prove the saying is true. She was faced with poverty, lack of job opportunities, raising two children alone, and yet through hard work, creativity, and determination, she triumphed.

    Write a paragraph that tells a story and proves the truth of another old saying. You can use a saying like, "Take time to stop and smell the roses," or "You never know what you can do until you try," or any other saying.

    Begin by freewriting about old sayings and what they mean to you. Then pick one that connects to your experience or the experience of someone you know. Use that saying as the focus of your paragraph.

Critical Thinking and Writing Topics

1. Mrs. Annie Johnson, the woman who found a "new direction" to success, identified a need (a fresh lunch for workers at the cotton gin and the lumber mill) and filled that need. Write about someone else who found success by meeting a need that others had not recognized. Before writing your paragraph, you may want to do a little research about a well-known inventor or entrepreneur.

2. If you could be a well-known inventor or entrepreneur, who would you choose to be? What do you admire about this person? What do you envy?

Name _____ Section _____

Peer Review Form for Writing from Reading

After you have written a draft version of your paragraph, let a writing partner read it. When your partner has completed the following form, discuss the comments. Then repeat the same process for your partner's paragraph.

This paragraph (circle one) (1) summarizes, (2) agrees or disagrees, (3) reacts to an idea connected to a reading selection.

I think this paragraph should include (circle one) (1) both the title and author of the reading selection, (2) the author of the reading selection, (3) neither the title nor the author of the reading selection.

The topic sentence of this paragraph is _____

_____

_____

The most effective part of this paragraph starts with the words _____

_____

One suggestion to improve this paragraph is to _____

_____

_____

Other comments on the paragraph: _____

_____

_____

_____

_____

_____

_____

_____

_____

_____

Reviewer's Name _____

WRITING FROM READING

> **Note:** Writing topics based on readings can be found at the end each selection.

Pet Therapy for Heart and Soul

Kerry Pechter

Pechter's essay shows how pet animals can affect our health. From the story of a pet parrot at a nursing home to the account of horseback riding for troubled adolescents, this essay explores how and why pet therapy can change people's lives.

Words You May Need to Know (Corresponding paragraph numbers are in parentheses.)

listless (2): indifferent, without energy

wolf whistle (2): a whistle that an admirer gives to an attractive person

alleviate (2): reduce or lessen

phenomenon (3): notable change

strife: (4): conflict

animal magnetism (5): the power that draws people to animals

reap (7): gain or gather

spouses (7): husbands and wives

siblings (7): brothers and sisters

biofeedback (8): a way to check a person's bodily functions

hypertension (9): high blood pressure

mortality and morbidity (11): death and disease

domesticating (14): taming

1   It's exercise hour at the Tacoma Lutheran Home in the state of Washington, and P.T., an exotic yellow-crested bird called a cockatiel, is having the time of his life. He's sitting on the foot of 81-year-old Ben Ereth, riding in circles when Ben pedals vigorously on an exercise bicycle. The bird likes it so much that if Mr. Ereth stops too soon, P.T. will squawk at him.

2   A bizarre sort of activity to find in a nursing home? Not at Tacoma Lutheran. Three years ago, the nursing home adopted an angora rabbit. Then a puppy. Then tropical birds. The home's elderly residents have taken to these animals with a passion. And, says Virginia Davis, director of resident services, the animals have breathed enthusiasm into what otherwise might have been a listless nursing home atmosphere. "The animals help in several ways," says Davis. "One of the cockatiels gives a wolf whistle whenever anyone passes its cage. That gives them an unexpected boost in morale. And the birds seem to alleviate the tension associated with exercise. They make exercise more acceptable and relaxing."

3   What's happening at Tacoma Lutheran is just one example of an increasingly popular phenomenon called pet therapy. Although humans have adopted pets for thousands of years, only recently have social scientists taken a close look at the nature of the relationship that people form with cats, dogs, and other "companion animals." At places like the Center for the Interaction of Animals and Society in Philadelphia and the Center for the Study of Human Animal Relationships and Environments (CENSHARE) in Minneapolis, they've discovered that there is something mutually therapeutic about these relationships. They say that pets

help relax us, help us communicate with each other, build our self-esteem, and comfort us when we're feeling down.

4   In fact, many people now believe that pets play a small but very significant role in determining how well, for example, a heart attack survivor recuperates, how a family handles domestic strife, whether a disturbed teenager grows up straight, or even whether a nursing home resident like Mr. Ereth enjoys and sticks to his daily exercise program. Pet animals, in short, may affect our health.

Animal Magnetism at Work

5   Pet therapists have put these capacities to work in a variety of ways. Pet therapy is very often used, for example, to combat the isolation and loneliness so common in nursing homes. At the Tacoma Lutheran Home, Davis has found that the pets help many residents break their customary silence. "Animals are a catalyst for conversation," she says. "Most people can remember a story from their past about a pet animal. And people are more comfortable talking to animals than they are to people. Sometimes a person who hasn't spoken for a long time, or one who had had a stroke and doesn't talk, will talk to an animal."

6   Animals also seem to draw everyone into the conversation. "Even in a nursing home, there are some people who are more attractive or responsive than others," says Phil Arkow, of the Humane Society of the Pike's Peak Region in Colorado, who drives a "Petmobile" to local nursing homes. "Human visitors try not to do it, but they inevitably focus on those who are more attractive. But animals don't make those distinctions. They focus on everyone equally."

7   A person doesn't have to live in a nursing home, however, in order to reap the benefits of a pet. Pets typically influence the communication that goes on between family members in a normal household. During a research project a few years ago, University of Maryland professor Ann Cain, Ph.D., discovered that pets help spouses and siblings express highly charged feelings. "When family members want to say something to each other that they can't say directly," Dr. Cain says, "they might say it to the pet and let the other person overhear it. That also lets the listener off the hook because he doesn't have to respond directly."

8   Though it's still in the experimental stage, researchers are discovering that watching or petting friendly animals—not only dogs and cats but almost any pet—can produce the kind of deep relaxation usually associated with meditation, biofeedback, and hypnosis. This kind of relaxing effect is so good that it can actually lower blood pressure. At the University of Pennsylvania's Center for the Interaction of Animals and Society, for instance, Dr. Katcher and Dr. Friedmann monitored the blood pressure of healthy children while the children were sitting quietly or reading aloud, either with or without a dog in the room. Their blood pressure was always lower when the dog was in the room.

9   The researchers went on to discover, remarkably, that looking at fish could temporarily reduce the blood pressure of patients with hypertension. In one widely reported study, they found that the systolic and diastolic pressure of people with high blood pressure dipped into the normal range when they gazed at an aquarium full of colorful tropical fish, green plants, and rocks for twenty minutes. This calming power of pets has found at least a few noteworthy applications. In Chicago, one volunteer from the Anti-Cruelty Society took an animal to a hospital and arranged for a surgical patient to be greeted by it when he awoke from anesthesia. "It's a comforting way to come back to reality," says one volunteer. "For children, pets can make a hospital seem safer. It's a reminder of home."

10   Animals may also have the power to soften the aggressive tendencies of disturbed adolescents. At Winslow Therapeutic Riding Unlimited, Inc, in Warwick, New York, where horseback riding is used to help handicapped children of all kinds, problem teenagers seem to behave differently when they're put on a horse. "These are kids who fight in school. Some of their fathers are alcoholics," says Mickey Pulis of the nonprofit facility. "But when they come here, they're different. When they groom and tack the horses, they learn about the gentle and caring side of life. The horse seems to act like an equalizer," she adds. "It doesn't care what reading level these kids are at. It accepts them as they are."

11   Ultimately, researchers like Dr. Friedmann believe that the companionship of pets can reduce a person's risk of dying from stress-related illnesses such as heart disease. "The leading causes of mortality and morbidity in the United States are stress-related or life-style-related," she says. "Pets, by decreasing the level of arousal and moderating the stress response, can slow the progression of those diseases or even prevent them."

Pets Are Comforting

12   But what is it about pets that make them capable of all this? And why do millions of people go to the trouble and expense of keeping them? Pet therapists offer several answers.

13   For one thing, animals don't talk back to us. Researchers have discovered that a person's blood pressure goes up whenever he talks to another person. But we talk to animals in a different way, often touching them at the same time, which minimizes stress.

14   Another theory holds that pets remind us of our ancestral link with other animals. "By domesticating an animal, man demonstrates his kinship to nature," Dr. Levinson once wrote. "A human being has to remain in contact with all of nature throughout his lifetime if he is to maintain good mental health." Dr. Corson, on the other hand, says that we love pets because they are perpetual infants. Human infants charm us, but they eventually grow up. Pets never do. They never stop being cuddly and dependent. Likewise, pets are faithful. "Pets can offer a relationship that is more constant than relationships with people," says Dr. Cain. "You can count on them."

15   Some argue that the most important ingredient in our relationship with animals is that we can touch them whenever we want to. "Having access to affectionate touch that is not related to sex is important," says Dr. Katcher. "If you want to touch another person, you can't always do it immediately. But with pets you can."

Topics for Writing from Reading: "Pet Therapy for Heart and Soul"

When you write on any of the following topics, be sure to work through the stages of the writing process in preparing your paragraph.

1. Do you have a pet? If so, write about the ways in which your pet improves your life. If you do not have a pet, write about why you do not have one.

2. Is pet therapy practiced in any nursing homes, children's hospitals, schools, or other institutions near you? Do a little research on Google or another search engine to discover how pets help people in your area. Then summarize your findings.

Computer

3. Working with a partner or group, make a list of what humans owe their pets. Once you have completed the list, work alone and write about the three most important things a pet owner must give to his or her pet.

Collaborate

Topics for Critical Thinking and Writing

1. Begin by working with a partner or group. Discuss the ways in which some pet owners relate to their pets. You may start with the trend toward pet costumes and pet contests. Then you may move on to other ways, such as agility competitions or dog shows, in which owners may go overboard in using a pet to fill an

Collaborate

emotional need. Then write individual paragraphs or essays about the benefits/damages of such relationships between people and pets.

2. Is America a pet-friendly country? Whether you feel that it is or is not, support your point with specific examples of the ways pets are treated.

NARRATION

Only Daughter

Sandra Cisneros

Sandra Cisneros, the child of a Mexican father and a Mexican-American mother, grew up in Chicago. She has worked as a teacher to high school dropouts and in other areas of education and the arts. A widely published writer of poetry and short stories, she has won many awards, but in this narrative, first published in 1990, she writes about a time when she craved a different kind of recognition: her father's approval.

Words You May Need to Know (Corresponding paragraph numbers are in parentheses.)

anthology (1): a collection of writing by various authors

mi'ja (3): my daughter

in retrospect (4): looking back

putter about (4): get busy in an ineffectual manner

philandering (5): unfaithful

woo (5): seek the affection of

bouts (6): periods

nostalgia (6): homesickness

flat (6): apartment

short-order cook (7): a cook specializing in food cooked quickly, on request, as in diners

fellowship (9): a grant of money for further study

Fellini (10): an Italian movie director who focused on strange characters and grotesque events

Chicano (11): an American of Mexican descent

colonia (11): neighborhood

1   Once, several years ago, when I was just starting out my writing career, I was asked to write my own contributor's note for an anthology I was part of. I wrote: "I am the only daughter in a family of six sons. *That* explains everything." Well, I've thought about that ever since, and yes, it explains a lot to me, but for the reader's sake I should have written: "I am the only daughter in a *Mexican* family of six sons." Or even: "I am the only daughter of a Mexican father and a Mexican-American mother." Or: "I am the only daughter of a working-class family of nine." All of these had everything to do with who I am today.

2   I was/am the only daughter and *only* a daughter. Being an only daughter in a family of six sons forced me by circumstance to spend a lot of time by myself because my brothers felt it beneath them to play with a *girl* in public. But that aloneness, that loneliness, was good for a would-be writer—it allowed me time to think and think, to imagine, to read and prepare myself.

3   Being only a daughter for my father meant my destiny would lead me to becoming someone's wife. That's what he believed. But when I was in the fifth grade and shared my plans for college with him, I was sure he understood. I remember my father saying, "*Que bueno, mi'ja*, that's good." That meant a lot to me, especially since my brothers thought the idea was hilarious. What I didn't realize was that my father thought college was good for girls—good for finding a husband. After four years in college and two more in graduate school, and still no husband, my father shakes his head even now and says I wasted all that education.

4   In retrospect, I'm lucky my father believed daughters were meant for husbands. It meant it didn't matter if I majored in something silly like English. After all, I'd find a nice professional eventually, right? This allowed me to putter about embroidering my little poems and stories without my father interrupting with so much as a "What's that you're writing?" But the truth is, I wanted him to interrupt. I wanted my father to understand what it was I was scribbling, to introduce me as "My only daughter, the writer." Not as "This is my only daughter. She teaches." *Es maestra*—teacher. Not even *profesora*.

5   In a sense, everything I have ever written has been for him, to win his approval even though I know my father can't read English words, even though my father's only reading includes the brown-ink *Esto* sports magazines from Mexico City and the bloody *!Alarma!* magazines that feature yet another sighting of *La Virgen of Guadalupe* on a tortilla or a wife's revenge on her philandering husband by bashing his skull in with a *molcajete* (a kitchen mortar made of volcanic rock). Or the *fotonovelas*, the little picture paperbacks with tragedy and trauma erupting from the characters' mouths in bubbles. My father represents, then, the public majority. A public who is uninterested in reading, and yet one whom I am writing about and for, and privately trying to woo.

6   When we were growing up in Chicago, we moved a lot because of my father. He suffered bouts of nostalgia. Then we'd have to let go our flat, store the furniture with mother's relatives, load the station wagon with baggage and bologna sandwiches, and head south. To Mexico City. We came back, of course. To yet another Chicago flat, another Chicago neighborhood, another Catholic school. Each time, my father would seek out the parish priest in order to get a tuition break, and complain or boast: "I have seven sons."

7   He meant *siente hijos*, seven children, but he translated it as "sons." "I have seven sons." To anyone who would listen. The Sears Roebuck employee who sold us the washing machine. The short-order cook where my father ate his ham-and-eggs breakfasts. "I have seven sons." As if he deserved a medal from the state. My papa. He didn't mean anything by that mistranslation, I'm sure. But somehow I could feel myself being erased. I'd tug my father's sleeve and whisper, "Not seven sons. Six! and one *daughter*."

8   When my oldest brother graduated from medical school, he fulfilled my father's dream that we study hard and use this—our heads, instead of this—our hands. Even now my father's hands are thick and yellow, stubbed by a history of hammer and nails and twine and coils and springs. "Use this," my father said, tapping his head, "and not this," showing us those hands. He always looked tired when he said it.

9   Wasn't college an investment? And hadn't I spent all those years in college? And if I didn't marry, what was it all for? Why would anyone go to college and then choose to be poor? Especially someone who had always been poor. Last year, after ten years of writing professionally, the financial rewards started to trickle in. My second National Endowment for the Arts Fellowship. A guest professorship at the University of California, Berkeley. My book, which sold to a major New York publishing house.

10   At Christmas, I flew home to Chicago. The house was throbbing, same as always; hot *tamales* and sweet *tamales* hissing in my mother's pressure cooker, and everybody—my mother, six brothers, wives, babies, aunts, cousins—talking too loud and at the same time, like in a Fellini film, because that's just how we are.

11   I went upstairs to my father's room. One of my stories had just been translated into Spanish and published in an anthology of Chicano writing, and I wanted to show it to him. Ever since he'd recovered from a stroke two years ago, my father likes to spend his leisure hours horizontally. And that's how I found him, watching a Pedro Infante movie on Galavision and eating rice pudding. There was a glass filmed with milk on the bedside table. There were several vials of pills and balled Kleenex. And on the floor, one black sock and a plastic urinal that I didn't want to look at but looked at anyway. Pedro Infante was about to burst into song, and my father was laughing. I'm not sure if it was because my story was translated into Spanish, or because it was published in Mexico, or perhaps because the story dealt with Tepeyac, the *colonia* my father was raised in and the house

he grew up in, but at any rate, my father punched the mute button on his remote control and read my story.

12   I sat on the bed next to my father and waited. He read it very slowly. As if he were reading each line over and over. He laughed at all the right places and read lines he liked out loud. He pointed and asked questions: "Is this so-and-so?" "Yes," I said. He kept reading. When he was finally finished, after what seemed like hours, my father looked up and asked: "Where can we get copies of this for the relatives?" Of all the wonderful things that happened to me last year, that was the most wonderful.

Topics for Writing from Reading: "Only Daughter" (Narration)

When you write on any of the following topics, be sure to work through the stages of the writing process in preparing your paragraph.

1. Have you ever wanted a parent's approval? If so, write about a time when you received or were denied that approval.

2. Write a narrative paragraph about a time when your place in your family (such as an only son, the oldest child, the youngest, one of three daughters, and so forth) gave you an advantage or put you at a disadvantage.

Collaborate

3. Cisneros writes of times when her father would say, "I have seven sons," even though he had six sons and one daughter. At such times, she says, "I could feel myself being erased." Working with a partner or a group, discuss what she meant by that comment. After your discussion, write individual paragraphs about a time when you felt as if you were "being erased."

4. Sandra Cisneros' father expected that his daughter would marry, and he believed that her college education was useful as a way for her to meet and marry "a nice professional." Have you ever imposed your own expectations on another person? For example, have you expressed disappointment when your child didn't make the best grades or wasn't interested in your favorite sport? Or have you (subtly) pressured a boyfriend or girlfriend to change goals or beliefs because they did not match yours? Write about a time when you tried to make someone what he or she is not.

5. Sandra Cisneros' essay includes many details about her life in opposing worlds: Spanish versus English, working-class background versus college-educated future, the traditionally male world of her father and six brothers versus a world with wider choices for women. Write your own story about an incident that placed you in a conflict between two worlds.

Topics for Critical Thinking and Writing

1. We live in a time when YouTube, Facebook, and other forms of instant communication can make anyone famous—at least for a short time. Do you believe that most people crave this kind of recognition? If so, why?

2. Sandra Cisneros' narrative is about the power of family ties. Although she had proved herself to be a successful student, writer, and independent woman, Cisneros still felt deprived of her father's approval. In your experience, is the need for approval from a person's peers stronger than the longing for parental approval? Explain.

NARRATION

Bullet to Blue Sky

Yesenia De Jesus

This essay, by Yesenia De Jesus, won First Place in the 2010 Pearson Education Writing Rewards Contest, a national competition for college students enrolled in basic composition classes. At the time, De Jesus was a Developmental English student at Palm Beach State College in Palm Beach Gardens, Florida. This essay is about an experience that changed her life, and thanks is extended to Professor Marilyn R. Tiedemann for encouraging Ms. De Jesus to enter the writing contest.

Words You May Need to Know (Corresponding paragraph numbers are in parentheses.)

flippantly (2): treating serious things lightly

feudal (4): a system of the Middle Ages in which powerful landowners ruled peasants with few rights

Al Capone, Bonnie and Clyde (5): Al Capone was a famous American gangster of the 1920s; Bonne and Clyde were well-known bank robbers of the same period.

double-dutched (6): verb form of jump-rope style

1   The sun was in the process of its morning stretch. While the residents of gated communities came alive to be greeted by the tropical heat of South Florida, the stragglers of the universe awoke to the sound of a 9mm dispersing its gunpowder to the blue sky. The ghetto houses that sheltered these citizens were painted different colors; some exposed faded paint, and others told stories in graffiti, inspired by gang artists marking their territories. Roll bars protected the windows covered by filthy bed sheets that not even dogs would lie on. The lanky, dark-haired girl lay in her bed twisting and turning, trying to catch a cool wave from the ceiling fan that spun and thumped overhead all night. She always heard the same dogs barking; her ears still rang from the sound of that gun. She still felt the warm, thin blood that stained her hands. She still felt a sharp, pounding pain along her left side; for every breath she took, the pain reminded her that she was human. She had witnessed many shootings before; she had seen more blood in her days. Why was this shooting any different? It was because for the first time she was the victim. I understood her pain, for I was that girl.

2   It all started with Mr. Tangye in the fall of 2004. He was an inspiring math teacher, who convinced me that I had more to offer this world than I thought. As the bell rang at Conniston Middle School, the students and I marched like zombies to our classes. I passed through the dark hallways of vandalized lockers with torn papers and ripped books scattered over the ground like a dump. I made my way past the miserable teachers and devilish students. The administrators surrounded the hallways like a S.W.A.T. team, commanding everyone to go to class. I walked into Mr. Tangye's math class; he had a bright, white smile that hurt my eyes every time I looked at him. Before I could make it to my seat, Mr. Tangye handed me a paper that itched my fingers; it was a math test. I stared at the test, and I begged my brain to wake up! The other kids shuffled the paper back and forth on top of their desks or used it as a pillow on which to lay their heads. I secretly tried my best at every problem and flippantly turned it in.

3   As the bell rang, I dashed for the exit. I swiftly dropped off my homework, but Mr. Tangye caught me and pulled me aside to show me my test. He said I was the only one who had passed the test. Mr. Tangye revealed my grade to me; I was on the border line of failing the class. I could pass. I listened to every word he said because I was tired of being perceived as an idiot.

4   As I finished out the rest of the day, all I could think about was whether to study or not to study. I hated being stuck between a world that offered happiness and stability, whose proverb was "anything is possible" and a world that followed the theory of Charles Darwin's "survival of the fittest." My world struggled for everything—money, power, respect, even for the last

piece of fried chicken. My world had an underground feudal system to follow with rules to be respected, lines not to be crossed. Although this world was violent, senseless, crazy, it was my world. This unmerciful, savage world … I was comfortable in it. I felt super-glued to this world, I felt guilty leaving it behind, like a crackhead quitting dope. I silenced that voice that begged to stay. I was going to make it out of my world of hardship and struggle and bullets.

5   When I got home, I was greeted by a warm aroma from the kitchen, where I always found my mother. We greeted each other in our usual exchange. After I gave my mother a brief overview of how school went, I rushed to my room to study. I was tired of the struggles, fight, problems, which by birth, I did not deserve. I was going to be somebody; I was going to do something with my life. I was not going to be another Al Capone or Bonnie with a Clyde. I was going to be somebody the way God intended. I was going to earn a living the right, clean way, but in order to be somebody, I needed an education. I would have to get an "A" on my chapter test in Mr. Tangye's math class. I had to do it. I would!

6   Four gruesome weeks passed. I slept, ate, and studied. The morning of the test, I woke up early. I studied some more, for I wanted to be alert in case an unusual math problem was on the test. I left early that day to ask a few questions. Usually, I took a longer route to school to avoid crossing enemy lines, but I rushed through a shortcut. The shortcut led me to the back of the school, where boys played basketball and girls double-dutched after school, but the recess court was empty. No one stood in the courtyard but me. My eyes locked on the formula sheet I memorized. Suddenly, I heard a familiar sound as gunshots sliced the morning air; tires screeched. As I walked toward the school build-ing, I felt something drizzle down the side of my torso. I grabbed my shirt; something slightly tickled me. It was wet. It was not sweat; it was blood. It happened so quickly. I threw my paper and books, bloody from my handprint, on the ground. I screamed at the top of my lungs, not because I had been shot, but because I knew I could not take my math test, the test I had studied so damn hard for. My memory faded before I collapsed. A former fire rescuer spotted me on the ground and got help.

7   As I lay in my bed at home, I exposed my secrets to myself. I tried to crawl around my brain; I wanted a reason why God led me to this path. I was not connected to these savages who shot me. These thugs just wandered around the neighborhood trying to find an ordinary person to become a victim, whose fate would carry a dark message.

8   When I was shot, it did not overpower my life; it empowered my spirit. As I got out of bed, I tried to convince myself I should stay there, but I could not find any good reason. My injuries were three-days fresh, but I was determined to make that math test. I reached to find the strength from deep within my soul to move. The pain gripped my side like five hundred needles repeatedly stabbing my ribs. I grabbed a chair so deeply that I bent my nails backwards. My arms and legs shook. I screamed with every movement I made, yet the agonizing pain only intensified. I gripped my book as I walked out the door. Slow steps minimized the pain. I gave my mother a kiss as the bus approached the curb. She touched my arm and reassured me I could make up the test after I healed completely. I objected because I was ready for this test.

9   I told my mom that morning that I had tried to better myself. This neighborhood, this ghetto, this hardship-world I lived in had tried to bring me down; it had tried to kill me. The shooting event that took place seven years ago answered the one question I had been asking myself since I was old enough to comprehend the world around me. Through the support of my mother and the leap-of-faith decisions I made, and even by beating death, God kept me alive to respond to a call. God wants me to be somebody. Even though I am excelling in life today, I will never forget who I am, where I came from, and how hard I have worked to get to this point. God gave me life again, for just like that morning in the courtyard, I stood out to those gang bangers because I was born to stand out. I will always stand out.

10   I dropped my coins into the bus depositor, found a seat, and quietly, painfully moaned along the ride. My mother waved to me as the bus drove off. She was staring at me with a satisfied expression upon her face, for she knew she was raising a fighter, a winner, and a believer. She was raising a somebody.

Topics for Writing from Reading: "Bullet to Blue Sky" (Narration)

When you write on any of the following topics, be sure to work through the stages of the writing process in preparing your paragraph.

1. What does the title of this essay mean? There is definitely a bullet in this story, but what does the reference to blue sky mean? How does the "blue sky" connect to the changes in Yesenia De Jesus' life? You can consider the changes that took place in one day or the changes that De Jesus *chose* to make before and after that day.

2. De Jesus writes vivid descriptions of her neighborhood, her school, and her suffering. These descriptions make her story convincing and hold a reader's attention. Write about a time when (a) you were forced to make a choice that could change your life or (b) you suffered great pain. Be sure to use sense details to enhance your narrative.

3. De Jesus writes that she "was going to make it out" of her "world of hardship and bullets," and she explains how a bullet "empowered" her spirit. Write a story about an incident that caused you to feel (a) empowered or (b) powerless.

Topics for Critical Thinking and Writing

1. Do a little research about a well-known person who made his or her way from poverty, illness, or abuse to a life that held meaning and emotional peace. Find several accounts of the transformation in the person's life. Then write a narrative of this person's journey from a dark past to a powerful present.

2. Begin this assignment with a partner or group. De Jesus' essay was based on the topic, "Write about a true experience that changed your life." Working with a partner or group, share at least one personal experience that changed you. Then answer any questions the member(s) of the group may ask, and be ready to provide details. After each person has shared his or her experiences, write separate narratives on the life-changing incident.

Collaborate

DESCRIPTION

The War Within (Excerpt)

David C. Botti

David C. Botti joined the Marine reserves while he was in college. Shortly after the September 11, 2001, attack on the World Trade Center, Botti's Marine unit was mobilized. After nearly a year of duty in the United States, Botti's unit was sent home, and he began a new life in New York City. However, after just a few weeks in the city, he was called to duty in Iraq. In this excerpt from his New York Times *article, Botti describes the day he was given his orders.*

Words You May Need to Know (Corresponding paragraph numbers are in parentheses.)

mobilize (1): to become prepared for war

contemplate (1): to consider carefully and thoughtfully

deployment (1): the time a soldier spends in action

infantry (3): the combat arm of units trained to fight on foot

1   After just one month of city living, the call to mobilize came. I was given the necessary information. And in an even tone, I replied that I understood, closing my eyes in my cubicle to contemplate the new phase of life I was entering. Word traveled quickly through the office that day. Friends and strangers approached me with words of encouragement and admiration. I left the office hours later, carrying a small flag signed by my coworkers that I would carry in the top flap of my pack throughout my deployment.

2   The city was beautiful my last night on the street, the chill making me appreciate the inviting warmth in a corner café or the familiar rock of a heated subway car. I headed south on Park Avenue, February numbing my hand as I held the cell phone to my ear. There was a marathon of calls through chattering teeth. Friends and family were confused, wanted to know more than I knew myself. Then I found a park bench and sat alone for the first time since the news came. I tried to remember everything I could, collecting memories for the times ahead.

3   I watched the day end, the people returning home or preparing for a night out. When it got late, I headed home, wishing I could line up every person in the city, shake each one's hand, say, "Good-bye, I've had a good time, maybe I can come back again some day." I spent the bus ride home that night consoling my mother by cell phone, telling her lies as I tried to persuade her they would never send a reserve infantry company into Iraq; we would only be asked to guard the supply lines throughout Kuwait. She didn't believe me, but pretended to.

4   After I hung up, a woman sitting in front of me turned and said she had heard my whole conversation. She promised to pray for me.

Topics for Writing from Reading: "The War Within" (Description)

When you write on any of the following topics, be sure to work through the stages of the writing process in preparing your paragraph.

1. Write about a time when you received surprising news (bad or good), and describe your immediate actions and reactions. If your instructor agrees, work with a partner to gather details. Once you have selected an incident, ask your partner to interview you. Your partner can ask questions such as the following:

   What exactly was the news?
   How was it delivered to you?
   Do you remember any sensations as you received the news?

   Your partner can write down your answers. Once you have been interviewed, trade places with your partner. Each partner should be prepared with five or more questions before the interview process begins.

   After both interviews, exchange the notes from the interviews so that each person can use the details to develop his or her paragraph.

2. On a life-changing day, Botti walks alone through New York City, noting how beautiful it is. Describe a time when you walked somewhere, alone or with

others, and suddenly felt the beauty of the place. Use the details of the place to explain your reaction.

3. Botti's description includes many references to telephones. For example, the orders to mobilize come on the phone at his office; later, he deals with "a marathon of calls" from friends and family as he walks in the city, his cell phone to his ear. Also, he consoles his mother by cell phone as he sits on a bus. Describe a dramatic moment in your life in which a phone or phones played a significant role.

4. An emotional moment in this description came when a stranger overheard Botti's conversation with his mother (in which he tries to comfort her about his deployment). The stranger promised to pray for him. Write about a time when you received unexpected sympathy or kindness from a stranger. Describe the circumstances, the act of kindness, and your reaction.

5. On the day Botti describes, he is saying goodbye to people, a place, and a new life he had barely begun. Describe a significant time in your life when you said goodbye. You may have been leaving a place, ending a relationship, giving up a dream, or breaking a dangerous addiction.

Topics for Critical Thinking and Writing

1. David Botti writes of the turmoil in his heart and mind as he prepared to leave for military duty in Iraq. Those who returned from such duties often faced the continuing stresses of battle (their own "war within"). Before you write on this topic, do a little research into post traumatic stress disorder (PTSD). Then describe what the symptoms of PTSD feel like.

2. When you think of war, what words come into your mind? Freewrite about these words until you are out of descriptions. Then see if you can find a cluster of those terms that reveal your attitude toward war. Then write about that attitude.

DESCRIPTION

Deep Cold

Verlyn Klinkenborg

Verlyn Klinkenborg writes a column called "The Rural Life" for The New York Times. *His regular descriptions of nature's beauty and harshness rely on exact details and sense descriptions. As you read "Deep Cold," note how the author's language draws the reader into the world of an icy day.*

Words You May Need to Know (Corresponding paragraph numbers are in parentheses.)

gnashing (1): grinding or grating
muted (1): softened, made less ringing or resonant
rime (2): white frost
reservoirs (3): a place where water is stored for future use

brood (3): think deeply and with gloom
current (3): stream of water
paradox (3): a situation or statement seemingly impossible but also true
trepidation (3): agitation or fear

1   If deep cold made a sound, it would be the scissoring and gnashing of a skater's blades against hard gray ice or the screeching the snow sets up when you walk across it in the blue light of afternoon. The sound may be the stamping of feet at bus stops and train stations, or the way the almost perfect clarity of the audible world on an icy day is muted by scarves and mufflers pulled up over the face and around the ears.

2   But the true sound of deep cold is the sound of the wind. Monday morning, on the streets of Cambridge, Massachusetts, the wind chill approached fifty below zero. A stiff northwest wind rocked in the trees and snatched at cars as they idled at the curb. A rough rime had settled over that old-brick city the day before, and now the wind was sanding it smooth. It was cold of Siberian or Arctic intensity, and I could feel a kind of claustrophobia settling in all over Boston. People went about their errands, only to cut them short instantly, turning backs to the gust and fleeing for cover.

3   It has been just slightly milder in New York. Furnace repairmen and oil-truck drivers are working on the memory of two hours' sleep. Swans in the smaller reservoirs brood on the ice, and in the swamps that line the railroad tracks in Dutchess County, you can see how the current was moving when the cold snap brought it to a halt. The soil in windblown fields looks—and is—iron hard. It's all a paradox, a cold that feels absolutely rigid but which nonetheless seeps through ill-fitting windows, between clapboards, and along uninsulated pipe chases. People listen superstitiously to the sounds in their heating ducts, to the banging of their radiators, afraid of silence. They turn the keys in their cars with trepidation. It's an old world this week.

Topics for Writing from Reading: "Deep Cold" (Description)

When you write on any of the following topics, be sure to work through the stages of the writing process in preparing your paragraph.

1. Write about heat. You can call the heat "extreme heat," "deep heat," or use another term to sum up the heat you are describing. Concentrate on using sense words to explain the power and impact of this heat.

2. Klinkenborg describes the negative effects of deep cold. Write a description of the positive effects and the beauty of deep cold.

3. If your earliest years were spent in a warm climate, write about your first experience of cold weather.

4. Describe your experience of some type of extreme weather: a flood, a tornado, a hurricane, a forest fire, a sandstorm, and so forth.

5. Describe some element of nature (such as snow or surf) to someone who has never experienced it.

Topics for Critical Thinking and Writing

Collaborate

1. Certain descriptions become so overused that they are called "clichés." Clichés include phrases like a "state-of-the-art" entertainment center, or a party dress "to die for." Working with a group, compile a list of some popular clichés. Then, working alone, write about one cliché. Explain how it is used today. Include what the words of the cliché are used to describe, and give several examples of this usage. (For instance, a dress may be something "to die for," but some people refer to "a vacation to die for," and others talk of "a pizza to die for.") Then suggest better, more specific words to describe some of the items now linked to the cliché.

2. Choose a product you like. It can be a specific food, a brand of sneakers, a model of car, and so forth. Write a paragraph to describe this product, and be sure to use sensory descriptions.

ILLUSTRATION

A Different Mirror (Excerpt)

Ronald Takaki

Ronald Takaki, born in Honolulu, is a historian known for his books on history, race, and multi-culturalism. The following excerpt is from his book A Different Mirror. *In the book, Takaki argues that in studying America's history, we must study all the groups who have created America so that we "see ourselves in a different mirror." This excerpt focuses on specific details that support the idea of America's diversity.*

Words You May Need to Know

ethnic diversity: variety of people, races, and cultures

discerned: recognized, perceived

Ellis Island: an island off the shore of New York City, where many immigrants first landed in America

Angel Island: an island off San Francisco

Chinatown, Harlem, South Boston, the Lower East Side (of New York City): places associated with a variety of ethnic groups and races

derived: originated from

Forty-Niners: people who joined the Gold Rush of 1849, when gold was discovered in California

vaqueros: cowboys

The signs of America's ethnic diversity can be discerned across the continent: Ellis Island, Angel Island, Chinatown, Harlem, South Boston, the Lower East Side, places with Spanish names like Los Angeles and San Antonio or Indian names like Massachusetts and Iowa. Much of what is familiar in America's cultural landscape actually has ethnic origins. The Bing cherry was developed by an early Chinese immigrant named Ah Bing. American Indians were cultivating corn, tomatoes, and tobacco long before the arrival of Columbus. The term *okay* was derived from the Choctaw word *oke*, meaning "it is so." There is evidence indicating that the name *Yankee* came from Indian terms for the English—from *eankke* in Cherokee and *Yankwis* in Delaware. Jazz and blues as well as rock and roll have African-American origins. The "Forty-Niners" of the Gold Rush learned mining techniques from the Mexicans; American cowboys acquired herding skills from Mexican *vaqueros* and adopted their range terms—such as *lariat* from *la reata*, *lasso* from *lazo*, and *stampede* from *estampida*. Songs like "God Bless America," "Easter Parade," and "White Christmas" were written by a Russian-Jewish immigrant named Israel Baline, more popularly known as Irving Berlin.

Topics for Writing from Reading: "A Different Mirror" (Illustration)

When you write on any of the following topics, be sure to work through the stages of the writing process in preparing your paragraph.

1. Interview three people in your class. Ask each to tell you about his or her family background. Before you begin, prepare a list of at least six questions such as "Were you born in this country?" and "Do you know how long your family has been in America?" Use the answers as the basis for a paragraph on diversity in your classroom. You may discover a wide range of backgrounds or a similarity of backgrounds. In either case, you have details for a paragraph about your classmates and their origins.

Collaborate

2. Write about the many foods that are considered American but that really originated in another country or culture. Give specific examples.

3. Write about some of the place names in America that came from one or more other languages. You might, for example, write about only Spanish place names

and group them according to the states where these places are located. On the other hand, you could write about names from several languages and group them into Spanish names, Native American names, French names, and so forth.

4. Write about what one ethnic group has contributed to American life and culture. You can use specific examples of contributions to language, music, dance, food, clothing, and customs.

Topics for Critical Thinking and Writing

Computer

1. Takaki gives examples of words Americans use, like *Yankee*, that originated in another language. Write about words or expressions that Americans use that originated in another language. You can visit *http://en.wikipedia.org/wiki/Lists_ of_English_loanwords_by_country_or_language_of_origin/*. Here you will find lists of words from such origins as African, Chinese, Hawaiian, Indian, Native American, Italian, and Korean languages. In your own words, give examples of at least three American words that have interesting origins. Be sure to click on each word in the list for interesting information about the word's original meaning, history, and present-day meaning.

2. Write about your name. It might be Patrick Andrew DeLucca. Look carefully at each part of it. Is any part of your name, such as *Andrew*, a common name in your family? Do you know if you were named after a particular relative or ancestor? Is "DeLucca" part of an Italian or Spanish heritage? What nationality tends to choose the name "Patrick"? Once you have done a little research about the meaning of your name and asked family members about the personal reasons for its choice, write about your findings.

ILLUSTRATION

Meet the Neighbors

Peter Lovenheim

In this article published in Parade *magazine, Peter Lovenheim talks about the power of a community in which neighbors know each other and concludes that "If ever there was ever a time to break down the barriers that separate us and take advantage of the potential for companionship, it is now."*

Words You May Need to Know (Corresponding paragraph numbers are in parentheses.)

accelerated (3): increased in speed
potlucks (7): a meal in which participants bring food to be shared
decentralized (7): separated

radius (7): limited area
stockade fences (10): an enclosure of upright fences

1   When Jodi Lee, a librarian, bought a home in 2004 near downtown Columbus, Ohio, neighbors told her about "Wednesdays on the Porch." From the first week after Memorial Day through early fall, residents take turns hosting a weekly porch party for their neighbors. It is a way to get to know one another, exchange information, and keep in touch. Jodi was encouraged to host one. She followed the advice and, a few weeks later, on her own front porch, met her neighbor Bill Sieloff. Four years later, he became her husband. "The wedding was almost like another Wednesday on the Porch," Jodi recalls, "so many neighbors were there."

2   Doug Motz, one of the founders, estimates that since these Wednesdays began eight years ago, about 75 different families have held more than 130 porch parties in the neighborhood. "It's a time for sharing—opinions on new restaurants, how to find good painters and home repair people—but it's primarily social," Motz says. "And the nice thing is, the hosts don't have to worry about cleaning up inside."

3   New traditions like these are a welcome exception to the trend favoring privacy over community, which goes back to the post-World War II flight to the suburbs. According to social scientists, neighborhood ties today are less than half as strong as they were in the 1950s. Recently, the trend has accelerated with suburban "McMansions," huge houses set back from wide streets with big backyards that further isolate neighbors from one another.

4   It was a tragedy ten years ago on my own street, in a suburb of Rochester, New York, that got me thinking about how we Americans live. One evening, a neighbor shot and killed his wife and then himself. Their two middle-school-age children ran screaming into the night. Soon, the kids moved in with their grandparents, and the house was put up for sale.

5   But life on our street seemed little affected. Asking around, I learned that hardly anyone had known the family well. In fact, few people on the street knew anyone more than casually. In an age of discount air travel, cheap long distance, and the Internet, when we can create community anywhere, why is it that we often don't know the people who live next door?

6   By not knowing our neighbors, we lose a crucial safety net. We also lose social and economic benefits: the ability, in a pinch, to borrow a cup of sugar or a dash of vanilla instead of making another trip to the supermarket, and the simple pleasure of daily, unplanned contact with people with whom we have become friends. Bucking the decades-long trend toward isolation, people around the country are finding new ways to break down the barriers that separate neighbor from neighbor.

7   In Reno, Nevada, during the last week of June, residents will celebrate their annual "Get to Know Your Neighbor Week." It's a celebration that has generated more than sixty-five simultaneous potlucks with thousands of participants. "We've created a decentralized model where neighbors invite neighbors from a three-block radius," Richard Flyer explains. "It's self-organizing; we provide a downloadable form for people to put the names and addresses on, and then everyone is invited to bring food."

8   Through these gatherings, Flyer says, neighbors have noted seniors among them who needed companionship and young people who lacked enough supervision. "These individuals were kind of invisible before," he says. "I know of two women who were recently widowed, and through the neighborhood gatherings, they connected with families for support. Another senior was alone, and neighbors helped him with shopping and landscaping."

9   When new people move into Hollywood/Grant park, a district of modest, single-family homes about two miles from downtown Portland, Oregon, the first thing Dennis Maxwell does is give them a homemade map of the neighborhood. It shows locations of families, names, children, pets, telephone numbers, and work numbers for emergencies. The effect has been to draw neighbors closer together. "Now we exchange child care, take care of mail and newspapers, and water plants during vacations," Maxwell says.

10   In Albany, New York's Center Square/Hudson Park, owners of six adjoining brick row houses have traded a bit of privacy for a lot of beautiful gardening. "Our tiny backyards were really shaded from the stockade fences between each unit," recalls one of the owners, Kathryn Sikule. "You really couldn't grow too much." Over time, neighbors agreed to take down their fences and merge gardens. Stone footpaths set among the joint garden now allow each resident access to the fully landscaped space and an uninterrupted view of a sunny garden scene. The result, Sikule says, has "brought us all together as a community."

11   In the U.S. today, more than 30 million people live alone. Add to that an economic recession that often puts travel and entertainment out of reach. If there was ever a time to break down the barriers that separate us and take advantage of the potential for companionship, it is now. As a woman from Jackson, Mississippi, who identified herself only as Pamela, wrote to me, "If we all cared about our neighbors, we could change the world one street at a time."

Topics for Writing from Reading "Meet the Neighbors" (Illustration)

When you write on any of the following topics, be sure to work through the stages of the writing process in preparing your work.

1. Write about two or more of your neighbors who have been part of your life. They can be good neighbors, bad neighbors, or both.

2. Have you ever been a good or bad neighbor? Write about your interaction with one neighbor. Illustrate this connection with specific examples of your relationship with this neighbor.

3. Would you prefer to remain detached from your neighbors? If so, explain your reasons with examples.

Collaborate

4. Begin this assignment by brainstorming with a group. Think about the many reasons why people in the suburbs do not spend much time getting to know their neighbors. For example, long working hours may have cut residents' time at home. Also consider what changes in daily life have made it easier to connect with people and establish friendships outside the neighborhood.

Topics for Critical Thinking and Writing

1. Think about one television series that depicted a happy family living in a suburb. Do a little research on the setting, characters, and plots typical of this series. Then write about the appeal of this series and how realistically it described life in the suburbs.

2. Peter Lowenheim writes that in our country today, "more than thirty million people live alone." What do you value more? Your privacy or your connection to others? Also consider why privacy has become an issue in recent years.

PROGRESS

Coming Over

Russell Freedman

In this selection from Russell Freedman's book, Immigrant Kids, *he describes the difficult and often frightening process European immigrants of the 1880s to the 1920s endured when they looked for a better life in America. From the dark conditions of the Atlantic crossing to the terror of the examinations at Ellis Island, the immigrants found strength in their dreams and in their first glimpse of the Statue of Liberty.*

Words You May Need to Know (Corresponding paragraph numbers are in parentheses.)

impoverished (1): poor
fervent (1): passionate
penniless (2): without any money
foul-smelling (3): having an offensive odor
lounges (3): public sitting rooms
New World (5): the Western Hemisphere
the Narrows (5): a narrow channel of water between Brooklyn and Staten Island in New York City
foredeck (6): the forward part of the deck of a ship
jabbered conversation (6): rapid talk that can't be understood

din (6): loud noise
veered (7): swerved
scowling (7): frowning
maze (10): a confusing network of interconnecting pathways
nationality (12): the country a person belongs to
flustered (12): nervous and upset
rigorous (13): harsh, severe
momentarily (13): for a minute
indomitable (13): not able to be overcome
teeming (14): crowded, filled to overflowing

1   In the years around the turn of the twentieth century, immigration to America reached an all-time high. Between 1880 and 1920, twenty-three million immigrants arrived in the United States. They came mainly from countries of Europe, especially from impoverished towns and villages in southern and eastern Europe. The one thing they had in common was a fervent belief that in America life would be better.

2   Most of these immigrants were poor. Somehow they managed to scrape together enough money to pay for their passage to America. Many immigrant families arrived penniless. Others had to make the journey in stages. Often the father came first, found work, and sent for his family later. Immigrants usually crossed the Atlantic as steerage passengers. Reached by steep, slippery stairways, the steerage lay deep down in the hold of the ship. It was occupied by passengers paying the lowest fare.

3   Men, women, and children were packed into dark, foul-smelling compartments. They slept in narrow bunks stacked three high. They had no showers, no lounges, and no dining rooms. Food served from huge kettles was dished into dinner pails provided by the steamship company. Because steerage conditions were crowded and uncomfortable, passengers spent as much time as possible up on deck.

4   The voyage was an ordeal, but it was worth it. They were on their way to America. The great majority of immigrants landed in New York City at America's biggest port. They never forgot their first glimpse of the Statue of Liberty. Edward Corsi, who later became United States Commissioner of Immigration, was a ten-year-old Italian immigrant when he sailed into New York Harbor in 1907. Here is how he later described the experience:

5   My first impression of the New World will always remain etched in my memory, particularly that hazy October morning when I first saw Ellis Island. The steamer *Florida*, fourteen days out of Naples, filled to capacity with 1600 natives of Italy, had weathered one of the worst storms in our captain's memory, and glad we were, both children and grown-ups, to leave the open sea and come at last through the Narrows into the bay.

6   My mother, my stepfather, my brother Giuseppe, and my two sisters, Liberta and Helvetia, all of us together, happy that we had come through the storm safely, clustered on the foredeck for fear of separation and looked with wonder on this miraculous land of our dreams. Giuseppe and I held tight to Stepfather's hands while Liberta and Helvetia clung to Mother. Passengers all about us were crowding against the rail. Jabbered conversation, sharp cries, laughs, and cheers—a steadily rising din filled the air. Mothers and fathers lifted up babies so that they too could see, off to the left, the Statue of Liberty.

7   Finally, the *Florida* veered to the left, turning northward into the Hudson River, and now the incredible buildings of lower Manhattan came very close to us. The officers of the ship went striding up and down the decks shouting orders and directions and driving the immigrants before them. Scowling and gesturing, they pushed and pulled the passengers, herding us into separate groups as though we were animals. A few moments later, we came to our dock, and the long journey was over.

8   But the journey was not yet over. Before they could be admitted to the United States, immigrants had to pass through Ellis Island, which became the nation's chief immigrant processing center. There they would be questioned and examined. Those who could not pass all the exams would be detained; some would be sent back to Europe. And so their arrival in America was filled with great anxiety. Among the immigrants, Ellis Island was known as "Heartbreak Island."

9   When their ship docked at a Hudson River pier, the immigrants had numbered identity tags pinned to their clothing. Then they were herded onto special ferryboats that carried them to Ellis Island. Officials hurried them along, shouting "Quick! Run! Hurry!" in half a dozen languages.

10   Filing into an enormous inspection hall, the immigrants formed long lines separated by iron railings that made the hall look like a great maze. Now the examinations began. First the immigrants were examined by two doctors of the United States Health Service. One doctor looked for physical and mental abnormalities. When a case aroused suspicion, the immigrant

received a chalk mark on the right shoulder for further inspection: L for lameness, H for heart, X for mental defects, and so on.

11   The second doctor watched for contagious and infectious diseases. He looked especially for infections of the scalp and at the eyelids for symptoms of trachoma, a blinding disease. Since trachoma caused more than half of all medical detentions, this doctor was greatly feared. He stood directly in the immigrant's path. With a swift movement, he would grab the immigrant's eyelid, pull it up, and peer beneath it. If all was well, the immigrant was passed on.

12   Those who failed to get past both doctors had to undergo a more thorough medical exam. The others moved on to the registration clerk, who questioned them with the aid of an interpreter: What is your name? Your nationality? Your occupation? Can you read and write? Have you ever been in prison? How much money do you have with you? Where are you going? Some immigrants were so flustered that they could not answer. They were allowed to sit and rest and try again. About one immigrant out of every five or six was detained for additional examinations or questioning. The writer Angelo Pellegrini recalled his own family's detention at Ellis Island:

13   We lived there for three days—Mother and we five children, the youngest of whom was three years old. Because of the rigorous physical examination that we had to submit to, particularly of the eyes, there was this terrible anxiety that one of us might be rejected. And if one of us was, what would the rest of the family do? My sister was indeed momentarily rejected; she had been so ill and had cried so much that her eyes were absolutely bloodshot, and mother was told, "Well, we can't let her in." But fortunately, Mother was an indomitable spirit and finally made them understand that if her child had a few hours' rest and a little bite to eat, she would be all right. In the end, we did get through.

14   Most immigrants passed through Ellis Island in about one day. Carrying all their worldly possessions, they left the examination hall and waited on the dock for the ferry that would take them to Manhattan, a mile away. Some of them still faced journeys overland before they reached their final destination. Others would head directly for the teeming immigrant neighborhoods of New York City.

Topics for Writing from Reading: "Coming Over" (Process)

When you write on any of the following topics, be sure to follow the stages of the writing process in preparing your paragraph.

1. Travel involves a number of processes. One of the most common today is the process of the security check at the airport. Using clear steps and specific details, describe this process to a reader who has never experienced it.

2. Write about the steps involved in another process that involves some local, state, or national agency. For example, you can write about the steps involved in obtaining a driver's license, paying for a traffic ticket, getting a marriage license, applying for a green card, or obtaining a passport.

3. Write about a process that was new for you. You might write about the first time you registered for college classes, went through Customs in a foreign country, prepared for surgery, or took a medical test that required local or general anesthesia.

4. As it was in the late nineteenth and early twentieth centuries, America today is filled with immigrants. If you began your life in another country, trace the steps of your first entry into (and first glimpse of) America.

Topics for Critical Thinking and Writing

Computer

1. Using Russell Freedman's steps as a guideline, write your own version of the journey of the immigrants from Southern and Eastern Europe to New York City. Make this version your own by adding details about Ellis Island you find in research. For such details, try these sources:

   http://www.nps.gov/elis/ (This address uses "elis" instead of "ellis.")
   http://www.history.com/minisites/ellisisland/

   Your details can include two or more photographs of different stages of the journey. For selected images of Ellis Island and of immigration, see this source:

   http://www.loc.gov/rr/print/list/070_immi.html

2. In Freedman's essay, he cites the experience of Edward Corsi, who came to America at age eleven. Corsi describes the joy of the immigrants as they held their children up to see the first glimpse of the Statue of Liberty. To them, the statue seemed the first glimpse of the "miraculous land of our dreams."

   Think about what a specific practice, process, or ceremony symbolizes about America. Then write about the power that this symbol has for you.

PROCESS

How to Stop a Car with No Brakes

Joshua Piven and David Borgenicht

Have you ever seen a movie in which a driver suddenly realizes that his or her car has no brakes? Usually, this scene is intensified by the setting: a winding mountain road or a railroad crossing with a train in sight. Such scenes tap into a universal fear of losing control. In "How to Stop a Car with No Brakes," Joshua Piven and David Borgenicht tell the reader what to do if the movie scene becomes reality.

Note that this piece from their instructional book, The Worst-Case Scenario Handbook, *is a numbered set of directions. It is not an essay, but it can serve an a springboard for directional process papers.*

Words You May Need to Know (Corresponding paragraph numbers are in parentheses.)

fail-safe (4): automatically compensating for a mistake or a failure

sheer (10): absolute, steep

1. Begin pumping the brake pedal and keep pumping it. You may be able to build up enough pressure in the braking system to slow down a bit or even stop completely. If you have anti-lock brakes, you do not normally pump them—but if your brakes have failed, this may work.
2. Do not panic—relax and steer the car smoothly. Cars will often safely corner at speeds much higher than you realize or are used to driving. The rear of the car may slip; steer evenly, being careful not to over-correct.
3. Shift the car into the lowest gear possible and let the engine and transmission slow you down.
4. Pull the emergency brake—but not too hard. Pulling too hard on the emergency brake will cause the rear wheels to lock, and the car to spin around. Use even, constant pressure. In most cars, the emergency brake (also known as the hand brake or parking brake) is cable-operated and serves as a fail-safe brake that should still work even when the rest of the braking system has failed. The car should slow down and, in combination with the lower gear, will eventually stop.

5. If you are running out of room, try a "bootlegger's turn." Yank the emergency break hard while turning the wheel a quarter turn in either direction—whichever is safer. This will make the car spin 180 degrees. If you were heading downhill, this spin will head you back uphill, allowing you to slow down.

6. If you have room, swerve the car back and forth across the road. Making hard turns at each side of the road will decrease your speed even more.

7. If you come up behind another car, use it to help you stop. Blow your horn, flash your lights, and try to get the driver's attention. If you hit the car, be sure to hit it square, bumper to bumper, so you do not knock the other car off the road. This is an extremely dangerous maneuver. It works best if the vehicle in front of you is larger than yours—a bus or truck is ideal—and if both vehicles are traveling at similar speeds. You do not want to crash into a much slower-moving or stopped vehicle, however.

8. Look for something to help stop you. A flat or uphill road that intersects with the road you are on, a field, or a fence will slow you further but not stop you suddenly. Scraping the side of your car against a guardrail is another option. Avoid trees and wooden telephone poles. They do not yield as readily.

9. Do not attempt to sideswipe oncoming cars.

10. If none of the above steps has enabled you to stop and you are about to go over a cliff, try to hit something that will slow you down before you go over. This strategy will also leave a clue to others that someone has gone over the edge. But since very sheer cliffs are sheer drops, you may fall just several feet and then stop.

Topics for Writing from Reading: "How to Stop a Car with No Brakes" (Process)

When you write on any of these topics, be sure to work though the stages of the writing process in preparing your paragraph.

1. Think about an emergency you've experienced that required quick thinking. Write about how you handled that situation. This writing assignment would *not* be a directional process (explaining how to handle such a situation) but an informational one, in which you trace the steps of your reacting to the emergency.

2. Choose a process you perform each day. This process should be so familiar that you perform it almost automatically. To begin, brainstorm with a partner or group and list such processes. They could be as simple as parallel parking your car in a city parking space, making your bed, or styling your hair. Once you have a list of such processes, work individually on writing an informational process on one of the topics.

3. Teach a reader the steps of a process that you know well. For example, you may be an expert on painting a room, giving a manicure, or packing a breakable object. Include the tools or other items that a person would need to complete this process.

Topics for Critical Thinking and Writing

1. Remember a time when you became frustrated because a specific process took too long. For instance, you may have had to wait for half an hour as you stood in line for movie tickets. First, describe the process you experienced. Then explain how this process could have been streamlined or at least improved.

Computer

2. Do some online research about two new and popular cars with similar prices. Print a photo of each car and list its most attractive features. Next, write about the process you followed in comparing the two and determining the better car.

NOUNS AND ARTICLES

A **noun** names a person, place, or thing. There are *count nouns* and *noncount nouns*.

> **Count nouns** refer to people, places, or things that can be counted.
> three *cookies*, two *dogs*, five *suitcases*

> **Noncount nouns** refer to things that can't be counted.
> *luggage, employment, attention*

Here are some more examples of count and noncount nouns.

count	noncount
joke	humor
movie	entertainment
dream	inspiration
automobile	transportation

One way to remember the difference between count and noncount nouns is to put the word *much* in front of the noun. For example, if you can say *much entertainment*, then *entertainment* is a noncount noun.

Exercise 1 **Practice: Identifying Count and Noncount Nouns**

Put **count** or **noncount** next to each word below.

1. _____ grandchild
2. _____ gas
3. _____ support
4. _____ coin
5. _____ money

6. _____ sympathy
7. _____ electricity
8. _____ animal
9. _____ interference
10. _____ idea

Using Articles with Nouns

Articles point out nouns. Articles are either **indefinite** (*a, an*) or **definite** (*the*). There are several rules for using these articles.

a. Use *a* in front of consonant sounds; use *an* before vowel sounds.

a filter	an orphan
a room	an apple
a bench	an event
a thought	an issue
a necklace	an umbrella

b. Use *a* or *an* in front of singular count nouns. *A* or *an* means *any one*.

I saw *an* owl.
She rode *a* horse.

503

c. Do not use *a* or *an* with noncount nouns.

> **not this:** I need a money.
> **but this:** I need money.

> **not this:** Selena is passing ~~an~~ arithmetic.
> **but this:** Selena is passing arithmetic.

d. Use *the* before both singular and plural count nouns whose specific identity is known to the reader.

> *The* dress with the sequins on it is my party dress.

> Most of *the* movies I rent are science fiction films.

e. Use *the* before noncount nouns only when they are specifically identified.

> **not this:** He wants ~~the~~ sympathy. (Whose sympathy? What sympathy? The noncount noun *sympathy* is not specifically identified.)
> **but this:** I need *the sympathy* of a good friend. (Now *sympathy* is specifically identified.)

> **not this:** ~~Generosity~~ of the family who paid for my education was remarkable. (The noncount noun *generosity* is specifically identified, so you need *the*.)
> **but this:** *The generosity* of the family who paid for my education was remarkable.

Exercise 2   Practice: Using *a* or *an*

Put *a* or *an* in the spaces where it is needed. Some sentences are correct as they are.

1. Once she started her new job, Elisa was filled with _____ enthusiasm.
2. Tommy offered me _____ cup of green tea.
3. On summer nights, _____ soft breeze cooled the back yard.
4. The neglected child was desperate for _____ affection.
5. There was nothing in the refrigerator except _____ apple and _____ box of stale crackers.
6. After listening to my girlfriend's obvious lies, I lost _____ control.
7. Mr. Stein has _____ allergy to _____ dust, so he avoids dusty rooms and objects.
8. _____ sense of _____ humor can break the tension at _____ interview.
9. _____ fuel can be expensive for anyone who needs _____ car to get to work or school.
10. I needed to see _____ counselor yesterday, but the counseling office was so busy that I had to make _____ appointment for Friday.

Exercise 3   Practice: Using *the*

Put *the* in the spaces where it is needed. Some sentences are correct as they are.

1. When Kevin gets a little older, he will have _____ physical strength of his father.
2. My mother never let me play near _____ canal behind my house.
3. Hank has _____ ability to meet a customer once and remember _____ person's name forever.
4. _____ city commission of _____ Forest Park met to discuss _____ possibility of building more low-cost housing.
5. _____ movies I prefer focus on _____ action rather than on _____ romance.
6. My father was _____ first person in his family to make _____ money in _____ real estate business.

7. With _____ help from his father, Matthew converted an old barn into an attractive house.

8. Tanisha is overcome by _____ anxiety every time she stands at _____ edge of a bridge or dock.

9. When my father died, my friends offered me _____ comfort I needed.

10. Sometimes Callie behaves foolishly because she wants _____ attention.

Exercise 4   **Connect: Correcting a Paragraph with Errors in Articles**   Connect

Correct the eleven errors with *a*, *an*, or *the* in the following paragraph. You may need to add, change, or eliminate articles. Write the corrections in the space above the errors.

The traveling can be a frustrating experience. Last week, I spent four hours at air-

port, waiting for plane that would take me to Atlanta. The person at the check-in counter

did not announce an delay until one hour after the plane was supposed to take off. One

hour later, we finally boarded the plane, only to sit for another two hours. During those

two hours, the air conditioning was turned off, and no one offered me the drink or the

snack. Pilot kept coming on the loudspeaker to say he had a news of bad weather ahead

and had to wait. Sitting in the tiny seat, sweltering in the heat, I felt the anger and an

impatience. I experienced bad side of travel.

NOUNS OR PRONOUNS USED AS SUBJECTS

A noun or a pronoun (a word that takes the place of a noun) is the subject of each sentence or dependent clause. Be sure that all sentences or dependent clauses have a subject.

> **not this:** Cooks breakfast on weekends.
> **but this:** *He* cooks breakfast on weekends.

> **not this:** My cousin was hurt when fell down the stairs.
> **but this:** My cousin was hurt when *he* fell down the stairs.

Be careful not to *repeat* the subject.

> **not this:** The lieutenant ~~she~~ said I was brave.
> **but this:** The lieutenant said I was brave.

> **not this:** The cat that bit me ~~it~~ was a Siamese.
> **but this:** The cat that bit me was a Siamese.

Exercise 5   **Practice: Correcting Errors with Subjects**

Correct any errors with subjects in the sentences below. Write your corrections in the space above the errors.

1. The ugliest part of my apartment it was the kitchen.

2. After finishes his work, he takes a train back to his house.

3. Likes to go shopping as a way to relieve tension.

4. Yesterday the copy machine at the office it didn't work.

5. My sister Isabella she has friends in the neighborhood.

6. A day at an amusement park is getting more expensive every day; can cost me a week's salary.

7. On Tuesday, got an email from an old friend in Albuquerque.

8. Extra pillows on a bed they are essential for a good night's sleep.

9. When my little boy started crying, my dog she started crying, too.

10. Makes a mess in the garage whenever he works on his car.

VERBS

Necessary Verbs

Be sure that a main verb isn't missing from your sentences or dependent clauses.

>   **not this:** Carlos extremely talented.
>   **but this:** Carlos *is* extremely talented.

>   **not this:** Bill called the police when saw the robbery.
>   **but this:** Bill called the police when *he* saw the robbery.

-s Endings

Be sure to put the *-s* on present tense verbs in the third person singular.

>   **not this:** She ~~take~~ a break in the afternoon.
>   **but this:** She *takes* a break in the afternoon.

>   **not this:** The plane ~~arrive~~ at 7:00 P.M.
>   **but this:** The plane *arrives* at 7:00 P.M.

-ed Endings

Be sure to put *-ed* endings on the past participle form of a verb. There are three main forms of a verb:

>   **present:** Today I walk.
>   **past:** Yesterday I walked.
>   **past participle:** I *have* walked. He *has* talked.

The past participle form is also used after *were*, *was*, *had*, and *has*.

>   **not this:** We had ~~talk~~ about this plan for several weeks.
>   **but this:** We had *talked* about this plan for several weeks.

>   **not this:** The baby was ~~amuse~~ by the new toy.
>   **but this:** The baby was *amused* by the new toy.

Do not add *-ed* endings to infinitives. An infinitive is the verb form that uses *to* plus the present form of the verb:

>   to suggest

>   **not this:** My husband wanted me to ~~suggested~~ a family party.
>   **but this:** My husband wanted me to *suggest* a family party.

to revise

not this: I finally learned how to ~~revised~~ a draft.
but this: I finally learned how to *revise* a draft.

Exercise 6   **Practice: Correcting Errors in Verbs: Necessary Verbs, Third Person Present Tense, Past Participles, and Infinitives**

Correct any errors in verbs in the sentences below. Write your corrections in the space above the line. Some sentences do not need any correcting.

1. Every time I drive for more than one hundred miles, my mother feel anxious.

2. Over the weekend, I was determine to finish my psychology assignment.

3. The cough syrup smell terrible, but I need something for my cold.

4. On Saturday mornings, my roommate wakes up at dawn so he can go to the gym.

5. My father was so sick that he was not expected to recovered.

6. By the time George arrived at the restaurant, the staff had lock the doors for the night.

7. A romantic setting for a wedding is the rose garden at Hamilton Park.

8. This semester, Emily will get better grades because she has learn about managing her time.

9. You can spend a day at the lake when get some vacation time.

10. A few months ago, Sammy and I were trick into buying an old, creaky table.

Exercise 7   **Practice: Correcting a Paragraph with Errors in Necessary Verbs, Third Person Present Tense, Past Participles, and Infinitives**

Correct the nine verb errors in the following paragraph. Write your corrections in the space above the errors.

Eileen is the most popular person in her department because she give so much to her fellow employees. Whenever she greets her officemates with a smile or a silly joke, Eileen has the power to turned a dull day into a happier one. Even when Eileen herself is feeling low, manages to make others laugh. She is also a good listener. She offer her total attention and does not judge those who confide in her. She been known to spend hours on the phone with someone in trouble. Everyone feel comfortable talking to Eileen, for she genuinely care about others. She is well liked because she knows how to responded to others and to brightened their lives.

Two-Word Verbs

Many verbs called **two-word verbs** contain a verb plus another word, a preposition or adverb. The meaning of each word by itself is different from the meaning the two words have when they are together. Look at this example:

I ran across an old friend at the ballgame.

You might check *run* in the dictionary and find that it means *to move quickly*. *Across* means *from one side to the other*. But *run across* means something different:

> **not this:** I ~~moved quickly from one side to the other of~~ an old friend at the ballgame.
>
> **but this:** I *encountered* an old friend at the ballgame.

Sometimes a word or words come between the words of a two-word verb:

> Yesterday I *took* my brother *out* to dinner.

Here are some common two-word verbs:

ask out:	I hope Steve will *ask* me *out* tomorrow.
break down:	If you drive too far, the car will break down.
call off:	I will *call* the game *off*.
call on:	He may *call on* you for advice.
call up:	Neil *calls* Marsha *up* on weekends.
come across:	Sometimes Joe *comes across* Nick at work.
drop in:	We can *drop in* on the neighbors.
drop off:	I can *drop* you *off* on my way to school.
fill in:	For this test, just *fill in* the blanks.
fill out:	You must *fill out* an application.
hand in:	Harry has to *hand in* his lab report.
hand out:	Marcy will *hand out* the tickets.
keep on:	We can *keep on* rehearsing our music.
look into:	The police want to *look into* the matter.
look over:	Tom intends to *look* the place *over*.
look up:	I can *look* the number *up* in the phone book.
pick up:	Tom went to *pick up* his dry cleaning.
quiet down:	The neighbors asked us to *quiet down*.
run into:	Maybe I will *run into* you at the park.
run out:	We have *run out* of coffee.
think over:	Thank you for the offer; I will *think* it *over*.
try on:	I like that dress; I will *try* it *on*.
try out:	Jack needs to *try* the drill *out*.
turn on:	*Turn* the radio *on*.
turn down:	Lucy wants to *turn* the proposal *down*.
turn up:	The lost keys will *turn up* somwehere.

Exercise 8   **Practice: Writing Sentences with Two-Word Verbs**

Write a sentence for each of the following two-word verbs. Use the examples above as a guide, but consult a dictionary if you are not sure what the verbs mean.

1. quiet down   _____

2. try out   _____

  3. fill in   _____

  4. run into   _____

  5. come across   _____

  6. turn up   _____

  7. hand in   _____

  8. drop off   _____

  9. keep on   _____

 10. look up   _____

Contractions and Verbs

Contractions often contain verbs you may not recognize in their shortened forms.

> **contraction:** *I'm* making cookies.
> **long form:** *I am* making cookies.

> **contraction:** *He's* been out of town for two weeks.
> **long form:** *He has* been out of town for two weeks.

> **contraction:** *He's* studying German.
> **long form:** *He is* studying German.

> **contraction:** *They'll* meet us at the beach.
> **long form:** *They will* meet us at the beach.

> **contraction:** The *cat's* in the basement.
> **long form:** The *cat is* in the basement.

Exercise 9   Practice: Contractions and Verbs

In the space above each contraction, write its long form. The first one is done for you.

  1. *She would*
     She'd make a fine manager of a large department store.

  2. Jimmie's making a mess in the kitchen.

  3. Jimmie's made a mess in the kitchen.

  4. My supervisor won't accept any excuses for lateness.

  5. Next week they'll perform at the Crystal Springs auditorium.

  6. I was sure he'd want some time alone.

  7. You're never home when I call.

  8. After a tough day at work, I'm too tired to study.

  9. Your truck's in better condition than my car.

 10. My neighbors were great; by the time I regained consciousness, they'd already called
     an ambulance.

Text Credits

Page 84: King, Dr. Martin Luther. From the "I Have a Dream" speech. Reprinted by arrangement with The Heirs to the Estate of Martin Luther King Jr., c/o Writers House as agent for the proprietor New York, NY. Copyright 1963 Dr. Martin Luther King Jr; copyright renewed 1991 Coretta Scott King.

Page 101: Mora, Pat. Excerpt from "Remembering Lobo." Copyright 1993 by Pat Mora. First appeared in *NAPANTLA: Essays from the Land in the Middle*, published by the University of New Mexico Press. Reprinted by permission of Curtis Brown, Ltd.

Page 161: Buchanan, Edna. Reprinted with the permission of Pocket Books, a division of Simon & Schuster, Inc. from *The Corpse Had a Familiar Face: Covering Miami, America's Hottest Beat* by Edna Buchanan. Copyright © 1987 by Edna Buchanan. All rights reserved.

Page 460: Klott, Gary. "Part Time Job May Do Teenagers More Harm Than Good," from *South Florida Sun Sentinel*, 1966. Reprinted by permission of the Estate of Gary Klott.

Page 478: Angelou, Maya. "New Directions," from *Wouldn't Take Nothing for My Journey Now*, copyright © 1993 by Maya Angelou. Used by permission of Random House, Inc. For online information about other Random House, Inc. books and authors, see the Internet web site at http://www.randomhouse.com.

Page 483: Pechter, Kerry. "Pet Therapy for Heart and Soul," from *Prevention Magazine*, 2004. Copyright Rodale Inc. 1985. All rights reserved. Used by permission.

Page 486: Cisneros, Sandra. Copyright © 1990 by Sandra Cisneros. "Only Daughter." First published in *Glamour*.

November 1990. By permission of Susan Bergholz Literacy Services, New York, NY, and Lamy, NM. All rights reserved.

Page 489: De Jesus, Yesenia. "Bullet to Blue Sky." Pearson Education Writing Rewards contest winner, 2010.

Page 491: Botti, David C. Excerpt from "The War Within," *The New York Times*, November 16, 2003 © 2003 *The New York Times*. All rights reserved. Used by permission and protected by the Copyright Laws of the United States. The printing, copying, redistribution, or retransmission of this Content without express written permission is prohibited.

Page 493: Klinkenborg, Verlyn. "Deep Cold," from *A Rural Life* by Verlyn Klinkenborg. Copyright © 2003 by Verlyn Klinkenborg. Little, Brown and Co.

Page 495: Takaki, Ronald. From *A Different Mirror: A History of Multicultural America*. Copyright © 1993. Courtest of Little, Brown, and Company and The Ward & Balkin Agency, Inc.

Page 496: Lovenheim, Peter. "Meet the Neighbors." © 2010 Peter Lovenheim. Initially published in *Parade Magazine*. All rights reserved. Reprinted by permission.

Page 498: Freedman, Russell. "Coming Over," from *Immigrant Kids*, copyright © 1980 by Russell Freedman. Used by permission of Dutton Children's Books, A Division of Penguin Young Readers Group, A Member of Penguin Group (USA) Inc., 345 Hudson Street, New York, NY 10014. All rights reserved.

Page 501: Piven, Joshua and Borgenicht, David. "How to Stop a Car with No Breaks," from *Worst-Case Scenario Handbook: Travel*, 2001. Reprinted by permission of Chronicle Books.

Photo Credits

Cover: China Images/Alamy; **Page 1:** Photos.com; **Page 23:** Photos.com; **Page 40:** René Mansi/iStockphoto; **Page 50:** Chris Schmidt/iStockphoto; **Page 59:** Photos.com; **Page 68:** Photos.com; **Page 79:** Photos.com; **Page 88:** Photos.com; **Page 100:** Photos.com; **Page 111:** Photos.com; **Page 133:** Photos.com; **Page 144:** Photos.com; **Page 154:** Christopher Futcher/iStockphoto; **Page 172:** Photos.com; **Page 185:** Photos.com; **Page 196:** Photos.com; **Page 231:** Photos.com; **Page 243:** Photos.com; **Page 260:** JupiterImages/Thinkstock; **Page 270:** Photos.com; **Page 271:** Photos.com; **Page 289:** Photos.com; **Page 300:** Photos.com; **Page 307:** Photos.com; **Page 314:** Graham Monro/Photolibrary; **Page 317:** Photos.com; **Page 347:** Bob Daemmrich/The Image Works; **Page 348:** Paul Edmondson/Stone/Getty Images; **Page 350:** Photos.com; **Page 374:** Photos.com; **Page 374:** Photos.com; **Page 375:** JupiterImages/Thinkstock; **Page 377:** Photos.com; **Page 396:** Photos.com; **Page 396:** Photos.com; **Page 396:** Photos.com; **Page 396:** Photos.com; **Page 396:** Photos.com; **Page 396:** Photos.com; **Page 399:** CandyBoxPhoto/Shutterstock; **Page 415:** Photos.com; **Page 417:** Photos.com; **Page 452:** Photos.com; **Page 452:** Photos.com; **Page 453:** Photos.com; **Page 453:** Photos.com; **Page 453:** Arthur Tilley/Taxi/Getty Images; **Page 454:** GK Hart/Vikki Hart/The Image Bank/Getty Images; **Page 458:** Photos.com; **Page 503:** Photos.com.

INDEX

Note: Reading selections are listed under "readings." Each selection contains vocabulary definitions, suggested writing options, and critical-thinking questions for discussion or writing topics.